BETWEEN TRADITION AND MODERNITY

Harvard East Asian Monographs, 133

BETWEEN TRADITION

AND MODERNITY:

WANG T'AO AND REFORM

IN LATE CH'ING CHINA

Paul A. Cohen

Published by COUNCIL ON EAST ASIAN STUDIES, HARVARD UNIVERSITY and distributed by HARVARD UNIVERSITY PRESS, Cambridge (Massachusetts) and London   1987

The Council on East Asian Studies at Harvard University publishes a mono-
graph series and, through the Fairbank Center for East Asian Research and
the Edwin O. Reischauer Institute of Japanese Studies, administers research
projects designed to further scholarly understanding of China, Japan, Korea,
Vietnam, Inner Asia, and adjacent areas.

Library of Congress Cataloging-in-Publication Data

Cohen, Paul A.
    Between tradition and modernity.

    (Harvard East Asian monographs ; 133)
    Bibliography: p.
    Includes index.
    1. Wang, T'ao, 1828–1897. 2. China—History—Reform
movement, 1898. 3. Scholars—China—Biography.
    I. Title. II. Series.
CT3990.W36C64 1987   951'.03'0924 [B]   87-13606
ISBN 0-674-06876-9 (pbk.)

TO MY PARENTS
ROSE J. COHEN AND
WILFRED P. COHEN

BOOKS BY PAUL A. COHEN

Discovering History in China: American Historical Writing on the Recent Chinese Past, 1984

Reform in Nineteenth-Century China, ed. and contrib. with John E. Schrecker, 1976

Between Tradition and Modernity: Wang T'ao and Reform in Late Ch'ing China, 1974

China and Christianity: The Missionary Movement and the Growth of Chinese Antiforeignism, 1860–1870, 1963

PREFACE TO PAPERBACK EDITION

When the idea of a paperback edition of *Between Tradition and Modernity* was first suggested, my initial response was one of hesitation. Almost fifteen years had elapsed since my completion of the original typescript, and I felt quite removed from the subject matter. Besides, I had already confessed in print my worries about the book's intellectual design, above all certain of the more problematic assumptions underlying the tradition-modernity polarity that serves as an important part of its conceptual framework.[1] On the other hand, I still felt that Wang T'ao, the subject of eight of the book's nine chapters, was a remarkable historical figure, and I remained no less convinced of his importance both as a promoter of change in the last decades of the nineteenth century and as a negotiator between civilizations. Although articles on Wang in Chinese and Japanese have appeared from time to time, in some cases adding details to the story,[2] and although Wang has a secure spot in the vast Chinese scholarly literature on the *yang-wu* (Westernization) and reform movements of the late Ch'ing,[3] no one has ventured to do another book on him in any language. This alone, I felt, was sufficient justification for keeping him in print.

Beyond this, I tried in the final chapter of the book to address some broader issues having to do with change in nineteenth- and

vii

twentieth-century China. And, although if I were writing that chapter today I would frame it somewhat differently, the issues themselves seem to me every bit as important now as they were a decade and a half ago. Indeed, it is arguable that, with the end of the Cultural Revolution and the accelerated opening of China to external influences, as part of the Four Modernizations policy of the post-Mao leadership, these issues have become more salient than ever.

Let me briefly summarize the main themes of the book's last chapter and then suggest some of the modifications I would be inclined to make if I were to rework it. The framework of interpretation that I advanced embodied three propositions: first, that sweeping culture change generally takes place in two phases, the first dominated by pioneers (or innovators), the second by legitimizers (or validators); second, that Chinese history since the Opium War may be viewed as a product of the interaction between two largely distinct and self-contained cultural environments, the littoral or coast (Hong Kong, Shanghai, and so on) and the hinterland or interior; and, third, that, in the nineteenth century, and for a while in the twentieth, the primary responsibility for the initiation of change rested with the subculture of the coast, the interior functioning mainly as a vehicle of legitimation. In an effort to clarify the ways in which the littoral served as an initiator of change in the late Ch'ing period, I shifted in this concluding chapter from individual to collective biography and probed the careers of a dozen pioneer reformers, eight of them (including Wang T'ao) closely affiliated with the culture of the littoral, four products of the Chinese hinterland.

I openly acknowledged this framework at the time to be "tentative and exploratory in nature" (p. 241) and hedged it with a fair number of qualifications.[4] It wasn't, however, until I was able to put some distance between myself and the book that I gained a clearer sense of where the soft areas were and how I might go about firming them up. The most critical of these soft areas, I would say, was a tendency, visible not only in the final chapter but elsewhere as well, to imply that the key measure of change in late Ch'ing China was the extent of the West's impact on Chinese institutions and on the world view of China's educated strata. Change, in other words, was overidentified with Western influence upon Chinese life, with the triple consequence that endogenous patterns of change were either overlooked or trivialized; that the process of institutionalizing change, referred to in the book as "legitimation," was too readily reduced to simple Sinicization (or de-Westernization); and, finally, that attention was diverted from social, economic, and political barriers to change to focus almost exclusively upon intellectual and cultural barriers.

If I were reconceiving this chapter today, I would retain the polarity between coast and interior and continue to insist upon the importance of distinguishing between the pioneering and legitimizing phases of culture change (using "culture" in a broadly anthropological sense). However, I would devote much more attention to patterns of internally powered change emerging in China in the latter half of the nineteenth century—commercial development,[5] growing politicization of local elites, and so on—and, even more crucially, I would say something about the special problems involved in validating such change and how these problems differed from those involved in the legitimation of foreign-influenced changes. To illustrate, Feng Kuei-fen's far-reaching proposals for the reform of Chinese local government, which were largely (if not entirely) endogenous in inspiration, encountered barriers to incorporation into the Chinese world of the 1860s, 1870s, and 1880s that were arguably no less formidable than those confronting the reform efforts of a man like Wang T'ao. In Wang T'ao's case, however, because so many of his reform proposals reflected the influence of the West, the obstacles to legitimation tended to be more cultural and social in nature, whereas in Feng's case they were apt to be more political and economic.

Greater recognition of the importance of internal *processes* of change in the late Ch'ing (as distinct from the indigenous "impulse to change" now stressed in the last chapter) would serve as a natural corrective to overstatement of the role of the West; it would also make it more difficult to misstate this role. In rereading the book, I note, for example, a tendency in places to assume, almost in spite of myself, that the more radical forms of change in the latter half of the nineteenth century were generally (if not invari-

ably) those stemming from the "Western challenge." Apart from
the fact that, from my present perspective, I would be inclined to
steer clear of the "challenge" terminology altogether, I would here
make the more basic point that Chinese promotion of Western-
inspired change (initially in the area of technology, but eventually
in many other sectors as well) was often justified, especially when
the promoters were members of the government or the social elite,
as a defensive strategy to block far more fundamental—and hence
more threatening—changes of partially or wholly indigenous origin.
Western-related change, in other words, could in certain circumstances be allied with forces of a relatively conservative nature in
Chinese society. There was no guarantee that, just because it was
Western in inspiration, it would necessarily be more "radical" or
"fundamental" or "system-threatening" in character.

Finally—and somewhat paradoxically in light of the points I
have just been making—if I were redoing the final part of the book
today, I would be less hasty in writing off the littoral as a major
source of innovation in China in the latter decades of the twentieth
century. One of the main features of the Teng Hsiao-p'ing (Deng
Xiaoping) era has been an opening to the outside world far exceed-
ing anything even remotely imaginable in the early 1970s when
the original edition of this work was completed. Although not all
of the foreign influences that have flowed into China in recent
years have been channeled through the littoral, a great preponderance of them have, and the contrast, in respect to accessibility and
receptivity to foreign-inspired innovation, between such coastal
urban entrepots as Shanghai, Tientsin (Tianjin), and Canton and
the more remote cities of the Chinese hinterland is still immense.

By the same token, the post-Mao years have also underscored
the persistence of the distinctive problems of incorporation and
acceptance presented by foreign-patented (especially Western-
patented) changes. The suppression of the "democracy movement"
in 1979, the campaign against "spiritual pollution" in 1983, and
the sharp attack on "bourgeois liberalization" that began in the
winter of 1986–1987 all bespeak an ongoing resistance to the legitimation of certain kinds of foreign-linked ideas in the Chinese
world. The sources of this resistance, however, are complicated and

differ in important respects from those that operated in Wang T'ao's day. Now, after all, it is the perception that the purity not of native cultural traditions but of a *foreign*-derived ideological system, Marxism-Leninism, is being threatened that provides a major justification for clampdowns on other foreign-derived ideological influences (such as capitalism or democratic liberalism). Moreover, where resistance is shown to such Western-grounded political demands as the right to demonstrate or greater freedom of expression or an independent judiciary, it seems clear that the basis for the resistance is only partly the Westernness of the demands; far more important is their challenge to a tradition of political authoritarianism that is at least as intractable today as it was under the emperors.

Proprietary feelings about China's cultural distinctiveness and self-sufficiency, on the other hand, are still a force to be reckoned with. In spite—and partly because—of all the foreign influences that have buffeted China over the past century and a half, a deep reservoir of ethnocentrism remains to be tapped, especially in the vast Chinese hinterland areas and sectors of the bureaucracy, and especially in situations of crisis. This ethnocentrism establishes an unstable standard of Chineseness that foreign ideas can negotiate with but cannot easily meet; also, it places individuals who have been profoundly influenced by such ideas (including maverick or unorthodox forms of Marxism) in a uniquely marginal, tenuous, and potentially illegitimate position in the larger Chinese world. Although the substantive ideas of these Western-influenced individuals are very different from those of the pioneer reformers of a century ago, the problems they encounter with respect to their own legitimacy in Chinese society and the legitimacy of certain of their intellectual orientations resonate palpably with the problems faced by Wang T'ao and his generation. In this sense, the themes explored, however preliminarily, in the final section of this book may speak not only to the late Ch'ing but also to the more recent situation in China.

P. A. C

March 1987
Cambridge, Massachusetts

NOTES

1. Paul A. Cohen, *Discovering History in China: American Historical Writing on the Recent Chinese Past* (New York, Columbia University Press, 1984), pp. xi–xii.

2. See, e.g., Nishizato Yoshiyuki, "Ō Tō to *Junkan nippō* ni tsuite" (On Wang T'ao and the *Hsün-huan jih-pao*), *Tōyōshi kenkyū* 43.3:508–547 (December 1984); Liu Shih-lung, "Ch'ing-mo Shang-hai Ko-chih shu-yüan yü tsao-ch'i kai-liang ssu-ch'ao" (The Shanghai Polytechnic Institute and Reading Room of the late Ch'ing and the early wave of reform thought), *Hua-tung shih-fan ta-hsüeh hsüeh-pao* 4:45–52, 84 (1983); Yang Ch'i-min, "Wang T'ao shang-shu T'ai-p'ing-chün k'ao-pien—chien yü Lo Erh-kang hsien-sheng shang-ch'üeh" (An inquiry into Wang T'ao's letter to the Taiping army—and a challenge to the view of Mr. Lo Erh-kang), *Chin-tai-shih yen-chiu* 4:241–261 (July 1985).

3. See, e.g., Ch'en Chiang, "Lun tsao-ch'i kai-liang-p'ai jen-wu tui yang-wu-p'ai ts'ung i-fu tao p'i-p'an te fa-chan" (The evolution of the early reformers from dependence upon to criticism of the *yang-wu* group), in Ts'ai Shang-ssu et al., *Lun Ch'ing-mo min-ch'u Chung-kuo she-hui* (Chinese society in the late Ch'ing and early republican eras) (Shanghai, Fu-tan ta-hsüeh ch'u-pan-she, 1983), pp. 197–221.

4. So many, in fact, that one frustrated reviewer charged me with "stretching the foot to fit the sock." See C. A. Curwen, *Bulletin of the School of Oriental and African Studies* 39.3:683–684 (1976). Another reviewer who found fault with the last chapter was W. S. Atwell, *China Quarterly* 67:640–643 (September 1976). The reactions of most people, on the other hand, were on balance quite favorable. See, e.g., Jerome B. Grieder, *Intellectuals and the State in Modern China: A Narrative History* (New York, The Free Press, 1981), pp. 130–131, 379.

5. Two important recent books that make a persuasive case for much higher levels of hinterland commercialization during the late Ch'ing than had previously been acknowledged are William T. Rowe, *Hankow: Commerce and Society in a Chinese City, 1796–1889* (Stanford, Stanford University Press, 1984), and Susan Mann, *Local Merchants and the Chinese Bureaucracy, 1750–1950* (Stanford, Stanford University Press, 1987). Mann, on the basis of her findings, explicitly questions (ibid., p. 27) the validity of my suggested division of late imperial China into two distinct cultural environments. This part of her argument I find less persuasive for two reasons. First, no matter how commercialized one judges the economy of the hinterland to have become by late Ch'ing times, it still rested on an economic base that was massively agrarian; these emphases are exactly reversed in the case of the littoral culture which, I remain convinced, "was more commercial than agricultural in its economic foundations" (p. 241). Second, even if it should be proved that the economic contrast between littoral and hinterland was very much less pronounced than I had once supposed, this still leaves the noneconomic terms of the contrast—degree of exposure to Western influence, elite value orientations, administrative and legal arrangements, and the like—basically intact.

ACKNOWLEDGMENTS

Much of this book was written at Harvard's East Asian Research Center. I want to take this opportunity to thank the successive directors of the center, John K. Fairbank and Ezra F. Vogel, for their generosity in providing me with office space over the years. I would also like to congratulate both men for their part in the creation of a uniquely successful working environment for scholars.

I am indebted to the many friends and colleagues whom I have troubled for information on specific points or for assistance in locating and procuring out-of-the-way materials. Some of these individuals are named in the notes. Others include: Adrian A. Bennett, the late Richard G. Irwin, Harold Kahn, Noriko Kamachi, Weiying Wan, and Richard Williams.

Part IV of the book, in a shorter and somewhat different form, was presented as a paper at the conference on "American Missionaries in China and in America," held at Cuernavaca, Mexico, in January 1972. For useful criticisms and suggestions, I should like to thank the participants in the conference, especially Kwang-Ching Liu, Philip West, and the conference's organizer, John K. Fairbank. Subsequently, in the course of reworking and expanding Part IV, I benefited from discussion of its main themes before two other forums of China specialists: the New England China Seminar at Harvard (March 1973) and the China colloquium at Princeton (May 1973).

I am grateful to the Association for Asian Studies, Inc., for permission to use material which originally appeared (in a quite different guise) in an article in the *Journal of Asian Studies* (August 1967); and to the Regents of the University of California for permission to draw freely (in Part II) on a chapter originally published in Albert Feuerwerker and others, eds., *Approaches to Modern Chinese History* (Berkeley: University of California Press, 1967).

The debt I owe my wife, Jane, is too great and too complicated to be easily expressed in words. I thank her for her help with the book. But, much more, I thank her for those qualities of intelligence, creativity, and human warmth that have made her companionship a treasure.

P.A.C.

January 1974
Cambridge, Massachusetts

CONTENTS

IV. LITTORAL AND HINTERLAND
IN MODERN CHINESE HISTORY

PART I. THE GENESIS

OF A NEW MAN

PROLOGUE

Early in 1894 a brash young man set out from his home in the south of China to present a memorandum on reform to Li Hung-chang, the most powerful official in the land. On his way north he stopped off in Shanghai and made the acquaintance of an elderly reformer of some prominence who helped him put his memorandum into acceptable form and agreed to write a letter of introduction to a member of Li's staff. The young man was Sun Yat-sen. The subject of this book is the older man, whose name was Wang T'ao.[1]

Wang T'ao's career prefigured Sun's in significant respects. Through his writings he may even have exerted a direct impact on some of Sun's ideas.[2] But the importance of the crossing of their lives in 1894 is more symbolic than anything else. Sun, full of the future, shortly went on to achieve world-wide fame as a Chinese revolutionary. Wang, after a long and productive career, died in obscurity in May 1897,[3] on the very eve of changes which he, as much as any Chinese of his day, had anticipated.

To "anticipate" change is, in some sense, to help bring it about, to make it possible. Before the kind of dramatic event called a revolution can take place, there must be a period of preparation, a period of incremental change during which increasing numbers of people are brought to the point where, for the first time, they can contemplate radical change as a real possibility. This is what happened in China in the last sixty years of the nineteenth century. Many of the basic patterns of Chinese life during this period remained, doubtless, much the same as before. But in certain realms, above all the intellectual, changes took place which, cumulatively considered, can only be described as revolutionary.

Scholars whose perceptions of nineteenth-century China are defined—one is tempted to say confined—by the comparison with Meiji Japan may balk at such a statement. From the vantage point of Japanese "success," the late Ch'ing epitomizes "failure," and next to the dynamism of the Meiji era, China, during the latter half of the nineteenth century, appears as the very embodiment of stasis. The trouble with this perspective is that it glosses over a very important fact, namely that China and Japan, in their respective encounters with the West in the last century, did not start out at the same point. Cross-cultural comparison is an elusive enterprise. It is enormously valuable for the identification of similarities and differences. But as a yardstick for the measurement of change (and speed of change) it presents problems. Modernization, after all, is not a horserace. And two cultures do not share a common "baseline" just because they both happen to be "premodern."

A much more valid way of measuring change in nineteenth-century China is by internal points of reference. It is not until we compare the China of 1900 with that of 1800-1840—the final phase of what Frederic Wakeman calls "High Ch'ing"[4]—that we begin to appreciate the scale of the transformation that occurred. In the early years of the nineteenth century, England, France, and America were as remote from China, intellectually and psychologically, as China had been from the West in Roman times. Many Chinese—and I refer to the educated—had never heard of these countries. Few had even a vague notion of where they were located on the map. And if there was anybody in the Chinese empire who knew about the French Revolution or had heard "the shot heard round the world," he guarded his secret well. The one point of contact between China and the West in these years was the regulated trade carried on at Canton. Unlike the Dutch trade at Nagasaki, however, the Canton contact did not serve as a funnel for the transmission of Western intellectual influences. Confucian China, isolated by choice and totally self-absorbed, had no way of knowing what was in store for it.

By the end of the nineteenth century—four foreign wars, five domestic upheavals, and dozens of imposed treaties later—this proud and comfortable world had been shattered. Not, perhaps, in outward physical terms: an imaginary visitor from the pre-Opium War epoch, if he steered clear of the Western-influenced littoral and riveted his gaze upon hinterland China, might not have found too much that was startlingly different. Juan Yüan could have survived in 1900. The great change was in the mental landscape of China's educated. The invisible bars which two or three generations earlier had locked the minds of Chinese scholars in a closed Confucian world had first been made visible and then, after much painful effort, had been pried apart, letting in a whole new universe of ideas, information, and values. Granted, there were learned Chinese in 1900 who still did not know the precise location of England, just as there are American college graduates today who, given a map of Southeast Asia, are unable to place Vietnam. But England, like Vietnam, meant *something* to everyone. And there were plenty of Chinese—easily numbering by 1900 in the tens of thousands—whose outlooks had been fundamentally transformed by sixty years of Sino-Western interaction. Sun Yat-sen could not have inhabited the Chinese world of 1800.

Nor could Yen Fu or K'ang Yu-wei or Liang Ch'i-ch'ao, the point being not that these men all happened to have been influenced by Westerners who lived and wrote after 1800, but that they were in a position—historically—to be influenced by Westerners at all. This circumstance, more than any other, distinguishes 1900 from 1800. Chinese, in 1800, had the sense of being a universe unto themselves, of literally encompassing the world. This sense was still alive in 1840. But by 1900 it had become moribund. During the intervening years an awareness had first been kindled of something very important happening, of change on a scale that it was not given to all generations to experience. Then, one or two people ventured to describe the change as "unprecedented"—something not experienced by *any* previous generation. Like Nietzsche's madman, wandering through the early morning dark with his lantern proclaiming "God is dead," these percipient individuals were unable, initially, to make people listen. In time, however, the number of madmen grew, and by 1900 they had become so numerous that to talk of revolutionary change was no longer considered mad at all. The unthinkable had happened. The civilization whose eternal validity no Chinese of the pre-Opium War period had for a moment doubted stood on the verge of disintegration.

To say that Sun Yat-sen was not a possibility in 1800 is simply to say that there are limits to what can take place in any given generation, limits which no individual, however extraordinary, is capable of transcending. This is the negative aspect of the process of historical change. On the positive side, every generation contributes something new to the world, thereby changing the limits—and the possibilities—for the following generation. According to this "logic of generations,"[5] what Sun Yat-sen thought and did at the turn of the century was built in part on what others had thought and done before him. Sun did not create a revolution (qua event) out of thin air. The China into which he was born (in 1866) was one in which revolution (qua process) was already immanent.

This was not true, however, of the China into which Wang T'ao was born (in 1828). Every generation produces its new men. But the *degree* of newness can vary greatly from one generation to the next. It did not take very long for man to get from trains to airplanes, but it took him thousands of years to get to trains. In these relative terms, Wang T'ao's generation, with one foot in prerevolutionary China, was newer than Sun Yat-sen's. For Wang's generation—and only Wang's—experienced the enormous leap in modern Chinese history from no trains to trains. The same applied, moreover, to Wang T'ao and Sun Yat-sen as individuals. Although Sun Yat-sen represented a later stage of the revolutionary process and in that sense was a newer man than Wang T'ao, in terms of the amount of cultural change each man encompassed in his lifetime—generational change viewed in relative, rather than cumulative, perspective—it was Wang who was the newer of the two.

Perspective, indeed, is everything. When we look at Wang T'ao from the vantage point of Sun Yat-sen, we catch ourselves using words like "limited," "not very advanced," "still quite tradition- al." But when we view him from the perspective of his origins, the China of his birth, we are impressed by Wang's newness. Both perspectives are legitimate. It depends on the book one is writing. This book is about the *beginnings* of the revolutionary process in modern China, the pioneer phase. Its focus, therefore, is not on why Wang T'ao failed to become a revolutionary, but on how he succeeded in becoming a pioneer.

1

THE EARLY YEARS

IN KIANGSU

Wang T'ao was born on November 10, 1828, in the town of Fu-li, about fifteen miles southeast of Soochow, in the coastal province of Kiangsu. The Wang family had flourished in Ming times. But after being decimated in the fighting that accompanied the Manchu conquest in the mid-seventeenth century, it was unable to recover its former strength and by Wang T'ao's day stood precariously close to extinction. The first three sons born to Wang's parents all died within ten days from smallpox, and it was only after the offering up of special prayers that Wang T'ao himself arrived on the scene.[1]

Throughout his adult life Wang T'ao remained deeply attached to the setting of his childhood years and visited Fu-li whenever the opportunity presented itself. One favorite spot was an old Buddhist temple on the outskirts of town, the grounds of which served as a focal point for the annual New Year festivities. As later recalled by Wang, the air at this time was filled with the din of gongs and bells, drums and flutes; there was an endless round of theatrical and magical performances; and, outside the temple gates, the venders of toys and puppets paraded their wares. For the children of Fu-li, this was plainly the happiest of seasons.[2]

Wang T'ao's "preschool" education was initiated by his mother

8

when he was around three years old.* It was she who taught him his first characters, and she also who regularly enlivened the long summer evenings with her stories of the famous men of the past and their deeds. Wang was deeply affected by these stories and claims, as a result of them, to have acquired by the age of seven or so a thorough foundation in Chinese fiction.[3]

Wang T'ao's father, Wang Ch'ang-kuei, earned his living as a teacher with the task of preparing young men for the government examinations. In the China of that day the one career that carried with it a promise of both wealth and prestige was membership in the bureaucracy. Almost all educated men therefore shared the dream of entering officialdom, and since the principal means of realizing this dream was passage of a succession of examinations in the Confucian corpus, training in the classics and histories became, for those who could afford it, the serious business of life from an early age. Wang T'ao's formal education, supervised by his father, began when he was seven or eight years old and lasted into his teens. Wherever Wang Ch'ang-kuei happened to be teaching, whether at home or in a nearby village or town, Wang always accompanied him, and in his later years, when he was too busy for intense study and reflection, he expressed his gratitude for the solid grounding in Confucian literature received at this time.[4]

There were three levels of government examinations. Wang T'ao passed the first level (held in the prefectural capital) with distinction in 1845 and was praised by the examining official for the exceptional flavor of his writing.[5] As a holder of the first degree (popularly termed a *hsiu-ts'ai* or "cultivated talent"), he was now entitled to consideration as a lower-ranking member of the gentry class. In the normal course of events, however, he was not eligible for an official appointment until he passed the second-level examinations, given triennially in the provincial capital.

Wang T'ao went with his father to Nanking in 1846 to take the examinations for the second (*chü-jen*) degree. But the competi-

---

*The Chinese text says "four or five *sui.*" Since Wang T'ao was born fairly late in the lunar year, his "Chinese age" was usually two years higher than his "Western age." Unless otherwise noted, age figures given in this book are based on the Western reckoning.

tion at the provincial level was much stiffer and this time he failed. Although failure in the examinations was far from being a sign of inferior intellectual gift—many Chinese took the very opposite position—it had a decisive effect on a candidate's immediate life prospects. The door to an official career was temporarily closed, and until the examinations could be taken again, an alternative career had to be considered. Wang T'ao, like his father and many others in similar circumstances, chose the honorable, if not particularly remunerative, profession of teaching.[6]

Wang T'ao's lack of success in the examinations provided him with a custom-tailored opportunity to strike out at "the system." The Ch'ing dynasty, he complained to his friend and brother-in-law, Yang Yin-ch'uan, in 1848, followed the old Ming practice of making examination candidates write in the stilted and highly formal "eight-legged" style. Consequently, numerous men of outstanding ability, who had studied the classics until gray in the hair, remained in obscurity and did not get appointed to official posts. Under the Han (206 B.C.-A.D. 220), when people had been elevated for their filial piety and spotless character, the officials had been good and the scholars true. That this was no longer the case was due not to a lack of able men (*jen-ts'ai*) but to the defective nature of the system used to pick people. How could one possibly get from the eight-legged essays men with a capacity to govern![7]

Wang T'ao's attack on the examination system may be viewed in a number of different ways. It is possible, of course, simply to accept it at face value. His point, after all, was well taken and had been made by numerous Chinese before him.[8] It is also possible to dismiss it as the spiteful reaction of a young man with a high opinion of his own abilities and a greater than average capacity for self-pity. The system had no room for him, so he rejected the system. A third possibility is that Wang had formed his hostile view of the examinations before ever taking them and was merely confirmed in this view by his failure. Wang later maintained that, even as a boy, he had hated writing in the eight-legged essay style.[9] Moreover, it appears that, despite the urging of friends, he refused to take the provincial examinations again, insisting that there were other and better ways to do honor to one's parents.[10]

Wherever the exact truth may lie, one thing is clear. By taking a critical stance toward the examinations and toward the general run of officials recruited by means of them, Wang T'ao, already at this early date, betrayed his partial dissatisfaction with the status quo. In the years ahead, this unhappiness would grow enormously.

In 1847 Wang T'ao's father had obtained a teaching position in Shanghai and early in the following year Wang went to visit him. Up to this point Wang had inhabited an exclusively Chinese world. The events of the early 1840's—the Opium War, the Sino-British Treaty of Nanking, the opening of Shanghai and several other coastal cities to foreign trade—had scarcely disturbed life in the Chinese interior. Nor, in 1848, was it a foregone conclusion that they ever would. The cosmopolitan flavor of Wang T'ao's description of his initial encounter with Westerners comes, therefore, as something of a surprise:

As soon as we got up the Whangpoo I found myself all at once in a different world. As I looked out from the boat I was in I could see an expanse of mist and water, and bristling through it a forest of masts. All along the bank of the river were the houses of foreigners, which seemed to me then to tower into the sky with their upper storeys . . . The foreign scholar Medhurst was at the time in charge of the London Mission Press, which was printing books by a machine from movable type. This was considered to be a great novelty, and I specially went to pay him a visit . . . I was brought into a room the walls of which were covered with bookcases full of Chinese books. Mr. Medhurst called his two daughters out to meet me . . . After I had been sitting there for a while they offered me some port wine in a glass and pressed me to drink. It tasted sweet and was red in colour and not inferior to Chinese wine. Then they played a foreign tune for me on the piano which I found very charming in its own way. After that Mr. Medhurst took me to see where the printing was done. The press was turned by an ox and could produce several thousand impressions a day.[11]

In a poem commemorating this first visit to Shanghai, Wang T'ao revealed an altogether different—and in some ways more predictable—set of feelings. Distressed at the suffering China had undergone in the war with England and fearful of the large number of "barbarian" traders gathered in the city, he castigated the policy of peace being pursued by the dynasty and laid stress on the urgent need to strengthen China's coastal defenses.[1 2]

Wang T'ao's responses to his introduction to the Shanghai environment were set down at different times—the first some years later, the second right afterward—which affords a partial explanation of their asymmetry. A more basic explanation, however, is that this is the way Wang T'ao was. Not only, as we shall see, did Wang play an astonishing array of outward roles during his career, he also led a number of very different intellectual, emotional, and social lives and was capable of moving back and forth among these lives with dazzling suddenness.

We have taken a brief glimpse at the external high points of Wang T'ao's youth. There was also an internal side. Between the ages of seventeen and twenty, Wang tells us, not a night passed in which he failed to dream about some experience that had particularly moved him during the day. In the spring or summer of 1849 these nocturnal flights abruptly ceased and he made up a small volume to which he gave the title, "Hua-hsü shih-lu" (A true record of my dreams). Wang's dream diary, unfortunately, was never published, but we do have the preface he wrote for it at the time. Here is a portion of it:

I have heard that the gods may be able to penetrate our thoughts and that the things which preoccupy them are not confined to this earth. Is this how dreams originate? If we pursue the matter more deeply, we find that it is all a question of emotions. Our destinies, having already been charted, invariably place limits on what we are able to experience. When we have reached the point where our longings cannot be satisfied and our desires cannot be attained, we concoct fantasy experiences out of nothing and communicate them in dreams. In this way we give expression to the words that we should like to utter but cannot, the objects we should like to see but have no means of seeing. What would it be like if we could not daily fulfill our wishes in our dreams? . . . Life's successes and failures are over soon enough . . . If I could but finish out my allotted span with a long dream, losing myself in sleep, the pleasure I should feel would be boundless.[1 3]

In the summer of 1849, around the time he wrote this, Wang T'ao faced the first real crisis of his life in the death of his father. As a result of this event, he had to assume immediate responsibility for the support of his mother and younger brother, as well as a wife and infant daughter. For a man in Wang's financial circumstances, this could mean only one thing: the season for dreaming was over. In the fall, Walter Henry Medhurst (1796-1857), whom Wang had met the year before, invited him to come to Shanghai to serve as a Chinese editor at the London Missionary Society's press (Mo-hai shu-kuan). Wang was full of misgivings. But the salary was good and he accepted.[1 4]

YOUNG MANHOOD IN SHANGHAI

At first, Wang T'ao was miserable in his new surroundings. Shanghai in the 1840's was not the exciting, bustling metropolis it was shortly to become, and the location of Wang's small cottage, adjacent to a graveyard on the northern outskirts of the city, was ill-calculated to keep him from being prey to morbid thoughts.[1 5]

Furthermore, although Wang soon moved to more suitable quarters and was joined by his family, it was not long before tragedy struck. In October 1850, a week or so after her return to Shanghai from a visit home, Wang's young wife, who had long been ill, took a turn for the worse and died. Wang was inconsolable. In a day of arranged marriages, when a man and a woman, as often as not, had to make the best of a bad pairing, Wang and his wife seem to have shared a deep mutual attachment. "If only I had known it would come to this," he lamented, "how could I have borne to be separated from her for a single day and go to another place!" The gloomy suspicion that, by moving to Shanghai, he had been partly responsible for his wife's untimely death continued to torment Wang, even after his remarriage some time later.[1 6]

Wang T'ao complained incessantly about his work at the London Missionary Society (LMS) press. Although the actual writing was done by him, it was closely supervised by the foreigners, and these last so butchered the Chinese language that, as Wang colorfully put it, "even Confucius, if resurrected, would [have found] it impossible to correct their composition."[1 7] More galling even than the work itself was the plain fact of being associated, on a daily basis, with the despised barbarian. In time, in port cities like Shanghai which had large foreign populations, a new Sino-foreign culture would emerge and it would become possible to work closely with Westerners without losing entirely one's sense of self-esteem as a Chinese. In the 1850's, however, this development still lay some distance in the future and scholars like Wang T'ao who "sold their writing" (*mai-wen*) to the foreigners were treated by their countrymen with a suspicion bordering on contempt.

Why, then, did Wang continue in the work? The most important reason, clearly, was money. The pay at the press was regular and far more than he could ever hope to make as a schoolteacher in Fu-li.[18] Another reason, very likely, was that the reality of working for the foreigners was not quite so bad as the stereotyped picture Wang painted. The physical surroundings were agreeable: "The place . . . had a most charming rustic air. All around it was a fence of bamboo, and inside there was a pleasant garden with trellises for flowers."[19] Wang, moreover, formed a genuine fondness for his employer, Medhurst, who was his father's age and appears to have treated Wang with much kindness at a time when it was needed. (Some years later, when the news of Medhurst's death reached Shanghai, Wang T'ao was deeply grieved and confided to a friend that this was one Westerner with whom he had felt truly intimate.[20])

One final factor that helped to make life in Shanghai tolerable for Wang T'ao was a growing circle of Chinese friends. Students of traditional Chinese society, in their stress on the centrality of the family, have sometimes overlooked the crucial place of friendship, especially in the lives of China's male elites. Not only did the work of these men frequently take them from their families, their "after-hours," too, were customarily spent outside the home. For men who, unlike their modern American counterparts, had little or no opportunity to unbutton within the family circle, friendship and other extrafamilial relationships thus provided essential vehicles for emotional release.

It did not take Wang T'ao very long to discover that Shanghai was full of people like himself. Wang's diaries (which are available in manuscript for most of the period from July 1852 to May 1855),[21] in addition to supplying a superb account of how he occupied himself in his off-hours, give ample indication of the importance to him of his friends:

August 20, 1852: Perused the *Ch'ien-Han-shu* [History of the former Han] in the afternoon. Toward dark Cheng-chai [Sun Ch'i-chü] stopped by and we went for a stroll together in the vicinity of the city gate. On reaching the Ta-ching Pavilion, we dropped in on Jen-shu [Li Shan-lan] . . .

October 1, 1852: Visited Cheng-chai in the afternoon. Went together to the Hua-fang Pavilion and sipped tea . . . After parting, I passed by the Catholic church and watched a dramatic performance. They did 'Sao-Ch'in' [The destruction of Ch'in]. Excellent . . .

October 9, 1852: . . . After dark I went to Cheng-chai's place. For several days I had been flat broke . . . Cheng-chai lent me two silver dollars to relieve the immediate crisis . . . I wonder when I shall be rid of this poverty demon![22]

October 30, 1852: Toward dark I accompanied my younger brother to a teahouse in the northern sector of the city . . . Cheng-chai, having bought some paddy crabs, had us over for dinner in the evening. To feast on crabs and wine, chatting freely with the candles extinguished—is there any greater pleasure?

December 5, 1852: . . . After consuming much wine, Chen-shu [P'an Ying], Jen-shu, and I toured the brothels together. But there weren't any beauties . . . We looked them over and then gave up and went home.[23]

June 3, 1853: Chiang Chien-jen [Chiang Tun-fu] came over in the afternoon. We talked about national affairs and he showed me his collected prose . . .

Mid-August 1853: Ying Yü-keng [Ying Lung-t'ien] came. He told me about his trip to England and the many sights he had seen abroad. So I wrote down what he said and called it "Ying-hai pi-chi" [Notes on the lands across the ocean].[24]

March 5, 1855: Went in the afternoon with Chien-jen and Jen-shu to visit Mei-po [Yao Hsieh]. We chatted together for a long while and then had some wine at a wineshop. Afterwards we went to the brothels and visited with the beauties . . . I was guided to the chamber of the courtesan, Fu-yün. Fu-yün was quite seductive in appearance. But unfortunately her lovely face was marred by pimples.

April 26, 1855: Drizzled in afternoon. Today Pastor Muirhead presented me with a gift of kumquats. Very courteous and thoughtful of him.[25]

Who were Wang's friends? Many of them were men who were trained in the Confucian classics, had taken the *hsiu-ts'ai* degree, and had come to Shanghai, at least in part, because of the new employment opportunities that the Westerner's presence there had generated. As individuals, they were an unconventional lot, often eccentric, sometimes brilliant. Collectively, they represented a new social phenomenon on the Chinese scene which was to become increasingly important as the years rolled by: the treaty port intellectual. Operating on the fringes of the Chinese world, the work of these men at first seemed to bear little relationship to the main stream of events in China. But, in time, a convergence developed between what they had to offer and what China needed. And, as this happened, they gradually acquired a modicum of status and self-respect.

Wang's closest friends during the first half of the fifties were two older colleagues at the LMS press, Li Shan-lan (1810-1882) and Chiang Tun-fu (1808-1867). So inseparable were the three that they were known as "The Three Odd Fellows" (San i-min) and a painting was done of them entitled "The Three Friends of Shanghai" (Hai-t'ien san-yu).[26] Chiang Tun-fu was a native of Pao-shan hsien, Kiangsu. According to Wang, he had been a child prodigy and was known for his bizarre behavior. In his youth, he spent some time in a monastery. But his friends urged him not to waste his talents in this way and he was finally persuaded to sit for the prefectural examinations. The examining official was greatly impressed by Chiang's essays and his name was soon on everybody's lips as a man to watch. Then, however, Chiang became addicted to opium and squandered all of his money on the drug. For a time, his sister helped him out, but when her husband died she entered a nunnery in Shanghai and he had to fall back on his own resources. On Wang T'ao's recommendation, Chiang in the early 1850's found employment assisting William Muirhead (1822-1900) of the LMS in the preparation of the latter's *Ta-Ying-kuo chih* (History of Great Britain). In the process Chiang himself is said to have compiled a more comprehensive history of England which remained unpublished. In addition to becoming something of an expert in foreign matters (he wrote brief biographies of Joan of Arc, George Washington, and Julius Caesar), he was known for his fine poetry, two collections of which were published while he was still alive. His prose writings appeared posthumously.[27]

More than two decades after Chiang Tun-fu's death, an essay by him attacking Christianity was reprinted in a collection of writings on statecraft and Chiang was roundly condemned in a letter published in the *North-China Herald.* Joseph Edkins (1823-1905), an LMS missionary who had been in Shanghai in the 1850's, came to Chiang's defense:

He was a man whom I knew well, ruined by opium smoking, and a clever writer . . . he worked with us, not because he loved Christianity, but to be able to continue the enjoyment of the opium pipe.

What was the reason of the bitterness shown by him in writing against Christianity? I suspect that he wished to gain the favour of Confucianist readers. He repeats no scandals. He writes politically from the Confucianist standpoint . . . Tsiang [Chiang] also had a partiality for Buddhist reading and that would prejudice him somewhat against Christianity . . . We need to allow a liberal discount in a writer like Tsiang for his way of employing forcible terms consecrated by long usage.[28]

Li Shan-lan was a native of Hai-ning, Chekiang. Like Wang T'ao and Chiang Tun-fu, he failed to go beyond the *hsiu-ts'ai* degree. From childhood, he displayed a rare ability in the field of mathematics. In a book on logarithms written in 1846 he developed a theorem which, according to the missionary-scholar Alexander Wylie (1815-1887), "in the days of Briggs and Napier would have been sufficient to raise him to distinction." In 1852 Li went to Shanghai and for the next eight years assisted missionaries of the LMS in the translation of Western mathematical and scientific works (Euclid, William Whewell, John F.W. Herschel, and Augustus de Morgan, among others). For a time, in the 1860's, Li served on Tseng Kuo-fan's staff. In 1869 he was made head of the

Department of Mathematics and Astronomy of the T'ung-wen kuan (Peking). He remained on the T'ung-wen kuan faculty until his death in 1882.[2 9]

In 1869 the American missionary, W.A.P. Martin (1827-1916) was appointed president of the T'ung-wen kuan and Li Shan-lan and Martin became good friends. Martin's impressions of him are therefore of interest: Li was "the most eminent mathematician China has produced." His "example . . . inspired our students with zeal for mathematical studies, though the difficulty of following his reasoning was aggravated by a villainous patois, which made him quite unintelligible to the people of Peking." While working with Wylie in Shanghai, Martin continues, Li came "very near professing Christianity. Deterred by fear of prejudice to his official preferment, he retained in considerable measure the impressions he then received . . . His faith, if he had any, was a compound of West and East." "Of stout unwieldy form, massive head, and heavy features, Professor Li so much resembled the viceroy Tso [Tsung-t'ang] that his likeness was once published for that of the conqueror of Kashgar."[3 0]

Another friend, with whom Wang T'ao became particularly intimate in the late 1850's, was Kung Ch'eng (b. 1817), son of the influential scholar and reformer, Kung Tzu-chen (1792-1841).[3 1] Henry McAleavy has translated one of Wang's sketches of Kung:

Mr. Kung was by nature very fond of wine, and as he was one of my very best friends, whenever I was free in the evening I would go to his place and stay there until the small hours drinking and talking about everything under the sun . . . He came from a very distinguished family, which, incidentally, had the biggest collection of books in Kiangsu or Chekiang, including many titles not found in the imperial collection . . . When he was a young man, Kung browsed about this collection, and made copies of a lot of rare material from it. In this way he absorbed an enormous amount of reading. Unfortunately the collection was all destroyed in a fire . . . Kung was . . . born in Shanghai . . . but he went with his father all over the country, making a specially long stay in Peking. It was there he learned Manchu and Mongol and was always in the company of those people and others from Central Asia . . . He was not interested in an official career, and in middle life he was reduced to such poverty that he had to pawn even his lutes and his books ... During the campaign of 1860 Kung [who was working at the time for Thomas Wade in the British consulate] went up to Tientsin with the British fleet. Such conduct aroused great dislike. The latter part of his life was even more unprosperous ... It was rare for him to find anything good to say of his contemporaries. These in their turn feared and disliked him as an eccentric, and shunned his company so much that they would go out of their way to avoid meeting him ... He went out of his mind before he died.[32]

Kung Ch'eng was, indeed, an eccentric. In another profile of him, Wang says that at one point he threw aside everything and began to study Sanskrit, chanting sutras day and night.[33] According to a widely circulated tale, he not only accompanied the British on the 1860 expedition, but was actually the first to suggest the burning of the Summer Palace—not, it should quickly be added, out of disloyalty to China, but because of an old family grudge against the Manchus! Whatever the truth concerning this and other questionable acts attributed to Kung, McAleavy is certainly correct in stating that Wang T'ao "must have been flattered by the familiar conversation of a man of distinguished family ... whose contempt for officials and the system by which they gained preferment came so conveniently to soothe his own disappointment and loss of self-esteem."[34]

WANG T'AO AND THE CHRISTIAN CHURCH

One of the most puzzling chapters in Wang T'ao's career was his relationship to Christianity. In July 1853 one of Thomas Wade's Chinese assistants at the British consulate, Ying Lung-t'ien, returned from abroad and, introducing himself to Medhurst, announced that he wanted to become a convert. Daily, thereafter, Ying went to the press and studied the Scriptures under Medhurst's guidance, soon being joined in this by another of Wang T'ao's friends, Sun Ch'i-chü.[35] There is an almost complete break in Wang's diary from the summer of 1853 to the fall of 1854. When the diary recommences, this is what we find:

October 15, 1854 [Sunday]: No work today. Went to hospital to hear Englishman preach. Received communion . . .

October 17, 1854: Pastors Medhurst and Muirhead were making an excursion to Yün-chien [hsien in Sungkiang prefecture, Kiangsu] and Tung-t'ing [mountain in Soochow prefecture], and asked me to accompany them . . .

October 18, 1854: . . . At noon we reached Min-hsing *chen* [near Chinshan hsien, Kiangsu]. Securing the boat and stepping ashore, we distributed Bibles . . .

October 19, 1854: . . . In late afternoon we reached T'un-ts'un. Went ashore with Pastors Medhurst and Muirhead and distributed literature. The people of the place crowded around to hear them preach. The literature we had with us was gone in no time . . .

March 18, 1855: Today Sunday. Went to Wu-lao-feng to hear Englishman expound Scriptures . . . [In afternoon] met Chiang Chien-jen [Chiang Tun-fu] and went with him to the brothel on the lefthand side of Rainbow Bridge [Hung-ch'iao]. The two courtesans [who entertained us] were visitors from Yangchow. They weren't very pretty . . .

April 1, 1855 [Sunday]: Went to church and received communion . . . [36]

These diary entries provide convincing evidence that Wang T'ao, as of late 1854, had become a practicing Christian, a fact duly confirmed in LMS records, where Wang is listed as having been baptized on August 26, 1854.[37] The remarkable thing is that, in the entire corpus of Wang's *published* writings, there is not the slightest hint of corroboration of this.[38] In fact, comparison of the printed and manuscript versions of a letter Wang wrote to James Legge reveals that Wang was willing to take considerable pains to conceal his Christian tie. The original text of this letter (which was written in 1873 on the occasion of Legge's departure for England) refers to Legge as "Pastor" (*mu-shih*), the printed text, as "Mister" (*chün*). At one point in the original Wang states of Legge: "His main purpose was to preach the Gospel to bring salvation to the whole world and to lead men to eternal life, so that the light of the Christian doctrine could shine in every corner of the earth." In the printed version this sentence is replaced by another which makes no reference whatever to Christianity. Only in the manuscript version, finally, does Wang reveal that the letter was written by him on behalf of the "members of the church of Hong Kong."[39]

Wang's apparent ambivalence toward Christianity was revealed in other ways as well. Through the remainder of his career, he continued to be closely associated with Protestant missionaries in a variety of enterprises (mostly secular). Moreover, he showed a decided preference for Protestant over Catholic Christianity and defended Jesus as one of the great men of Western history, the man principally responsible for giving to Westerners their knowledge of *tao* (the Way, norms of civilized behavior).[40] Yet, in the later decades of his life Wang T'ao voiced criticism of both the missionary movement and Christianity,[41] and he consistently pointed to Confucius as the historical figure whose elucidation of *tao* came closest to perfection.

What, then, are we to make of Wang's Christianity? Was he "sincere" or was he an opportunist? We have seen, in Edkins' apology for Chiang Tun-fu and Martin's assessment of Li Shan-lan, the obstacles that stood in the way of any sort of public profession of Christianity by a Chinese with scholarly or official pretensions. The fact that Wang T'ao went to some lengths to conceal his Christian affiliation cannot, therefore, be taken as solid proof that he was a "bad" Christian. There is precious little evidence, on the other hand, to show that he was a good one. Certainly, Wang's behavior, from a Christian standpoint, left something to be desired. Moreover, although he may have remained a church member until the end of his life (the latest positive evidence of affiliation is the 1873 letter to Legge), he does not (as do T'an Ssu-t'ung and K'ang Yu-wei) lead one, at any point, to believe one is in the presence of a personality with a strong religious orientation.

So much for Wang T'ao's commitment to Christianity. What were the forces that induced him to become a convert in the first place? One of these, certainly, was the nature of the work in which Wang was engaged at the LMS press during the first several years. This was a new Chinese translation of the Bible, to become known popularly as the Delegates' Version. The preliminary work on this translation had been done by local committees representing much of the Protestant missionary body. Then a smaller committee of five was delegated to see the work through to completion. This committee, which was headed by Medhurst, met daily at the latter's home in Shanghai beginning in June 1847. The work on the New Testament was completed in July 1850, that on the Old Testament in 1853.[42] W.C. Milne of the LMS, who was a chief participant throughout, described the procedure followed: "Our sessions occurred daily, opened with reading a portion of the Sacred Scriptures and prayer, and extended from 10 o'clock A.M. to half-past 2 o'clock P.M. The method of proceeding . . . was to consider verse by verse, word by word, allowing each individual opportunity to propose any alteration that he might deem desirable. The several members of the delegation had their native tutors with them . . . rendering most valuable assistance."[43]

The Delegates' Version of the New Testament was adopted by the British and Foreign Bible Society and rapidly became the most widely circulated version in China. By 1859 it had already gone through eleven editions and, as late as the 1920's, was still in use.[44] A speaker at the general missionary conference of 1890 expressed the opinion of many when he remarked: "As a literary work it has altogether a new flavor. It is comparatively free from harsh and forced constructions . . . a monument to the erudition of its authors . . . The most frequent adverse criticism of it is not against its literary polish, but that it does not sufficiently conform to the rule . . . of strict adherence to the sense of the original always . . . that too often combinations of characters are found more suggestive of the doctrines of the sages than of the mysteries of the kingdom of heaven . . . that . . . the inexperienced unspiritual reader, deceived by the familiarity of the rhythm, is liable to mistake Christ for Confucius, to his peril."[45]

It is very probable that the literary merit of the Delegates' Version was due, in substantial measure, to the skill of Wang T'ao. The translation, according to Alexander Wylie, could "well be considered [Medhurst's] production,"[46] and Wang had started working as Medhurst's "Chinese teacher" some eight or nine months prior to the project's completion, giving him ample time to exert an impact at least in the realm of style.[47] Further evidence of Wang's contribution, although indirect, is provided by the high regard in which he was held by his employers, who obviously sensed that in Wang T'ao they had struck gold. "He is a man of first-rate abilities," they wrote in 1854, "and should he continue in his present inquiring state of mind, he will be of the greatest service to us in a literary point of view."[48] The following year Wang was given the responsibility of revising all of the Society's Chinese hymns and "putting them into such a form that they might not be repulsive to the ears of the most refined poetical genius."[49]

Wang T'ao's conversion to Christianity can only be partially explained in terms of the nature of the work in which he was engaged at the LMS press. Equally important was the high-powered group of missionaries with whom he labored. A half-century later, Griffith John (1831-1912) of the LMS, recalling his early years in Shanghai, described William Muirhead as "one of the great evangelists the Christian Church has given to the Chinese people" and Medhurst as "the corypheus among the sinologues of his day . . . a very prince among the missionaries."[50] Daily contact with missionaries of this caliber generated its own kind of pressure. The missionaries did not insist upon their "native assistants" becoming Christians. But their preference was plain enough and many a Chinese employee must have felt that a discreet show of interest in the Christian religion was called for in the situation. It is unlikely that Wang T'ao's Chinese friends, most of whom were employed by Westerners and several of whom had themselves evinced a desire to convert, would have prized his companionship any the less for it. One of the most significant features of the newly emerging culture of the treaty ports, after all, was its comparative freedom from the constraints and taboos of the old hinterland culture.

A PRELIMINARY ASSESSMENT OF THE WEST: 1859

Wang T'ao's writings, for the first decade or so of his sojourn in Shanghai, contain almost no discussion of the West, certainly no hint that he viewed the West as a major "challenge." This may seem odd in light of the fact that Wang worked for Westerners and lived in a city in which Western influence was growing by the day. In order to understand why it was so, two things must be kept in mind. First, China in the 1850's (and Kiangsu province especially) was in the throes of an internal upheaval, the Taiping Rebellion (1850-1864), which dwarfed in importance all other contemporary developments. Of this more will be said in the next chapter. A second factor was that educated Chinese, in the middle of the last century, still lived under the influence of a world view in which little or no provision was made for the possibility of a fundamental challenge to Chinese civilization.

The key element in this world view was an unquestioning faith in China's centrality. On a geographical plane, it was widely held that the earth was a flat expanse with China (Chung-kuo: "Central Kingdom") at the center. This sense of geographical centrality had its political counterpart in the view that, in a properly ordered world, China would be the ultimate source of authority. Finally, the whole edifice rested on the conviction that Chinese values and cultural norms (all that the Chinese subsumed under the concept *tao*) were valid for all men and all time. Chinese standards were civilized standards; one became civilized as one became Chinese.[51]

Certainly the Chinese were not unique among the world's peoples in identifying their particular values with universal human norms. Christians, Moslems, Marxists, and Americans have all operated on the assumption that what is good for "us" is good for all. The uniqueness of the Chinese view lay in the pervasiveness of its grip and the degree to which, for largely geographical reasons, it had been permitted to develop unchallenged through the centuries. China had succumbed to superior military power (Mongols, Manchus), and Chinese civilization had been deeply influenced by contact with at least one other high civilization (India). But at no time prior to the nineteenth century had the Chinese world been challenged by an alternative center of civilization coupled with immense power resources. Moreover, when Chinese looked about them and observed the extent to which Chinese civilization had left its mark on the whole East Asian realm, there was little enough to keep them from concluding that what *had* not happened *could* not happen.

One effect of this world view was to discourage any serious intellectual preoccupation with "non-China." The very idea of "barbarian studies" was self-contradictory, since barbarians were by definition not worth studying. Chinese, therefore, not only were ignorant of the West in 1840. They remained ignorant of the West long after the Opium War was over. A second effect of the prevailing world view, inseparable from the first, was to structure Chinese perceptions of the West in such a way as to attribute all value to China and little or none to the West. The West might be superior to China in this or that area and it might even be necessary for Chinese to delve into such areas for security purposes. But, in themselves, these areas were unimportant.

In the latter half of the 1850's unresolved tensions between China and the West brought on a renewal of conflict. The *Arrow* and Chapdelaine incidents of 1856 provided the British and French with the needed pretexts. In the fall the British began their bombardment of the yamen of Canton Governor-General Yeh Ming-ch'en. Early in 1858, after a delay occasioned by the outbreak of the Sepoy Mutiny in India, Canton was taken and Yeh carted off to Calcutta. An Anglo-French expedition then proceeded to Tientsin where, in June 1858, a new set of treaties was negotiated with the Manchu government, providing for the residence of foreign envoys in Peking on terms of diplomatic equality. The Russians and Americans obtained almost identical treaties soon after. As it turned out, the Manchu court was unwilling to yield so easily on the residence issue, and when the allied negotiators returned to Tientsin in the summer of 1859 to exchange ratifications, new fighting broke out. A much larger foreign expedition finally forced the outcome in 1860. Supplementary conventions were negotiated and the Tientsin treaties ratified.

The events of the late fifties brought about a temporary (and of course only partial) shift in the focus of Chinese concern from the internal to the external menace. In the wake of this shift, the market value of expertise on the West rose and, with it, the self-esteem and confidence of men like Wang T'ao. In 1859, on hearing that a friend, Chou T'eng-hu,[52] was in line for an official assignment, Wang took it upon himself to write a long letter to Chou outlining his ideas on Sino-Western relations. He began by attacking three views which apparently were already current among treaty port Chinese: (1) that the growth of foreign trade benefited China by bringing in large customs revenues; (2) that China would advance in wealth and power (*fu-ch'iang*) by adopting the West's superior technology: its guns, steamships, railways, and textile and agricultural machinery; and (3) that it would be of practical advantage for Chinese scholars to master such fields of Western learning as astronomy, mathematics, geology, biology, water conservancy, and medicine.

Wang criticized each of these views in some detail. Whatever the immediate advantages of Western commerce, he argued, the opening up of China to the West exposed the Chinese people to great harm in the long run. Look what had happened to India! The Chinese court generously permitted the Westerners to trade at Canton and, as soon as the destruction of the opium occurred, they turned around and attacked China. The court, then, bending over backward to accede to their wishes, granted them five ports in which to trade. How grateful they should have been! But, no, on some flimsy pretext, they commenced hostilities in the region of the capital (that is, Tientsin) and demanded permission to trade in the interior. It all began, Wang tells us, with the giving up of Macao to Portugal. Now the Westerners were strategically situated in a number of ports and when conflicts broke out China could no longer control the situation.

Nor was the Western menace exclusively a military one. There was also the larger danger to Chinese customs and mores. Ever since the beginning of trade relations, the rotten elements of society had found a haven in association with the Westerners. The doctrines of the Taiping rebel chiefs, with whom people's minds were being poisoned, had been influenced by the teachings of the church in Kwangtung. "It is to be feared," Wang wrote, "that as time goes on Chinese customs will gradually become Westernized, resulting in great harm to Confucian values" (*ming-chiao*).

Wang T'ao was well aware of the benefits of Western technology and, to his credit, he did not fall into the trap of rejecting it because of its foreign origin. The reasons why China could not adopt it were of a practical kind: China's internal harbors were too narrow for steamship navigation, her topography was unsuited to the construction of railway lines, the introduction of time-saving agricultural machinery would put millions of poor peasants out of work, and so on.

Although, in a letter written the previous year, Wang had judged Western proficiency in astronomy and mathematics to be "ten times" higher than Chinese,[5 3] he now took a deprecatory view of Western science in general:

As for astronomy and astrology, in terms of relative refinement, it is true that Chinese methods are far from equaling Western methods and modern methods are vastly superior to ancient methods. But I am of the opinion that the ancient methods are useful while the modern methods are of no use, for the modern methods must undergo a constant process of change whereas the ancient methods last a long time without becoming obsolete . . . As for mathematics, it is but one of the Six Arts . . . Even if the whole world were to study it, of what benefit would it be in matters pertaining to the life of the body and mind or to the principles involved in governing a country and setting the world in order? If, on the other hand, man were to be deprived of this discipline altogether, it would be no great loss. As for the sciences of zoology and botany, skilled practitioners are said to be able to reconstruct an entire skeleton from a single bone or identify a whole plant on the basis of a solitary leaf. But I've only heard this said. I've never seen the man who could do it.

Did this, then, mean that Western methods (*Hsi-fa*) ought not to be introduced in China under any circumstances? Not at all, Wang answered. The past had known wise men who had adopted barbarian methods, and even Confucius had gone to the four corners of the realm in his quest for knowledge. A successful policy hinged on selecting those methods that were applicable and rejecting those that were not. Wang then proceeded to discuss three areas in which it would be to China's advantage to learn from the West. First, she should adopt Western firearms, so that her armies could compete on even terms. Second, she should introduce Western steamships to defend her coastline against pirates and other dangers. Finally, she would do well to establish interpreters' colleges in each of the treaty ports so that a better class of people could be trained in Western languages for service as interpreters and translators.

Having proposed these three measures, Wang hastened to add that he favored them only because China had no alternative. The adoption of certain of the West's methods was necessary in order to control the West, but it could hardly be justified on any other grounds. If the Westerners had never come to China, there would be no advantage in emulating their methods—and a great deal of harm. Wang had little patience with those who maintained that, as the whole world was now one (*t'ien-hsia ta-t'ung*) and the Westerners, in revealing the secrets behind their new methods, had done much to enlarge China's knowledge, Chinese should bear them no ill will. He reminded such persons that China herself had produced a long line of individuals of technological ingenuity, such as Mo-tzu, who devised elaborate defenseworks, and Chu-ko Liang, who had invented a self-propelling vehicle for transporting grain. All of these inventions, however, had died with their inventors, the Chinese view being that man's intelligence was best directed along other lines. "Therefore, I say: China excels in the higher realm, *tao* [norms of civilized conduct], while the Westerners excel in the lower realm, *ch'i* [technology]."

Reproaching those who praised everything Western and deprecated everything Chinese, Wang pointed to three basic defects in Western (he really meant British) governmental institutions: (1) that state and church were joined in one body (*cheng-chiao i-t'i*); (2) that men and women could both succeed to the throne; and (3) that the monarch and the people shared in the governing power (*chün-min t'ung-chih*).[54] He then listed a number of other features of Western life which he found deplorable: the wealth of merchants gravitated to the people at the top, yet the national debt frequently figured in the millions; when women married they had to pay dowries, with the result that those who had no wealth sometimes spent their entire lives single; youth was prized and old age disesteemed; Westerners revered a Lord of Heaven (God) but were remiss in the carrying out of their obligations to their secular rulers; they revered a Great Father (God) but the affection shown by sons to their own fathers was niggardly. "Is there anything worthy of praise in mores as contemptible as these?"

In the final portion of his long letter, Wang placed the Sino-Western confrontation in broader perspective and found reassurance for the future in a cyclical view of history. China's ultimate defense, he reasoned, was her moral (*te*) rather than her physical power (*li*). When the government of China flourished, the countries on her peripheries submitted; when the Great Way prospered, foreign teachings perished. The reason why the Westerners had come to China was that China's physical power was, for the moment, in a state of decline. But this was nothing new. Throughout her long history China had been invaded by barbarians who were temporarily stronger than she. Yet, invariably, after entering China, their power wilted. Where were the Liao, the Chin, and the Yüan today? "Indeed! From ancient times down there has never been a country that has perpetuated its power" (*wu ch'ang-ch'iang chih kuo*).[55] And the same law held for European history. In Han times it was Rome that was dominant, in T'ang-Sung times, Spain, in Ming times, Holland, and now, England. But just as Rome, Spain, and Holland had declined in the past, so would England in the future. Arrogance and self-satisfaction invited destruction. This was Heaven's Way (*t'ien-tao*).[56]

In January 1859, the governorship of Kiangsu was taken over by one of China's most eminent mathematicians, Hsü Yu-jen (1800-1860). Hsü was an admirer of Li Shan-lan (who served on his staff for a while in 1859-1860),[57] and very likely it was through Li that he heard about Wang T'ao. Wang, during the first half of 1859, began to ply Hsü with advice concerning China's current difficulties, and it appears that Hsü encouraged him.

In Wang's first letter to Hsü he opened with a statement of priorities which in 1859 could probably only have been made by a man who had lived for some time in the treaty ports: "At present China's greatest problem does not consist in pacification of the rebels but in withstanding the barbarians, for the rebellion's birth had its roots in the outbreak of difficulties with the barbarian. Yet, if we are to withstand the barbarians, we must first pacify the rebels . . . and if we are to pacify the rebels we must begin by preserving peaceful relations with the barbarians." The barbarian peril, in short, was the more profound of the two, but it was also the less urgent.

Wang was incensed at the humiliations to which China had been subjected in the previous year and reproached China's high officials for their seeming indifference to the fate of Canton and its erstwhile governor-general, Yeh Ming-ch'en. Yet, consistent with his initial remarks, his advice was strongly conciliatory. Noting the military preparations being made by Seng-ko-lin-ch'in at Tientsin, he warned that if the dynasty contemplated war with the foreigners, it was making a huge mistake.

The central issues at dispute were the foreigners' demands for an increased number of treaty ports and for ministerial residence in the capital. The court, it seemed to Wang, while willing to concede the first demand, viewed the second as a danger of indescribable proportions. Wang felt differently, and argued that China should yield on the second issue as well. His reasons were two. First, and most basic, China was not strong enough to defeat the foreigners militarily. If she yielded on the residence issue without resorting to hostilities, the foreigners would be grateful for the court's kindness. But if she insisted on going to war, the foreigners would still get their way, and there would be no gratitude. Second, although China was not accustomed to having foreign officials reside in her capital, this was the normal practice in foreign countries. The interest of the Westerners in China, for the time being at least, was confined to trade, and their purpose in wishing to reside in Peking was to enable them more easily to look after their commercial interests. It was not, as feared, to spy on China.[5 8]

In a second letter to Hsü, Wang went straight to the heart of China's problem. The reasons for her continuing difficulties with the West were, first, military weakness, and second, internal unrest. Therefore it was essential that measures for self-strengthening be adopted without delay. Some court officials did not view the barbarians as an urgent problem, because unlike earlier barbarians the Westerners did not seem to be interested in Chinese territory. But was the granting of treaty port privileges really so different from the cession of territory? The calamity in the first instance might be slower and less apparent, but it was no less real. Others, Wang went on, believed that the old strategy of playing off one barbarian against another could still work. But, while it was true that there was plenty of friction among the Western countries at home, could one seriously imagine the United States siding with China in an attack on England? In concluding, Wang reiterated his belief that no country in the world could remain powerful and prosperous forever. But, in the same breath, he cautioned against the complacent view that a country could *acquire* power and prosperity without taking definite measures. China, in other words, could not just sit back and wait for the balance of power to turn in her favor. The only way in which she would ever be able to neutralize the Western challenge would be by taking over and applying the specific Western strengths on which this challenge was built.[59]

Wang T'ao's maiden assessment of China's confrontation with the West contained certain ideas, such as the cyclical perspective on history and the clear recognition of Western power superiority, which he was never to relinquish. Many of the other ideas he expressed at this time, however, would eventually undergo radical revision. Although it is clear that by the late 1850's Wang already perceived the West as a major physical threat to China, he was not yet ready to concede (at least openly) that it might also represent a challenge of a more fundamental kind. The West had to become a respected civilization before such would be possible. Barbarians with "high noses and deepset eyes," "cruel and crafty by nature"[60]—phrases Wang still was using in his correspondence of the 1850's—would have to become full-scale human beings.

2

THE AMBIGUITIES OF REBELLION:

WANG T'AO AND THE TAIPINGS

The Taiping Rebellion was possibly the greatest civil upheaval in world history. Its causes were complex. Some of them, such as official corruption, overtaxation, and excessive land rents, were typical manifestations of Chinese dynastic decline, while others, notably population explosion and economic dislocation induced by foreign trade, were specific to the first half of the nineteenth century. The Taipings differed from most other peasant movements in Chinese history in that they challenged not only the reigning dynasty but the entire traditional order. In this sense, they are better described as revolutionaries than as rebels. Their ideology was a bizarre alchemy of militant Old Testament Christianity, utopian Confucianism, sexual puritanism, and primitive communism. The movement's founder and early leader was a Hakka from Kwangsi, a visionary who called himself the younger brother of Jesus Christ and was convinced that he had been divinely charged to rid the world of demons and institute the Kingdom of Heaven on earth.

The rebellion began in 1850 in South China, where conditions were particularly ripe for revolt. The insurgents quickly drove north, piling success upon success against the hapless imperial forces, until they reached the Yangtze River. They then turned eastward and in March 1853 established the capital of the Heavenly Kingdom of Great Peace (T'ai-p'ing t'ien-kuo) in Nanking. Nanking remained the Taiping capital until the movement's collapse in 1864. Although the main area of rebel control was in central China, in fifteen years of fighting some sixteen Chinese provinces were affected. A northern expedition in the mid-fifties was able to reach the environs of Peking before being turned back, and in the early 1860's, as the center of rebel strength shifted toward the coast, Shanghai was threatened on a number of occasions.[1]

In its human and physical destructiveness, the Taiping Rebellion had few parallels in history. Large portions of the Lower Yangtze region, rural and urban, were totally devastated, and both sides in the conflict, the imperialists even more than the rebels, treated human life with unbelievable abandon. Millions of people were butchered. Millions more fell victim to famine and disease. Contemporary foreign estimates placed the total of lives lost at between 20,000,000 and 30,000,000. Although these figures were arrived at by guesswork, and may well be exaggerated, there is strong evidence that in individual districts substantial portions of the population were eliminated. Local survivors from Kuang-te in southern Anhwei, for example, described the outcome in the following stark terms: "Within a radius of several tens of li there was no vestige of humanity. The county's original population was over 300,000. By the time the rebels were cleared only a little over 6,000 survived. This was a catastrophe unique for the locality since the beginnings of the human race."[2]

Kuang-te, in Ping-ti Ho's view, was representative of a much larger area in southern Anhwei. Other regions that were especially hard hit were northern Kiangsi, northern Chekiang, and southern Kiangsu. "The once rich and densely settled southern Kiangsu area," according to Ho, "was so depopulated that whole villages of peasants from some Hupei counties rushed in as settlers in the hope that they might 'cultivate ownerless fertile land and occupy ownerless nice houses.' "[3]

Holocausts like the Taiping impinge not only on their immediate victims, but also, in countless ways, on the lives of their

survivors. Certainly this was so in Wang T'ao's case. Wang followed
the rebellion closely from start to finish and eventually became
one of its most important contemporary chroniclers.[4] It first
affected him directly in September 1853 when the Small Sword
Society, a secret society offshoot connected with the Taipings,
seized the walled Chinese city of Shanghai. For many months now
Wang's movements were confined to the foreign-protected International Settlement. Several friends from the Chinese city (among
them Chiang Tun-fu) came to live with him in his home in the
Settlement.[5] Shanghai's history as a haven for refugees from
war-torn areas began, as the Chinese population in the foreign
sectors of the city swelled from 500 in 1852 to 20,000 in 1854.[6]

It took 20,000 imperial troops almost a year and a half to
suppress the Small Sword Society uprising.[7] In contrast, rebel
forces were able to take cities like Kiukiang and Nanking in a
matter of days. What was the cause of the disparity? In part, Wang
T'ao thought, the squandering of China's wealth by yamen clerks,
opium addicts, and Buddhist and Taoist clerics was to blame. But
the principal source of the government's difficulties, in his view,
was the shortage not of money but of men. What China most
needed was able military commanders and competent officials.
The ease with which the Taipings occupied the Lower Yangtze
area was due to popular alienation and low gentry morale. And
alienation and poor morale, he complained to Kung Ch'eng in
1860, were the outgrowth of weak official leadership at the local
level.[8]

In 1860, after a period of waning vigor, the Taipings obtained a
new lease on life under the brilliant command of Li Hsiu-ch'eng.
Li, in the summer of this year, occupied Soochow and much of
the territory between it and Shanghai. The Chinese population of
Shanghai rapidly soared toward the half-million mark,[9] as the city
was inundated by refugees, many of them officials and gentry
from the provincial capital (Soochow). Wang T'ao described the
change that now came over the city: "The bustling gaiety of
Shanghai far surpassed that of former days. Men of prominence
fled their native places and came there to take up refuge. And
through gambling and drinking, conversation and poetry, they
almost forgot the ravages of the war."[10]

WANG T'AO'S ADVICE TO THE AUTHORITIES

During the 1850's Wang T'ao, as far as is known, remained aloof from the struggle against the Taipings.[11] The rebels' occupation of his home place and convergence on Shanghai in the summer of 1860, however, impelled him to take a more active part. For a while he assisted the local officials of Chu-chai, west of Shanghai, in organizing and training that town's militia units.[12] In the fall of 1860, moreover, he began to ply the authorities with advice on how to deal with the rebels.

The wealth of Shanghai, Wang observed in his initial communication, was a prize the rebels would spare no effort to get their hands on. Preparations therefore had to be made for the city's defense. But to concentrate on defense alone would leave the initiative to the rebels and permit them to attack the city at a time of their own choosing, thus depriving the government of an important advantage. The rebels had not yet consolidated their gains in southern Kiangsu and popular morale (*min-ch'i*) in the region was still high. The government side, therefore, had everything to gain by an immediate counterattack. Shanghai's best defense was to take the offense.

Wang's specific proposals were set forth in two groups of ten each. The first group may be summarized as follows: (1) Induce mercenary fighters who have fled Kwangtung and Kwangsi to support the imperial side. (2) Devise means to liberate those portions of the population that have been coerced into joining the rebels. (3) Encourage stray boats from Ch'ao-hu (a large lake in Anhwei) to join the government side, so that the rebels will not be able to develop a naval force. (4) Put refugees from Nanking to constructive use so that they do not constitute an unnecessary strain on government resources. (5) Keep the spheres of operation of popular militia units and government forces separate, so that they cannot shift responsibility back and forth. (6) Appoint as militia heads men of proven courage and resourcefulness. (7) Employ foreign officers to assist Chinese commanders in enforcing discipline in the field. (8) Disguise government troops as rebels so that in battle the latter will be thrown into confusion and caught off guard. (9) Protect Shanghai by strengthening the supply network and volunteer defense system in the surrounding countryside. (10) Secure Shanghai against subversion from within by carefully investigating all recent arrivals and searching all incoming boats.

Wang's second set of proposals dealt largely with guerrilla tactics. The peasantry knew the countryside better than anyone, he argued, but they needed intelligent military leadership in order to provide effective resistance. Wang's specific suggestions were as ruthless as they were ingenious: seduce the rebels into penetrating deep and then mousetrap them; scrutinize the movements of the rebels and attack them when they are fatigued; instruct villagers to abandon their homes prior to the arrival of rebel forces and then launch surprise attacks; sabotage rebel boats; and so forth.[13]

One gets from Wang's proposals a vivid sense of the fluidity of the situation in the combat area. This was no ordinary war, where the two sides looked different, spoke different languages, and represented radically different commitments. It was a civil war. To be sure, as in other civil conflicts, there were those, especially among the educated, who fought to preserve or destroy something larger than themselves: an idea, a set of values, a political regime. But for vast numbers of participants the line separating friend and foe, progovernment and antigovernment, was extremely blurred. The principal concern, at the level of peasant decision, was personal survival, and it was not always clear on which side one's interests were likely to be best served.

One of Wang's proposals brings this out with particular sharpness. When rebel units approached a new village, he notes, they sometimes made a pretense of being righteous and compassionate and, if the villagers responded with money and provisions, refrained from looting and burning. The villagers, "desiring only the protection of their families and having no sense of any larger obligations [ta-i]," then reposed trust in the rebels and disbanded their militias. To counteract this, Wang recommended that militia chiefs, posing as ordinary villagers, present gifts to the rebels and then ambush them. Then, when the villagers presented *their* gifts, the rebels would kill the villagers, whereupon the villagers would lose all trust in the rebels![14]

Shortly after submitting the foregoing, Wang T'ao pressed upon the local authorities another set of proposals, this time focusing on the problem of severing lines of communication and supply between Shanghai and rebel-held areas. The special character of the jurisdictional situation in Shanghai made this an exceedingly complex problem, for it involved controlling the activities not only of rebel spies entering the city and Chinese traitors living in the sanctuary of the International Settlement, but also of those Western merchants who surreptitiously supplied the rebels with arms and provisions. The problem was rendered even stickier by the large number of overland and riverine accesses to the metropolis. Wang's solution embraced a wide range of measures, including the registration and investigation of refugees, inspection of the cargoes on all incoming and outgoing vessels, the establishment of riverine checkpoints where merchants would be required to furnish inspectors with details concerning their trading transactions, and the like. Above all, he maintained, it was essential that Chinese and foreign authorities cooperate closely.[15]

One other letter, probably written by Wang in late 1861, deserves brief mention, though it appears never to have been sent. This was addressed to the commander in chief on the government side, Tseng Kuo-fan (1811-1872). Its main point was that the recent successes of the Taipings in the southeast were due not to rebel military prowess but to a basic flaw on the government side, namely that the authority of the chou and hsien magistrates was not proportionate to the critical nature of their functions. If government-controlled cities were to be adequately defended and rebel forces put to rout, it was necessary for magistrates in charge of urban defenses to be given not only full responsibility but also greatly increased powers.[16]

In a number of essays written around this time Wang T'ao gave more systematic expression to his views. One, which he claims to have submitted to the authorities just prior to the rebel seizure of Soochow, noted that there were three general strategies for dealing with rebels: extermination, blockade, and pacification. Blockade and pacification, however, could work only if the capacity to exterminate existed, and the strategy of extermination, to be effective, had to be implemented with intelligence. Wang made it quite clear that, in his view, this was precisely where the government fell short of the mark.[17]

The empire, Wang wrote in a second essay, was beset by three great maladies. Yet, like the man who conceals his illness and refuses medical attention, the authorities persisted in letting matters drift and in lulling people into thinking everything was fine. The three maladies were the impoverishment of the people (due to the extraordinary tax burden required to finance the suppression campaign), the devastation of Kiangsu and Chekiang (China's richest rice-producing area), and a wooden, inflexible adherence to form and precedent on the part of Chinese officials (the last, according to Wang, a "chronic malady").

These maladies required urgent treatment or they would become incurable. To relieve the pressure on popular livelihood, Wang proposed that the government encourage development of China's natural, manufactured, and commercial wealth. Once the government pointed the way, private individuals would quickly follow, and in ten years time there would be something to show. The economic rehabilitation of war-torn Kiangsu and Chekiang, of course, could be accomplished only after the destruction of the rebels, but the mere fact that Wang underscored the urgency of the problem must be counted to his credit.

The malady that was most distressing to him, as might be guessed, was the excessive rigidity of the bureaucracy and its recruitment policy. The great peril to China, he wrote, was not the rebels in her midst but the relative absence of gifted men in government. "Men of ability are the vital force of the country. The people depend on them for their livelihood. If it could really and truly be seen to that there were no free-riders among the officials and no neglected talents among the population, what hardship would there be in a paltry handful of rebels!" Wang had in mind men who could do more than shuffle documents back and forth, who were willing and able to give substance to government measures. But such men, he caustically concluded, were to be found only in the everyday world of practical affairs. They would never be brought to light through the regular examinations.[18]

PRESUMPTUOUS TALK

In January 1862, Wang T'ao received word that his mother was ill and immediately departed for home. His stay in Fu-li was prolonged, allegedly because of bad weather and severe fighting, and it was not until May that he returned to Shanghai. During the three and a half or so months that he was in Fu-li, despondency over the course the war was taking and frustration at the government's ineptitude prompted him to write a searching critique of China's ills.

Entitled "I-t'an" (Presumptuous talk) and written in forty-four parts, the critique was consciously patterned after two political works of the T'ang and Sung periods (Tu Mu's *Tsui-yen* and Su Hsün's *Ch'üan-shu*). Although Wang apparently hoped to present his views to the authorities, this hope never materialized for reasons that will shortly be made clear. He did, however, publish a portion of the work some years later.[19]

In the "I-t'an" essays Wang T'ao brings under scrutiny three broad areas of government policy: economic, military, and political. His economic views are a blend of old and new. The aim of the government, he tells us, is to enrich the state and satisfy the basic needs of the people (*fu-kuo erh tsu-min*). Four paths should be followed to reach this goal: reduction of expenditures, expansion of revenues, elimination of extravagance, and encouragement of frugality. Wang also recognized the value of developing, through application of Western methods (*Hsi-fa*), such new sources of wealth as mining, shipbuilding, and machine weaving. But this would take much time. For the present, more traditional approaches were needed. Wang noted, for example, a number of actions the government could take immediately to cut down on spending: removal of supernumerary officials from the bureaucracy, termination of the practice of padding troop registers, and shipment of tribute grain by sea in order to eliminate the huge expense of maintaining the Grand Canal.[20]

The condition of the Ch'ing military was criticized by Wang on several counts. Troop registers were falsified in order to get additional rations, the ranks were filled with men too old or too weak to fight, training was neglected, weapons were of poor quality, volunteers were brave when it came to brawling but cowardly in combat. In order to remedy these defects Wang proposed that rations be increased, that training be improved, and that more attention be paid to the general problem of morale and discipline. Above all, he insisted on the need for better generals: "A thousand troops are easily obtained but one general is hard to find."

Generals, moreover, should have different fields of expertise. Some should be held responsible for overall strategic planning, others for field command, and still others for military engineering, weapons use, and so on. To encourage such specialization, Wang proposed that the military examinations be completely overhauled, separate examinations being designed for the different types of military leaders. He further urged that a military training academy (*wu-pei yüan*) be founded, where future officers could study and undergo periodic examination. Every three years men could be recruited from the academy and assigned ranks in the army. China's military preparedness would thus be placed on a regular footing and she would not again have to fear being taken by surprise.[21]

Wang T'ao's primary concern in the "I-t'an" essays was with China's system of government. Repeatedly he gave expression to a strain in the Chinese political tradition that might be loosely characterized as "radical feudalism": "radical" in its thoroughgoing critique of the practice (if not theory) of the existing imperial bureaucratic state, "feudalism" because the model for the critique, by and large, was the period of the Three Dynasties when a political arrangement sometimes described as feudal prevailed in China.

The nub of the problem, as Wang saw it, was the great chasm that had grown up between the monarch, on the one hand, and the officials and people on the other. In antiquity, when there was a close relationship between ruler and people, the people were able to communicate their grievances to the ruler. The monarch, in turn, was privy to the innermost thoughts of his ministers. Beginning with the Ch'in, however, all of this changed. It became more and more difficult for officials to get the ear of the monarch except by servile flattery, and ordinary people came to view the imperial palace as being no less distant than Heaven.[22]

Wang felt that the solution to this problem lay, first, in increasing the quality and effective power of the officials, and second, in fostering a greater sense of solidarity of interest between the governing and the governed. The two approaches were, of course, inseparable. The establishment of a more energetic and resourceful officialdom would automatically have the effect of repairing broken lines of communication between the sovereign and society.

In ancient times, when the monarch was more approachable and less awesome, officials spoke their minds freely and admonished the throne with regularity. Now, however, although there were officials (censors) specially charged with the task, the incentives to flatter and fawn were so great that candid criticism was rarely encountered at court. As a consequence, there was no way for the throne to gain a faithful picture of what was going on in the empire. To remedy this situation, Wang T'ao urged that fearless criticism by censors be rewarded and that the *yen-lu* (avenue of criticism) be opened, thereby encouraging all officials to report frankly on affairs in their jurisdictions.[23]

Wang also opposed the frequent transfer of officials from one post to another, arguing that this practice prevented officials from familiarizing themselves with local problems and devising long-term programs for dealing with them. Again Wang harked back to the ancients—this time to their practice of employing or dismissing officials on the basis of "public opinion" (*yü-p'ing*). Ordinary people might be simple but they were the most fair-minded, and where reliance was placed on their judgment good government was sure to prevail.[24]

Wang's concern with the creation of a more effective administrative system naturally led him to consider the question of the chancellorship. Prior to the Ming dynasty the post of chancellor had been the highest in the bureaucracy and the men who occupied it often wielded very great executive power. The autocratic founder of the Ming, for this very reason, abolished the post in perpetuity. But although the name was done away with, the reality (we are told by Wang) was preserved in the guise of the grand secretaries, who worked closely with the emperor and whose head sometimes exercised power comparable to that of the chancellors of old. Wang dwelt at some length on the pivotal role of the chancellor. Indeed it was so pivotal that from the degree of good fortune enjoyed by the populace, the relative worth of the chancellor could be divined. The logical conclusion from all this, which he explicitly drew, was that China had for some time been deprived of the benefit of good chancellors. He urged, therefore, that the throne ignore the rules of seniority and routine bureaucratic promotion and search far and wide for the very best men to fill the "chancellor" post.[25]

Such proposals as the preceding were all concerned, directly or indirectly, with enhancing the effective power of the bureaucracy. Equally important to Wang was the matter of improving the caliber of Chinese officials. Owing to widespread corruption and the common practice of selling rank and office to raise government revenues, the law of the market place had come to prevail among officials and the true functions of officialdom had been lost sight of: "Are there any officials who act in behalf of the state? There are none. Are there any who act in behalf of the people? There are none. All that the officials are concerned about is their own interests. Alas, in such circumstances, how can the state remain unharmed? How can the people not be alienated?"[26]

The short-term way to deal with this problem was to tighten up enforcement of the laws against corruption and eliminate nonfunctional posts from the bureaucracy so that the salaries of the remaining officials could be raised. The long-term approach involved a fresh consideration of the means by which officials were recruited, the chief, of course, being the examination system. This system, in Wang's view, was deficient in two basic respects. First, too many scholars were selected by it, thereby lowering standards, diluting scholarly prestige, and undermining the government's ability to provide for the scholars' support. Second, the subject matter of the examinations was too narrow and impractical, with the result that numerous individuals who might make excellent officials failed, while others with no apparent administrative gifts passed.

To rectify the first shortcoming, Wang recommended that the quotas for successful candidates be reduced and the time lapse between examinations lengthened. The second defect, he felt, could be eliminated by broadening the range of subjects covered in the examinations to include the classics, the histories, poetry, "questions and themes," administration, current affairs, geography, astronomy, natural science, mathematics, military and penal matters, and fiscal affairs. With such an arrangement, no man possessing any special competence would be lost to the government.

Wang cautioned, however, that even the best of examination systems was bound to be imperfect, for no examination could test a man's character or his ability to apply his knowledge in practical situations. Almost all of the great reformers in Chinese history had made this point and almost all had encouraged greater use of the ancient practice of recommendation (*chien-chü*) as a supplementary mode of official recruitment. No exception, Wang T'ao wrote with enthusiasm about the operation of the recommendation system in Han times and voiced the belief that no method was better suited to bringing into government service men of good character and practical ability.[27]

Implicit in a number of Wang's proposals was the assumption that, if the Chinese polity as a whole was to be fortified, the throne would have to relinquish some of its power. In one essay this assumption was made explicit. The great strength of the "feudal" system, he declared paradoxically, was its diffusion of power, for when the royal house shared its power and territory with influential families and clans throughout the realm, the latter had a more tangible stake in the fortunes of the dynasty and were more likely to come to its assistance in time of danger. Wang lamented the decline of this ancient system, and argued for its partial revival through an increase in the power of the imperial clansmen.[28]

In the "I-t'an" essays Wang T'ao seems to have been under the spell of the brilliant early Ch'ing thinker, Huang Tsung-hsi

(1610-1695), and, to a lesser extent, of Huang's contemporary, Ku Yen-wu (1613-1682). Many of the specific reforms Wang urged—reinvigoration of the chancellorship, a broadened examination system, the use of recommendation as an alternative channel for entry into the bureaucracy, greater stress on specialization and practical knowledge among officials—echoed ideas found in Huang's classic critique of imperial despotism, *Ming-i tai-fang lu* (A plan for the prince), a work which Wang knew well.[29] Like Huang Tsung-hsi, moreover, Wang's framework for approaching the problem of reform rested on the premise that Chinese government, since the Ch'in unification, had undergone a steady process of deterioration. It was not enough, therefore, in treating the wounds left by the Taiping upheaval, to restore the status quo ante bellum. Restoration would only postpone the moment of truth. What was needed was a more fundamental reconstruction of the system, guided by an idealized projection of Chinese political behavior in remote antiquity.

The "I-t'an" pieces mark the end of an important phase in Wang T'ao's development. Up to this point, despite his extensive contact with Westerners and conversion to Christianity, his perception of "China's problem" seems to have been only slightly intruded upon by a sense of "Western challenge." Wang's scattered references to Western gunnery or shipbuilding techniques or agricultural machinery, even when favorable, conveyed little idea of urgency. The pressing problem of the day—rebellion—was all-too-familiarly Chinese, and the natural impulse was to search for Chinese solutions. Still, if the thinking in "I-t'an" was pre-Western, it was not on this account any the less radical. Unlike the traditionalist, who conceives of the past as static and whose rigid attachment to this past bars the adoption of new ways,[30] Wang's devolutionary view of history permitted him to use the past as justification for far-reaching change. The commitment to tradition, in his case, instead of negating innovation, actually facilitated it.

THE CHARGES AGAINST WANG T'AO

While Wang T'ao was still in Fu-li an incident took place that was to affect the entire subsequent course of his career. On April

4, 1862, Ch'ing forces under the command of Hsiung Chao-chou defeated the Taipings in battle at Wang-chia-ssu (in Ch'i-pao), just southwest of Shanghai. Among the items which fell into the victors' hands at the time was a long letter written by one Huang Wan (with the courtesy name of Lan-ch'ing), a native of Su-fu province (the Taiping equivalent for eastern Kiangsu). Dated February 3, 1862, the letter was addressed to the Taiping official in charge of civil affairs for Su-fu province, Liu Chao-chün, for retransmission to Li Hsiu-ch'eng.[31] Li, who was then in Soochow, had publicly announced to the people of Shanghai early in January that the Taipings were about to take the city. He had urged the government forces to submit, the Westerners to remain neutral, and the populace to be calm.[32] It was against this background that Huang Wan's letter, which dealt with the impending attack, was written.

The letter began by stressing the strength and thoroughness of foreign defense arrangements in Shanghai. The author hazarded the opinion that the foreigners had no desire to make trouble for the Taipings and that, as long as their own area remained unthreatened, they would keep their troops in check. However, he continued, it was well to remember that the English and French were the strong men of Europe and would sooner suffer the deaths of ten thousand of their soldiers than submit to humiliation. The Taipings, therefore, would be wise to follow the time-honored military doctrine of avoiding confrontation with the enemy where he was strong and attacking him where he was weak. It was the Manchus they were fighting for control of China, not England and France.

The writer of the letter hastily added that this did not mean Shanghai *could* not be taken by the rebels. It was all a question of proper timing and planning. He then proceeded to outline a four-point program which, while averting any immediate confrontation between Taiping and Western forces, would ultimately bring Shanghai under rebel control. First, Li Hsiu-ch'eng should write to the consular representatives of England and France, indicating his awareness of the importance of Shanghai to foreign trade and emphasizing the Taiping desire for a continuation of peaceful relations with the Westerners, but requesting the foreigners not to compromise their neutrality by giving aid and comfort to the enemy.

Second, rebel troops should, for the time being, be deployed elsewhere. With Shanghai under threat of attack, foreign troops were concentrating in the city and were in a high state of readiness. But if the Taipings were to retreat, foreign defense preparations would be relaxed. Then, later on, rebel soldiers disguised as civilians could infiltrate the city and establish residence in the International Settlement, and on a prearranged date these fifth columnists could rise up within the city while the regular forces of the Taipings attacked the city from without.

As his third and fourth points, Huang Wan outlined a comprehensive strategy for establishing Taiping control over Chinkiang and other cities further up the Yangtze; this accomplished, the rebels could then occupy the food-producing area surrounding Shanghai and starve the city into submission.

The author of the letter, in conclusion, reiterated his belief that the rebels should for the time being concentrate their attack against the Manchus and do everything possible to maintain cordial relations with the foreigners. The foreigners had formidable military power and would not be humiliated. If defeated at Shanghai, they could be counted on to join sides with the Ch'ing and take the offensive against the Taipings. Thus, the price of a quick rebel victory at Shanghai might well be the empire.[33]

The Huang Wan letter has been viewed as an extremely important document by modern scholars of the Taiping movement, for it is generally agreed that if the advice in the letter had been followed, the outcome of the rebellion might have been substantially different.[34] This judgment is borne out by the alarmed response of contemporary Chinese officials (despite the fact that, in complete disregard of Huang Wan's advice, the Taipings in mid-March launched a full-scale assault on Shanghai). Hsüeh Huan, outgoing governor of Kiangsu, immediately forwarded the letter to the court. The throne, in an edict of April 25, ordered that the British and French consuls in Shanghai be notified of the plan; that Hsüeh, together with incoming Governor

Li Hung-chang, take stern measures of defense against internal subversion; and that Tseng Kuo-fan promptly determine the whereabouts of Huang Wan and have him placed under arrest.[35]

It did not take the local Shanghai authorities long to arrive at the conclusion that Huang Wan was none other than Wang T'ao. Apparently, however, Wang's foreign employers at the LMS press knew nothing of the letter, and after Wang had been away for some time, William Muirhead asked him to return. When Wang responded in the affirmative, Muirhead, fearing that his long sojourn in rebel-held territory might excite the suspicion of the authorities, took the precaution of obtaining from the powerful customs taotai, Wu Hsü, a written guarantee that no harm would befall Wang. Nevertheless, on his return (around May 23), Wang narrowly missed being arrested by Wu's men and had to be given refuge in the British consulate, which at this time was in the charge of Walter Henry Medhurst, son of Wang T'ao's former employer.

There now ensued a protracted exchange of diplomatic correspondence between the chief British representative in China, Sir Frederick Bruce, and the Tsungli Yamen. The Yamen demanded that Wang T'ao be delivered over to the Chinese authorities. But Bruce refused. By May 6, the date on which Wu Hsü issued the safe conduct guarantee, Bruce argued, over a month had lapsed since the discovery of Huang Wan's letter and the authorities must have already identified Huang Wan as Wang T'ao. Therefore, in still issuing the guarantee, Wu was shamelessly exploiting British trust. Whether Wang T'ao was guilty or innocent was not the issue. The issue was the Chinese taotai's breach of good faith.[36]

Wang T'ao remained in the consulate for 135 days. On October 4, the case still unsettled, he secretly took passage for Hong Kong on a British steamer.[37] Almost two decades passed before he again set foot in Shanghai.

A REEXAMINATION OF THE CASE

The evidence against Wang. It is possible to argue that the significance of the Huang Wan letter for Taiping history has been overstated, inasmuch as a similar strategic plan had been put forward two years earlier by one of the foremost Taiping leaders, Hung Jen-kan.[38] The significance of the letter for Wang T'ao's life, on the other hand, can hardly be exaggerated. It is imperative, therefore, that we take a closer look at the evidence identifying him as the author.

First, let us examine Wang's own position. Wang readily admitted, on a number of occasions, that he had indeed established contact with the Taipings while in Fu-li. But he explicitly denied having written the letter.[39] Moreover, he insisted that his sole purpose in contacting the rebels was to further the government cause. Some of the officials appointed by the Taipings in the Soochow area were old acquaintances of his. Meeting with them in secret, Wang hoped to persuade them that it was only a matter of time before Tseng Kuo-fan's forces would be directed against Soochow and that they should therefore demonstrate their loyalty to the Ch'ing by sowing dissension among the rebels. Then, when the government armies attacked, recovery of the region would be a relatively easy matter.

As he was preparing to go back to Shanghai, Wang learned of the charge against him. Still, braving the lions' den, he elected to return. In a self-vindicatory letter to James Legge a few years after, he wrote (with customary melodrama): "He was willing to advance and be punished with decapitation, but he was not willing to retreat and suffer condemnation as a collaborator. By retreating he could have gained a reprieve from death; by advancing he was certain to lose his life. From the fact that T'ao forsook life and chose death, his true intentions may surely be discerned."[40]

Among Taiping scholars who have seriously looked into the matter of the Huang Wan letter's authorship, only one, Wu Ching-shan, has taken Wang's statements at face value and defended his innocence.[41] However Wu's main argument—that if Wang were truly guilty he would never have returned to Shanghai—can easily be disposed of. By May, when Wang finally returned, it must have been perfectly plain to him, first, that his advice was not being heeded by the rebels, and second, that the rebels' chance of ultimate success had grown exceedingly dim. In these circumstances, there was every reason for Wang, once having received a formal guarantee of safety, to return to Shanghai and resume his former life. No doubt he anticipated that Wu Hsü's guarantee, by itself, would be worth little. But he probably also anticipated that, with British prestige on the line, he could count on the protection of his foreign friends.

Wu Ching-shan's study was made without the benefit of having seen the original letter of Huang Wan. The letter was discovered in the Palace Museum archives and published in facsimile form in 1933. Subsequent analyses of it, made by Hsieh Hsing-yao, Lo Erh-kang, Hu Shih, Chien Yu-wen, and Shang Yen-liu all conclude that Wang T'ao was without any doubt the letter's author.

The evidence is fairly massive. First, there is the matter of the name, Huang Wan, which was accompanied on the original seal by the courtesy name Lan-ch'ing. The surname "Huang" poses no difficulty. Since the character "Wang" in Taiping-controlled areas was reserved only for the rebel kings, ordinary people with this surname generally replaced it either with a differently written "Wang" (with the water radical) or with "Huang." As for the given name "Wan," in addition to rhyming with Wang T'ao's given name, which at the time was Han (T'ao having been assumed by him only after his arrival in Hong Kong), it is affiliated in the famous poem *Li-sao* (Encountering sorrow) with the first character in Wang's courtesy name (Lan). And there is conclusive independent evidence that in 1862 Lan-ch'ing was in fact Wang T'ao's courtesy name.[42]

Lo Erh-kang and Hsieh Hsing-yao, through a careful comparison of the Huang Wan letter with Wang T'ao's writings, established Wang's guilt even more conclusively by showing that (1) the biographical circumstances of Wang T'ao and Huang Wan were identical (Huang Wan identifies himself as a Confucian scholar from the Soochow area who has been living in Shanghai and whose mother, wife, and children have all been sent back to the family's native village); (2) the phrasing and style of the Huang Wan letter closely paralleled Wang T'ao's; and (3) the overall strategy in the letter of maintaining friendly relations with the foreigners was a constant theme in Wang T'ao's writings from the late 1850's on.[43] (The reader will recall Wang's correspondence with Hsü Yu-jen, discussed in the preceding chapter.) The clincher in the case against Wang was provided by Hu Shih and Chien Yu-wen, both of whom judged Wang's calligraphy to be very similar to the calligraphy of the Huang Wan document.[44]

There remains, of course, the remote possibility that, as Wang T'ao himself suggested, he was framed. Wang certainly must have had plenty of enemies among the local officials of Shanghai. He could be extremely abrasive when he had had too much to drink (a weakness to which he succumbed with great regularity). Moreover, the criticism of the bureaucracy, with which he tactlessly interlaced his written advice to the authorities, was ill-calculated to win him their affection and gratitude, and in the case of a small-minded bureaucrat like Wu Hsü (to whom some of Wang's proposals were submitted), was likely to give considerable offense.[45] The hypothesis that Wang was framed by local officials, nevertheless, rests on three extremely fragile supports *all* of which would have to be fully confirmed before the hypothesis could be taken seriously. It assumes, first, that the authorities, with all their power, could not have dealt with Wang by simpler, more expeditious means; second, that Wang's writing style, life circumstances, ideas, and even calligraphy were well known to the person (or persons) who framed him; and, third, that the Huang Wan letter was never, in fact, either submitted to the rebels or discovered at Wang-chia-ssu. The ideas in the letter were too subversive of the Ch'ing cause to be presented gratuitously to the rebel leaders. Moreover, if the document had indeed been submitted, there could be no guarantee that it would ever again fall into Ch'ing hands.[46]

Wang's motives. Another approach is to consider the range of motives that might have impelled a man like Wang T'ao to involve himself in so risky a business. Treason, in China as elsewhere, was a capital offense.

One possibility, suggested by Sir Frederick Bruce at the time, is that Wang did it to secure protection for his family. After the death in the fall of 1860 of his younger brother, Wang's mother, who had been living in Fu-li, came to Shanghai to live with him. Late in 1861, however, when Shanghai was under threat of attack by Li Hsiu-ch'eng's armies and foreign reinforcements had not yet arrived, Wang apparently sent his mother, wife, and two small daughters back to Fu-li, which, although situated in rebel territory, was free of fighting. Then, in order to make sure that his own previous identification with the dynasty's cause (through militia work, for example) did not jeopardize his family's safety, he drafted a letter sympathetic to the rebels and submitted it to the Taiping administrator of civil affairs in Soochow, Liu Chao-chün, with whom (there are indications in the letter) Wang was personally acquainted.[47]

Another possibility, this one advanced by Lo Erh-kang, is that, in seeking to persuade the Taipings to leave Shanghai alone or at least postpone their attack, Wang was acting in the service of British interests—possibly even on British instructions. In the spring of 1861, when British and French officials went upriver to Nanking to implore the rebel leaders not to attack Shanghai, Wang accompanied them. There is even some evidence that the formation of the Ever Victorious Army for the defense of Shanghai was done at Wang's suggestion.[48] None of this, however, need be taken to mean that Wang had become a mere "running dog" of the "foreign aggressors," as Lo Erh-kang brands him. It would be nearer to the truth to say that, after having worked for the British in Shanghai for some thirteen years, Wang's personal interests and the interests of the British were, for all practical purposes, inseparable.

A more basic problem with Lo's interpretation is its underlying premise (dictated by the strictures of Chinese Communist historiography) that as long as Wang T'ao's action accorded with foreign interests, it could not possibly accord with the interests of the Taipings. Doubt is cast on this premise, however, by those scholars (such as Hsieh Hsing-yao) who maintain that, had the rebels followed the advice in the Huang Wan letter, the rebellion's outcome might have been quite different. This is not to suggest that Wang T'ao was a sincere partisan of the Taiping cause. But it seems equally unlikely that he was a staunch Ch'ing loyalist. Indeed, we are probably safest in assuming that, at least for a flickering moment in the winter of 1861-1862 when it seemed that the civil war might go either way, Wang T'ao's loyalties were sufficiently diffuse to permit him to go either way too.

Wang T'ao's personal circumstances at the time lend support to this conclusion. Although Wang prided himself on his understanding of practical affairs and had a strong sense of political vocation, his advice seems only rarely to have received a sympathetic hearing and he was never offered an official position commensurate with his high conception of himself. Some of Wang's closest friends were much more fortunate. Li Shan-lan had been a member of Hsü Yu-jen's staff in the period just preceding Hsü's death (in 1860). Another friend, Chao Lieh-wen (Chou T'eng-hu's brother-in-law), became an adviser to Tseng Kuo-fan in the summer of 1861, a month after he and Wang had become "sworn brothers." It must have angered and depressed Wang to see the ambitions of his friends thus fulfilled while his own remained thwarted. When, on returning early in 1862 to the Soochow area, he was given a favorable reception by Liu Chao-chün (as several phrases in the Huang Wan letter suggest), the temptation to seek his fortunes with the rebels was probably strong enough to overcome any lingering sense of loyalty to the dynasty.[49]

This temptation was doubtless nourished by an additional circumstance which so far has escaped scholarly notice, namely the friendly intercourse that had taken place between Wang T'ao and several Taiping leaders before 1862. Most important in this respect was Hung Jen-kan, who between 1859 and 1864 was one of the leading figures in the Taiping movement. Hung Jen-kan (1822-1864) was a cousin and close friend of the Heavenly King (T'ien-wang), Hung Hsiu-ch'üan.[50] When the Taiping Rebellion broke out he tried unsuccessfully to join the insurgents and in 1852 took refuge in Hong Kong. In the British colony he studied Christian doctrine with the Reverend Theodore Hamberg, whose book, *The Visions of Hung-Siu-Tshuen and Origin of the Kwang-si Insurrection* (1854) was largely based on Hung Jen-kan's accounts of his notorious relative's early history.

In May 1854 Hung Jen-kan (after being baptized by Hamberg) took passage for Shanghai in hope of making contact with the rebels in Nanking. This hope was frustrated. But during his sojourn in Shanghai, which lasted until the winter of 1854, he had close relations with the LMS missionaries there and for a period of several months "read for an hour every day with Dr. Medhurst."[5 1] Inasmuch as Wang T'ao was at this time Medhurst's principal native assistant, it would have been impossible for him not to come to know Hung at least superficially. This is confirmed by an entry in Wang's diary, dated October 29, 1854, where he casually notes: "In the evening I went to the lodging of the visitor Hung to read a portion of the Scriptures."[5 2]

During the years 1855-1858, Hung Jen-kan, back in Hong Kong, was employed as a catechist and preacher by members of the LMS. Aside from continuing his theological studies, he applied himself assiduously to extending his knowledge of world geography and history. The evaluations of two foreign missionaries with whom he worked closely (and with whom Wang T'ao was later to work even more closely) may be taken as representative of the high opinion in which Hung was held. James Legge remarked of him: "He soon established himself in the confidence and esteem of the members of the mission, and the Chinese Christians connected with it. His literary attainments were respectable; his temper amiable and genial; his mind was characterized by a versatility unusual in a Chinese. His knowledge of Christian doctrine was largely increased, and of the sincerity of his attachment to it there could be no doubt." According to John Chalmers, "Whenever you see anyone having long and frequent intercourse with Hung-jin [the name by which Hung Jen-kan was known in missionary writings], you may be sure there is something good going on in him."[5 3]

In the summer of 1858 Hung Jen-kan again set out for Nanking, his main objects, according to Legge, being to correct the religious errors of the rebels and to urge on them a conciliatory policy toward foreigners. After an arduous overland journey Hung reached his destination in April 1859. The Heavenly King was delighted to see his relative and promptly appointed him to the office of prime minister with the title of Shield King (*Kan-wang*).

In the summer of 1860, four Shanghai missionaries, among them Joseph Edkins and Griffith John of the LMS, made a trip to Soochow (which had just fallen into rebel hands) for the purpose of "gaining information respecting the opinions and feelings of the Insurgents . . . and also of communicating . . . information on Christianity." The missionaries had an audience with Li Hsiu-ch'eng and came away with the feeling that the religious commitment of the rebels was still high. Edkins and John prepared, "with Wung lan king's [*sic*] assistance, a theological statement on several important subjects," asking Li, after reading it himself, to submit it to Hung Hsiu-ch'üan in Nanking. "Persuaded that our proper course was to present a plain statement of truth, . . . without adopting the tone of the censor," Edkins wrote, "we allowed our talented native secretary to place it in a form and style, such as would appear melodious to readers of that amount of literary attainment which we know the rebel leaders to possess."

The missionaries were cheered to learn in Soochow of the high place Hung Jen-kan had been given in the Taiping inner councils and Edkins wrote Hung "reminding him of the instruction he had received . . . from the late Dr. Medhurst" and congratulating him on "his accession to his present dignity." This letter "was prepared by Wang-lau-king [*sic*], who accompanied us, and who was Dr. Medhurst's assistant in translating the Scriptures."[5 4]

After returning to Shanghai, Edkins received letters from both Li Hsiu-ch'eng and Hung Jen-kan, stating that Hung had come from Nanking to Soochow expressly to see his former missionary mentors and awaited their arrival. Edkins and John left immediately for Soochow and on August 2 and 3 had long interviews with the Shield King, who made "kind inquiries about his old friends in Shanghae, both native and foreign." The missionaries returned to Shanghai on August 5, "much pleased with the Kan-wang" whose "knowledge of Christian truth" they judged to be "remarkably extensive and correct." Hung, for his part, implored them to send missionaries to Nanking to work among the population.[5 5]

The "talented native secretary" referred to by Edkins was of course Wang T'ao, known in missionary records by his courtesy name Lan-ch'ing (here variously misspelled "lan king" and "lau-king"). In March-April 1861 Edkins made another trip into insurgent territory, this time to Nanking "to bring to the attention of the rebel chief the views held by the Christian Church on the divinity of our Saviour, and of the Holy Spirit." Again (according to his diary) Wang T'ao went along.[56]

The writings of the LMS missionaries in combination with Wang T'ao's diary bring out several points that bear directly on the whole matter of Wang's connection with the Taipings. They reveal, first, that, on at least two occasions *prior* to 1862, Wang was placed in immediate contact with rebel leaders; second, that he assisted in the drafting of friendly communications to two of these leaders; and, third, that he had a personal acquaintanceship—how close we cannot tell—with the man who, for a time at any rate, was second in command of the entire Taiping movement. All of this must have suggested to Wang that, if he were to throw in his lot with the rebels, his chances of winning a position of power and influence would be significantly greater than they had been on the Ch'ing side. The attractiveness of such a move could only have been enhanced by the mood of Wang's closest missionary associates, which as late as 1861 was still one of tempered hopefulness regarding the Christian potentialities of the Taipings.[57]

COMPETING MORAL CODES AND THE CONCEPT OF BETRAYAL

Labels like "running dog," "opportunist," and "traitor"—all pinned on Wang T'ao at one time or another—may suffice as partial descriptions of men's outward acts. But they can reveal little about the inner motives which bring men to act in certain ways. Such motives are bound to be complex under any circumstances. Their complexity is intensified many times over when the actor finds himself enmeshed in a pluralistic moral environment, where, as one writer has framed it, the "difficulties lie not in the violation of a particular code, but in conflicts between codes, each compelling loyalty."[58]

By 1862 Wang T'ao had, for more than a decade, been tossed about in a sea of competing moral and cultural pressures. For others, more snugly ensconced in the traditional society, a rebellion like the Taiping could only be viewed as a terrible threat to everything held dear. But for a Christian convert, in daily association with Westerners not unsympathetic to the rebel cause, the issue was bound to be less crisply defined.

This was all the more so for one who lived in Shanghai, with its uniquely ambiguous moral climate. Shanghai, in the mid-nineteenth century, was not just a Westernized port city. It was also a frontier, "where two civilizations met and . . . neither prevailed."[59] In such a context, with parochial commitments under daily assault, the possibilities for the transformation of *ressentiment* into rebellion were maximal. *Ressentiment*, according to Robert K. Merton, embraces three interlocking elements: (1) diffuse feelings of hate, envy, and hostility; (2) a sense of powerlessness to express these feelings actively against the person or social stratum evoking them; and (3) a continual reexperiencing of this impotent hostility. The essential point distinguishing *ressentiment* from rebellion is that the former does not entail a true change in values. It involves, instead, a sour-grapes pattern which asserts that desired but unobtainable objectives (such as, in Wang T'ao's case, success in the examinations and appointment as an official) do not actually embody the prized values. Rebellion, on the other hand, connotes a genuine transvaluation—a full denunciation of previously prized values. Briefly stated: "In *ressentiment*, one condemns what one secretly craves; in rebellion, one condemns the craving itself."[60]

It would be nice, perhaps, if we could neatly conclude that by 1862 Wang T'ao, after suffering from *ressentiment* for many years, had made the full transition to rebellion. But clearly this was far from being the case. On the other hand, if we think of *ressentiment* and rebellion not as two mutually exclusive concepts but as the endpoles of a continuum, we can say with assurance that, however fitfully and hesitantly, Wang was beginning by the early sixties to move in the direction of rebellion. During the last thirty-five years of his life, Wang would never again come as close to active rebellion as he did in 1862. But, after the fall of the Taipings, his intellectual rebellion against the prevailing order of things gained progressively in momentum, and he became one of China's most vocal advocates of far-reaching reform.

3

THE YEARS IN EXILE:

HONG KONG AND EUROPE

After Wang T'ao's dalliance with the Taipings had become past history, some friends, treating the matter as a joke, nicknamed him "The First-Ranking Metropolitan Graduate of the Long-Haired Rebels" (Ch'ang-mao chuang-yüan).[1] For Wang himself, however, the affair was anything but a joke. His mother, ailing and grief-stricken, died in August, while he was still confined to the British consulate. The enforced departure from Shanghai separated him from a large circle of friends and a city he had grown to love. And any hopes he may still have cherished of becoming a somebody in the China of his day had finally to be laid to rest: great officials were not made in Hong Kong. Wang's writings in the first months of his stay in the British colony teemed with self-reproach and bitterness over his fate. So intense was his psychic anguish at times that one scholar believes he may even have experienced a temporary mental breakdown.[2]

TRANSLATION OF THE CLASSICS:
COLLABORATION WITH LEGGE

At the beginning, Wang T'ao grumbled constantly about living conditions in Hong Kong (where he arrived on October 11, 1862). The people were vulgar, the climate unbearable, the language barbarous, the food barely edible. Although provided with board and lodging by LMS missionaries, he was in straitened circumstances financially, and with his family and books still in Shanghai, there was little to divert him from loneliness and self-pity. In time, matters improved somewhat. Wang's living quarters were pleasant enough. By the end of the year his family had joined him, followed some time after by his books. Also, he began to make regular trips to Canton and soon acquired a new coterie of literary friends.[3]

But the factor which, probably more than any other, made life in Hong Kong endurable for Wang was his association with the supremely gifted missionary-sinologue, James Legge. Born in northern Scotland in 1815, of nonconformist parents, Legge after completing his university education and theological training, had joined the London Missionary Society and been sent to Malacca. There, on top of his duties as principal of the Anglo-Chinese College and superintendent of the Society's printing press, he applied himself assiduously to the study of Chinese. His linguistic abilities, earlier revealed in his attainments in Latin, were stupendous, and by the time he arrived in Hong Kong in 1843, he had already developed a considerable mastery of the language. In the British colony Legge embarked on the Herculean task of translating into English "the entire books of Confucius," "in order that . . . our missionary labours among the people should be conducted with sufficient intelligence and so as to secure permanent results."[4] Over a hundred years have passed since the publication of the first edition of Volume I of *The Chinese Classics*. Yet, for all their stiffness and inadequacy, Legge's translations are still considered standard by sinologists everywhere.

Before Wang T'ao left Shanghai, arrangements were made for him to assist Legge in his labors. As Medhurst's scholar-helper in the early 1850's, Wang had played a key role in the transmission of the West's *tao* to China. Now, changing hats, he took an equally important part in the transmission of China's *tao* to the West. Years later, obviously pleased at least with the second half of his role as a broker between civilizations, Wang wrote: "Who would have expected the Way of Confucius to be transmitted from the

East to the West! In the future, the statements in the *Chung-yung* [about world unification] are certain to be fulfilled."[5]

Wang T'ao remained in Legge's employ for the better part of a decade. Although at first Legge appeared to him rather stern and forbidding, these initial impressions rapidly gave way to others of a more favorable nature. Legge, for his part, was broadminded enough to overlook Wang T'ao's personal vices (which for a Christian were considerable), and the two men became fast friends.[6]

There were several important schools of classical interpretation current in the nineteenth century. But Wang T'ao, eclectic as always, adhered to no one school. When still in his teens he had written to a friend: "The School of Empirical Research, fathered by K'ung [An-kuo] and Cheng [Hsüan of the Han], and the School of Principle, originating with the Ch'eng brothers and Chu [Hsi of the Sung period], constitute two separate traditions of classical scholarship. The Han tradition, however, suffers from being too sticky and stubborn, while the Sung tradition errs in being excessively abstract. Both thus have their defective aspects."[7] In Wang's view (and possibly in part because of his influence), James Legge shared this eclecticism. "As a general rule," Wang tells us, "[Legge] weighed the materials he took from K'ung and Cheng against the opinions of the Ch'eng brothers and Chu. His attitude toward the teachings of the Han and Sung schools was one of impartiality."[8]

By the time of Wang T'ao's arrival in Hong Kong, Volumes I and II of *The Chinese Classics*, containing Legge's translations of the *Ssu-shu* (Four books), had already come off the press, and Legge was apparently fairly well along in the preparation of Volume III, the *Shu-ching* (Classic of documents). In his preface to the third volume (dated July 12, 1865), he indicates nevertheless that Wang T'ao's contribution was considerable. "This scholar," Legge wrote, "far excelling in classical lore any of his countrymen whom the Author had previously known, came to Hong Kong in the end of 1863 [*sic*], and placed at his disposal all the treasures of a large and well-selected library. At the same time, entering with spirit into his labours, now explaining, now arguing, as the case might be, he has not only helped but enlivened many a day of toil."[9]

Greater still were the services rendered by Wang T'ao in the preparation of the later translations, in particular the *Shih-ching* (Classic of songs), which comprised Volume IV of *The Chinese Classics* (first published in 1871); the *Ch'un-ch'iu* (Spring and Autumn annals) and *Tso-chuan* (Tradition of Tso), comprising Volume V (first published in 1872); and the *Li-chi* (Record of rituals), which first appeared in 1885. There is frequent reference to Wang's textual interpretations in the footnotes to these volumes.[10] Moreover, at Legge's request, Wang assembled exhaustive commentaries for each classic, paying special attention to opinions which, being buried in out-of-the-way works, would otherwise have escaped the notice of a foreign scholar.[11] Legge appreciated and gave full recognition to these compilations, typical being his reaction to the first of them (on the Mao version of the *Shih-ching*): "There is no available source of information on the text and its meaning which the writer has not laid under contribution. The Works which he has laid under contribution,— few of them professed commentaries on the *She* [*Shih-ching*],— amount to 124. Whatever completeness belongs to my own Work is in a great measure owing to this . . . I hope the author will yet be encouraged to publish it for the benefit of his countrymen."[12]

In 1867 Legge returned home because of poor health and the translation work was interrupted momentarily. He soon issued an invitation to Wang T'ao to join him, however, and by year's end Wang, after sending his family back to Shanghai, was on the high seas bound for Scotland. The two men returned to Hong Kong in March 1870, so that Legge could supervise personally the printing of the final two volumes. After years of close collaboration, Legge's estimation of Wang, if anything, had grown. In a letter of 1871 he wrote: "We have printed 380 pages [of Volume IV], but the expense is heavy, about 105 dollars a month—including 20 dollars to Dr. Wong my native assistant. Sometimes I grudge keeping him on, as a whole week may pass without my needing to refer to him. But then again, an occasion occurs when he is worth a great deal to me, and when I have got the Prolegomena fairly in hand, he will be of much use. None but a first-rate native scholar would be of any value to me, and here I could not get anyone comparable to him."[13]

In 1873 Legge returned to England for good, thus bringing to a close one of the most remarkable relationships to have been formed in the last century between a Chinese and a Westerner. Legge went on to become the first occupant of the Chinese Chair at Oxford. In 1877, ready to begin his translation of the *I-ching* (Classic of changes), he again invited Wang T'ao to join him. But by this time Wang, too, had become launched on a new career and the invitation was declined.[14]

Wang T'ao's contribution in the field of classical studies was not confined to the help he gave Legge. Indeed, on the Chinese side, far more important was his research into the calendar and eclipses of the Spring and Autumn (Ch'un-ch'iu) period, done while he was staying at Legge's home in Scotland in the late 1860's. Accurate determination of the chronology of this period had long been a problem for Chinese scholars. Wang T'ao, under the influence of the missionary-sinologue John Chalmers (1825-1899), became possibly the first Chinese to investigate the problem with the aid of Western astronomical and mathematical knowledge. Legge, commenting on one of Wang's treatises on the subject, stated: "There is certainly no Work in Chinese on the chronology of the Ch'un-Ts'ëw [Ch'un-ch'iu] period at all equal to this."[15] A leading Japanese student of the history of Chinese astronomy, Shinjō Shinzō, claimed that, in his own study of the Spring and Autumn calendar, he had used the same methods as Wang and arrived at roughly the same conclusions. In the People's Republic of China, also, Wang T'ao's work has been hailed as "epoch-making."[16]

THE MISSIONARY IMPACT ON WANG T'AO'S WORLD VIEW

When Wang T'ao left for Europe in December 1867, he could look back on almost two decades of continuous association with Protestant missionaries. This was a unique experience for a Chinese scholar in those days and, as could be expected, it had a profound impact on the evolution of Wang's world outlook. What was the nature of this impact?

Prior to the Opium War, Chinese tended to view China more as a world than as a nation. Consequently, it could not be part of anything bigger, as France for example might regard itself as part of the larger entity, Europe. If China did not literally encompass "all under heaven" (*t'ien-hsia*), it did include all that was worthwhile under heaven. So when Chinese were asked by Westerners, uninitiated in the Chinese way of looking at things, to join the world, they could only blink in bewilderment or become outraged at the impudence of the invitation. They could not really understand what the question was all about.

Such was the China into which Wang T'ao was born. Because it was a self-contained universe, the very concept of nationhood was strange to it. Before Chinese could view themselves as a nation, they had to acknowledge the existence of something of value in the world that was not Chinese, for only then could they respect themselves *merely* for their Chineseness.[17] It is significant, in this light, that the Chinese who gravitated toward a more nationalistic world view *before* the Sino-Japanese War of 1894-1895—Kuo Sung-tao, Wang T'ao, Cheng Kuan-ying, Hung Jen-kan, and a small handful of others—all displayed, in their attitudes toward the West, a curious blend of sharp resentment and more than grudging respect. Prenationalistic xenophobes shared the resentment. But the respect was hard to come by in the absence of a very special kind of experience.

The most important ingredient in this experience was significant exposure to the West, attained either through travel, close relations with Westerners in China, or (later on in the nineteenth century) books and newspapers. Wang, Kuo, Cheng, and Hung each had this exposure in one form or another. In Wang T'ao's case it was particularly intense. The missionaries with whom Wang had been associated since 1849 were an extraordinary collection of men, so extraordinary that they might aptly be characterized as the scholar-elite of the Protestant missionary body in China.

Like other missionaries, they were all committed to the transformation of China along modern lines; some of them (notably

Wylie, Edkins, and Muirhead) even took an active part in the extension of China's knowledge of the West. Where they differed (with the possible exception of Muirhead) from the common run of missionaries, and differed decisively, was in their sincere admiration for Chinese civilization and their recognition of it as an object worthy of serious study. The sinological contributions of Legge and Chalmers have already been noted. Medhurst, aside from compiling dictionary aids for the study of Mandarin, "Hokkien" (Fukienese), and Japanese, was one of the first to try his hand at translating the *Shu-ching* (Shanghai, 1846).[18] Joseph Edkins, while making Chinese Buddhism his special field of interest, published on a wide variety of esoteric matters in the learned journals of the day.[19] Alexander Wylie took as his subject the entire range of Chinese writing, and his monumental *Notes on Chinese Literature* (Shanghai, 1867), with descriptive notices of over two thousand major Chinese works, has still to be superseded.[20]

Yet—and this was something new—the esteem in which these missionary-sinologues held China had no implications for their Western cultural commitments. Unlike Jesuit missionaries of an earlier age who, lacking complete confidence in the superiority of their own culture, could think in terms of a happy fusion between Christian theology and Confucian ethics, the missionary intellectuals of the nineteenth century held Confucianism at arm's distance. James Legge's view of Confucius was typical: "I know . . . that I have been forward to accord a generous appreciation to him and his teachings. But I have been unable to make a hero of him. My work was undertaken that I might understand for myself, and help others to understand, the religious, moral, social, and political condition of China, and that I might see and suggest the most likely methods of accomplishing its improvement. Nothing stands in the way of this improvement so much as the devotion of its scholars and government to Confucius."[21]

Wang T'ao could not view his Western friends as barbarians, for they had gone to great lengths to acquaint themselves with the teachings of China's Sage. Yet, for the very reason that they regarded Confucian doctrine as an object of study only and not as a repository of living truth, it was equally impossible for him to view them as Confucians. One can imagine the unsettling effect this had. Instead of confirming Wang in the comfortable thought that all of civilization was Chinese, it forced him to contemplate a world larger than China. As his knowledge of this wider world grew, and admiration followed, it became less and less plausible for Wang to make a simple equation between China and civilization. China became one version of civilization among a variety of possible versions. And, *pari passu*, an intellectual basis for nationalism was laid.

The transition in Wang's outlook was gradual. In his published writings of the late 1850's, as we saw in Chapter 1, he had taken a generally negative attitude toward Western culture. At the time he still opposed the expansion of foreign trade, adoption of the West's (admittedly superior) technology, and study of Western science and mathematics. Indeed, apart from firearms and steamships (for coastal defense only) and Western languages, there was nothing, in his view, that Chinese could profitably learn from the West.

After his arrival in Hong Kong, Wang continued, for a while, to pay scant heed to the Western challenge. In 1863 he and Wong Shing (Huang Sheng), who had been one of the first Chinese to study in the United States (along with Yung Wing) and was employed at the LMS press in Hong Kong,[22] collaborated in translating into Chinese some materials on Western firearms. But the context for the compilation was still the crusade against the Taiping rebels in east central China.[23] It was only with the final collapse of the great rebellion in 1864 that Wang T'ao's concern shifted visibly to the long-term challenge offered by the West. In a letter to Li Hung-chang, written in 1865 on behalf of a friend,[24] Wang revealed the degree to which his thinking had changed since the 1850's:

Countries from all over the globe . . . have thronged to China. This is an event without precedent in the annals of time and represents a vast change in the world situation . . . People either scorn the Westerners, regarding them as subhuman, or dread them as if they were tigers. As a result, we pay no attention to matters pertaining to the Westerners, and we end up suffering the harm [of foreign intercourse] without enjoying any of its benefits . . . The things in the world that bring people harm can also bring them good. Although poisonous snakes and ferocious scorpions are able to kill people on the spot, physicians use them to eliminate leprosy and to fight ulcers. If, on account of the harm Westerners may cause, we abruptly adopt a policy of exclusion and resistance, it is tantamount to throwing away the whole dinner because one has choked on a mouthful . . . Heaven's intent, in causing several dozen Western nations all to converge on China, is not to weaken China. Quite to the contrary, it is to strengthen China.[25]

Wang went on to note that Japan, although it had been trading with the United States for only a few years, was already able to manufacture weapons, ships, trains, and machinery that, in quality, were equal to those produced in the West. How could a great empire like China fail to match the achievement of this petty island country!

The major part of Wang's letter dealt with the reconstruction of his native Kiangsu, of which Li was then governor. Most Chinese reform thought of the mid-sixties, especially in the domestic field, was profoundly conservative in orientation. This was the time of the T'ung-chih Restoration (1862-1874). The Taiping experience had stunned and unnerved Chinese leaders, and in the effort to restore Confucian order, their natural tendency was to seek the safe ground of the ante-bellum past. In the area of economic rehabilitation, for example, the overriding emphasis in Restoration thinking was on revival of the traditional economy. Agricultural recovery was to be achieved by the conventional methods of reducing imperial expenditures, repairing water works, and the like. It was taken for granted, moreover, that agriculture was the only truly important sector of the economy. Wang T'ao's recommendations contrasted sharply with this view. Reversing his earlier stand, Wang called for the manufacture of Western-style agricultural and weaving machinery and instruction of Chinese farmers in their use. He also urged that Chinese merchants be taught the commercial value of steamship transport and, even more important, that the Chinese government adopt a new attitude toward merchants.

Some might raise the objection, Wang continued, that after China introduced steamships on her waterways and firearms in her armies, increased the productivity of her farmers and weavers by the application of modern agricultural and textile machinery, and instructed her officials in astronomy, science, and Western languages, the country would virtually become Westernized. Wang did not put much stock in this reasoning, feeling that as long as imitation of the West was confined to those skills in which the Westerners excelled, it would do no harm to basic Chinese customs and sentiments (*feng-su jen-hsin*).

Another possible objection was that, if China adopted all of the West's good points, Sino-Western relations would become so intimate and harmonious that the Westerners would remain in China indefinitely. To this, Wang replied that the Westerners' primary purpose in coming to China was material gain (*li*). When China expanded her production of commodities through the application of machinery and forced down the price of imported opium by planting her own poppy, the sources of Western profit would gradually be wrested away. At that point, deprived of their material incentive for staying in China, there was every reason to believe that the Westerners would leave.[26]

Wang T'ao, by 1865, had lived for some sixteen years in the Westernized cities of Shanghai and Hong Kong, all the while in close working contact with Western missionaries. The effect was marked. Well before most of his contemporaries, he perceived that the Western challenge was without precedent in Chinese history and that unprecedented measures would have to be taken to counter it. Even more significant, by the mid-sixties we find Wang already launched on the difficult journey from a culturalistic to a nationalistic view of the world. His emphasis, in the letter to Li Hung-chang, on the acquisition of Chinese economic control (*wo li-ch'üan*) and the building up of China's national prestige (*shu kuo-wei*), as well as his clear recognition of the need to engage in active economic competition with the Western nations, bore the stamp of a radically altered view of China's place in the world. This transformation in Wang's outlook would be carried one step further by his sojourn in the West.

WANG T'AO IN EUROPE

Wang T'ao was probably the first classically trained Chinese scholar in the modern era to spend a meaningful period of time living in the West. A handful of Cantonese with missionary connections—Yung Wing, Wong Shing, and Wong Foon were the most famous—had been educated in the West in the 1840's and 1850's, but they were not, as Wang, steeped in the learning of China. It was not until the 1870's that Chinese with more substantial Confucian credentials began to visit Europe and North America for lengthier periods, as students and as diplomats.

Wang T'ao left Hong Kong by steamer on December 15, 1867. Aboard ship, after recovering from an initial spell of seasickness, he quickly made friends with two of his fellow passengers, a French physician and a German sea captain (who had at his command a smattering of Chinese). The ship made stops at Singapore, Penang, Ceylon, Aden, and Suez, and at each stop Wang and his companions disembarked and took in the sights. An enthusiastic traveler, Wang kept a detailed diary of his experiences, peppering his account with observations on the continuing commitment to Chinese ways of Singapore's Chinese population, the peculiar character of Ceylonese Buddhism, the strategic importance of Aden to Britain, or whatever else happened to strike him.

For one who was as well-schooled as Wang T'ao in Biblical literature, the trip overland by train from Suez to Alexandria (with a three-day stopover in Cairo) naturally had its special fascination and Wang found space in his diary for a recital of the story of the exodus of the children of Israel from Egypt.[27]

The six-day trip across the Mediterranean in January was rough and Wang was relieved when his boat finally pulled into Marseilles. Not yet having experienced Paris or London, Marseilles was quite an event for him: "The buildings, all bright and glittering, were seven and eight stories high . . . The luxuriousness of the service and the elegance of all the arrangements in my inn were without parallel."[28] Touring the city in a horse and carriage, in the company of a Western friend, Wang was especially impressed by the throngs in the streets and the abundance of goods in the market places.

Marseilles is as far from Paris as Canton is from Foochow, and Wang T'ao was left breathless when the midnight train out of Marseilles arrived in the French capital by noon the next day. Wang spent a week or so sightseeing in Paris, with an Englishman as his guide. He was fascinated by the city's magnificent museums and public libraries—China had no exact counterpart for either institution—and spent much time wandering through the Louvre. In the evenings he made the rounds of the city's more famous amusement spots and on a number of occasions attended the theater. Wang's stay was capped by a dinner party thrown in his honor by his guide at one of Paris' five-star restaurants.[29]

For a Chinese who had seen his country bend twice before British might and who had spent the greater part of his mature years working with missionaries from Britain in cities that had grown up under the tutelage of British wealth, London was bound to be the crown jewel in any visit to the West. As Wang T'ao himself indelicately put it, after having seen something of the city: "True it is that England is the fat man of the West and London, England's bay window."[30]

Wang made a minor splash in Britain. A London photographic studio, hearing of his presence, asked if it might grace its shop-walls with his picture. (For his acquiescence in this bit of crude commercialism, Wang received twelve free copies of his photograph.) Later, in Aberdeen, he was followed through the streets by youngsters who, unaccustomed to Chinese garb, mistook him for the wife of a Chinese "giant" then on tour in Europe and shouted: "There's the Chinese lady!" "My oh my," Wang interjected only half-humorously, "once I was a virile, full-blooded male, and now, dwelling in a foreign land, I have become a timorous old hen. How telling are the words of these young people!"[31]

On a more serious plane, while still in London, Wang was invited to address the graduating class at Oxford. Speaking in Chinese, presumably with Legge interpreting, he took as his theme the commencement of Sino-foreign intercourse in modern times. In his concluding charge, he expressed the hope that the top-ranking members of the class would go on to serve their government as high officials, while the academically less gifted would propagate the Holy Way (that is, Christianity). (We may assume that, out of courtesy to Legge, Wang, in his original address, strove for somewhat more equal treatment in his phraseology.) At this point in his speech, Wang reports, the walls of the assembly hall fairly shook with the appreciative clapping and stomping of his audience.

Afterwards, some of Wang's listeners asked him to compare the *tao* of Confucius and the *tao* of Heaven (Christianity), to which he responded:

> The *tao* of Confucius is the *tao* of humanity (*jen-tao*). There are human beings, and so there is *tao*. As long as mankind is not extinguished, *tao* will persist unchanged. Western gentlemen, when they discuss *tao*, invariably derive it from Heaven. Yet those of them who propagate it invariably posit its basis in man, [reasoning] that if men do not first exhaust their own efforts, they cannot seek the blessings of Heaven. Thus, [in the West], too, *tao* is ultimately bound to man . . . As a former wise man once said: "The East has its sages, and in mind and principle they are one; the West has its sages, and in mind and principle they are one." If, then, I may be permitted to sum it all up in a word: The *tao* of the East and the *tao* of the West form a great unity (*ta-t'ung*).[32]

Although in this setting, Wang T'ao's cross-cultural reductionism may have stemmed partly from considerations of tact, the notion of a unified world order would eventually become one of his favorite themes.

Shortly after arriving in London, Wang had been met by Legge, who took him to see all the sights a conscientious tourist should see—the British Museum (where Wang talked with the curator of the Chinese collection), Madame Tussaud's wax museum (with its stunning likeness of Lin Tse-hsü), St. Paul's Cathedral (from the top of which Wang had a magnificent view of the city), and so forth. Wang was as openminded socially as intellectually and was willing to learn from anyone who had anything to teach him. Thus, he tells us, whenever he took the train out to the Crystal Palace (four times in all), he made it a point to stop in for a drink at a particular public house along the way, where he was waited on by a pretty young bargirl who pestered him incessantly with questions about China. Once, the girl's father, a bearded engine-driver, happened to be present, and Wang engaged him in conversation about the benefits to Great Britain of the introduction of railroads. At the outset, Wang learned, everyone had been apprehensive lest the railroads put herdsmen and coachdrivers out of work and create hardships for the population. But in time it had become apparent to all that, in addition to its advantages in the realms of public safety and war, the railroad was a source of great wealth for both the state and the people. After Wang had quenched his thirst, the engine-driver accompanied him back to the train station. Pointing to one of the cars, he explained that in the early days of the railroad, the sparks caused by the rapid revolution of the wheels often started fires, but that later a man had invented a cooling oil that enabled trains to go for long periods of time without the wheels heating up. Wang's response: "In this we see exemplified the exacting and subtle quality of Western manufacture."[3][3]

From London Wang T'ao journeyed to Legge's home in Dollar. Known then as now principally for its academy and its lovely mountain scenery, Dollar is a small town in the county of Clackmannanshire in central Scotland. During the two years Wang spent there he was mainly occupied with translation work. But he had ample time off and made frequent excursions into the surrounding countryside. Also, on several occasions, he went with Legge on longer trips, visiting among other places Edinburgh, Glasgow, Leith, Aberdeen, and Legge's boyhood home in Huntly.

In Edinburgh Wang renewed his acquaintance with his old friend, Muirhead, who took him on a tour of the university. Examinations happened to be in progress at the time and the visit of a Chinese scholar to the examination hall was considered sufficiently newsworthy to make the daily papers the following morning. In his diary Wang took special note of the fact that the candidates were tested in mathematics, military science, astronomy, geography, art and music, and foreign languages, and commented approvingly: "What the British study is thus of a practical nature."

During his stay in Edinburgh Wang also had the opportunity to visit a medical clinic, a public bathhouse, a law court (while in session), and a large printing outfit. In light of his past experience, the printing firm was what interested him most. It employed over 1,500 men and women and, by means of a new chemical process, was capable of manufacturing several thousand pieces of type a day. All of its operations, moreover, from the pouring of type and the casting of plates right through to the printing and binding, were fully mechanized.[3 4]

On another occasion Wang T'ao traveled with Legge to Aberdeen and stayed at the home of John Chalmers. Wang was just then in the midst of working through some of the problems of the Ch'un-ch'iu and profited from the chance to discuss them with Chalmers. Aberdeen itself struck him as a rather cold and dreary place. But he was duly impressed by its famed granite quarries, noting especially the use of machinery to grind down and polish the blocks of granite. Wang also found time to visit a large textile factory, the operations of which were so highly mechanized that the two thousand or so employees had little to do except stand to one side and run the machines.

After three days in Aberdeen, Wang went with Chalmers and Legge to Huntly, where they visited with Legge's family. While in Huntly, Wang was invited to give a talk at a local church, with Legge translating. Before leaving Huntly, the death of an elderly member of the Legge household gave him an unexpected opportunity to attend his first Western-style funeral. Next the party journeyed to Dundee, a sizable commercial city on the eastern coast of Scotland, and here again Wang took note of the impact of the machine on local industry.[3 5]

Three months after returning to Dollar, Wang T'ao made a short excursion to Glasgow. Then, on January 5, 1870, after a last trek through the Dollar hill country of which he had become very fond,[3 6] he began the long journey back to China, in the company of Legge and his daughter, Mary. Proceeding at a leisurely pace, the party stopped long enough in Edinburgh for Wang to visit with Alexander Williamson (a former LMS missionary just returned from Shanghai) and, at Legge's invitation, give two lectures on

Confucianism at one of the city's churches. On route from Edinburgh to London, they paid a call on the widow of Wang's first missionary mentor, Walter Henry Medhurst. They also had occasion, on the way, to inspect a British prison, conditions in which were so attractive in comparison with those in China that Wang was moved to liken it to Paradise. In London Wang was entertained lavishly by friends of Legge, one of them a prominent paper manufacturer. He was staggered, on a tour of this man's plant, by the speed with which the pulp was converted into finished paper, and the paper cut and neatly stacked for distribution.[37]

Wang T'ao claims that before leaving Great Britain, he presented the books he had with him (amounting all told to some eleven thousand chüan) to a London museum. The museum in question would almost certainly have been the British Museum, but the only record that institution has of any such transaction is an invoice (dated October 1869) noting the acquisition from Wang of 203 works in 712 chüan for £65.10.0.[38]

The high point of Wang's return trip through Paris was a meeting at the Sorbonne with the grand old man of French sinology, Stanislas Julien. Wang had long been an admirer of Julien's prodigious accomplishments in Chinese and had corresponded with him earlier from England. Julien greeted him with a warm French embrace and, probably with Legge interpreting, chatted with him animatedly for several hours. Years later, after Julien had died, Wang paid hommage to his French friend in an adulatory biographical sketch.[39]

Wang T'ao returned to Hong Kong in March 1870. In the twenty-eight months that he spent abroad, he had often gotten homesick and sometimes even depressed. Yet, on balance, he seems to have enjoyed himself immensely, commenting at one point in his diary: "Alas, here I am living in exile far from home, and yet the marvels of travel, the beauty of the scenic surroundings, the delights of literature, and the pleasures of friendship provide me with joy enough almost to forget that I am abroad."[40] Wang's peregrinations furnished the setting and subject matter for many of his short stories, three collections of which were published in his lifetime. These stories, part fact and part fancy, often revolved around the hackneyed Buddhist theme that men reap the consequences of their acts. Modeled in style after the tales of the renowned early Ch'ing writer P'u Sung-ling (1640-1715), they sold well enough in the last decades of the nineteenth century to net their author a not inconsiderable income.[4][1]

Wang T'ao's travels did not radically alter his vision of the West. This had already happened before he left Hong Kong. They did, however, contribute in an important way to his career preparation. As in the case now of the graduate student in area studies who caps his training by living for a year or two "in the field," Wang's stay in Europe provided him with a feel for the concrete realities of Western life and culture. In the 1870's and 1880's other Chinese would join Wang T'ao in advocating the introduction of railroads, modern industry, and the like. The difference was that Wang had actually ridden trains himself and personally inspected a range of different kinds of factories. As he began to devote more and more of his time to writing about the West for a Chinese audience, this direct practical experience gave Wang T'ao an invaluable edge over his fellow "Westernizers."

WANG T'AO AND THE ORIGINS OF
MODERN CHINESE JOURNALISM

Wang T'ao was forty-one years old when he returned to Hong Kong. For twenty years he had depended on Westerners for a living. Yet, although his services to his missionary employers had been of incalculable value to them, he had produced little that he could really call his own. His working life so far had been the working life of an apprentice. But it was by no means clear what he had been apprenticing for. He had no vocation. Before too many months had passed, Legge's departure for Europe would leave him without even a visible means of support. Faced with this rather bleak prospect, Wang, almost immediately on arriving in Hong Kong, pressed into service his two greatest assets: his ability to write with ease and his unparalleled knowledge of the West.

Appalled at the provincialism of his fellow Chinese—a provincialism that, in the standard history of the Ming (*Ming-shih*), resulted in France's being lumped together with the island king-doms of the South Seas—Wang in 1868 had written Stanislas Julien and invited the French scholar to collaborate with him on a history of the French nation.[42] Julien declined, but Wang, nothing daunted, set to work on his own and by 1871 completed an introductory history of France (*Fa-kuo chih-lüeh*) in fourteen chapters. Working at an intense pace, he also compiled at this time a lengthy record of the Franco-Prussian War of 1870-1871 (to be discussed, along with the work on France, in Chapter 5).

Wang was strongly encouraged in these endeavors by the governor of Kiangsu, Ting Jih-ch'ang, with whom he kept up a lively correspondence. Through the efforts of Ting and another official friend, Ch'en Lan-pin (soon to become the first Chinese minister to the United States), Wang's talents were brought to the attention of Tseng Kuo-fan and Li Hung-chang, and he was almost offered a position in the Translation Department of the Kiangnan Arsenal. The whole thing fell through, however, when Tseng died in March 1872 and Li's soundings disclosed the existence of lingering local opposition to Wang's return to Shanghai.[43]

Determined to make his living by writing, Wang T'ao, around this time, took the fateful decision to embark on a career in journalism. Wang was a natural for this choice. Apart from his adventurousness and interest in all kinds of people and topics, he had the classic newspaperman's mixture of idealism and skepti-cism, of crusading spirit and shrewd business sense. Wang had learned the printing trade over the years through his work with Medhurst (who had originally been a printer by profession) and Legge. While aiding Legge in the mid-1860's, moreover, he appears to have served concurrently as editor of the *Chin-shih pien-lu* (Hong Kong news), a Chinese-language adjunct of the *China Mail*, and a paper which, according to Britton, "influenced the develop-ment of modern newspapers not only in South China but at Shanghai and in the Chinese communities in the Straits Settle-ments."[44]

Wang T'ao had numerous affiliations with the infant world of Chinese journalism. His two principal collaborators in the com-pilation of *P'u-Fa chan-chi* (Account of the Franco-Prussian war),

Chang Tsung-liang and Ch'en Yen (Ch'en Ai-t'ing), had both been translators for foreign-controlled newspapers. Ch'en was a particularly interesting figure. Equally incensed at the humiliations inflicted on China by the West and the "compradorism" of so many of his countrymen in Hong Kong, he was convinced that China must become strong to survive and that, to become strong, her people must become enlightened. In 1864, therefore, with a font of type purchased from some missionaries, he started his own newspaper, the *Hua-tzu jih-pao*. Although the *Hua-tzu jih-pao* was printed and published by the *China Mail*, the editorial direction remained largely in Ch'en's hands. In later years, when Ch'en Yen served as attaché to the Chinese legation in Washington and as China's consul-general in Cuba, his son assumed management of the newspaper.

Although it was one of the most successful and long-lived of Chinese-language dailies—it did not cease publication until 1940—the *Hua-tzu jih-pao* for many years needed all the help it could get. Two men who are said to have been especially generous in their support of the paper were Ho Kai (Ho Ch'i) and Wu T'ing-fang, both of whom Wang T'ao knew well.[45] The son of a Chinese businessman and pastor connected with the LMS, Ho Kai (1859-1914), after some early schooling in Hong Kong, obtained advanced degrees in medicine and law in Great Britain. One of Hong Kong's most distinguished Chinese citizens, he became a pioneer advocate of basic political reform in China. Wu T'ing-fang (1842-1922) was Ho Kai's brother-in-law and was also related to Ch'en Yen. Like Ho Kai, he went to school in Hong Kong and then studied law in England (1874-1877). His importance in the early history of modern journalism in China has been largely overshadowed by his service as minister to Washington in the last years of the Ch'ing and his close association with Sun Yat-sen in the early Republican period.

Ho Kai and Wu T'ing-fang—one could add Yung Wing (1828-1912), Wong Shing, and their boyhood schoolmate at the Morrison Education Society school in Macao and Hong Kong, Tong King-sing (T'ang T'ing-shu, 1832-1892)—represented a wholly new breed of "treaty port Chinese," closer in many ways

to a Sun Yat-sen than to the treaty port intellectuals with whom
Wang T'ao had been surrounded in Shanghai in the 1850's. In
contrast with the latter, most of whom hailed from Kiangsu and
Chekiang, these men were all from southern Kwangtung—the part
of China that had been in contact with the West longest. They
were, in most cases, a good bit younger. And they tended, as a
rule, to be sober-minded men of action rather than bookish
eccentrics or neurotic dilettantes. Educated as youths in Western-
operated schools in China and in academies and universities
abroad, they had little exposure to Chinese learning and literature.
Yung Wing, the first Chinese graduate from an American university (Yale, 1854), actually had to relearn spoken Chinese on
returning to China, and Ho Kai's command of the literary language
was so poor that he needed a collaborator to put his Chinese
writings into presentable form. Socially and culturally deracinated,
these men were as apt as not to take Western women for wives
(Yung Wing and Ho Kai), and many of them were professed
adherents of the Christian religion. Cosmopolitan in outlook,
nationalists before their time, their attachment was less to Confucian culture than to the Chinese nation.[46]

It is hard to say how much this new treaty port personality was
a consequence of generational change, how much a matter of
different social and geographic background. For our purposes, the
important thing is that Wang T'ao, though doubtless preferring the
Shanghai litterateur to the Hong Kong man of affairs, was able to
work smoothly and profit from his relations with both. In 1873
Wang and Wong Shing, who for twenty years had been superintendent of the LMS press in Hong Kong, pooled their resources
and, with help from others, purchased the press' printing equipment and type for $10,000 (Mexican). The name of the press was
changed to Chung-hua yin-wu tsung-chü (Chinese printing company) and Wang began to use its facilities to bring out his own
works (the first edition of P'u-Fa chan-chi, for example). The most
important function of the new press, however, was the publication
of Wang T'ao's newspaper.[47]

With the assistance of Wong Shing and Wu T'ing-fang, Tsun-wan
yat-po (Hsün-huan jih-pao) began publication on January 5,

1874.[48] The *hsün-huan* of the paper's name means "to come full circle, to make a complete revolution (as in the case of heavenly bodies)." Wang T'ao's choice of this name apparently reflected his deeply grounded cyclical outlook on history, as well possibly as his conviction that China would come into her own again as a great country. It certainly did not connote—as Wang's twentieth-century compatriots, in their zeal to make of him a fully accredited revolutionary, would like us to believe—that, the revolutionary enterprise in the guise of the Taiping Rebellion having suffered a momentary setback, the seeds of revolution would again be sown by the new paper.[49]

Tsun-wan yat-po was the first successful Chinese daily to be published completely under native auspices.[50] As co-founder and editor-in-chief, Wang T'ao was from the start its guiding spirit. For a brief time he was assisted by his friend and son-in-law, Ch'ien Cheng, who was associated with the newly founded Shanghai daily, *Shen-pao* (established April 30, 1872), and had been sent to Hong Kong to reconnoiter the native newspaper scene. Ch'ien, however, soon returned to Shanghai to become *Shen-pao*'s chief editor, and from 1875 until 1884 Wang T'ao's principal assistant was Hung Shih-wei (Hung Kan-fu), a Cantonese *hsiu-ts'ai* who had previously served on Governor Chiang I-li's staff.[51] Better known perhaps than either Ch'ien Cheng or Hung Shih-wei, though he played a less important part in the development of the *Tsun-wan yat-po*, was Hu Li-yüan, who contributed his excellent command of Chinese and English to the paper's translating staff between 1879 and 1881. Hu later became a well-to-do merchant in Hong Kong and won fame in the 1890's as Ho Kai's literary amanuensis.[52]

Tsun-wan yat-po was published daily except Sunday and cost its subscribers HK $5 per annum (or HK $.50 per month). It contained, aside from advertisements and public notices, two categories of news: commercial and general. Wang T'ao was well aware of the value to a community like Hong Kong of the latest market prices and shipping information. The commercial section (which was printed on native paper) therefore came first. It was usually twice as large as the general news section. And it was probably in consequence of the commercial section, which was in steady demand among Chinese traders and merchants in the Hong Kong-Canton-Macao area, that Wang's paper derived most of its income and so maintained its independence.

The general news section was printed on imported paper and ordinarily took up about a third of the total space. It was divided into three subsections: (1) excerpts from the *Peking Gazette* (which, in line with the general practice in Chinese newspapers until the fall of the dynasty, occupied the position of honor); (2) news of Canton and Kwangtung province; and (3) news from other parts of China as well as foreign news (both drawn largely from the foreign press in Hong Kong).

Wang T'ao was an enterprising businessman and was willing to experiment. In the *Tsun-wan yat-po*'s second year, he added a monthly supplement (priced at HK $1 per annum) in which selected news concerning important events was brought together in a convenient format. This venture was soon dropped because of insufficient sales. Somewhat more successful was the practice, begun in 1878, of putting the *Tsun-wan yat-po* out in the evening, thus gaining a twelve-hour jump in news circulation on rival papers. This was Hong Kong's first Chinese-language evening paper. The evening edition could not, however, be printed in time to make the last boats departing for Canton and Macao, and in 1882 Wang went back to a morning edition.

During the early history of the modern Chinese press, newspapers were generally published as money-making ventures exclusively, with little effort being made to take stands on issues or to influence public opinion. One of the rare exceptions was Wang T'ao's paper, the most distinctive characteristic of which was its periodic inclusion of editorials, written in most cases by Wang himself. Wang used his editorials, the choicest of which were reprinted in 1883 in book form, alternately to criticize the Chinese court and bureaucracy (which, under the protection of foreign law, he could do with impunity), to advocate reforms, to influence China's foreign policy, or simply to spread information on this or that phase of Western life. The editorials were written in an elegant, unadorned literary style—much less popular than that of Liang Ch'i-ch'ao a few decades hence but still simple enough to permit them to be read by the widest possible spectrum of literate Chinese.[53]

Wang T'ao was well aware of the importance newspapers had in Western countries and bemoaned their poor performance in China.[54] Aside from the general function of the press as a vehicle for assembling and spreading information on all matters, he felt that it had a number of critical roles to play in the political arena. Wang knew, for example, of the sensitivity of Western governments to public opinion. He urged, therefore, that Chinese envoys to foreign countries have on their staffs translators whose job it would be to scan the Western press. Significant material would be translated by them into Chinese and dispatched to the Tsungli Yamen, which could then use it to good advantage in negotiations with Western countries.[55]

Wang went still further and recommended (on several occasions) that a Chinese effort be made to influence Western opinion directly on matters affecting relations between China and the West. Western papers in China, he observed, tended to report Sino-foreign news with a distinctly pro-Western slant. This distortion was then carried over to papers in the West, which depended for China news on their China-coast counterparts. The Western public therefore never really got the Chinese side of things. To correct this situation, Wang proposed that China produce her own Western-language newspaper and circulate it in Europe. Then, if a situation arose in which China was treated unfairly by one of the Western powers, Western public opinion could be mobilized and pressure exerted on the government involved.[56]

In the domestic political field also, Wang T'ao felt that the daily newspaper had an important part to play. In his "I-t'an" essays of 1862, Wang had expressed dismay over the great gap in communication that existed in China between the ruling stratum and the people (see Chapter 2). Anticipating the views of Liang Ch'i-ch'ao, he eventually came to look upon the newspaper as an ideal means of narrowing this gap. For the newspaper not only communicated official and governmental news downward to the populace at large, it also provided an upward channel for the transmission of popular attitudes and responses to the government. When newspapers were well-edited and widely circulated—Wang cited as examples the London *Times* and the leading dailies of Paris—they could influence events and provide an effective curb on the excesses of those in power.[57] For a Chinese like Wang T'ao, whose search for power and influence by the traditional channels had been frustrated, the newspaper thus became a new vehicle for self-realization.

After Hung Shih-wei joined the staff of the *Tsun-wan yat-po*, Wang T'ao was freed from many of the day-to-day chores connected with the running of a newspaper and was able to devote much of his time to other writing and publishing.[58] Nevertheless, Wang remained a practicing journalist right up to the eve of his death, and his circle of journalistic contacts steadily widened. On a four-month visit to Japan in 1879, he befriended Kurimoto Joun (1822-1897), Fujita Mokichi (1852-1892), and other members of the staff of *Hōchi shimbun* (a leading Japanese paper of the day).[59] After moving back to Shanghai in 1884, Wang joined the editorial board of that city's most respected and influential Chinese-language daily, *Shen-pao*,[60] and in the first half of the 1890's he was a regular contributor to the reform-oriented missionary periodical, *Wan-kuo kung-pao* (Review of the times).[61]

Wang T'ao's seminal position in the history of modern Chinese journalism has been widely recognized. Roswell Britton judges him to have been "the chief figure in the early development of Chinese newspapers at Hongkong"—the man who did for the newspaper press in China what Liang Ch'i-ch'ao later did for the magazine press. Lin Yutang describes Wang as "the father of Chinese journalists," and Hung Shen regards him as such a masterful editorial writer that it would be hard to find his better even in twentieth-century journalistic circles.[62]

In narrowing the focus to the place occupied by Wang T'ao within the field of journalism, however, Wang's modern-day assessors have tended to overlook the broader significance of his journalistic career. Prior to Wang's time, "making it" (*ta*) in China generally had meant becoming an important official. Wang himself shared this psychology during the early part of his career and, whatever his misgivings about officialdom in the abstract, clearly was disappointed over his failure to be invited into the club. In time, however, Wang's attitude changed. Beginning in the early 1870's, his newspaper editorials and writings on "foreign matters" (*yang-wu*) brought him growing recognition from contemporaries. As officials began to seek him out for advice and young Chinese reformers to send him their works for criticism, Wang's sense of social worth naturally grew. Wang had "made it" as a journalist and publicist. And in so doing, he helped to establish a new career model for Chinese intellectuals in general. He showed, as Lü Shih-ch'iang puts it, "that even if one did not become a big official, one could still do big things."[63]

THE CONVERGENCE OF HISTORY AND BIOGRAPHY

It takes a special combination of historical and biographical circumstances to enable an individual to break with familiar cultural patterns and chart new paths. Historically, China in the latter half of the nineteenth century was at a major crossroad in her development. Beset with enormous problems and confronted with unprecedented challenges, the possibilities for fundamental change were present as they had never been before. And yet, prior to the 1890's, few Chinese were able to accept this and act on it. Why was Wang T'ao different?

The question is a difficult one, and I shall return to it in the last chapter. In part, of course, it was a matter of endowment. In the opinion of Young J. Allen, editor of the *Wan-kuo kung-pao*, Wang T'ao was "one of the ablest men in China,"[64] and others were prepared to echo this assessment.[65]

In part, also, it has to do with the fact that Wang was more directly exposed to the Western challenge than most of his contemporaries. Living in Shanghai and Hong Kong, traveling in Europe and Japan, and working closely with Westerners, he was sufficiently detached from his own culture to detect the need for change and, at the same time, familiar enough with Western culture to discover new instrumentalities for making change a reality.

Finally, Wang T'ao, in manhood, found himself at a personal

crossroad that intersected China's in a potent way. Wang, too, had reached the end of the line, a dead end. And, in his case, the clichés had a starkly literal significance, as the following passage from an autobiographical statement written in 1880 makes plain:

Lao-min [another of Wang's many names] had a younger brother ... but he died at only twenty-seven years of age [by Chinese reckoning] ... He had an elder sister who ... in the summer of 1873 also predeceased Lao-min. Lao-min's [first] wife ... died in Shanghai after only four years of marriage ... Lao-min has no sons. He had two daughters. The eldest ..., who was married to ... Ch'ien Cheng, died prematurely. The next ... was born a mute. Alas! It is not enough for Lao-min to be without sons. He must be deprived of his daughters as well. How can the Creator (*tsao-wu-che*) treat him with such cruelty!

From the time of the first ancestor ... to the present, some 240 years have passed ... and there have been only fifteen male children in all. In the generation after Lao-min, three sons were born to a first cousin on the paternal side, but they died as boys, one after the other. Thus, the sole remaining representative of this noble line—which has lasted from the Ming to the present—is Lao-min. What Heaven destroys, none can restore. Heaven not only visited calamity upon Lao-min personally, it seems intent on finishing off the Wang family as well. With Lao-min, it is to be feared, the Wang line will be terminated.[66]

Wang T'ao's resentment against a system which stupidly failed to recognize his talents was thus compounded by anger at an unfeeling Heaven which, by denying him a son, prevented him from fulfilling his filial obligations. These obligations were of paramount importance in premodern China, and the psychological stress resulting from failure to meet them must have been great. Had Wang been a deeply religious man, this stress might have been alleviated somewhat. He appears, however, not to have been such a man, as evidence for which we may quote a letter he wrote to a friend in the early 1870's, detailing his views on life, death, and life after death. Although the religious references are specifically to Buddhism, the overall spirit of skepticism displayed in the letter would appear to say something about Wang's Christianity as well:

As a hanger-on I live among the numberless people of this vast universe . . . Humanity is not augmented by my existence . . . ; nor would it be diminished by my absence . . .

When my parents died, I could not die with them. I continued to eat and dress. I sought recreation and cavorted with friends as before . . . When people are alive, the vital forces (*ch'i*) come together; when they die, the vital forces disperse. It cannot be known whether there is any existence after death. The Buddhist theory of transmigration is nonsense.

When my wife died, I could not, for her sake, avoid remarriage. I continued to enjoy the pleasures of married life and visited the brothels as before. In all of time we will never again meet, and over the long twenty years [since her death] not one night has she appeared in my dreams. When life is exhausted, death follows; and if it should take place prematurely, that too is unavoidable. The Buddhist notion that people who are deeply in love can have their destinies united again in another life is absurd.

Man experiences personally every phase of life. But it is impossible for him to experience death and tell people about it. When we see others die, we count our lucky stars that we still live, but we also become apprehensive over our own inevitable deaths.[6][7]

The personal psychological pressures under which Wang T'ao lived may account, in some measure, for his intemperate drinking, his frequent debauches, and the fondness he eventually developed for opium.[6][8] But the same pressures, by straining to the utmost Wang's links to his past, also had the constructive effect of moving him into a strategic position to pioneer a new life pattern. Wang T'ao's personal misfortune and China's historical misfortune reinforced each other. For someone who had found fulfillment in the old society, there would have been everything to lose by doing what Wang did. But for Wang, who found all the old doors shut, there was everything to gain in trying to open new ones.

PART II. PERSPECTIVES

ON A NEW WORLD

PROLOGUE

Wang T'ao represented something very new on the Chinese scene. The life crises he faced—failure in the examinations, the abrupt death of a father-provider, the charge of *lèse majesté*—were such as could have been encountered by Chinese in any age. But the specific means by which he worked his way out of these crises were available only after the mid-nineteenth century.[1] Similarly, although there were Chinese in all ages who were critical of dynastic policy, their capacity to give vent to this criticism was, in general, scrupulously limited. Wang T'ao, operating through a new medium, the daily newspaper, and protected (whether in Hong Kong or Shanghai) by a new institution, foreign law, was restricted in his criticisms only by his own cultural presuppositions. Finally, Wang's extensive exposure to the West and to Westerners, while it did not serve to uproot him, did serve to give him perspectives that were not accessible to Chinese of earlier epochs or, for that matter, to most of his contemporaries.

For all his newness, on the other hand, Wang T'ao remained in some ways profoundly steeped in the culture and learning of the Chinese past. In fact, it could be argued that it was precisely the security afforded by this immersion in the past that permitted him to entertain certain highly untraditional notions without experiencing the shock of cultural dislocation. As Erik Erikson has said, "it takes a well-established identity to tolerate radical change."[2]

The fragile, often strained, equilibrium maintained by Wang T'ao between new perspectives and older habits of thinking that continued to crowd his mind is plainly revealed in his writings on Western history and the contemporary world. These writings are extensive and, spanning the period from the early 1870's to the early 1890's, afford us ample opportunity to reconstruct the world view arrived at by Wang T'ao in his mature years. In doing so, however, we shall encounter a number of pitfalls and it is best to make these as explicit as possible beforehand.

First, although Wang T'ao had an extremely nimble and wide-ranging mind, he was not a systematic thinker. Asked to dilate on the current world scene or the shape of things to come in Asia or Europe, Wang could—and quite regularly did—give his views at the drop of a hat. But if someone tried to pin him down concerning his "conception of world order" or his "theory of history," it is doubtful whether he would have been able to respond comfortably. In talking about Wang's "world view," then, we have to be especially careful not to overschematize, not to impose rigor and order where in fact there is untidiness, even inconsistency.

The second pitfall—really a syndrome of pitfalls—is much more formidable, involving the relationship between "tradition" and "modernity" and the complex process of transition from the one to the other. It is common to think of tradition and modernity as well-defined sociocultural landmarks, having wholly different, often mutually antagonistic, qualities, and of "transition" as the bridge connecting the two. The trouble is that this is too rigid and mechanical. It overlooks the fact that transition has been a perennial characteristic of the history of mankind. It suggests a simplistic view of tradition as a self-contained organic entity, homogeneous and more or less static. And it excludes from consideration the possibility that certain facets of a traditional culture, not being intrinsically "traditional," may survive quite comfortably the corrosive pressures of modernization.

C.E. Black cautions that "tradition" and "modernity" are at bottom abstractions from the "continuum of variables" that make up reality, "single frames in the motion picture of history that have been enlarged for purposes of study."[3] Like all historical concepts, they thus stand in an ambiguous relationship to the actual record of human experience. Clearly, they are needed in order to make sense out of this record. But just as clearly, in the process they oversimplify and to varying degrees misrepresent the very thing they are designed to elucidate.

This quandary, characteristic of historical inquiry in general, is additionally complicated in the case of the application of "tradition" to the Chinese past by two special circumstances. First, there is the fact that among modern Chinese, "tradition" (the Chinese equivalent for which is *ch'uan-t'ung*) has of necessity been much more than a simple organizing generalization. In the kaleidoscopic whirl of nineteenth- and twentieth-century Chinese history, it has also been an object of deep emotional involvement— something to believe in, defend, or reject. In a situation where a Mao Tse-tung can ideologize tradition as an incessant struggle between oppressor (the feudal-autocratic-landlord ruling class) and oppressed (the peasantry), a Lu Hsün can curse it as a record of hypocrisy with the words "Eat men!" scrawled over every page, and a Chiang Kai-shek can enshrine it as the Confucian pursuit of virtue, China's gift to the civilization of the world, it becomes immediately apparent that the past is being drafted (consciously or unconsciously) into the service of present needs and purposes. Such angular visions of tradition, from the standpoint of the scholar, can only be viewed as caricatures of the real past.

A second kind of caricaturization (somewhat less severe usually) is contributed by Westerners who, as beneficiaries of a seductive heritage of romantic exoticism, are easily drawn to those aspects of another culture that least resemble our own and seem "unique." For students of the Sino-Western encounter of the last century, this hypnotic power of the unfamiliar is reinforced by historical reality. For there is no denying that the civilizations of China and the modern West did indeed contrast sharply at many points. Given this weighted situation, a special effort is required not to overlook those aspects of the Chinese past which, because they parallel facets of modern Western civilization, have less visibility and are harder to single out. Such points of convergence between cultures that in other respects are so far apart may be significant in at least two ways. For one thing, there is always the possibility that in them we have a reflection of basic human responses to inherently *human*—and hence to a degree supracultural—predicaments. For another, we are doubtless safe in assuming that, in those areas where the cultures of China and the modern West have tended to overlap, the need of modern Chinese to abandon earlier habits of thinking has been weaker and the predisposition toward continuity or revival stronger.

The real Chinese past, before being dramatized as "Chinese tradition," was fluid and dynamic, rich in variety and permeated with unresolved strains and tensions. Alongside of the assumptions and views that, at any given point in time, most Chinese shared were others that were embraced only by select classes or individuals. Even in the minds of single persons, moreover, there were often areas of inconsistency—assumptions and attitudes that, when scrutinized, appear to be logically (though not necessarily psychologically) incompatible.

Some of these phases of Chinese reality were brought into sharp focus by the West's intrusion and their continued viability threatened. Others, however, because they were not inherently "Chinese" or irretrievably "traditional," were less brightly illuminated by the impingement of the West. To a degree, these muted, less exposed areas of the Chinese past lay outside of the conflicts between "traditional" and "modern," "Chinese" and "Western"— as normally depicted—and injected an added dimension of complexity into the whole process of intellectual transition in nineteenth-century China. In the ensuing consideration of Wang T'ao's mature perceptions of the world, a special effort will be made to capture this extra dimension.

4

VIRTUE AND POWER

IN THE CONTEMPORARY WORLD

The spatial and temporal aspects of Wang T'ao's world view were intimately joined in his mind. In fact, a major part of Wang's historical output was devoted to what would ordinarily be classified as contemporary history. There are, nevertheless, different issues to be raised in connection with the two aspects, which is why I have chosen to treat them separately. The focus of Chapter 5 will be on Wang's understanding of historical causation and change. The present chapter will concentrate on his views of the contemporary world and its constituent countries.

MIGHT AND RIGHT IN INTERSTATE RELATIONS

For Confucian thinkers, the question of the relationship between morality and power was always of critical importance. Mencius made a distinction between two kinds of power: (1) power that was derived from virtue and exercised in just ways (*wang-tao*), and (2) power that was grounded in brute force and exercised without reference to moral considerations (*pa-tao*). Both kinds of power could exist. But the latter kind, in Mencius's view, necessarily became the agent of its own destruction; only the former was capable of providing the basis for a stable and lasting social order.

The Mencian view left a deep mark on Chinese attitudes toward power. But Confucian monarchs, for all their lip service to the ideal of government by virtue, knew full well the value of force. The resulting commitment to a Mencian idealism tempered by hardheaded appreciation of practical political realities found expression not only in the domestic arena but also in China's relations with other countries.[1] The tributary system, within which these relations were generally conducted, reflected the Mencian belief that if the Son of Heaven were demonstrably virtuous, the countries on China's peripheries would spontaneously assent to Chinese primacy. Real power, however, also played an essential part in the system's operation.

In the nineteenth century the tributary system disintegrated. This had happened before in Chinese history. But now, for the first time, China was confronted with an entirely different mode of handling interstate relations. In certain respects—for example the Western notion of a world of legally equal nation-states—Chinese adjustment to the new order proved exceedingly difficult. In other areas, however, the adjustment was made rather easily because there simply was not that great a disparity between Western and Chinese conceptions to begin with. An example of this was the common ability of Chinese and Westerners to appreciate the part played by sheer power in the *actual* ordering of world affairs ("world" of course being taken in a relative sense), despite very radical differences between their conceptions of the basis on which the world *ought* to be arranged. Thus Western countries in modern times have abided by international law when it has been in their interests to do so, but have ignored or defied it when it has conflicted with national goals. Similarly, the Chinese worked through the tributary system when it yielded results but resorted to other means, such as war, when their political objectives could best be achieved outside of the system.

This underlying tension in the Chinese view of power comes through with great clarity in the analyses of the international scene periodically put forward by Wang T'ao. The basic framework through which Wang viewed power was solidly grounded in the Mencian tradition. Yet always counterposed to this idealist strain was a high degree of sensitivity to the operation of "real power factors" in the shaping of world affairs. This was revealed in the elaborate parallels he often drew between the political situation in Europe and that of the Spring and Autumn (722-481 B.C.) and Warring States (403-221 B.C.) periods in ancient China. For example, in arguing against the advisability of a Franco-Russian alliance against Germany, Wang wrote (around 1873-1874):

The general situation in Europe today is no different from that which prevailed in earlier times in the Spring and Autumn and Warring States periods. Russia corresponds to Ch'in, France to Ch'i, England to Ch'u, and Germany [which Wang still referred to as Prussia (P'u)] and Austria to Han and Wei. If Germany and Austria are strong, Russia cannot advance a step into Western Europe. Similarly, if Han and Wei had been strong, Ch'in would have had to be content with making a lot of noise in her own backyard . . . Thus, the failure of the Six States [Chao, Wei, Han, Ch'i, Yen, Ch'u] consisted in their inability to strengthen Han and Wei in order to keep Ch'in in check. As respects the peace of Europe, formerly it rested on England and France helping Turkey to fight Russia [in the Crimean War], but today it depends upon Germany and Austria combining to withstand Russia. If France allied with Russia to attack Germany, would she not be sacrificing the very means of her protection?[2]

The astuteness of Wang T'ao's analyses of foreign affairs is not of primary concern to me. What interests me much more is the fact that in his combing of Chinese history for analogies Wang fastened upon the late Chou rather than some other period. Although we are used to thinking of China as a single country, a nation, there was a time, from the late Spring and Autumn period until the Ch'in unification in 221 B.C., when the Chinese culture area was not coterminous with anything that could properly be called a Chinese state but was divided up into a number of independent political units, much as has been the case with the European culture area in the modern era.[3] The concept of a unified Chinese state existed during these centuries, to be sure, but the reality was one of a plurality of competing states with sovereign attributes whose relations with one another were expressed in terms of treaties, alliances, exchanges of envoys, and war.[4] Little wonder, then, that, upon observing the contemporary European scene, Wang T'ao was reminded of this early period.[5]

Nor was it just the existence of a multitude of sovereign or quasi-sovereign states in the late Chou that made comparison natural. It was also the corollary fact that in this period there was no effective supranational restraint upon the behavior of the individual sovereign units. As Richard Walker has put it: "The moral code of the former Chou feudal age had meaning only when it added to the power and prestige of the state which claimed to adhere to it. The ritual framework of the feudal tradition could at times serve as a code of conduct for the individual states, but this code carried little weight unless power considerations argued in favor of adherence."[6] Might, in short, was the ultimate arbiter in interstate relations, not right.

Keeping this situation in mind, let us examine Wang T'ao's attitude toward the role of international law and treaties in his own day. At times Wang seems to have attributed to international law a modicum of usefulness, as a means of justifying certain kinds of actions and inhibiting others. In the mid-1870's, for example, during the controversy over the Ryūkyū Islands affair, he urged the Tsungli Yamen to use international law to apply pressure on Japan.[7] But there is every indication that Wang's underlying view of international law was one of extreme cynicism. Thus, prefacing a criticism of the Western powers for not speaking out in favor of justice in connection with the Ryūkyū question, he editorialized: "Alas, the countries beyond the seas, as numerous as the stars in the firmament or the pieces on a checkerboard, all scheme to realize their private interests. The great dominate the small, the strong coerce the weak, the countries of others are annexed and their rulers mistreated. This goes on all over. Though there is international law, it exists on paper only."[8]

Wang's comments on the effectiveness of international law in intra-European relations reflected the same mistrust. Using the example of Russia's helplessness in the face of England's refusal to participate in a general conference on matters pertaining to the conduct of war, he generalized: "When a country is strong it can dispense with international law or promote it, but when a country is weak, though it may wish to use international law, international law remains inaccessible to it. Alas, today's world may be summed up in two words: profit (*li*) and power (*ch'iang*)."[9]

A similar pattern of thinking was evidenced in Wang T'ao's stand on the value of treaty agreements. Such agreements might be of use in some circumstances, but at bottom they were untrust-worthy. For "if one country is strong and the other is weak the first will not be willing to adhere to a treaty agreement forever, while if the first is weak and the other is strong the first will not be able to adhere to it over the long run. In the case where both countries are strong and the treaty is not to the first's advantage, again the first country will certainly not be inclined to adhere to it indefinitely." Wang documented his point by referring to Russia's unilateral repudiation (in October 1870) of the Black Sea clauses of the Treaty of Paris (1856). These clauses, which forbade Russia to maintain a fleet or construct fortifications in the Black Sea, had been imposed on her after her defeat in the Crimean War. But that had been a weak Russia. Now, Wang T'ao observed, Russia had become wealthier and stronger, enabling her to act with im-punity.[10]

Wang T'ao's skepticism over the capacity of a "moral code" or "ritual framework" to act as a restraining force in a world of power-hungry sovereign states is one reason why he saw the interstate relations of his day, to some extent at least, through late Chou eyes. But I think there is another. We must be wary of focusing on Wang T'ao the "detached" foreign affairs analyst at the expense of Wang T'ao the man. It is possible to argue that the analogy with the late Chou represented for Wang something more than just a cool perception of two seemingly parallel historical realities, that it was also, at least implicitly, a moral judgment against the West by a Chinese who was incensed over the injustices perpetrated against China in recent times.

It will be recalled that for the Confucian historian, as indeed for Confucius and Mencius themselves, the latter part of the Chou period stood condemned as a degenerate and politically immoral age, an age in which the *tao* did not prevail. This was the period which, through the shortsightedness and turpitude of its rulers, had rejected Confucius and Mencius and all that they represented. It was a period in which brute power was worshiped and moral power held up to ridicule, in which kings augmented their territories not through humane government but through military conquest. The general character of the age was expressed quintessentially in the rise to dominance of the geographically peripheral state of Ch'in, a state which, because of its militant anti-Confucianism and its glorification of war, came to be viewed by Confucians of subsequent ages as something very near to a moral monstrosity.

Presented with this highly negative image of late Chou political life, it seems fair to infer that, in suggesting certain similarities between the late Chou and contemporary Europe, Wang T'ao was passing judgment on the latter. This inference would be less supportable if nineteenth-century China had been included, along with the states of Europe, in Wang's analogies. But it was not. Wang was of course vitally concerned with the implications for China of the policies and actions of the world's states. But these states remained in a separate universe, subject to separate rules. Like the late Chou, it was a world that had been tendered the opportunity to operate according to Confucian canons of political behavior and had rejected the offer hands down.

IMAGES OF INDIVIDUAL NATIONS

The collective condemnation of the contemporary non-Chinese world implicit in Wang T'ao's writings did not keep him from making significant distinctions among nations. On the contrary, Wang's images of the world's countries were as numerous and diverse as the countries themselves and, considered in the aggregate, represented a sharp departure from the relatively monochromatic view of "non-China" characteristic of earlier generations of Chinese. This new flexibility of outlook may be illustrated by examining Wang's perceptions of Russia, America, and Japan, the first two briefly, the last in some depth.

Russia. Although Russia, after the Sino-Japanese War, would come to stand for many things in China, in the several decades prior to the war, most Chinese tended to depict their northern neighbor in stridently negative terms.[11] Wang T'ao was no exception. He portrayed Russia as a much poorer country than England, in spite of her great territorial sweep. On the rare occasions in which he discussed Russian internal conditions, his choice of subject matter—the persistence of certain features of serfdom ("a very bad institution") despite its abolition, rifts within the royal family, the severity of czarist rule, the disruptive activity of dissident religious groups—was anything but flattering.[12] And when, as was much more frequent, he spoke of Russia's foreign policy motives, the focus generally was on czarist territorial designs.[13] Over and over, Wang tagged Russia as a "predatory Ch'in devoid of moral principles" (*wu-tao chih hu-lang Ch'in*) and when he compared late Chou and contemporary European interstate relations it was invariably for Russia that the pejorative Ch'in symbol was reserved.[14]

Why so bleak a picture? It is possible that Wang's negative image of Russia was, to some extent, fed by a long-standing Chinese tradition of viewing the Russians as semibarbarous "man-eating demons."[15] Generally, however, Wang T'ao was not one to take his cues from folklore. Much more convincing is the argument that the anti-Russian bias of Wang and other late nineteenth-century reformers was a direct reflection of Anglo-American anti-Russian sentiment. As Wang Shu-huai has pointed out, most of the Westerners who wrote in Chinese on current affairs were British or American, and Anglo-American opinion tended in this period to be strongly anti-Russian in orientation.[16] In Wang T'ao's case the possibility of such influence was especially great because of his close personal associations with British missionaries.[17]

It is perfectly plausible to argue, on the other hand, that Anglo-American opinion merely served to reinforce a viewpoint arrived at by Wang T'ao independently. Wang, after all, was no tyro when it came to observing and analyzing the international scene. And if his association of Russia with Ch'in sometimes seems a trifle forced, the analogy was not entirely without grounds:

Russia, like Ch'in, was situated on China's northern border and her growing appetite for Asian real estate in the 1870's and 1880's had been manifested in countless ways.

America. Although Wang T'ao claims to have prepared a manuscript history of Russia in eight chapters, his knowledge of the country remained superficial. He never visited Russia. He seems to have known no Russians personally. And, prior to the turn of the century, there was little in the way of published materials (aside from newspapers) that a curious Chinese could turn to for further enlightenment. The situation in regard to America was much the same. Wang says that he wrote a brief history of that country, too.[18] But he did not go there. Nor, with the exception of Young J. Allen, were close associations with individual Americans part of his life experience.

In contrast with Russia, however, Wang T'ao's images of America were uniformly favorable. Not one to take up the cudgel in behalf of exploited minorities, he was duly impressed by the "civilizing" mission performed by the English among the Indians and also marveled at the economic productivity of the American South, which he insisted on describing (conveniently overlooking the condition of black people) as a land free of sorrow.[19]

America's political institutions and traditions were, in Wang's view, without peer among foreign countries. He noted, with satisfaction, the low level of government expenditures (manifestly a sign of frugal and compassionate administration); the smooth and efficient way in which local conflicts were resolved by village and town elders (who served without pay); the provisions made for the support of widows, orphans, and handicapped and sick people; and the small size of the standing army.[20] Wang also applauded the tradition of "abdication" established by George Washington, drawing the inevitable parallel between Washington's lack of personal political ambition—"he let go a land of ten thousand chariots as if it were a pair of old shoes"—and that of the great heroes of Chinese antiquity, Yao and Shun.[21]

Although Wang T'ao never made explicit why he was so well-disposed toward America, the reasons are easily enough surmised. As a nation with a favorable land-population ratio and a government that was both inexpensive and noninterventionist, America must have appealed to the "Jeffersonian" strain that formed part of every Confucian's vision of the good society. America, moreover, was closely associated in Chinese minds with Great Britain, a country for which (as we shall see in later chapters) Wang T'ao had the highest admiration. Last, but by no means least in importance, America, unlike Russia, did not pose an immediate threat to the Chinese empire.

Japan. Linguists say that the hardest sounds to master in a foreign language are those that approximate, but do not quite duplicate, sounds in one's native tongue. For countless Chinese in the nineteenth century, Japan posed a similar problem. In culture, writing, race, and geography, Japan was closer to China than any other major country. And in her forced acquiescence in treaty relations with the Western powers, she shared with China a common sense of historical grievance. These considerations drew Chinese and Japanese together. But other considerations drove them apart. Japan's conspicuous enthusiasm for things Western and the crisp efficiency of her modernization efforts inspired, among Chinese onlookers, an uneasy mixture of admiration, envy, and contempt, while her increasingly assertive behavior on China's peripheries in the closing decades of the century produced alternating feelings of anger and shame. The paternal attitude Chinese had for their island neighbor made Japanese encroachments all the more painful; but it also served to inhibit total Chinese rejection of Japan. The upshot was a deepseated sense of ambivalence that many Chinese found it hard to shake even in the twentieth century.

This ambivalence—polyvalence would perhaps be more accurate—was vividly reflected in Wang T'ao's discordant images of Japan. One such image, based partly on reality but also nourished by a fusion of Chinese egocentrism and Japanese sinophilism, portrayed Japan as a sort of cultural province of China and individual Japanese as fellow participants in a shared Sinic order. The reality-dimension of this image was sizable. For one thing, many educated Japanese in Wang T'ao's day were still doing much of their reading and writing in literary Chinese. This gave them direct access to the whole corpus of Chinese writing; it also provided Chinese (or at least the more venturesome among them) with an easy entrée into the intellectual world of Japan. Thus, Wang T'ao's books were widely read in Japan, several of them even appearing in Japanese editions in the 1870's and 1880's, and Wang, for his part, on a number of occasions, made use of Japanese-produced works to document or provide source material for his own writing.[22]

Another reality-component of the "cultural cousin" image—and one that was singularly rich in meaning for a man of Wang T'ao's life-style—was the strong resemblance that existed between Chinese and Japanese modes of friendship and social intercourse, at least where literary men were concerned. The incessant banqueting and return-banqueting, visiting and countervisiting, the geisha, the wine-drinking and poetizing, the sightseeing excursions, the ritual requests to read the manuscript works of friends and compose prefaces or colophons in their honor—such activities, which literally filled Wang T'ao's days when he visited Japan for four months in the spring and summer 1879, seem like a re-enactment, on a much grander scale, of Wang's social life in Shanghai in the 1850's.[23]

The reception Wang got and the friendships he contracted on his trip added a warm, personal dimension to his image of Japan. Cast off by his own countrymen and perennially starved for recognition, Wang experienced a considerable lift of the ego when he was welcomed in Japan as a celebrated Chinese man of letters. Wang had become known there partly through the reports of Japanese returning from Hong Kong, but mostly, it appears, through his book on the Franco-Prussian War (*P'u-Fa chan-chi*). Kurimoto Joun, who was editor of the *Hōchi shimbun* (News-dispatch), a leading Japanese newspaper, had acquired a copy of *P'u-Fa chan-chi* some years before in Shanghai and was so impressed both with the book's true-to-life depiction of the events of the war and the freshness of the author's commentaries—he judged the work to be of a caliber seldom seen since the writing of Ou-yang Hsiu's *Hsin wu-tai shih* (New history of the five dynasties)—that he got the Japanese Army Ministry to reissue the book in 1878.[24]

When word reached Japan that Wang T'ao, in need of recuper-
ation from what appears to have been a tubercular condition, had
expressed a desire to see for himself the beauty of the Japanese
landscape and the fabled charm of Japan's womenfolk, a group of
Japanese literary figures seized the opportunity to invite him
formally and to offer their services as hosts.[25] Aside from
Kurimoto, the group included Sada Hakubō (1832-1907), a man
of fiery temper who in the early 1870's had been a leading
advocate of a Japanese expedition against Korea;[26] Shigeno
Yasutsugu (1827-1910), an influential historian of the *k'ao-cheng*
(*kōshō*) or "empirical research" tradition, whose rigorous
methods led him to question many accepted "facts" of Japanese
history and earned him the nickname, Doctor of Obliteration
(Massatsu Hakase);[27] Oka Senjin (1832-1913), a romantic, China-
oriented scholar, with strong contemporary interests, who in the
1880's headed a private academy in Tokyo at which instruction
was given in the Confucian classics;[28] and Nakamura Keiu
(1832-1891), a prolific early Meiji author and educator of note,
whose translations of such works as Samuel Smiles' *Self-Help*
(1870) and John Stuart Mill's *On Liberty* (1871) were known to
all Japanese students.[29]

If Wang T'ao was flattered by the royal treatment he received in
Japan, his visit was no less flattering to his Japanese hosts. One
reason for this was the manner in which Wang conducted himself.
Unlike many Chinese, Wang T'ao, while abroad, did not sequester
himself in an exclusively Chinese ambiance. To be sure, some of
his time was spent in the company of fellow Chinese. (Ironically,
although still *persona non grata* to the Ch'ing government at
home, Wang was warmly received by the chief of Peking's newly
established Tokyo legation, Ho Ju-chang, and became fast friends
with Ho's subordinate, Huang Tsun-hsien, later to achieve fame for
his reform activities and pioneering history of Japan.)[30] But, by
and large, Wang placed himself at the disposal of his new Japanese
friends. Ever the curious traveler, in the early stages of his trip, he
took due note of the usual Japanese exotica: the odd style of
dress, the dwarf-trees, and such. But after reaching Tokyo, he
quickly settled down and behaved as if Japan were a second home.
With politeness, if not enthusiasm, he dined on Japanese fare, and

in contrast with the typical Chinese sojourner, he stayed in a Japanese home (that of his friend, Shigeno Yasutsugu).[31]

One reason, then, why his Japanese hosts were so pleased with him was Wang's insistence on "going native," on experiencing Japanese life from the inside. A second, and probably more basic, reason is that visits to Japan by name Chinese writers were still events in 1879. When, at a welcoming party in Wang T'ao's honor, Nakamura Keiu observed that Wang was the most prominent Chinese to visit Japan in a hundred years, and Oka Senjin embellished the compliment by extending the dry spell back to T'ang times,[32] there was more to their words than unctuous display. Aside from a handful of Ming loyalists who had fled to Japan at the time of the Manchu conquest, the Tokugawa period had not been conspicuous for its hospitality to foreign visitors. And in the succeeding Meiji era, although Chinese were welcome, few at first seemed to share Wang T'ao's spirit of adventure: it was not until the turn of the century, when a combination of new circumstances suddenly propelled Japan to the forefront of Chinese attention, that sizable numbers of educated Chinese went there either for study or political refuge.

Wang T'ao's summer in Japan was fittingly climaxed by a grand farewell party at the Nakamura Restaurant, attended by over sixty Japanese friends and acquaintances.[33] Following his return to China, Wang maintained his affection for his Japanese friends. He corresponded with them frequently, wrote prefaces and postfaces to their works, and, after resettling in Shanghai, played host to them when they had occasion to visit China.[34]

Among Wang T'ao's Japanese friends (some of them acquired in Shanghai in the 1880's) were several who were actively involved in Pan-Asianist causes. Although Japanese Pan-Asianism, in the last decades of the nineteenth century, meant many things to many people, there was a broad substratum of sentiments which most Pan-Asianists shared. Chief among these were (1) an awareness of the special historical and cultural relationship between China and Japan, (2) a strong sympathy for the cause of Chinese reform, and (3) vigorous opposition to Western domination of Asia. Since these were sentiments which, as long as they were not construed in a manner that was detrimental to Chinese interests, Wang T'ao heartily endorsed, it was natural that as the forces of Pan-Asianism began to assume more organized expression, he should respond with interest. Thus, in 1880, shortly after the formation in Tokyo of a society for the promotion of Sino-Japanese cultural interchange, the Kōa kai (Rise Asia society), Wang, in a letter to Oka Senjin, spoke of the urgent need for such an organization and commended the vision of its founders. Significantly, however, in another letter written around the same time, but to a Chinese friend (Cheng Tsao-ju), Wang noted that although the ostensible purpose of the Kōa kai was to foster friendly relations between China and Japan, the organization's true purpose was an enigma.[35]

This, of course, was precisely the problem with Pan-Asianism. What was its true purpose? Was it really, as claimed, to liberate Asian countries from the yoke of imperialism or was it just a camouflage for the replacement of Western domination by Japanese? To many Japanese Pan-Asianists, blinded by their own righteousness, the distinction probably seemed invidious: domination by Japan *was* liberation. There were some, nevertheless, like Sone Toshitora (1847-1910), whose commitments to China were deep and sincere. A naval officer who in the 1890's became involved in Sino-Japanese revolutionary activities, Sone first visited China in 1873. After the Formosan Expedition (1874) he remained in Shanghai for some years on official business and became so expert in Chinese affairs that, after returning to Japan, he was granted an audience with the Meiji Emperor. One of the founders of the Kōa kai, Sone had the reputation of being very pro-Chinese. He is said to have been a regular reader of the *Analects* and to have referred to himself as a native of Confucius' home province of Shantung.[36]

Wang T'ao first met Sone Toshitora in Shanghai either just before or after his trip to Japan. Sone's romantic leanings and fierce sense of loyalty were qualities Wang liked,[37] and a warm friendship soon sprang up between the two men. Unlike many of Wang's Japanese friendships, this one had a strong political side to it. Thus, when Sone, in early 1883, came up with a scheme for reducing the strain in Sino-Japanese relations, he turned to his Chinese friend and asked him to use his connections with Li Hung-chang's staff to bring the plan to Li's attention. After some initial reluctance—Wang appears to have been apprehensive lest involvement in anything political should jeopardize his chances of returning to Shanghai on a permanent basis—Wang in the summer described Sone's plan to one of Li's leading lieutenants, Sheng Hsüan-huai, and told Sheng that if Li approved of the plan and were willing to shoulder all responsibility, he, Wang, would be willing to go to Tokyo personally to try to persuade the Japanese authorities.[38]

Although the Sone-Wang effort fizzled, Sone's credentials as a China-sympathizer received fresh authentication at the time of the Sino-French crisis over Annam. He was an official observer of the conflict for the Japanese military and, at Wang T'ao's urging (according to Wang), wrote a book on it in which he came out strongly against France and picked fault with the Japanese government for its wooden indifference to the fate of China's erstwhile tributary.[39]

Although Sone Toshitora, Oka Senjin, Wang T'ao, and others like them viewed China and Japan as natural allies and wanted the two countries to form a close alliance in order to withstand foreign insult and work for the strengthening of the rest of Asia,[40] the general drift of Sino-Japanese relations from 1870 on was in a very different direction. Friction, first over the status of the Ryūkyū (Liu-ch'iu) Islands and later over Korea, mounted steadily as the century wore to a close, and by 1894 the two countries found themselves at war.

Wang T'ao, while preserving his friendships with individual Japanese, smarted with resentment in his reaction to the Meiji government's foreign policy. His editorials on the Ryūkyū crisis of the 1870's provide a case in point. Unlike numbers of his countrymen, Wang was prepared to accept the Japanese claim that her dispatch of envoys to China in the earlier years of the Ch'ing had merely been for the purpose of making inquiries and was not to be taken as an expression of vassalage.[41] He also granted that the Ryūkyūans had, in the past, sent tributary embassies to Japan. He insisted, however, using such Japanese works as the *Dai Nihon shi* (History of great Japan) to strengthen his case, that the Ryūkyūan tributary relationship with China was older and that, in any event, the Ryūkyūs had never actually *belonged* to Japan.[42]

Wang was almost as vehement in his denunciation of the Western penchant for taking Japan's side in the Ryūkyū embroilment. Ever since the Japanese began their policy of all-out imitation of the West, he ruefully declared, the Western response had been to extol Japan and deprecate China, and now, whenever some difficulty emerged in Sino-Japanese relations, the Westerners automatically accepted Japan's point of view. Wang was shrewd enough to see another and more directly self-serving motive for Western support of Japan: successful Japanese incorporation of the Ryūkyū Islands, after all, would provide the French and British with a clear precedent for any future colonial claims they might wish to press in Southeast Asia.[43]

Wang T'ao's fulminations against Japan and the West in the Ryūkyū affair were grounded in his perception of the rights and wrongs of the matter. But Wang was never one to stray very far from the practical world, and when he descended from the rarified heights of principle, the extremity of his response was greatly tempered. Wang saw several things very clearly: first, the Ryūkyū Islands were not worth going to war over; second, even if they were, China would have to become a lot stronger before she could risk such a course; third, although Japan was not to be trusted and the Japanese threat to China was not likely to subside, it was nothing as compared to the Russian threat; and, fourth, since Russia threatened Japanese and British interests as well, there was still something to be said for an anti-Russian coalition of the three countries.[44]

Wang T'ao's images of Japan reflected not only that country's foreign policy but also its domestic accomplishments. If, at the time of writing, Wang's dominant emotion was one of frustration over China's lack of accomplishment, he was all praise. Nothing, for example, impressed him more than Japan's uncanny ability to set strict limits upon Western penetration:

As in China, the commercial firms of the West now proliferate in Japan and its missionaries are actively engaged throughout the country. Yet the Westerners dare not intimidate or insult the Japanese. Why is this? It is because the Japanese strive for mastery over the entire range of Western methods (*Hsi-fa*). They have not yet been able to deprive the West of its foothold [in their country], but they have adopted the West's strengths and have shown a marked ability, in so doing, to rely on their own efforts (*neng tzu wei chih*).[45]

Wang wrote admiringly of Japan's "progressive" response to the times, her desire to learn from the West, the close attention she paid to practical matters, and her avoidance of the Chinese disease of just drifting along and responding to events as they occurred.[46] He often pointed to Japanese successes in this or that sphere of modernization and, in some of his writings, expressly enjoined China to follow the Japanese precedent of giving urgent consideration to plans for reform.[47]

At other times, however, Wang T'ao censured Japan in the harshest terms. When he wrote out of bitterness over the aggressive thrust of Japanese foreign policy or rancor over the Westerners' cynical preference of Japan to China or wariness over what, for the moment at least, he conceived to be Japan's slavish and excessive dependence on "Western methods," Wang retreated into the smug, cocoon-like world of the Confucian moralist and condemned the whole edifice of Japanese "Westernization" as resting on a foundation of quicksand. The following blast could as easily have come from the brush of a Wo-jen:[48]

Since the [Meiji] Restoration [1868] Japan has revered Western learning and copied Western methods, completely changing her received traditions and making everything over new. She has even gone so far as to change her calendar and style of dress, to the extent that there is almost no difference between her and the countries of Europe. For she feels that if she does not act in this way, she will be unable to compete with them.

Yet, in consequence of this, Japan's financial resources have become depleted and her treasury increasingly empty. Her national debt has mounted to a staggering level. Outwardly strong but rotten at the core, Japan will find it difficult to persist [in her present course].

Formerly, what [the government] took from the people [in

taxes] did not exceed two parts in ten [of a family's output].
Now it has practically gotten to the point where they "pound the
people's fat and suck out their marrow"; every last cent is taken
from them and then squandered as if it were worth no more than
mud or sand . . .

When a country is governed by harsh, rigid policies, it is certain
to be destroyed. When a country is governed by flexible, pliant
policies, it is certain to endure. [The Japanese] think nothing of
altering the model of their forebears and lay waste to the choicest
products of Heaven and Earth. They grind down hard on their
people in order to impress men from afar and exhaust their riches
in order to acquire foreign things. Outwardly they seem fat, but
within they are hungry. The disease . . . has become fixed in the
vital regions, yet the cure still eludes them.[49]

One has the decided impression that Wang T'ao was often too
angered and perplexed by the Japanese to be entirely consistent in
his assessments of them. The level of reasoning which he descended to in the editorial just quoted would have exasperated him
thoroughly if it had been presented as a conservative argument
against Chinese reform. Context and mood were everything.
Sometimes Wang mocked Japan for the superficiality of her
Westernizing efforts; on other occasions he praised her for the
depth of her understanding of the West.[50] Sometimes, as we have
seen, he applauded Japan's ability to achieve an independent
mastery over Western techniques; sometimes, however, the same
Wang T'ao disparaged the Japanese for their excessive reliance on
Western technicians and advisers.[51]

In one respect, moreover, Wang's doctrinaire attachment to
Confucian political wisdom caused him to badly misread the
Japanese situation. Over and over, Wang resorted to the stock
phrase *wai-ch'iang chung-kao*—"outwardly strong but rotten at the
core"—to epitomize the Japanese condition.[52] He saw some of the
strains that accompanied Japanese modernization and what he saw
seemed to be confirmed by the complaints of the more disaffected
of his ex-samurai friends. But Wang exaggerated the strains greatly
and the conclusions he drew were all wrong. He supposed that if
Japan's domestic problems were to be compounded by additional
difficulties abroad, her whole house would cave in.[53] Wang's

Confucian logic, in this instance, blinded him to the vast potential of Japanese nationalism as a unifying force.

It is understandable, in such circumstances, that Wang T'ao, for all his familiarity with Japan, should have been as startled as everyone else by the outcome of the war of 1894-1895. On a personal level, it must have been small comfort to Wang to see in Japan's victory the vindication of a lifetime of effort to get China to reform. In national terms, on the other hand, Wang shared the hope of others that the ultimate shame of defeat by a small Asian country would awaken China, at last, to the need to mend her ways. In tragedy there was opportunity; in calamity, the seed of hope. Wang's conviction that China was the leading country of Asia was not disturbed; nor was he shaken in his belief that Sino-Japanese friendship was the essential precondition for Asian peace. He contented himself, therefore, with rebuking Japan for stupidly acting against her own best interests and warning her that, sooner or later, she would have cause to regret the predatory course of her policy.[54]

From Wang T'ao's understanding of contemporary interstate relations and his perceptions of individual countries, we can extrapolate the vision of a world in which justice counted for little and brute power was set at a premium. What were the implications of this vision for China? Wang T'ao's answer to this question was neither simple nor entirely consistent. For the foreseeable future, he clearly believed that China had no choice but to challenge the West at its own game. She could try, through such dubious expedients as international law, to stave off further depredations at the hands of Europe and Japan. Certainly she should establish legations and consulates abroad[55] and do anything else, within the bounds of reason, that might have the effect of strengthening her position in a hostile world. In the final reckoning, however, Wang knew that all such measures could amount to little more than an extended holding operation—a means of buying time. China's only prudent course, ultimately, was to become wealthy and powerful like the West.[56]

As an illustration of his reasoning on this score, we may cite

Wang's discussion of the question of stationing Chinese consuls in California, Peru, and Cuba, where there were sizable communities of poor Chinese. Wang cautioned that, whatever the other merits of such a plan, it would not make the lot of the overseas Chinese laborer any sweeter. Analogy with the Western position in China failed in two respects: first, the social standing of Chinese who settled in the West was much lower than that of their Western counterparts in China, and, second, Western consuls in China were able, in the last resort, to back up their demands with force. "In short," Wang concluded, "if we wish to provide Chinese people who have gone abroad with protection, and to have our laws respected and our prestige upheld, there is no better place to begin than by making ourselves strong (*tzu-ch'iang*)".[5 7]

And yet, for a patriotic Chinese, the mere acquisition of wealth and power could hardly be a satisfying solution in the long run. For how would China then differ from the West? Pertinent here was the double-edged nature of Mencian logic. The West, according to this logic, was unvirtuous because it had used force to expand. But, in a world that was so manifestly unresponsive to Chinese monarchical virtue, there was the nagging inference, in terms of the same logic, that the Chinese monarchy might also be unvirtuous. Wang T'ao, if one excepts his obscure involvement with the Taipings, never to my knowledge openly advanced this suggestion. But his frequent criticism of the court and bureaucracy, along with his persistent advocacy of rather sweeping changes in Chinese governmental policies and practices, amounted to such a suggestion in fact. Here, then, we have a clue to the question of how China would ultimately differ from the West. A thoroughly renovated China would be strong—as was the West. But it would also be virtuous—as the West was not. And this combination would enable China, which had started out by responding to the West on Western terms, to end up by compelling the West to respond to China on Chinese terms.

5

HEAVEN AND MAN

IN THE MAKING OF HISTORY

Wang T'ao's vision of a future world shaped by China found strong support in his perspective on history. Inevitably, this perspective was conditioned by the new situation that confronted China in the nineteenth century. But it was equally a product of older attitudes.

THE PATTERN AND MOTIVE FORCE OF HISTORY

Traditional Chinese attitudes toward history were replete with problems. As was perhaps natural in an agrarian society, ever subject to the seasonal rhythm of growth and decay, Confucian scholars had a tendency to see history in cyclical terms. The rise-and-fall principle was deeply embedded in the Chinese outlook, embracing virtually everything human. Change, from this viewpoint, did not consist in becoming, but rather in "an endless round of alternating, recurrent conditions." The concept of progress was alien. The overriding purpose of civilized society was to arrest decay.[1]

The notion of arresting decay suggests a second view of change that had currency among Confucian historians. This was the concept of history as a process of decline from a utopian age in the past. Logically considered, the cyclical and devolutionary views can be construed as mutually contradictory, for the former denies the possibility of "upward" or "downward" movement except in relative terms, while the latter seems to imply a steady, nonrepetitive, "downward" flow of change. True, there were ways in which the two views could be rendered less incompatible. Confucian historians, for example, might choose to see the world not as progressively degenerating, but merely as having suffered an initial fall in remote antiquity.[2] Nevertheless, it appears that most Chinese did not pay too much attention to these scholastic niceties and were able to live in comfort with potentially inconsistent views.

Another issue in regard to which traditional Chinese attitudes were far from consistent is the related question of how historical change occurs. Many, in the Confucian-Mencian mold, would have agreed with the famous historiographer, Liu Chih-chi (661-721) that man is the primary shaper of his own destiny and "if one must bring fate into one's discourse . . . reason is outraged."[3] Good actions, for those who took such a stand, produced desirable consequences, while bad actions produced results that were undesirable. The extent of a man's capacity to influence events varied directly with his standing in society. Hence the rulers of society were in a particularly strategic position. Virtuous rulers, by the power of their example and by the enlightened policies which their humaneness prompted them to formulate and promote, would succeed in fostering social harmony and well-being, while conflict and disorder would ensue when the throne was occupied by men of inferior moral stature.[4]

Here again we find a potential inconsistency. For if history is part of a larger cosmic process and this cosmic process operates according to fixed, determined patterns—as most Chinese views of the universe seem to presuppose[5] —there would appear to be little room for human beings to influence the course of historical change. This is not the place to enter into a discussion of this dilemma, which, though it has taken different forms, has been no less prominent in the West. The main point to be made, as before, is that numerous Chinese thinkers seem to have been either unaware of its existence or (assuming they were aware) capable psychologically of embracing both of its horns, at times assigning a large role in historical causation to man (*jen*), at times laying almost everything at the foot of fate or Heaven (*t'ien*).[6]

Strains and stresses similar to these were rampant in Wang T'ao's perception of history. But, while this may be perfectly plain to us, there is no indication that Wang himself experienced them. It is essential to distinguish between the way in which a man looks at history intellectually—his understanding of it—and the way in which, as it were, he wants history to go. If the former concern is the primary one, inconsistencies will tend to generate strains; but if the latter dominates, there is no reason why views of the past which are incompatible by themselves cannot be harmoniously pressed into the service of a vision of the future that is utterly consistent.

Chinese society in the last decades of the nineteenth century was in the throes of a general crisis of unprecedented dimensions. Unlike many of his contemporaries, Wang T'ao sensed this crisis acutely, and it was extremely important for him, from a psychological standpoint, to be able to visualize a time when the crisis would be surmounted to China's advantage. Faced with such a transcendent goal, it is little wonder that he at times leaned one way, at times another, clutching at every straw that could give some comfort for the future.

WANG'S HISTORICAL WRITINGS

Although Wang T'ao is not ordinarily thought of as a historian, his historical writings made up a sizable share of his total output as an author. Wang's histories were a curious mixture of old and new. The stylistic conventions and organizational forms which he adhered to were essentially those which Chinese had been using since the time of Ssu-ma Ch'ien. But in his choice of subject matter, Wang broke fresh ground. Characteristically present-oriented, he left it to others, more timid and parochial than himself, to rework the histories of the Han and T'ang. In an age dominated by the Western challenge, Wang T'ao wrote about the West.[7]

Unpublished works. Several of Wang's historical compilations, though never published, deserve mention as evidence of the scope and quantity of his work. As we have already seen, Wang claims to have written (presumably in the 1870's) brief histories of the United States and Russia, each in eight chapters. It is possible that these were included in the much more ambitious work, "Ssu-ming pu-ch'eng" (Supplementary annals of the countries beyond the four seas), apparently intended by Wang as an updating of Wei Yüan's *Hai-kuo t'u-chih* (Illustrated gazetteer of the maritime countries). This compilation, which he hoped would serve as a principal reference for the section on foreign countries in the standard history of the Ch'ing, eventually ran to 120 chapters. Its contents were described by Wang in an annotated bibliography of his works which he printed in 1889: "The research for this book has been extensive. Recent times are covered in detail, remote times in outline form. Everything of consequence that has happened in the past forty years in connection with governmental affairs, popular sentiment, court embassies, treaties, war and peace, and reform has been recorded for future reference, special attention being paid to Sino-foreign intercourse."[8]

In the same bibliography Wang furnished brief characterizations of two other historical works which he had never gotten around to publishing. The first, "Hsi ku-shih" (The ancient history of the West), in four chapters, focused on the ancient land of Judea and supplied information on frontier changes, developments of different periods, and the evolution of learning and the arts. The second, "Hsi-shih fan" (Miscellaneous Western events), also in four chapters, brought together traditions and anecdotes which Wang had not been able to incorporate in his regular histories of the nations of the West. Wang concluded his discussion of "Hsi-shih fan" by observing that "the Western scholar understands the modern but is ignorant of the ancient, while the Chinese literatus loves the ancient but is contemptuous of the modern." "If both can remedy their respective shortcomings," he enjoined, "perhaps it will stop them from discrediting each other."[9]

P'u-Fa chan-chi (Account of the Franco-Prussian war). In this work, Wang T'ao amply fulfilled his own injunction. Based largely on Western newspaper coverage of the war and written with the help of Chinese colleagues skilled in English (principally Chang Tsung-liang), it was initially published in 1873 in fourteen chapters and later expanded to twenty chapters. This was the book that first brought Wang fame as a foreign affairs expert. It was reissued periodically in the last decades of the nineteenth century in China and Japan and won the praise of Tseng Kuo-fan, Li Hung-chang, Ting Jih-ch'ang, Liang Ch'i-ch'ao, and a host of lesser contemporaries.[10]

P'u-Fa chan-chi, as one of its prefacers pointed out, represented a radical departure from previous Chinese accounts of the West. The best of these, the works for example of Wei Yüan and Hsü Chi-yü, had tended to be extremely broad in scope and general in nature.[11] Wang's book was the first to subject to close scrutiny a single major episode in recent European history. It was also noteworthy for having been written under the explicit assumption that, in the wake of recent events, the histories of China and Europe were, for better or worse, inextricably joined, so that henceforth a major change in the European situation would automatically have consequences for China.[12]

Operating on this new premise, Wang T'ao did not have to make continual reference to China in *P'u-Fa chan-chi*. The important thing was to present information about Europe, which, having entered the stream of world (Chinese) history, could now be regarded as a useful subject of study in its own right. The resulting product, when read today, undeniably has something of the character of an "amateurish hotch-potch."[13] But in terms of its expressed purpose, it was a resounding success. It literally teems with information—however ill-digested and disorganized—about the histories and national customs of France and Germany (including a translation of "La Marseillaise"), European political institutions and their day-to-day operation, the latest advances in military technology and tactics (such as the extensive use of charts and maps by the Prussian armies, the besieged Parisians' use of balloons outfitted with cameras for air reconnaissance, the military advantages of the telegraph and railroad), the conduct of European diplomacy, the events of the war itself, and so forth.

Were this all, *P'u-Fa chan-chi* would be of only passing interest.

But Wang went further and, particularly in his two prefaces (both dated August 1871), placed the Franco-Prussian War in the framework of a more generalized perspective on history. In format this perspective was unequivocally cyclical. The war was viewed as yet another chapter in the unending saga of the rise and fall of states,[14] Prussia having risen from a condition of extreme weakness to send France plummeting from her accustomed position of strength. Nor was this likely to be the end of the matter: "Those who are good at probing the fortunes of nations (*kuo-yün*) do not take victory as an auspicious sign or defeat as an omen of doom. [They know that] upon reaching its most flourishing point [a country] begins to decline and that upon attaining a point of maximum weakness it gradually gains in strength."[15] France, in short, would rise again and Prussia would once more fall.

With cyclical change in the political arena elevated virtually to the status of a natural law, did this mean that there was no room for man to shape developments? No. Here Wang T'ao implied a kind of division of jurisdictions. General problems of historical timing apparently fell under the jurisdiction of Heaven and were therefore beyond man's control. Thus, the reason why hostilities between France and Prussia broke out just when they did was that Heaven did not wish France, because of a private grievance, to bring harm to China (*t'ien-hsia*).[16] (Possibly Wang had in mind the Tientsin Massacre of June 1870, which might have led to war between France and China had not the European outbreak intervened.)[17] The cosmic intelligence (lit. "the mind of Heaven" [*t'ien-hsin*] or "the course of Heaven" [*t'ien-tao*]) also dictated the overall pattern of history and the basic ground rules of causation, in this respect superseding national fortune (*kuo-yün*) as a determining agent in history. On the other hand, in the actual operation of the cause-and-effect nexus man's role loomed large. For example, Heaven established the iron rule that immoral actions had unfavorable consequences, but whether to act morally or immorally in any given situation was up to man.[18]

The influence that the "actions of men" (*jen-shih*) could have on the outcome of historical events was best illustrated in Wang's analysis of the reasons for Prussia's victory and France's defeat. It was understandable that Wang should be intrigued by this question. He had passed through France only a few months before the outbreak of the war and had been sufficiently impressed to write a history of the country on his return to Hong Kong (see below). Prussia, by contrast, was an unknown quantity in China and certainly was not viewed as one of the major European powers. Consequently, when in the early weeks of the war Prussia rode roughshod over the French colossus, Wang T'ao was both puzzled and fascinated.[19]

In sorting out the many causes for the sudden collapse of French power, Wang of course gave extensive attention to the strictly military side—tactics, weapons, training, and the rest. Also—perhaps with the contemporary Chinese situation in mind— he revealed a profound appreciation for the political strength derived by Prussia from the unification process.[20] One senses, nevertheless, that for Wang the moral element was more fundamental than any of these immediate power factors, power as such being less crucial in his mind than the manner of its employment. "Only through right," he stated, "can [a country] exert control over world developments. How can it value might alone? When [a country] uses might to coerce people it is rare for it not to be destroyed." The fate met by France, Wang added, was clear evidence of the truth of this proposition.[21] For France had relied on her preeminent strength to act so tyrannically that the countries of Europe had come to look upon her virtually as "a predatory Ch'in devoid of moral principles" (*wu-tao hu-lang Ch'in*).[22]

Wang again touched on the question of the proper use of power in his examination of the internal policies of the French and Prussian governments in the period leading up to the war. It was here that the human factor assumed for him a place of overriding importance. For example, in discussing the Prussian government's effective utilization of Prussia's human resources, he remarked: "If something uncommon is to be accomplished in the world there must be men who are uncommon to assist. Hence if a country is to rise it must recruit courageous military leaders to defend it and officials of undivided loyalty to shoulder the heavy burdens of state. In recent times the outstanding quality of Prussian leadership has been quite without match among the countries of Europe." Wang went on to present biographical profiles of Bismarck, Moltke, and others, and concluded: "With talent of this order Prussia's rise as a nation was predictable. Even without her successes in battle, informed people could see that her national situation was steadily improving. Ah, the connection between men of ability (*jen-ts'ai*) and national fortune (*kuo-yün*) is no thing of chance."[2 3]

Was France then devoid of talented leaders? Not at all. Though she may not have been blessed with a Bismarck or a Moltke, she certainly had men of outstanding caliber (Wang especially admired Thiers). The trouble was that Napoleon III either failed to use these men or, in using them, too often ignored their counsel.[2 4]

Napoleon III in fact came in for a major share of the blame for the French debacle. Wang recognized him to have been a ruler of some ability. But his rule had been flawed by his love of war, and this fatal defect had brought on "the depletion of [French] territory, the surrender of his army, the loss of his throne, and the weakening of his country."

Napoleon's penchant for waging war was not, however, the sole cause of France's defeat. Equally to blame were the deep divisions that plagued the French body politic. Mencius had once asserted: "A state sows the seeds of its own destruction before others finally destroy it. It first occasions an attack upon itself before others finally attack it." In Wang's view these words had been fully borne out by the situation in France on the eve of the war—a situation marked by growing popular discontent with Napoleonic policies and increasing dissension between ruler and ruled.[2 5] What a contrast to the steady augmentation of strength and prosperity that had distinguished Prussia's development since the accession of William I in 1861![2 6]

Fa-kuo chih-lüeh (General history of France). It may be recalled that, after getting to England in 1868, Wang T'ao had invited the French sinologist, Stanislas Julien, to pioneer with him in the writing of a Chinese "gazetteer" of France. Julien, for reasons unknown, declined. But Wang, embarrassed at his countrymen's near total ignorance of French history and culture, persisted in his goal. Shortly after returning to Hong Kong in 1870, he was asked by Ting Jih-ch'ang to revise and expand an illustrated world geography which Ting had had translated from an American original. Wang, seeing his opportunity, started out with the section on France and in six months' time was able to report to Ting the completion of a provisional draft.[27]

Of the fourteen chapters of this original version of the history of France, six were based on Ting's book, while eight were entirely new. It is not clear, however, whether the work was ever published in this form. The first published version that I have encountered references to—and the only version I have seen personally—is a completely revised and much enlarged edition which Wang brought out in 1890. This edition, entitled *Fa-kuo chih-lüeh*, is in twenty-four chapters. Aside from the original preface (written by Wang in early 1871) and the chapters on French geography and Anglo-French relations (which appeared in the original version of 1870), it seems to be largely a product of the 1880's.[28]

Although *Fa-kuo chih-lüeh* is, on the whole, a very different book from *P'u-Fa chan-chi*, the overview of history expressed in it is essentially the same. This is particularly evident in the original preface, where Wang gives forceful articulation to the central tension between the cosmic law of cyclical movement and individual responsibility for the shaping of events:[29]

Alas, France has been an independent nation in Europe for over a thousand years ... [She] took the lead and managed everything, for in the course of time her prestige and power had come to be held in awe by everyone.

[All countries], however, when they reach the pinnacle of success begin to decline (*sheng chi erh shuai*). Such change is governed by laws as constant as those which cause the sun to go down after reaching its zenith or the moon to darken by degrees after it has passed through its full phase ...

From ancient times on, once the chance to act has passed wise men and stupid have been frustrated together, but when it has been possible to seize an opportunity gifted men and mediocrities alike have been aroused. Which is only another way of saying that events, although patterned after the Way of Heaven (*chun chu t'ien-tao*), are also subject to the influence of men's actions (*ch'üan   chu   jen-shih*). Could [something as momentous as France's defeat in the war with Prussia], then, be the work of a day and a night?[30]

History, Wang seems to be saying in this passage, is an intelligible process and great historical events do not happen by accident or without warning. The causes of such events, however, operate over long stretches of time and are very deepseated in character. Therefore only the most experienced eye can discern the direction history is taking at any given moment.

Wang also, here, approaches the question of the scope of man's role in historical causation in a way that parallels Marx's handling of the same predicament. "Men make their own history," Marx wrote in *The Eighteenth Brumaire*, "but they do not make it just as they please; they do not make it under circumstances chosen by themselves, but under circumstances directly encountered, given, and transmitted from the past."[31] In Wang T'ao's vocabulary, men were free to make what they could of the opportunities presented by history. But whether such opportunities would in fact be presented, and what kinds, were matters that were determined by larger, more impersonal forces.

Wang T'ao's original preface to *Fa-kuo chih-lüeh* clearly was written under the spell of the Franco-Prussian War. Most of the book proper, however, was assembled just before the war or long after and is much broader in focus. Following the traditional Chinese format, the first part is devoted to a chronological account, dynasty by dynasty, of the political history of France, while in the later sections, assorted topics are subjected to monographic treatment. The history is comprehensive, detailed, and surprisingly free of factual errors. Although, as we shall shortly see, Wang is critical of certain aspects of the "French tradition," no effort is made to minimize in any way the greatness of individual French heroes or of French culture. Such would have been entirely contrary to the central purpose of *Fa-kuo chih-lüeh*, which was to break away from the smug parochialism of past Chinese history-writing. As Wang put it:

The Japanese scholar, Kihara Genrei, says: After Ssu-ma Ch'ien paved the way by incorporating chronicles of the Hsiung-nu and the southern and western barbarians into his history, this procedure was adopted in the standard histories of all subsequent dynasties, [information on] frontier tribes being included in the chronicles of foreign countries (*wai-kuo chuan*) . . . Unfortunately, the accounts in these sections were mostly based on hearsay and half-truth and could not be taken as authoritative . . . People from faraway places were not deemed fit for serious study . . .

I think Kihara Genrei's criticism of the provincialism of the official historians of the past is truly correct. Europeans arrived in China to trade . . . as early as the Wan-li period of the Ming. Yet when it came to writing the chronicles for the *Ming-shih* [History of the Ming], [the compilers] were still unable to show the location of France, treating it as if it were one of the island kingdoms of the South Seas. They failed to consult Giulio Aleni's *Chih-fang wai-chi* or any of the other works [on foreign geography]. Is it any wonder that the foreigners laugh at them?[32]

When Wang T'ao asked his readership not to laugh at him for trying, in the space of a dozen or so chapters, to do justice to the whole sweep of French history from the Merovingians to his own day,[33] he served notice that a radically changed Chinese outlook on the world had dawned. Wang's unequivocal endorsement of a *Japanese* indictment of the narrowness of past Chinese historiography was the perfect symbolic expression of this new outlook.

To note the cosmopolitanism embodied in *Fa-kuo chih-lüeh* is, however, only to tell part of the story. How did Wang T'ao perceive French history? What factors influenced what he saw (as well as what he failed to see)? And how did he respond to his own perceptions? It cannot be too strongly emphasized that Wang T'ao did not respond to an objective reality called "French history." He responded to his perceptions of French history, and these in turn were the end-product of a complex process of selection governed by Wang's general understanding of historical process, his particular concerns as a Chinese in the nineteenth century, and the amount and kinds of information to which he had access.

As regards the last factor, aside from the daily newspaper and a variety of unnamed Chinese-language works by Westerners, Wang identifies three sources which he used in compiling *Fa-kuo chih-lüeh*: Oka Senjin's *Fa-lan-hsi chih* (Gazetteer of France), Okamoto Kansuke's *Wan-kuo shih-chi* (An account of world history), and a Kiangnan Arsenal publication, *Hsi-kuo chin-shih hui-pien* (A classified compilation of recent Western events; published serially).[34] The most important of these sources, Oka's work, was itself a composite translation of several French secondary accounts. Thus, Wang T'ao's depiction of French history was at best several removes from the original data.

Judged by present-day historiographical canons, *Fa-kuo chih-lüeh* was not only third-hand but also third-rate. But of course it is not to be so judged. Probably there was not a single case in the nineteenth century (and I dare say precious few in the twentieth) of a Chinese history of the West based on research in primary sources. In the context in which Wang T'ao wrote, the relevant fact was Chinese ignorance, and the relevant standard for judging the product of his efforts was the effectiveness with which he dispelled this ignorance.

If *Fa-kuo chih-lüeh* were nothing more than a repository of available information on France, nevertheless, its interest today would be strictly limited, regardless of how valuable it might have been to contemporary readers. It is fortunate for us, therefore, that Wang T'ao chose to follow the time-honored Chinese procedure (also harking back to Ssu-ma Ch'ien) of enlivening his narrative with personal commentary, the opinions of "Wang T'ao, chronicler of neglected history" (i-shih shih Wang T'ao) always being kept scrupulously divorced from the text proper.[35] Wang's running interpolations are nowhere more absorbing than in the opening six chapters, which chronicle the political history of the Merovingians, the Carolingians, the Earlier and Later Capetians, the Bourbons, and the Bonapartes. For he based the contents of these chapters largely on the work of Oka Senjin and on several occasions juxtaposed his own comments to Oka's, treating us to a most illuminating comparison, in microcosm, of Chinese and Japanese reactions to the West.

Here, for example, is how the two men read the history of the Earlier Capetians:

[Oka Senjin], chronicler of unfamiliar history, comments: When I noted Louis's protection of popular rights (*min-ch'üan, minken*) and Philip's declaration to his countrymen of their freedoms and privileges (*tzu-yu ch'üan-li, jiyū kenri*), I heaved a big sigh and exclaimed: Here is the reason for the increasing strength and prosperity of the European nations!

... The mentality of freedom comes from Heaven and is not something that can be limited by other men. The European countries recognize this, and so, in the allocation of authority and the establishment of laws and institutions, they have seen to it that everyone enjoys the right of freedom without interference ... Since freedom belongs to all, the condition of society and the state of men's minds steadily improve, however mean the age or turbulent the times ... In substance if not in name, the tradition of the Three Dynasties still survives in the laws of the countries of Europe ...

Since all laws are made in the national assemblies, the process is one in which central importance is attached to protecting the rights (*ch'üan-li*) of the people. As the rights of the people steadily expand, the vitality of the nation steadily increases. Since there is communication between those above and those below, and the relationship between the sovereign and the people is a secure one, when the nation faces an important matter, the hearts of a thousand times ten thousand people are as one heart. It is for this reason alone that the countries of Europe in recent times have been contemptuous of the entire world. Those who would discuss the virtues and shortcomings of different governmental forms ought certainly to consider [the European example].

Wang T'ao, chronicler of neglected history, comments: France is truly a war-loving country. Her kings and nobles, through the ages, have all striven for glory and victory in the hope of establishing their merit. They attack abroad and extend their frontiers at home ... [It may in fact be said that the French] carry on the tradition of Ch'in. By acting so outrageously, they are often able to get their way in the short-run, but I fear that they cannot sustain [their successes] on a long-term basis. For they suffer from the defect of precipitousness.

After France broke away from the control of Rome and became an independent nation, she had six or seven brave and martial kings, all of whom were able to extend her frontiers and develop her land. Victorious in battle after battle, they looked upon the [rest of] Europe with contempt ... But [later French rulers] reposed confidence in the clergy and gave them a share in the governmental power. Heeding [the clergy's] rash advice, they paid armies to go long distances to fight [in the Crusades]. In the end, the national treasury was depleted and the soldiery exhausted, to the point where several hundred thousand young braves were slaughtered and the nation almost perished. Was it not the church that caused such harm?

There were three essential ways, Wang concluded, in which the West differed from China: the monarch and the people shared in the governing process, men and women both could accede to the throne, and church and state were joined.[36] He restated his conviction that much of France's trouble in the political sphere stemmed historically from the excessive power of the church and he charged Queen Clotilda with primary responsibility for establishing this noxious precedent.[37]

Wang's and Oka's comments could scarcely have been more different. Oka, the déclassé samurai living in a rapidly changing society under an authoritarian regime, was full of admiration for a system of government in which (as he saw it) authority was divided justly and the rights and liberties of all were secured. His overall view of France was a highly positive one: French laws embodied the spirit of the Three Dynasties and French history offered lessons for all of humanity to emulate. By contrast, for Wang T'ao, French history, at this point, was paridigmatic only in a negative sense. Wang decried the militaristic orientation of France, likening her not to Oka's Three Dynasties but to the dreaded Ch'in. And he was especially sensitive in an area where Oka's notice was not attracted at all, namely, the political involvement of the Catholic church.

Wang's preoccupation with the church-state issue can be attributed partly to his long association with Protestant missionaries, who tended in the nineteenth century to be militantly anti-Catholic. It can also be attributed to anger over the behavior of Catholic missionaries in China, who, under the official protection of France, showed a marked inclination to get involved in local political matters.[38] It would be a mistake, nevertheless, to take Wang's negativism toward France entirely at face value. At this juncture, Wang was not just responding to France; he was also responding to Oka Senjin. Although Oka was a close friend, he was Japanese, and there were a lot of things about Japan that Wang T'ao did not like. This is made amply clear toward the end of the chapter on the Later Capetians, where both men again furnished commentaries:

[Oka Senjin], chronicler of unfamiliar history, comments: The beneficial aspects of a thing can be realized only when there is resistance power (*ti-k'ang-li*) present. Electricity sends messages in a split second because of the power of resistance provided by the two qualities, dryness and dampness. Steam propels ships and trains huge distances because of the power of resistance provided by the two substances, water and fire. It is amazing how great the benefits realized from resistance power are!

Now soldiers are the resistance power of human beings. After reading the history of the Earlier and Later Capetians, I realized how necessary soldiers are. The benefits that accrue from skill in the use of soldiers are displayed before the world with lightning speed. Thus, as long as the Earlier Capetians continued the warring states pattern [of the preceding era], they were barely able to defend their borders. But once the Crusades started, . . . the entire situation in Europe was transformed, the Mediterranean growing into a vast commercial hub. [Similarly, in the case of] the Later Capetians, the Hundred Years' War between England and France stimulated the study of navigation, the invention of firearms . . . , leading in turn to intercourse with the southern part of Africa and to trade with the tribal states south of the equator . . .

People say that wars are dangerous affairs and armies cruel weapons. But this refers only to the harmful aspects of warfare. When we consider the wonderful benefits it confers on the world, do we know that these "dangerous affairs" and "cruel weapons" are not in fact harbingers of good?

Unable to contain himself, Wang at this point breaks in to admonish Oka:

This is the myopic view of a Japanese scholar. Military power, however great, must rest on a foundation of righteousness and virtue. The Japanese thought, when Toyotomi [Hideyoshi] announced his Korean expedition, that it would stimulate the growth of national power. They failed to realize that in the aftermath their armies would be exhausted and their supplies depleted. Ultimately, Japan derived nothing from this venture ... When [a country] insists upon using armed struggle as a means of training its troops, its troops are sure to be defeated in the process. This is not the way to govern a country.

In his formal commentary, which follows this, Wang hammers away again at French militarism, this time focusing on the Later Capetians. He then turns his spotlight directly on Japan:

The scholars of Japan have eyes only for their country's imitation of the military arts of the West ... Having tested their [new] weapons in the annexation of the Ryūkyūs, the expedition against the Formosan aborigines, and the plotting against Korea, the Japanese are convinced that they can become strong. They don't realize that, in fact, their strength is on the surface only and that they are weak within. When Japan first opened her ports to the Western countries and began to trade with them, it was with France that she was friendliest. Perhaps, then, she caught the disease from the French! That she should regard French militarism as something to be copied rather than avoided is too bad ... It is surprising to hear such things from the mouth of a Confucian scholar. I find nothing of value in [Oka's discussion].[39]

The gulf between Wang and his Japanese counterpart is again revealed in their comments on the French Revolution. (The author of the comment preceding Wang's, in this case, is not identified and may be another Japanese scholar. But the thinking is close enough to Oka's.) Both men seem to feel that it would have been better had the Revolution never taken place; that is, neither is committed to the cause of revolution as such. But their analyses of the Revolution's origins and the lessons they draw from the event are fundamentally different. Here is the Japanese comment:

When, in my reading of the history of the Bourbons, I got to the point where Louis XIV exclaimed, "The government is me, I am the government," I sighed and said: "This is the cause of Louis XVI's misfortune."
... In the *Analects* it is said that one word can destroy a state. Louis's statement may perhaps be taken as an example of this. It aroused the anger of the multitude and brought on the overthrow [of the government]. The law of retribution made it inevitable

that the people would reciprocate with "The government is the people, the people are the government."

... Now the way to keep a ruler from abusing his might and mistreating his subjects is to limit his authority by means of a constitution. And the way to keep the people of a nation from summoning up their strength and coercing their ruler is to fix their duties by means of a constitution. Since Louis was not averse to abusing his might and mistreating his subjects, why should the people have been averse to summoning up their strength and coercing their ruler? If a country is long to experience peace and good government, the first order of business must be the preparation of a national constitution to delimit the powers of the ruler and the people.[40]

The distinctive feature of this analysis is the emphasis it places on the institutional basis for good government. The Revolution of 1789 is seen as resulting from the French monarch's abuse of his power. But the way to prevent future revolutions is not to find kings who are less despotic. It is to establish a constitution which, by clearly delimiting the monarch's—any monarch's—authority, will function as an automatic check on royal despotism.

Constitutionalism was, of course, a major issue in Japan during the first half of the Meiji period (when the above comment was written). In China, however, it did not become a subject for public discussion until well into the 1890's. It is understandable, therefore, that Wang T'ao's analysis of the Revolution should point in a different direction entirely. For Wang, writing in the 1880's, it seems that the formula for good government still consisted in getting the right men to serve as rulers:

After getting to this point in my perusal of French history, I could not help closing the book and heaving a deep sigh. Does the calamitous violence engendered by republican governments (*kung-ho chih cheng*) always reach such an extreme? When rebel parties, in their cruel fury, brazenly dare to commit regicide, where are a country's laws? What has happened to the rules of nature? It is almost as if Heaven and Earth had been reversed and high and low had traded places ... There is a similarity between this and the killing of King Charles by the members of the English

House of Commons. In all of history surely there have been no rebellions worse than these.

And yet, if we search out the origins of these calamities, we find them to have resided in the inability of [the monarchs concerned] to conciliate the masses and win the hearts of the people. Presuming upon their positions high above the people, they failed to identify with popular fortunes. And the resentment which mounted [in consequence] sufficed [in each instance] to bring about the king's demise . . . Such being the case, can those who serve as men's rulers do as they please and behave irresponsibly?[4 1]

It would be too much, perhaps, to expect Wang T'ao to see anything of positive value in the French Revolution or in English and French experiments with republican (kingless) government. "Revolution," for which the Chinese language in the 1880's did not even have a proper word,[4 2] looked, especially in its regicidal variant, like the worst form of rebellion (*luan*). And "republicanism," a new word for which (*kung-ho*) had just been coined, was bound to be associated with chaos in a culture that viewed monarchy as part of the natural order of things.

Nonetheless, it is significant that, in his discussion of the origins of the Revolution, Wang did not hesitate to place the blame squarely with the French monarchy. Mob violence was always a terrible thing, in his eye, and he never failed to condemn it.[4 3] But, at the same time, the Confucian side of his thinking precluded the possibility of spontaneous, self-generated mob violence. The people were ultimately a passive, reactive force. It was the monarch who was the pivotal figure in the Confucian political cosmos. The people disposed, the monarch proposed. Thus when the people rebelled, it was not because they were rebellious by nature but because the monarch's behavior had driven them to rebel.[4 4] Confucian monarchs did not, like their divine right counterparts in Europe, have to wait until they got to Heaven to have their sins computed.

Kings and dynasties, rebellions and wars—these were the all-too-familiar stuff that history had always been made of. And when Wang T'ao wrote about them, it was hard for him to break through the old crust. French political history offered much new information, because it was French—and that was a breakthrough not to be minimized. But it did not, in Wang's hands (as it had in Oka Senjin's), furnish any new lessons. Instead, it provided new confirmations of lessons that had long since been learned.

It was quite a different matter when Wang T'ao addressed himself to French institutional life. Freed from having to respond somewhat defensively to a more "progressive" Japanese intelligence—Oka's comments cease after the sixth chapter—and freed as well from the burdensome conventions that strait-jacketed the writing of political history in China, Wang, in the later chapters of *Fa-kuo chih-lüeh* produced glowing accounts of French banking, penal practices, transportation and communication facilities, the French educational system, parliamentary government, and other institutions. These treatises (*chih*) were reasonably detailed and systematic. And in a number of cases, as the following discussion of Western penal and legal institutions makes plain, Wang was venturesome enough to draw comparisons that were far from flattering to his own country:

. . . The finest aspect of Western law consists in the provision it makes for witnesses. Before it is decided whether the plaintiff or the defendant is in the right, witnesses must be called. Also public opinion must be in accord. Only when absolute certainty has been reached in a case is a final judgment rendered . . . Therefore, there are never cases of adversaries falsely implicating each other to the point where the [real] grievances are impossible to determine.

Except in cases of exile, [criminals] are simply imprisoned. They are not subjected to such punishments as severance of the nose or ears, cutting off of the legs, branding, ear-piercing, and cutting off of the feet. Punishment goes no further than the individual [criminal]. Fathers, sons, and brothers are never involved. Even in cases of rebellion and other major crimes, they execute the individual—and that is all. Wives and children are not punished. Relatives and neighbors are not implicated. Moreover, when a culprit is dead, that is the end of it, there being no such thing as posthumous punishment. Such Chinese practices as extermination of the immediate family and opening the coffin and beheading the corpse [of a criminal who died while awaiting execution] are regarded as barbarous and are prohibited. In such matters [the Westerners] still exhibit the traditions of the ancients and the abundant virtue of the sage kings!

. . . As for their prison arrangements, the regulations are very comprehensive and the punishments are humane. Prisoners must be treated with great leniency. They are given food and drink every day and clothing and shoes yearly, so that they are all warm and well-fed and do not have to fear cold and hunger. Some impoverished families [on the outside] are less well-off [than prisoners]. In fact, poor people and beggars sometimes steal on purpose so that they can get into prison, where a modicum of comfort and nourishment can be obtained.

. . . The prison inmates are tested to see what kind of work they can do and are asked to make various things. Sometimes artisans are hired to teach them so that they can acquire special skills. Then when they get out of prison they won't gravitate into the ranks of the unemployed. The things made in prison are sold in the marketplace, and the [money realized from this] is sometimes used to defray prison expenses. One [advantage] of this is that [the prisoners] don't just fill their stomachs and have a good time; another [advantage] is that their minds are occupied and they don't misbehave. This is truly an excellent idea.

Those selected for the job of prison warden must be honest and careful. If they mistreat the prisoners without cause, they are immediately dismissed . . .

If a prisoner is truly repentant and the prison warden believes him to be sincere, the warden may petition the authorities on his behalf to pardon him and let him out early; the prison need not necessarily adhere to the scheduled term of the sentence.

On Sundays a pastor or priest comes to the prison to preach. The prisoners all have to sit in a circle and listen quietly, so that their refractory minds will be transformed and their tyrannical dispositions softened . . .

As between [Western] and Chinese prisons, the distance is greater than that separating the sky and the sea. Here is good government which still embodies the traditions of the Three Dynasties and earlier.[4][5]

It is doubtful whether there were many prisons in nineteenth-century Europe that measured up to Wang's idealized description. But the frank suggestion of Western superiority in a sphere which, because it had to do with government, was supposed to be something of a Confucian preserve, represented a significant advance over the usual Chinese hymn in praise of Western technology. If the West had institutions, too, that were worth emulating, her history must have lessons to teach after all. It could not just be kings and dynasties, rebellions and wars.

Hsi-hsüeh yüan-shih k'ao (An inquiry into the beginnings of Western learning). Early in 1889, after returning from his first and only visit to North China (Shantung), Wang T'ao, aging and ill, was urged by friends in Shanghai to publish his life's writings. On being assured of financial assistance, he consented, and in this and the following year a number of manuscripts which he had worked on sporadically over the years were printed for the first time. Among them were six treatises on various phases of "Western studies," including *Hsi-hsüeh yüan-shih k'ao* in fifty folio pages. Although we shall be expressly concerned with Wang T'ao's promotion of Western learning in Chapter 6, since this particular piece is framed in historical terms, it seems appropriate to discuss it briefly at this point.[46]

Hsi-hsüeh yüan-shih k'ao is not a history in the usual sense of the term. What it is, in essence, is a chronological chart of Western cultural developments from the third millennium B.C. to A.D. 1874. "Western" is taken to include everything from India to the Americas. The dates are given according to the Western calendar, with the corresponding Chinese dates following. Under each date, Wang enumerates the important developments of that year in technology, science, religion, architecture, literature, commerce, and so forth. Relatively little space is devoted to political events—the French Revolution and the Opium War, for example, are not even mentioned—and, with the approach of the modern period, increasing coverage is given to scientific and technological advances. Although in terms of the kinds of material included the reach of the work is extremely broad, it contains only a meager supply of substantive information. The flavor may be gleaned from a few random excerpts:

In the late tenth century B.C., corresponding to the time of King Hsiao of the Chou, the Greek poet Homer (Ho-ma) wrote poetry in celebration of war exploits. He was followed in the same period by Hesiod (Hai-hsiu-ta), whose ballads were mostly about matters pertaining to the fields and the gods. The two men together are referred to as the fathers of Greek poetry. The Western custom of holding poetry and song in high regard begins with them.

In the late seventh century B.C., corresponding to the time of Kings K'uang and Ting of the Eastern Chou, Greece had seven worthies ["The Seven Wise Men of Greece"] all of whom excelled at metaphysics. One of them, named Thales (T'a-li-ssu), was skilled in astronomy. The solar eclipse . . . of the fourth year of King K'uang of Chou [609 B.C.] was accurately predicted by Thales.[47] Thales may properly be regarded as the founding father of Greek astronomy, mathematics, and science.

Around 300 B.C., corresponding to the time of King She of the Chou, the famous Greek, Euclid (Ou-chi-li-te), wrote the *Elements of Geometry* in fifteen books. The science of geometry was founded by the Greeks. Thales and Pythagoras (Pu-shih-ko-la) were both versed in its theorems. Throughout history men have all held them in high esteem.

In 1348, that is, the eighth year of the Chih-cheng period of the reign of Yüan Shun-ti, there was an earthquake in Europe. In England it rained for a long time and there was a flood. [The result was] an epidemic of the plague—a disease like China's *huo-luan* [that is, cholera] and commonly referred to as the black death. It spread through Europe and the dead numbered 2,500,000. In the city of London 100,000 people died in all and in a single day and night there were 200 dead. This was truly an extraordinary calamity, the likes of which had seldom been witnessed in European history.

In 1669, that is, the eighth year of K'ang-hsi of the present dynasty, Newton (Nai-tuan) first devised a method for refracting light. When white light was passed through a three-sided glass [that is, a prism], it divided into seven colors; when a second three-sided glass was added, [the seven colors] joined to become white light again.[48]

Hsi-hsüeh yüan-shih k'ao is noteworthy in a number of respects. First, there is no effort to begrudge the West its great antiquity or to suggest, as was customary among Wang's contemporaries, that the superior achievements of Western civilization all had Chinese prototypes.[49] True, in two or three instances, Wang observed that China had invented a given item first or had been in possession of it since time immemorial. But usually, in such cases (the magnetic compass and gunpowder are examples), he was right. Most of the time, when he noted a particular discovery or invention, China was left out of the discussion altogether.

Wang's immunity to the "China had it first" argument—to be discussed in greater detail in Chapter 6—was reiterated in other of his writings too. In a short piece on ancient Egypt (written prior to 1875) he conceded that arts and letters had appeared in that country before the Hsia dynasty and that, according to archeological evidence, the first ancestors of mankind had originated not in China but in southwestern Asia, near the juncture of Asia, Europe, and Africa.[50] In one of his later writings, moreover, Wang dismissed with little patience the widely held opinion that Western astronomy and algebra derived from China.[51]

Another respect in which *Hsi-hsüeh yüan-shih k'ao* is significant is its strong implication that civilization in the West was developmental in character, its forward march punctuated by one new discovery after another. This was a far cry from cyclical history, which demanded recurrence and thus foreclosed the possibility of anything truly new happening. Still and all, if Wang was willing to depart from the cyclical view in his treatment of the march of civilization in general, when it came to particular *civilizations*, he still seemed more comfortable with the older outlook:

My study of the ancient history of the West shows that in olden times there were many Western countries that achieved renown. The larger ones, numbering more than ten, alternately flourished and declined, contesting each other for mastery. Sometimes one would rise and another perish; sometimes they would unite and then divide. Examples are Babylonia, Egypt . . . , Greece . . . , Rome . . . , Macedonia, Syria, Judea, Palestine, Phoenicia, Tyre . . . , India . . . , and Persia. In the remote past all of these places were famous for their civilization. As the Occident's Ch'i-Feng [the homeland of the Chou people] and Tsou-Lu [the states in which Mencius and Confucius were born], they supplied the ancient models for [the West's] writing, institutions, rites and music, laws and punishments, astronomy, calendar, technology, and natural science. And yet, how often they collapsed in the wake of barbarian subjugation, the examples that had been handed down from generation to generation being utterly destroyed and the people restored to barbarism! Countries which formerly were imitated by Europeans are now dominated by Europeans. Is not the cyclical pattern of the Way of Heaven (*t'ien-tao hsün-huan*) predictable then? Does it not always come to this?

Nor, Wang went on, did this law hold true only for very ancient times. When America had been "discovered" four centuries earlier, everyone called it a "new land." But, on the basis of archeological evidence, it was indisputable that highly civilized peoples had once lived in such places as Mexico. "Such being the case," Wang asked rhetorically, "can a state long hold on to its strength and prosperity or a people to its wisdom and intelligence?"[5][2]

HISTORY AND CHINA IN A CHANGING WORLD

Theoretically, if Wang T'ao were to be utterly consistent in his application of the cyclical law of history, he would have to entertain the proposition that China, like every other civilization, would one day be faced with extinction. Emotionally, however, this was unthinkable. How did Wang extricate himself from this quandary? Were there exceptions to historical laws? Could China somehow be exempt from their operation?

The truth of the matter is that Wang T'ao was not especially bothered by such difficulties. If it suited his purposes, he was not above issuing lofty pronouncements on the universal laws of history. But he was equally willing, when the occasion demanded, to make the assumption—presumably essential to anyone who believed in the possibility of reform—that man's fate (history) was determined by his own actions. Context, here as elsewhere, was everything. And only by keeping this clearly in view can any sense be made of Wang's thought.

To illustrate, in *P'u-Fa chan-chi*, where Wang T'ao was largely concerned with the West as a world unto itself, it was quite possible for him to identify France as a declining power and Prussia as a state on the rise, Napoleon III as a predatory and oppressive monarch, William I as an enlightened and just one. As long as he kept within the bounds of an intra-Western context he could be reasonably detached, for it was ultimately unimportant to him whether a war was won by France or Prussia or whether any given nation was strong or weak. Yet, as soon as his concern shifted back to the world as a whole, as soon as the lines of battle were again drawn between China and the West, Wang's desires as a Chinese began to shape his judgments as a historian. The West as a whole could not be in the right, and Wang was sublimely confident that China would reassert her supremacy in the world of the future.

It is easy enough to see how the voluntarist element in Wang T'ao's view of history could be summoned to the support of this vision: through consciously directed change (that is, reform), China would again become powerful. Less obvious is the manner in which Wang's vision derived sustenance from the tacitly determinist cyclical conception. In one of his early editorials, Wang argued that the world primacy of China (by which he apparently meant Chinese civilization) was a constant element in history. This primacy could not always be asserted, however, for China was subject to the general cyclical alternation of strength and weakness and, when weak, was prey to the depredations of non-Chinese peoples. A review of the long history of Chinese-"barbarian" relations, nevertheless, revealed something that was supremely comforting: One foreign people after another had used its momentary strength to intimidate a momentarily weak China, but sooner or later foreign aggressors, like the waters of a flood, had receded into the oblivion of time, while China, imperturbable and timeless—a mountain periodically submerged beneath the torrent—had always endured. In the future, as in the past, wise rulers might be counted on to come to the fore and renovate the country, at which point, Wang tells us, "the strong will again lose their strength, and the distinction between superior and inferior will be made clear."[53]

The latest representative of "the strong" (which, in this context, of course, had negative connotations) was the West, and Wang T'ao never tired of pointing out that Western strength was doomed to destruction. This was so on general cyclical grounds because military technology was rapidly approaching the point where the total destruction of the human race could result. Since "every phenomenon upon arriving at its limit enters upon a return course"[54] and Western military science was obviously nearing such a limit, its development had of necessity to be arrested and reversed.

Another reason why Western power was doomed—and this was the reason most often cited by Wang—was that it was used in immoral ways. Relevant in this connection was Wang's attitude toward war as a principal manifestation of power. As a patriotic Chinese reformer, Wang saw clearly that China must pull abreast of the West in general military capability and his writings were saturated with information on military matters. But as a Confucian moralist—and, perhaps, a human being—he regarded all war as evil and was particularly horrified at the potentialities for mass destruction inherent in modern warfare.[55]

Nevertheless, man, being the sort of creature that he was, had always engaged in wars—even sage kings had been forced to take up arms[56]—and the problem ultimately came down to the familiar one of distinguishing between just and unjust wars. In Wang's words:

When [a ruler] is bent on extending his territory and increasing his wealth, with only his own gain in view, it is in the interest of one party but not of all ... Even if his might is unrivaled, at length there will surely be an uprising of the people and he will be killed. When [a ruler] is on good terms with large countries and protects small states, with a view to remaining at peace with the one and to preserving the other from destruction, this is in the interest of all parties rather than only one. And if at length he encounters an external threat, even though his might is not great enough to repulse the enemy, he can vanquish it with right. For where right is followed the masses will spontaneously come to [a ruler's] aid ... Then, will he still have to worry about his army being too small?[57]

Clearly the selfish application of a state's power for purposes of extending its territory or increasing its wealth was not moral. Hence the whole process of Western expansion in modern times had been by definition an immoral one.[58] But it was equally plain, in Wang's view, that history was on the side of the angels. Consequently the trend toward domination of the world by Western power would have to be reversed if history were to continue to have meaning.

Would the world of the future, then, be a replica of that of the past? Was the intrusion of the West *simply* the latest manifestation of an age-old cyclical pattern of "barbarian" invasion? Yes and no. The Western intrusion was similar to previous "barbarian" assaults in that its instrument was force and the intruder was insensitive to the Chinese view of things. But it was also significantly different from earlier incursions on account of the West's high and constantly rising technological level. It was, after all, Western technology which formed the essential underpinning of the West's great military power, and it was this technology which had for the first time in Chinese history made massive foreign intrusion by sea possible.[59]

In one basic respect, then, the future world would be very different from the world of the past. For China and other countries, if they were to defend themselves against the encroachments of Western power, would have to assimilate the West's technology. Wang T'ao, after a brief period of hesitation, became fully committed to technological revolution, arguing that China had undergone sweeping changes before (witness the Ch'in-Han unification)[60] and that Confucius himself, were he alive, would certainly "not cling rigidly to antiquity and oppose making the changes required by circumstances."[61] It may be difficult for us to reconcile this view of change with the straightforward cyclical view put forward by Wang on other occasions. Yet there is no indication of his ever having abandoned the latter. In fact, in some of his writings the two views are found side by side.[62]

Technological development thus played the ambiguous role of being at once the cause of Western political ascendancy in the world and the means by which this ascendancy would eventually be ended. It also served the related function of providing the material basis for the establishment of a single universal world order. Wang T'ao used the term *ta-t'ung* or "great unity" to describe this order and has sometimes, in consequence, been viewed as a forerunner of K'ang Yu-wei (1858-1927). Without denying this possibility, it should nevertheless be pointed out that Wang's *ta-t'ung* thought, compared with K'ang's, was extremely rudimentary, containing no counterpart to the fully developed concept of human progress found in K'ang's utopia.[63]

In one other respect, also, the *ta-t'ung* thought of the two men differed significantly. Although K'ang Yu-wei's *ta-t'ung* ended up being much more radical than Wang's, it had its origins in a pedigreed, if somewhat unorthodox, interpretation of the Confucian canon, that of the Kung-yang school. One of the chief tenets of this school postulated that society developed through Three Ages, the last of which was the Age of Universal Peace (*t'ai-p'ing*) and Great Unity (*ta-t'ung*). Taking their cue from this notion, Kung-yang adherents maintained that government must periodically adapt to changed social conditions. Hence, the justification for reform.

Wang T'ao was certainly familiar with these theories—Kung Tzu-chen, the father of one of his closest friends from the early days in Shanghai, had been a prominent Kung-yang scholar—and one would expect, given his sympathetic attitude toward reform, that he would have been strongly attracted to the whole Kung-yang approach. Yet, while his *ta-t'ung* was very probably influenced by Kung-yang thinking, Wang never identified himself with the Kung-yang school in any explicit fashion. What is more, there is every reason to believe that a major source of inspiration for his *ta-t'ung* thought was not Confucian at all, but Western. Wang's prediction that, in the distant future, the principal teachings of the world would come together to form a great unity (*tao pi ta-t'ung*)[64] was cut from the same piece of cloth as John Fryer's statement alluding to "the great *Universal* religion that is gradually being evolved, and which will eventually embrace all people and nations and tongues."[65] Similar statements can be found in the writings of other Westerners with whom Wang was closely affiliated. In fact, speculation on common pasts and common futures was a favorite Victorian pastime.[66]

For Victorians, however, the universal culture of the future was most decidedly going to have a Western patent, and this was where Wang T'ao parted company with his foreign friends. His vision of the future, like theirs, was culture-bound. Only it was bound by a different culture. Wang was convinced that, in the absence of a supreme source of authority, the world would be visited by endless chaos,[67] but he was also convinced that this supreme authority would not be the West. When the technological gap had been closed and the Westerners had lost their military and economic advantage, he wrote with confidence, "by land and by sea, in fear and trembling," they would "hasten in droves to come and share with us universal peace (*t'ai-p'ing*)."[68] Or, in more strident language, on being deprived of their superiority in strength, the Western countries would all "bow their heads in submission to [Chinese] authority" (*fu-shou i t'ing-ming*).[69]

What was the philosophical basis for this China-centered world of the future? Clearly not technology. Technology (*ch'i*) could conquer geography and draw the world together, but it could not be regarded as "the basis for the governance of a state or the setting in order of all under Heaven." An object of such grand dimensions could be accomplished only by *tao*. *Tao*, a central concept in Chinese philosophy, signified ultimate truth, which for Wang T'ao meant the code of values natural and proper to all human beings. *Tao* was unchanging in character and in a sense therefore lay beyond the pale of history. Yet, it was also coterminous with history in that, as Wang put it, "without man there can be no *tao*, and without *tao* there can be no man."[70]

Tao was universal: "There is only one *tao* in the world. How could there be two?"[71] Thus it was valid for all of humanity and could not be a Chinese monopoly. Wang T'ao was very explicit on this score, insisting that *tao* was known to the West too and that Western history had produced sages of its own.[72] Still, the representations of *tao* to which other civilizations, since the beginning of history, had given their loyalties had been marked by imperfections. If there was any sense in which Wang may be said to have held to an idea of human (as distinguished from technological) "progress," therefore, it was in his very un-Condorcetian vision of the gradual extension to all men of a standard of perfection that had so far been grasped only by a limited number.[73]

The political implications of this conception of *tao* were fairly straightforward. Since *tao* embodied the loftiest ethical precepts, the world would be properly and justly ordered only when supreme authority emanated from *tao* or from that person or country most conversant with it. The term "country" is not entirely appropriate in this context, because the sphere of *tao*'s operation could conceivably—and should ideally—be coextensive with the whole world of man. But however one chose to define its limits, its center of gravity was Chinese. For *tao*, in Wang T'ao's view, though necessarily prior in time to Confucius, had found its most perfect historical expression in the teachings of China's Sage. Indeed, it was identical with these teachings (*K'ung chih tao jen tao yeh*).[74]

If we return now to our earlier question concerning the character of the future world, Wang's *ta-t'ung*, our answer must necessarily be in the nature of a paradox. Plainly, in the lower, more mundane realm, where change had always occurred, the world of the future would be different—and radically so. But in the higher realm, the home of the changeless, where ultimate human values resided, it would still be a world which Wang T'ao could inhabit comfortably. For here the past would live on. And it would be a familiar past, a Chinese past.

PART III. PRESCRIPTIONS

FOR A NEW CHINA

PROLOGUE

When the *Clermont* steamed up the Hudson River in August 1807, throngs of excited Americans lined the banks to cheer it on its way. The mood was festive; the onlookers felt good. It was a far cry from the atmosphere of suspicion and fear that greeted the first appearance of steamboats in Chinese waters. And yet, each response was intelligible in its own terms. "In our new land," John Fairbank has written, "we helped invent the modern world; the Chinese had it thrust upon them and rammed down their throats."[1] As the West closed in on China in the last century, it caught the Chinese off-balance, so off-balance that it took decades before they began to comprehend, even dimly, the nature and depth of the challenge facing them. In these circumstances, it was far from self-evident how the challenge was to be met, and it was not uncommon to encounter approaches such as the following:

According to Taoism, softness can overcome hardness and the way to advance is by retreating. Therefore, if one uses one's weakness with skill, it can be turned to strength. When something becomes too hard it must snap; when one advances too hastily one must stumble. Therefore, if one uses one's strength imprudently it will invariably turn to weakness. A glance at history shows that no dynasty ruled longer than the Chou, despite the fact that after the shift [of its capital] eastward under King P'ing [r. 770-719 B.C.],

143

the [Chou] was weakened to the point of being virtually power-less . . . [Similarly], the Sung was the feeblest of houses, yet it was able to contend successively with the Liao, Chin, and Yüan, and to prolong its rule for over three hundred years. Through weakness, it was able to survive.[2]

This passage appeared in a Hong Kong newspaper article in the late 1860's. The intent of the article was to show that Chinese were fooling themselves if they believed that the way to meet the Western challenge was to exchange the time-honored usages of China for those of the West. China's best defense consisted not in training armies, manufacturing weapons, and constructing fortifi-cations, but in the exercise of Taoist passivity and such hallowed Confucian virtues as righteousness, loyalty, and trust.

The editor of the newspaper sent the article to Wang T'ao in Scotland and Wang wrote a lengthy rebuttal, spelling out his position on the need for change and articulating an intellectual framework for coping with the Western menace.[3]

Wang began by boldly proclaiming that the world was under-going changes of such magnitude that the customs and institutions that had been preserved by Chinese for three thousand years were in real danger of being destroyed. He then drew a comparison between the northwestern portion of the globe (the West) and the southeastern portion (China): "The southeast is soft and qui-escent, the northwest, hard and active. Quiescent [civilizations] are adept at conserving; active ones are adept at changing . . . Soft [civilizations] are able to maintain themselves; hard ones are able to control others. Therefore, the [countries] of the northwest have always been able to visit harm upon those of the southeast, but the [countries] of the southeast have never been able to hurt those of the northwest."[4]

Wang was prepared to grant that sometimes change could be countered by nonchange (conserving) and hardness overcome by softness. But this was at best a slow and uncertain process, and the West, in the meantime, could be counted on to seize every opportunity to make trouble for China. China's only sensible course of action, therefore, was to beat the West at its own game by mastering its strengths (*shih ch'i so ch'ang*). This would, of course, mean change. But it was change necessitated by circumstance, and such change, according to Wang, had always been sanctioned: "When the course of Heaven changes above, the actions of men must change below. The *I-ching* [Classic of changes] states: 'When the possibilities inhering in a situation have been exhausted, change must take place; when there has been a change, things will run smoothly again.' "[5]

If China had to change before she could stand firm as a nation, did this mean that she must abandon her traditional customs, government, and culture and undergo a process of all-out Westernization? "No," Wang answered emphatically, "when I speak of change, I mean changing the outer, not the inner, changing what it is proper to change, not what cannot be changed. The change I have in mind, [moreover], must proceed from us . . . If they make us change, the advantage will be reaped by them; only if we change of our own volition will we retain control over our affairs."

Wang went on to note that, just as China had started out as a small country and gradually expanded, reaching its greatest extent under the Ch'ing, a parallel development had now taken place in European history. Like a great tidal bore, the Europeans, in a century's time, had spread from India to Southeast Asia and from Southeast Asia to South China, their knowledge advancing all the while.

A change of so fundamental a character could not have been programmed by man; it had to have been designed by Heaven. And since it was Heaven's will at work, it could not but be for China's good, one of the deepest strains in Wang T'ao's "belief system" being the assumption that Heaven (or destiny) was on China's side: "Heaven's motive in bringing several dozen Western countries together in the single country of China is not to weaken China but to strengthen her, not to harm China but to benefit her. Consequently, if we make good use of [this opportunity], we can convert harm into benefit and change weakness into strength. I do not fear the daily arrival of the Westerners; what I fear is that we Chinese will place limits upon ourselves. We have only one alternative, and that is to undergo complete change (*i-pien*)."

Earlier Wang T'ao had specified that what he meant by

"change" was change of the outer (*wai*), not change of the inner
(*nei*). Now he called for "complete change." How was this
inconsistency to be resolved? Actually, I think the inconsistency is
more apparent than real. Wang, if I understand him correctly, used
i-pien to signify not change of *everything*, but change of everything that was *capable* of being changed. *I-pien* did not embrace
the realm of *nei*, the inner, the essence, for *nei*, which was
comparable in value to *tao*, was not subject to change. It did, on
the other hand, encompass *wai*, the outer realm, the realm of the
changeable, and since *wai* included everything that was not *nei*,
the potential scope for change was considerable. So considerable
that, without impinging on the security of *nei*, Wang was able to
envisage a fairly sweeping transformation of the Chinese landscape:

> . . . in the military sphere we should make a complete conver-
sion (*i-pien*) from swords and spears to firearms; in the field of
navigation we should make a complete conversion from [old-
style] boats to steamboats; in the sphere of overland travel we
should make a complete conversion from carriages and horses to
trains; and in the realm of work we should make a complete
conversion from [traditional] tools to machines. Although . . .
[the old and the new means in these several areas] are alike in
regard to their end results, they cannot be compared in respect to
speed, precision, relative difficulty, and amount of labor required.
[The Westerners] have all four of these things; we do not have a
single one. If the situation were one in which we lacked them and
they had them and there were no relations between us, our lack of
them would not be a shortcoming and their possession of them
would give them nothing to brag about. We could carry on in our
accustomed fashion and it would be perfectly all right. But when
they insult us in an overbearing manner and on comparison we are
found to be inferior, when they constantly insist upon contending
and competing with us so that there is mutual wrangling and
recrimination, can we afford for a single day to be without these
things? . . . We may be certain that before a hundred years are out,
all four will be in China's possession, functioning as if they had
always been with us and viewed [by everyone] as commonplace
contrivances. It is not that I *want* this prediction to come true; it
cannot help but come true. Circumstances and the times make it

so. It is Heaven's wish that the eastern and western halves of the globe be joined in one.

The significance we attach to these paragraphs will depend on the framework of assumptions with which we approach them. It has been common among students of nineteenth-century China to assume that Confucianism and "modernity" were incompatibles;[6] that the traditional order had to be torn down before a new modern order could be built up; and that any commitment to reform that stopped short of a fundamental critique of Confucian values and institutions was, by implication at least, inadequate. Those who accept this sequence of assumptions have tended to deprecate the mere advocacy of technological change: Technological change is tinkering; only through value-change can a major systemic overhaul be effected.

I find this line of reasoning defective on a number of counts. First, there is a growing body of scholarly opinion which, in defining the relationship between "modern" and "traditional," rejects the implication that they are necessarily antithetical, mutually repellent conditions. As Michael Gasster has summarized it:

Most societies, Western as well as non-Western, are dualistic, in the sense that they are *mixtures* of the modern and the traditional, not *either* modern *or* traditional. They are "systems in which culture change is taking place," and they are distinguished from each other in terms of the type of relationship between the "modern" and the "traditional" components that exists in each ... From this point of view, modernization is best understood as a process *leading toward* a condition of modernity but never quite reaching it; indeed, there is no final condition of modernity but only a continuing process of adjustment among many modernizing and traditional forces.[7]

To this, I would only add that I see no reason why we must limit ourselves to the two categories, "modern" and "traditional." Presumably, there are elements in the make-up of every society which do not fall neatly under either rubric.

If it is accepted that modernity is a relative concept and that all societies, however modern, still retain certain traditional features, two questions arise: How much of the Confucian order, *objectively* considered, had to be abandoned before substantive change could take place in nineteenth-century China, and was it necessary, as a prelude to such change, for this order to be *openly* challenged? These questions uncover a hornet's nest of further questions: Granting that Confucianism and the traditional order were not coterminous, where do we draw the line between the two? Did the conscious rejection of the Confucian order (however defined) necessarily immunize against continued contamination by it? Conversely, did refusal to take open issue with Confucianism have the ineluctable effect of protecting it against attrition? What, to put it more succinctly, is the relationship between real change and perceived change? Between perceived change and desired change?

My object, in posing these questions, is to warn against overhasty acceptance of the answers that have already been given them. These are fiendishly difficult questions. Some of them may be ultimately unanswerable. None of them, certainly, can ever be answered with finality, and therefore it is essential to keep asking them.

The tendency to deprecate the "ships-and-guns" stage of Chinese reform thought also reflects the widely held assumption that Chinese reform efforts prior to 1895 were a "failure." This assumption was fed initially by treaty port opinion, which was consistently impatient with Chinese "bungling." In more recent times it has been reinforced by scholarly misinterpretation of the meaning of the Japanese example. Comparison of Chinese and Japanese modernization efforts can, as suggested at the outset of this book, be invaluable. But it must be done with extreme caution. If, from the fact that Japan defeated China in 1895 and went on to become a world power while China continued to flounder in weakness, we conclude that Japan's "response to the West" was rapid and successful, China's, slow and unsuccessful, we ignore a fundamental fact about modern Japanese history, namely that Japanese modernization had begun long before the arrival of the Westerners.[8] It is useful, as a corrective to such reasoning, to broaden our comparative perspective and measure the modernizing experiences of China and Japan not merely against each other but against those of the rest of the world's nations, the impact of the West being taken as only one variable among many. When we do this, we find that both China *and* Japan come off relatively well.[9] China is still way behind Japan, but she started much later.

Words like "failure" and "success," "rapid" and "slow," have a relative value only, and it is essential to keep this in mind when making comparisons. Perhaps, the key question to ask, in comparing the modernizing experiences of China and Japan, is not why the two countries responded to the West with such differing rates of speed and degrees of success, but why China's modernization began in earnest only *after* the intrusion of a substantial outside stimulus while Japan's began long before.[10]

Partly as a result of the pervasive influence of assumptions such as those discussed in the foregoing paragraphs, there has been a general reluctance to bear down on the technological aspects of reform in nineteenth-century China. In the upshot, some of the most elementary distinctions have been obscured. Technological change, as an objective fact, has been confused with *commitment* to technological change, which is subjective and indicates a value preference. Also, there has been relatively little effort to distinguish different *kinds* of commitment to technological change. People may advocate limited changes in technology or they may favor what amounts to a technological revolution. They may have warm, positive feelings toward technological change, viewing it as a natural concomitant of the "forward march of civilization," or they may see it as an unavoidable misfortune, something required by the pressure of circumstances but not desirable in itself. Finally, the commitment to technological change may be entered into for a variety of specific reasons (not all mutually exclusive): to improve living conditions, to compete more effectively with other countries, to increase state power, to preserve existing values and institutions, and so forth.

Assuming it to be true that the nature of a person's commitment to technological change reflects, to a greater or lesser extent, his orientation toward change in general, where did Wang T'ao stand as of the late 1860's? Relative to what other Chinese were proposing at the time, how radical was his reform program? His prognosis for the future? While it is impossible to say *exactly* how far Wang was prepared to go at this juncture—he probably did not know himself—it was certainly a lot farther than his contemporaries. Other reformers agreed on the necessity of introducing Western firearms and steamships. But leading Chinese officials were unanimous in their opposition to the building of railways,[11] and, with the exception of a few highly Westernized treaty port types, no one in the late 1860's, as far as I know, was ready to advocate extensive mechanization of the Chinese economy.

Equally important were the specific reasons Wang gave for advocating technological change. Many late nineteenth-century reformers, identifying the West with "matter" and China with "spirit," argued that only by the adoption of Western material civilization could China's spiritual civilization be saved from extinction. This was the *t'i-yung* approach, immortalized in the 1890's by Chang Chih-tung in the famous phrase, "Chinese learning for the essential principles (*t'i*), Western learning for the practical applications (*yung*)."

While it would be incorrect to say that Wang T'ao was wholly invulnerable to the *t'i-yung* approach—here as elsewhere he was capable of inconsistency—the central thrust of his thinking pointed in a quite different direction. Wang assumed that the essence of Chinese civilization—the core values, China's *tao*—was indestructible. Therefore he was theoretically free to take any position he wished in regard to technological change. He could reject even token technological change as being unnecessary. Or, with equal logic, he could espouse massive technological change on the grounds that it could do no harm. If he chose the latter course, however, it would necessarily be for reasons other than the preservation of Chinese essence. And in fact this is precisely what we find to have been the case. In the above-summarized article, Wang gave two justifications for technological revolution: first, that this was the only way in which China could compete with Western countries that had already undergone such a revolution, and second, that Heaven demanded it as the means to future world unification. In either instance, the preservation of Chinese values was viewed less as the justification of technological change than as its limiting condition.

In proposing sweeping technological change, was Wang, then, merely advocating the inevitable or was he to some extent using the argument of inevitability to buttress his advocacy? In other words, did he view such change as desirable because it was going to happen anyway or did he simply say it was going to happen anyway because he felt it to be desirable? On the face of it, it would appear that Wang regarded technological revolution as a necessary evil. It was not, he insisted, that he *wanted* his predictions to come true; they *had* to come true, as a result of "circumstances and the times." In a context like this, however, we must be very wary of accepting Wang's words at face value. This was not, after all, a letter to a friend or a private diary; it was a newspaper article. Wang's object was to persuade the newspaper's readership. And since it had to be assumed that this readership was opposed to massive technological change, it only made sense, tactically speaking, to portray such change as inevitable. Wang's personal feelings about the advent of the "machine age" were probably more accurately reflected in the travel diary he kept at this time, where, it will be recalled, his response was one of unqualified admiration and awe (see Chapter 3).

The radical quality of Wang T'ao's commitment to technological change brought him, quite early, to the recognition that other kinds of change would also be necessary. Wang became one of the first proponents, in the 1870's, of institutional change (*pien-fa*) and it was not long before his commitment to innovation widened still further to embrace basic social, economic, educational, and political reforms. Inevitably, as this happened, the old sanctions for change proved increasingly inadequate and Wang was obliged to seek new ones.[1][2]

One such, historical in character, reflected the developmental, noncyclical side of Wang's view of history:

Westerners who have perused the annals of Chinese history think that for five thousand years there has been no change. When, on the contrary, has China not experienced change? First, Yu-ch'ao, Sui-jen, Fu-hsi, and the Yellow Emperor cleared the wilderness and gave China governmental institutions. Then, Yao and Shun, following in their footsteps, styled China the center of the firmament and provided her with the attributes of civilization. From the Three Dynasties to the Ch'in there was another complete change and from the Han and T'ang to the present yet another complete change.[13]

Wang's defensiveness, in the face of Western criticism of Chinese stasis, is interesting. He could, after all, have turned the criticism into a backhanded compliment—a glorification of China eternal. The fact that, instead, he chose to respond with an insistent "We too have had change" implied an emotional identification with the idea of change that was not commonly encountered in the traditional Chinese setting.

The same positiveness of spirit may be seen in another of Wang's sanctions for reform, his assertion that it had always been the Way of the Sages (that is, the Confucian Way) to make proper accommodations to the times and that if Confucius were living in the nineteenth century he would certainly have lent his support to the introduction of Western technology and the general cause of reform.[14] The view of Confucius as a would-be reformer—here again Wang anticipated K'ang Yu-wei—was potentially revolutionary. For it not only provided a powerful justification for particular changes but also introduced into Confucianism a more affirmative attitude toward change in general.

Just as revolutionary, though much less obvious, were the implications of Wang's universalistic conception of *tao*. As we have seen, the prevailing tendency among his contemporaries was to equate China with *tao* and the West with *ch'i* (technology). Wang's conviction that *tao* was an attribute of *human* civilization, and therefore the property of the West as well as of China, injected something very new into the picture. It brought the West into a Chinese world of discourse and, willy-nilly, in the process it furnished China with a rationale for borrowing more than mere *ch'i* from the West.

Did Wang T'ao's dynamization of Confucius and his universalization of *tao* modify the Confucian tradition to the point where it could no longer be called Confucian? In his efforts to find a basis of legitimacy for China's modernization, did Wang reinterpret Confucianism to death? It is easy, when faced with such questions, to lapse into a kind of retrospective determinism which, starting from the conscious rejection of Confucianism in the May Fourth period, sees all modifications of Confucianism in the immediately preceding decades as leading inexorably to this conclusion. One antidote to such reasoning is to remind ourselves that radical changes in Confucian doctrine had taken place before in Chinese history without bringing an end to the tradition. It is very possible that neither Han nor Sung Confucianism would have been recognizable to Confucius, but this did not keep their adherents from seeing themselves as authentic followers of the Sage. Similarly, in the case before us, there is probably no way of determining whether the liberties Wang T'ao took with Confucianism were fatal to it in any objective sense. All we can say for sure is that Wang continued to regard himself as a Confucian.

6

EDUCATIONAL REFORM

One measure of Wang T'ao's newness is that he defies simple classification. Although he had a wide range of bureaucratic connections, he never served in an official capacity. Nor, despite his work for James Legge, could he really be called a scholar in the classical sense. For a brief period, in the late 1840's, Wang was technically a member of the "lower gentry" class. But once he moved to Shanghai and began to work for the London Missionary Society, the "gentry" label rapidly became anachronistic—even granting the gentrylike character of the militia work he engaged in in the late 1850's. Wang wrote short stories and histories, but certainly he was much more than a short story writer and something less than a historian. As for his newspaper activity, although it clearly fell within the confines of what would today (and in his own day) be accepted as journalism, it was rarely a full-time occupation; Wang's goals as a journalist, in any case, far transcended mere commercial success. Even the word "reformer," while manifestly applicable in Wang's instance, fails to distinguish adequately between power of advocacy and power of implementation. The former kind of power Wang T'ao had in abundance and put to good use. But Wang was seldom in a position to carry out his reformist ideas in practice.

"Reform," nevertheless, describes better than any other word Wang T'ao's central preoccupation. Wang wanted change. He wanted a more effective bureaucracy, staffed by abler men; higher status for merchants and acknowledgment of the growing importance of commerce in the economy; revision of court policies toward foreign countries and of the educated public's attitudes toward foreign learning; a greater political voice for people outside the government; and countless other modifications of the existing system. Finding the present at best frustrating, at worst intolerable, Wang pictured a future which, though still framed in the immutable norms (*tao*) of bygone eras, would be utterly different from anything previously known. He wanted China to take the lead in designing this future; otherwise, he feared, she would be devoured by it.

In this chapter and the two that follow, I propose to break up Wang T'ao's reform thought into three broad categories: educational, economic, and political. This is, to some extent, an artificial division. Reform of the examination system naturally had political as well as educational implications, while the establishment of schools for women was as important socially as educationally. Such artificiality is heightened by the fact that the divisions used are derived from modern Western culture, where, to cite but one instance, the political and educational realms tend to be much more clearly differentiated than they were in nineteenth-century China. I shall try to counter this difficulty, as it arises, by exploring the multiple ramifications of Wang's individual reform proposals.

Two other problems relating to the specific sociocultural context in which Wang T'ao operated are those of means and audience. Reformers of all times and places share the impulse to change things for the better. But the means available to them to express this impulse and the possibility that such expression will have a significant impact vary greatly from society to society. The range of variation is probably somewhat smaller in the case of the bureaucrat-reformer, by virtue of the fact that he works within a bureaucracy and all bureaucracies share certain fundamental features in common. It is enormous, however, in the case of the nonofficial, independent reformer. At one extreme we have the ordinary American citizen who, if he wishes to register general dissatisfaction with things as they are or to press for a specific change, has unlimited avenues open to him. He can write his congressman, give a speech, organize a pressure group, place an ad in a newspaper, draft and circulate petitions, demonstrate, picket, take his case to the courts, or campaign and vote for political candidates who share his views. The political system under which he lives is expressly designed to be responsive to public opinion. Therefore, he frequently tries to bring about change by influencing, mobilizing, or claiming to articulate this opinion.

This is necessarily an oversimplification. The United States government does not merely *respond* to public opinion. It sometimes takes a leading part in developing it, it sometimes manipulates it, and it sometimes ignores it. On balance, nevertheless, it is true to say that public opinion is a crucial factor in the American political process.

Can the same be said of China in the final third of the last century? Was there a public opinion at all? If so, what was its nature, how was it formed, and to what extent was it capable of exerting influence on government policy? If not, was there a functional substitute for a "public" opinion—an influential audience to whom a nonofficial reformer interested in changing government policy could address himself in his writings? These are important questions in the context of this book, because, although it is not my purpose to study the extent of Wang T'ao's influence, the fact is that, as an advocate-reformer, the only way Wang could make any mark at all was by influencing someone.

The problem, in Wang's case, is complicated by the circumstance that major shifts were taking place in China during the last phase of his career. In the 1890's, and certainly in the first decade of the twentieth century, a genuine public opinion was unquestionably starting to assert itself. Its means—boycotts, protest demonstrations, petitioning, elections, reform clubs, newspapers, and journals of opinion—were utterly modern. And the Ch'ing court, less out of natural susceptibility than out of desperation, began to be significantly affected by it.[1]

By the 1890's, however, Wang T'ao had slowed down considerably. During the period of his most active involvement in reform
promotion, the 1870's and 1880's, these modern vehicles for
the expression of public opinion were, with the important exception of the newspaper, not yet on the horizon. The means Wang
had to work with and the audience he could hope to reach were,
therefore, by comparison severely limited. Public opinion, in the
1870's and 1880's, was still, for all intents and purposes, "literati"
opinion, the opinion of the educated community. Therefore, when
Wang T'ao was not writing or speaking directly to officials or their
staff members—something he did with great frequency—he wrote
for this larger educated community, in the hope that, once
enlightened, it would, if not actively foster change, at least be less
resistant to it.[2]

THE PURSUIT OF EXCELLENCE

To the extent that persuasion was his principal business and the
written word his principal instrument, it could be argued that *all*
of Wang T'ao's reform efforts were at bottom educational. There
are, however, several more specifically educational concerns that
run through his reform writings, and it is to these that the present
chapter is addressed.

Men of ability. The whole question of the importance to society
of trained human talent is one which straddles premodern China
and the modern West in an awkward way. "In the conditions of
modern life," wrote Alfred North Whitehead, "the rule is absolute,
the race which does not value trained intelligence is doomed." The
same perception was echoed in 1906 by William James: "The
world ... is only beginning to see that the wealth of a nation
consists more than in anything else in the number of superior men
that it harbors."[3] The odd thing is that both of these statements
could have been subscribed to by a Chinese Confucian centuries
earlier. The backward-looking statesmen of the T'ung-chih Restoration, Mary Wright tells us, "were positively obsessed with the idea
of 'human talent.' "[4]

What, then, are the differences? One difference, certainly,
pertains to the prescribed locus of operation of human talent. The

Confucian view was expressed by Tso Tsung-t'ang: "Chaos in the Empire results from the fact that civil government is not properly maintained. That civil government is not properly maintained results from the fact that men of ability are not in office; that men of ability are not in office results from the fact that men's hearts are not upright; that men's hearts are not upright results from the fact that learning is not expounded."[5] The same idea is given even more succinct expression in *Chung-yung* (The mean): "When the right men are available, government flourishes; when the right men are not available, government declines."[6] "Human talent," then, in the premodern Chinese setting had reference almost exclusively to the capacity to govern, and the idea that an able man might not make a good official was a contradiction in terms.

Modern societies, of course, have a much more diversified conception of human talent, due in part to the vastly greater range of career goals to which educated people can aspire. When Whitehead talked of "trained intelligence" and James, of "superior men," we may be certain that they were not thinking just of the qualifications necessary for making good officials. For in modern societies it is axiomatic that the kinds of talent required for effective performance in one field may be entirely different from the kinds required in others. We do not expect a Nobel Prize-winning scientist and a leading government official to be able to exchange jobs and maintain their previous performance levels.

This suggests a second major difference between premodern Chinese and modern Western views of human talent. In imperial China talent was defined as mastery of the theoretical principles and moral dicta found in the Confucian Classics. It was felt that if one understood these principles and had studied their practical applications, as revealed in the dynastic histories, one would automatically be equipped to cope with any situations that might arise in one's official career. Thus, the commanders chiefly responsible for the suppression of the rebellions of the mid-nineteenth century were civil officials with no special military expertise. And it was precisely this kind of "omnicompetence" that had always been upheld as the ideal. Specialists there were, in fiscal, judicial, and other matters, but their specialized knowledge had to be acquired on the job, as there were no schools to teach it. Moreover, expertise, as such, never became an acknowledged pathway to social prestige and status. Confucius's dictum that "The superior man is not an implement" (*chün-tzu pu ch'i*) had lasting impact.

The contrast with modern society is striking. The complexity of economic life, the degree of societal differentiation, and the unprecedented expansion of knowledge that characterize the condition of modernity have made specialization one of its principal hallmarks. Indeed, things have reached such a state that the dangers of *over*specialization in a rapidly changing society have attracted increasing notice. "Nothing," cautions John W. Gardner, "contributes more damagingly to the unemployment of educated talent than rigid specialization and rigid attitudes supporting this specialization . . . If technological innovations reduce the demand for [an individual's] specialty, he has nowhere to go. On the other hand, if he is broadly trained in fundamental principles, and knows that he may have to apply these principles in varying contexts over the years, he is in a position to survive the ups and downs of the job market."[7]

The pendulum seems to have swung back to the old Chinese view that training in fundamental principles was the best kind of training a man could receive. Appearances, however, are deceptive. For one thing, Gardner's warning against specialization derives from the fear that overspecialized talent might lose its marketability—never the basis, certainly, for the Confucian complaint. For another thing—and here is a third basic distinction between Chinese and Western conceptions of human ability—the content of the "fundamental principles" differs markedly in the two cases. For Confucians, these principles were essentially ethical in character, with the consequence that the man of ability and the moral man were one and the same. "No one," as Wright put it, "could with impunity suggest that a morally superior man might be incompetent in office, or that a morally inferior one might be possessed of great ability."[8]

Modern societies, of course, have their moral codes too, and it is expected (at least in some quarters) that government officials will adhere to them. But few people would argue that there is any logical or necessary connection between morality and talent. In any event, the fundamental principles Gardner speaks of clearly have nothing to do with the former. What he appears to be saying, quite simply, is that the man best equipped to adjust to the mercurial and unpredictable changes of modern society is the man with general, as well as specialized, training—at least within his own field.

A final point of divergence between Chinese and Western views of talent focuses on the role to be played by human beings relative to such impersonal factors as technology, institutions, and law. Here, as elsewhere, the contrast is by no means a black-and-white one. But there are important differences of stress. On the Chinese side, certainly there were always some individuals who felt that laws and institutions were of great consequence. But there was a stronger tendency, the roots of which can be traced back to Confucius himself, to emphasize the human ingredient. The response of the Tung-lin reformers at the end of the Ming to the deterioration of government was to call for better men, not new institutions. And the same was true of the T'ung-chih Restoration leaders two and a half centuries later.

A similar pattern emerges in reference to technology. The notion that the Chinese were ever oblivious to technology is of course a modern Western myth. It is true, nonetheless, that in many contexts, especially the military, much less weight was assigned to technology than to men. A typical motto of the Restoration period stated that "The conduct of war rests with men, not with implements."[9] And among the more bellicose opponents of the West in the late Ch'ing it was not uncommon to hear statements like the following: "The superiority of China over foreign lands lies not in reliance on equipment but in the steadfastness of the minds of the people."[10]

Modern Westerners, while not underestimating the importance of able men, have generally insisted on the need for a proper institutional and legal setting if society is to function effectively. When society fails to function effectively in a given area, the critic *may* call for new men. But he is just as likely to diagnose the failure as systemic and to prescribe institutional modifications. The man-technology relationship in modern societies is equally complex. It is axiomatic that as technology becomes more and more sophisticated, increasingly high levels of human skill are required both to operate existing technologies and to invent still more sophisticated ones to replace them. Yet, as part of the very same process, manpower needs are reduced quantitatively, and in many spheres the tendency over time is to replace human beings with machines, resulting in a situation directly opposed to that prevailing in traditional China.

To sum up, the importance attached to men of ability in modern societies is at least as great as it was in imperial China. But there are fundamental differences in the kinds of ability valued and the societal roles talent is asked to play. In premodern China talent—or, as the Chinese called it, *jen-ts'ai*—was occupationally circumscribed, qualitatively homogeneous, and highly moral in constitution; moreover, in any given situation, it, rather than technology or institutions, tended to be viewed as the key factor. In modern societies, almost the reverse is true. The occupational outlets for talent are unlimited. Talent is heterogeneous in quality and amoral in make-up. And, although talent is felt to be necessary for the effective functioning of technology and institutions, it is seldom thought of as a sufficient substitute for such factors.

We are now in a position to evaluate the part played by talent in Wang T'ao's reform thought. How much importance did Wang attach to human talent in relation to impersonal factors? What goals did he think might be achieved by the application of talent? When Wang spoke of gifted men, what kinds of men did he have in mind? Men of high moral stature or men of "trained intelligence"? Men with specialized training or men of general ability?

Throughout his long career and in every conceivable context, Wang T'ao insisted that China's great need was for men. Sometimes he specified "gifted men" (*jen-ts'ai*); sometimes he just said "men." But it amounted to the same thing. "Men of ability are to a nation," he wrote Li Hung-chang in 1865, "what energy is to a human being." Deprive a nation of its gifted men and impotence will result.[11] In 1880, Wang wrote to a Vietnamese official that the only way for Vietnam to protect herself against France was by self-strengthening. At the same time, he warned, such a policy would remain mere verbiage unless the right men were found to implement it.[12] Hong Kong, Wang stated in another context, had within recent memory been an uninhabitable clump of rocks in the sea. Now, as a consequence of man's efforts, its prosperity was growing daily. Thus, whether a place was to prosper or not depended upon man alone; it was not dictated by physical conditions.[13] In a letter to the authorities (before 1883) Wang expressed the same thought more succinctly: It is well and good to esteem technology (ch'i), "but the use of technology depends on men. If you have the technology but not the men, it will be all empty show."[14] And, as late as the 1890's: "The business of empire depends entirely on obtaining men (te-jen). If the right men are found, good government will prevail. If the right men are not found, even with fine methods and the best of intentions, failure will generally ensue, on account of everything being in the hands of people who follow the old ways."[15]

It is clear from these statements, and many others like them, that Wang attached enormous importance to the human ingredient. There is no question, moreover, but that at times Wang got carried away with his own rhetoric and hinted that human beings alone—the right ones of course—could solve any and all difficulties. I am convinced, however, that this was only rhetoric. More and more, as time went on, Wang was faced with the problem of explaining why, despite China's extensive efforts to emulate Western methods and borrow Western technology, it seemed of no avail. His answer—and it was probably the correct one—was that the right men had not been found to use the new technology and to make the new methods work.[16] There was all the difference in the world between this and the conservative argument that the West's technology and methods were not needed by China at all.

Another respect in which Wang T'ao's concept of human talent diverged from previous Chinese attitudes was in the realm of purpose. Here, there was a decided shift in Wang's viewpoint over time. In his earlier writings, his calls for abler officials and generals were in direct response to the tide of rebellion that was then sweeping the country. Better officials were necessary if government was to be improved, and only by an improvement in government could domestic order and tranquillity be restored (see Chapter 2). After the destruction of the Taiping movement, Wang continued to lay stress on the importance of gifted men in government. But his view of the tasks of government underwent a perceptible change. As he grew more and more concerned with the Western challenge, his focus shifted to the problem of how China could hold her own in a world of hostile nation-states. And to the degree that the solution to this problem lay in the creation of a wealthy and powerful Chinese nation, Wang's whole conception of the societal value of human talent underwent a subtle transformation. Human talent now became the precondition for national power as well as good government: "What is the cause of the relative power of nations? Is it the extent of a nation's territory? The size of its armed forces? Is it the caliber of its weaponry? Or the quantity of its material wealth? In my opinion it is none of these. The basis of a nation's power is the relative abundance of its human talent."[17]

This statement, with its emphasis on national power and its unembarrassed relativism, could not have been made by a Confucian untouched by the modern world. And along with it came an equally posttraditional conception of the kinds of talent society should encourage and reward. In one sense Wang's views in this area did not change much over the years. From the very first, he had been adamant in the belief that talent should, above all, be useful, that the men who made good officials were men who had experience in dealing with practical problems.[18] What did change were the problems themselves. As the traditional challenges of rebellion and rehabilitation receded from view, they were replaced by a new set of challenges that could only be met by fundamental reform. For reform to become a reality, however, men who understood the requirements of change had to be found. "Why is it," Wang asked, "that though we have an arsenal for making weapons and a school for teaching foreign languages, though we send our youth to America to study Western learning and train our soldiers to do battle with modern firearms, we are as sluggish and feeble as ever? It is because we still haven't found men who understand the changes of the times and possess the resourcefulness to deal with them. [Not seeing this], however, people leap to the conclusion that Western methods aren't worth following at all, either because they are too wasteful or too much trouble or because they are useless to the rulers and injurious to the ruled. Alas! It isn't that Western methods are no good; the deficiency lies with those who have copied them. This is what is meant by not grasping the laws of change."[19]

Wang T'ao never explicitly rejected the ideal of omnicompetence. He was much too busy attacking the incompetence he saw all around him. Wang did, however, frequently give voice to the belief that knowledge must be practical—and practical knowledge, willy-nilly, meant specialized competence.[20] In a letter to the authorities, written in the 1880's, Wang spoke plainly on this point: "There are various categories of talent. There is the talent of the official, the talent of the general, the talent of the artisan, the talent of the diplomat. There are men who have a talent for subduing the enemy and resisting insult, for comprehending fundamental principles and applying them in practice, or for dealing with crises and saving difficult situations. Every man must be used in a manner appropriate to his talent; then only will his talent be made manifest."[21] Wang also espoused the natural corollary to this proposition, that when there were special tasks to be performed people should be given the training required to perform these tasks.

Recruitment of talent: the examinations. "If we accept the common usage of words, nothing can be more readily disproved than the old saw, 'You can't keep a good man down.' Most human societies have been beautifully organized to keep good men down."[22] It would not have taken much persuasion to get Wang T'ao's endorsement of this statement. Wang was convinced, doubtless with himself in mind, that there existed in China a superabundance of talent. But he was just as convinced that the prevailing system of recruitment was utterly incapable of identifying this talent, raising it up, and putting it to constructive use. The first order of business, then, was a complete overhaul of the examination system. And a new examination system inevitably meant a new system of schooling.

Criticism of the examination system, like concern with men of ability, was a phenomenon that bridged pre- and post-Western-impact China. But the thrust of the criticism changed greatly over time. Back in the 1840's, when Wang T'ao was still personally involved in the "examination life,"[23] his complaints were the same stale fare that had been served up by countless other traditional critics of the examinations. Exclusive reliance on the suffocating eight-legged essay style suppressed talent instead of elevating it. People could study the Classics for a lifetime and still not make the grade, as a result of which ministers of high integrity, who dared to speak their minds without fear, were seldom any longer heard at court.[24]

By the early 1860's Wang's criticisms, as well as his proposals for reform, acquired greater specificity. First, he argued, the standards of the existing system were too low, with the threefold consequence that too many scholars passed the examinations, the prestige of scholarly status was lowered, and the government's capacity to subsidize scholars had diminished. To deal with this problem, Wang recommended a reduction in the quotas for successful candidates and an extension of the time period between examinations. Second, Wang maintained that the subject matter of the examinations suffered from undue narrowness and impracticality. Too many men who might otherwise make superb officials, therefore, failed, while others with little or no administrative talent passed. This shortcoming, Wang felt, could be removed by enlarging the scope of the examinations to embrace, in addition to the usual subjects, administration, current affairs, geography, astronomy, natural science, mathematics, military and penal matters, and fiscal affairs. Also he urged that greater use be made of the Han system of recommendation, as a supplementary mode of recruitment.[25]

Excessive reliance on recommendation, on the other hand, was strongly opposed by Wang. In Kiangsu province in the mid-1860's the examination system had long been inoperative due to the

Taiping Rebellion and recommendation was the mode of recruitment in general use. The result was that only people who were well-known got tapped for official posts and many gifted individuals were overlooked. Wang, in a letter to the then governor of the province, Li Hung-chang, urged that eight categories of examinations be instituted, each testing a different kind of talent, and that the outstanding candidates in each category be recommended for positions appropriate to their special gifts. The categories suggested by Wang included judicial and fiscal administration, geography and the military arts, astronomy and science, machinery and manufacture, and the conditions and languages of the Western countries.[26]

In the 1870's and 1880's, as Wang T'ao became more convinced than ever of the need for Chinese scholars to learn about—and from—the West, his exasperation over the lack of visible motion in this direction deepened and his rhetoric became increasingly blunt:

Most Westerners who come to China study the Chinese language. Even if they don't learn the language they in all cases develop an intimate knowledge of Chinese conditions and a precise sense of our advantages and defects. Chinese, on the other hand, remain utterly ignorant of Western government, public opinion, geography, and customs. Most of them don't even know where [a country] is on the world map or how far it is [from China]. There is really no cause for surprise in this. What is incomprehensible is the fact that when you ask them about such important Chinese concerns as the Yellow River conservancy and the grain transport system or military and penal matters or financial and fiscal affairs, they beg off answering on the ground that they are too busy for such things. Why is this? It is because [mastering] the eight-legged essay style has so deprived them of time and energy that even the most learned scholars are able to do no more than browse through the works of the sages and the historical records of three thousand years. Thus I have said that China's scholars are acquainted with the past but do not know the present, while the scholars of the Western nations comprehend the present but do not know the past. Yet, *it is essential that scholars who want to be of use to society place comprehension of the present first.*[27]

In a society which had always revered the past and regarded knowledge of the past as the *sine qua non* for service in the present, these were strong words. Equally strong were Wang's final recommendations on reform of the examination system, presented in the 1880's in a *Shen-pao* editorial entitled "Chiu-shih ch'u-i" (My proposals for saving the times). Wang now envisaged an examination system that would place equal emphasis on Chinese learning (*Chung-hsüeh*) and Western learning (*Hsi-hsüeh*) and require of successful candidates that they demonstrate competence in both. On the Chinese side, the Five Classics and the Four Books would be combined to form the Six Classics, first importance being given to the *I-ching* (Classic of changes). On the Western side, the lead subject would be geometry, followed by chemistry, physics, astronomy, geography, military science, zoology, international law, and so forth. Realizing that not everyone would be able to master all of these subjects, Wang suggested that those who attained a thorough knowledge of two classics (the *I-ching* and one other) and two branches of Western learning (geometry and one other), and a general acquaintance with the main outlines of the remaining classics and divisions of Western learning, be entitled to official appointment. He suggested, further, that provision be made for selection by recommendation of people who had mastered one subject only, so that no one with any useful talent would be passed over.

In justification of his proposal, Wang revealed how far he had advanced beyond the still popular *t'i-yung* mode of thinking toward a new spirit of relativism:

The Six Classics embody the *tao*, and the way to make the *tao* prevail is to study the Classics thoroughly. The spirit of three thousand years of Chinese [culture] is entirely contained in the Six Classics. Western learning delineates what is not contained in the Six Classics; it is something which China's philosophers were not able to discuss. The superficial, applied aspects of Western learning pertain entirely to matters of ordinary everyday use, but the broader, more theoretical, aspects of Western learning have to do with the basic principles of life and of the human body and mind. By changing the examination system so as to incorporate

Western learning, we will master the strengths of both civilizations and combine the finest aspects of the entire world's [learning]. With our huge territorial expanse and our several hundred thousand gifted scholars, after fifty or sixty years, when we have become proficient in Western learning, all under Heaven will honor China. This is not, however, something that can be realized overnight. It must come about gradually.

The most impressive—and radical—part of Wang's proposal was his insistence that Western learning be made part of the *regular* examination curriculum: "If Western learning is made the subject of a separate examination," he cautioned,

the gentry will all misconstrue it as the clever techniques and novel tricks of foreigners, something at variance with the ideas found in the Six Classics of the sages, and they won't dare to try their hands at it. Those who do dare, moreover, will for the most part be drawn from the half-educated, irresponsible category. The evil may well arise, then, where these people use Western learning to denigrate the Six Classics, causing those who have studied the Six Classics in turn to make a laughing-stock of them. Will we be able, [in such circumstances], to look forward to a steady yield of truly gifted people from the empire?[28]

Wang demonstrates here his firm grasp of the problem of incentive,[29] the failure to take serious account of which bedeviled so much well-intentioned reform activity in the late Ch'ing. In a society in which the pathway to power and influence was as narrowly charted as it was in China, the establishment of alternative paths was bound to be ineffective as long as the alternatives remained optional. Good social engineering, in such a situation, necessitated an element of coercion.

Production of talent: the schools. Since the examination system, in the nineteenth as in previous centuries, dictated the curriculum of Chinese schools, it was to be expected that a person who found fault with the former would also be unhappy with the latter. Although Wang T'ao was familiar with the educational systems of France and England,[30] in his most sustained critique of Chinese education (written in the late 1880's or early 1890's), he took the school "system" of ancient China as his paradigm. In so doing, he fell back for the moment on a devolutionary view of history, which enabled him, quite conveniently, to press past tradition (idealized) into the service of present innovation.

China has numerous schools, Wang observed, yet her customs remain unwholesome. She has countless students, yet those with more than average ability seldom emerge. In such a situation what is the use of having schools? All they serve to do is provide a facade of prosperity, not the reality. Wang advanced five specific objections to the prevailing school arrangement, in each instance comparing it unfavorably with the ancient model. First, there was too much emphasis on book-learning, not enough on action, too much theory and not enough practice. Products of the schools were good at talking, in high-flown language, about human nature and life; they could lecture on benevolence and righteousness; they could do painstaking analyses of the most trivial minutia. But if you asked them something about taxation or finances, they not only evinced complete ignorance but, worse, were unashamed of the fact.

The second and third points of Wang's critique, closely related to the first, dwelt on the lack of relevance of the school system to the actual affairs of government. In antiquity government and education had emanated from the same source. There was no such thing as an "educational official," for all officials were educators. In the course of time, however, a distinction had grown up between scholars (*ju*) and officials (*li*), and as scholars who knew nothing about governing gained control over the schools, the content of education became increasingly divorced from the needs of administration. In such circumstances, even if everyone in the empire were sent to school, it would do little to upgrade the quality of Chinese government.

Wang's fourth criticism pointed to a similar process of splitting between civil (*wen*) and military (*wu*) governmental personnel. In the remote past prospective officials had been trained in both areas. But, now, military men had no understanding of ceremony and politeness, while scholars, for their part, declined to have anything to do with military matters. In time, as a direct consequence of this, a terrible deterioration had taken place in the morale of the Chinese military.

Finally, Wang attacked the schools for the broadness and superficiality of the education they provided. Long ago, scholars had specialized in one aspect of government or in one classic, with the result that they developed a profound knowledge of the thing they studied. At present, however, they were required to study all of the classics together and, if they became officials, to change posts every few years. The goal of the system, ostensibly, was omnicompetence, but the result, in Wang's view, was the worst sort of incompetence: "Today in charge of Rites, tomorrow in charge of Punishments—could even a Po I or a Kao Yao accomplish anything worthwhile? Today laboring on the *Shih-ching* [Classic of songs], tomorrow laboring on the *Shu-ching* [Classic of documents]—even a Fu Sheng or a Shen Kung could not thoroughly comprehend the meaning."* [31]

Believing that education should, above all, relate to the practical needs of government, and that one of the greatest of these needs in the last decades of the nineteenth century was mastery of Western learning, Wang naturally favored the inclusion of Western subject matter in school curricula. The regular course of study, he proposed in one of his reform editorials, should have two parts. One, headed literary studies (*wen-hsüeh*), should provide instruction in the Classics and Histories, political and institutional history, and literary style, while the other, headed technical studies (*i-hsüeh*), should embrace geography, natural science, astronomy and mathematics, and law. [32] Wang suggested at another point that schools be set up by the government at the district, prefectural, and provincial levels and that the traditional academies (*shu-yüan*), which no longer taught anything useful

*Po I was the minister in charge of Rites under Emperor Shun. Kao Yao, another famous minister under Shun, is said to have been the first to introduce laws for the repression of crime. Fu Sheng was a student of the *Shu-ching* who, according to tradition, was instrumental in saving this work from complete destruction at the time of the Ch'in book-burning (213 B.C.). Shen Kung, who lived at the same time, was a famous student of the *Shih-ching.*

anyway, be converted into educational institutions of the new style.[33]

Education for modernization. As has often been pointed out, a society may engage in the enterprise of educating people for the most diverse reasons.[34] Education may be undertaken for the purpose of making good citizens or loyal, well-indoctrinated subjects. It may be undertaken in order to train people in the range of skills necessary for modernization. In some societies education is prized as a means of enabling the individual to attain greater personal fulfillment. In others it is engaged in for the purpose of welding the members of the society into a more cohesive national group. And in still others education has as its main goal the provision of society with a reservoir of leadership—religious, political, social, as the case may be.

In China, especially in Ming and Ch'ing times, education was intimately tied to the government examinations and people went to school in the hope of passing the examinations and becoming officials. Since only a tiny fraction of those who received formal schooling ever actually got into the bureaucracy, however, from the standpoint of the individual, there had to be other motives for making the effort. And there were. Education, even if it did not lead to success in the examinations, generally was translatable into economic advantage and, at the local level, nearly always meant enhanced prestige for oneself and one's family—a consideration of some moment in a society which attached supreme importance to filial obligation. If it did result in passage of the examinations, on the other hand, it meant (in Ch'ing times) automatic entrance into the gentry class (again for one's family too). And gentry status, apart from (if not because of) the social privileges and legal immunities it conferred, enabled the individual to exercise considerable powers of leadership on the local scene.

The purpose of education, from the standpoint of the Chinese state, was somewhat different. The state, too, was principally interested in creating leaders, both formal (official) and informal (gentry). But its motives for doing so were to ensure social stability and the security of the dynasty. Thus the privileges and immunities accorded the gentry by the state were not in the nature of a gift. They constituted, by implication, one half of a contract, the other half of which consisted, broadly speaking, in the gentry's obligation to preserve order at the local level.

This is, no doubt, a greatly oversimplified picture of educational objectives in late imperial China. There were individuals, at all times, and emperors, on occasion, who valued education for sincere scholarly reasons, and education, from the point of view of neo-Confucian ethical philosophy, was the necessary prelude to individual self-perfection. On the whole, nevertheless, the picture stands up. Whatever an individual emperor's predilections, from the vantage point of the state, the overriding purpose of education was to provide the kind of political and social leadership that would best ensure dynastic longevity.

How did Wang T'ao's concept of education square with this picture? Was education, in his view, something for officials and gentry only, or was it for other classes as well? And what of the goals of education? Should education be engaged in essentially for maintenance purposes, as in the old society? Or should it be geared to change and aim at equipping people with new kinds of knowledge to deal with new kinds of problems?

The last set of questions we have really already answered. Wang T'ao was forever beseeching his countrymen to awaken to the revolutionary changes that had taken place in the world and to the inadequacy of existing institutions and practices for coping with these changes. Consistent with this point of view, Wang had the utmost scorn for the common run of officials who puttered along as if nothing had happened and responded to everything with the pat formulas of bygone ages. Change, he was convinced, had to be met by change. And nowhere was this more true than in education. Wang's vocabulary did not contain a word for "modernization." But it was clear, from the substance of his proposals for educational reform, that his objective was nothing less than a modernized China.

Education for modernization was a far cry from the educational goals of premodern China. What impact did this have on Wang T'ao's notion of *who* should be educated? At times, it would seem,

very little. Certainly, Wang believed that the process of modernization should be initiated and led by the state, and in much of his
thinking on educational reform, the implicit, if not explicit, goal is
a better trained, more modern officialdom.

At the same time, in line with his overall view that no talent
should remain untapped, there are numerous indications in Wang's
writings of support for a much broader distribution of educational
opportunity. As part of his general program for army and navy
modernization, for example, he advocated setting up military
academies (*wu-pei yüan*) to produce better commanders and
naval academies (*shui-shih yüan*) for the training of captains and
navigators, the content of the instruction in both cases to be
thoroughly modern in character.[35]

More innovative by far was Wang T'ao's suggestion (first made
in the mid-1880's) that state-supported technical schools for
commoners be erected in each of the treaty ports, mainly for the
purpose of stimulating manufacture. Instruction in these institutions would be exclusively in technical subjects, emphasizing
science and engineering. The schools would be fully equipped with
books, maps, charts, and instruments, as well as the latest
scientific and technical journals. Western experts would be hired as
instructors, to be replaced as soon as feasible by Chinese. Students
attending the schools would be provided with stipends, and
financial rewards would be granted to those who excelled. On
graduation, each student would be placed in a job which suited his
particular area of skill. If a student at one of these schools were
clever enough to invent something really useful to the state, Wang
added, he should be handsomely rewarded and his invention
placed under protective patent for a fixed period of years.[36]

On one point Wang T'ao was adamant. This was his conviction
that schools of this sort must be publicly financed. When it came
to his attention in the early 1890's that a *yang-wu* (foreign
matters) school had been inaugurated by the taotai of Chungking
for the benefit of that city's residents, Wang was full of praise for
this official's initiative. But he deplored the fact that the school
was supported entirely by the taotai's own funds. After all, he
asked, who was to guarantee that the next Chungking taotai would

be equally magnanimous and enlightened? Would it not be far better for the school to be funded from surplus customs revenues or some other public source?[37]

Although Wang T'ao never formally proposed that education at public expense be made available to the entire population, the ideal of an educated populace obviously appealed to him. When Yung Wing took the lead in organizing a "public school" (*i-hsüeh*) in his native village (near Canton) in the early 1870's, Wang greeted the enterprise with warm enthusiasm. Such schools, he commented, were the surest guarantee of an honest and law-abiding populace. Also, by bringing education to segments of society which the government schools ordinarily failed to reach, they ensured the fullest possible exploitation of the country's talent.[38]

Wang's belief that, somehow or other, learning must be made more generally available was again expressed in his reaction to the establishment in Hong Kong of the first public library for Chinese books. Although the institution of the free village school had been known in China from time immemorial, the concept of a public library was new. In Wang's opinion, it was a far better idea than the Chinese practice of forming private collections. For one thing, the expense of accumulating and maintaining a private library was borne by one person, making it hard to keep such libraries intact for more than a generation or two, whereas public libraries were collective undertakings and therefore much more permanent in character. For another thing, the books in private collections benefited a few people only. How could this be compared with public libraries, the benefits of which were reaped by all? In the great libraries of Europe, Wang testified from experience, the shelves were filled with books and the reading rooms were invariably jammed with people. This was one reason why learning flourished there.[39]

Wang T'ao also took his cue from the West in the vital matter of education for women. The Western nations, he observed (in the late 1880's), placed great stock in female education and erected special schools for the purpose. China should do the same. The education provided, moreover, should be substantive: "There is no use in educating women if they don't know how to read, and there is no use in their knowing how to read if they don't read the Six Classics." Wang took issue with the ancient lament that talent was hard to come by and female talent doubly hard to come by. "Set up schools for women and educate them," he dared his fellow countrymen, "and female talent will make its appearance."[40]

In these last words there is a larger message that might be missed. Running through all of Wang T'ao's thinking on educational reform—and, indeed, his reform thought in general—is the unstated assumption that, for meaningful change to take place, the institutional machinery of society must be overhauled. Now there was nothing revolutionary about institution-building per se. Chinese history was full of it. What was unsettling and threatening was the conscious connection drawn between new institutions and societal change. It was no accident that the great social engineers of post-Chou China—Li Ssu, Wang Mang, Wang An-shih—were uniformly excoriated as exponents of Legalism (which was still a dirty word in the nineteenth century). For extensive social engineering carried with it the implication that there were gross imperfections in the existing order. And this, more than ever at a time when the existing order was under challenge, was precisely what most Confucians were unwilling to acknowledge.

We began this section by emphasizing the importance Wang T'ao attached to men. As we conclude it, the accent has shifted demonstrably to institutions. The real change that took place, however, cannot be framed in such starkly dichotomous terms. Wang's growing commitment to institutional change (*pien-fa*) did not signify a shrinking commitment to the need for gifted men. Quite to the contrary, the whole purpose of institutional innovation, in the educational field, was to introduce greater rationality into Chinese manpower recruitment. What really changed was something else: it was the nature of the relationship *between* men and institutions. Where premodern Chinese tended to see this relationship in either/or terms, men and institutions being alternative emphases, Wang T'ao saw the two as being mutually dependent, each equally necessary to the other. This was a subtle shift, but it was a critical one that had to be made before a more modern approach to reform could be formulated.

THE PROMOTION OF WESTERN LEARNING

I have described Wang T'ao as an advocate-reformer, because of his lack of power to carry out his reform ideas. While in general this is an accurate characterization, there were several exceptions, one being Wang's journalistic activity (see Chapter 3), another his energetic promotion of Western learning (Hsi-hsüeh). Wang's activities in the latter area included the actual transmission (through his writings) of knowledge of the West and involvement in the affairs of the Shanghai Polytechnic Institute and Reading Room (Ko-chih shu-yüan).

The transmission of Western scientific learning. Since we have already examined Wang T'ao's principal works on Western history (Chapter 5), I shall confine myself here to his scientific writings. Wang was fascinated by modern science and understood certain of its branches sufficiently well to undertake the work of popularization. He wrote biographical profiles of figures like Francis Bacon, John Frederick William Herschel, and Mary Somerville,[41] and brief accounts of such curiosities of applied science as Western dentistry (which he judged to be far superior to Chinese), the properties of the diamond, the formation of snowflakes, and Western experiments with flying machines (which he called *t'ien-ch'uan* or "sky ships" and predicted would one day be used for military purposes).[42] Wang also published a number of popular scientific treatises.

Only one of these popularizations, *Hsi-hsüeh t'u-shuo* (An illustrated exposition of Western learning), was entirely the product of his own hand. The others were collaborative efforts, in which Wang's function was to transpose the oral accounts of his Western associates into acceptable Chinese. Works of this category included "Ko-chih hsin-hsüeh t'i-kang" (An introduction to the new theories of natural science), written in collaboration with Joseph Edkins in the 1850's; "Kuang-hsüeh t'u-shuo" (An illustrated exposition of optics), also in collaboration with Edkins;

Chung-hsüeh ch'ien-shuo (A popular exposition of mechanics), with Alexander Wylie (1850's); and *Hsi-kuo t'ien-hsüeh yüan-liu* (The origins and development of Western astronomy), with Wylie (1850's). The Edkins popularizations were never published,[43] but those done with Wylie and Wang's own *Hsi-hsüeh t'u-shuo* appeared in print in 1889-1890.

In *Hsi-hsüeh t'u-shuo*, Wang discussed such subjects as the sun, the equator, the planets and their revolution around the sun, dense star clusters, the precession of the equinoxes, air, acoustics, and the movement of light. His accounts were accompanied by illustrations and were, in the main, simple, lucid, and accurate. An excerpt from the section on planetary motion, setting forth the heliocentric theory of Copernicus, may be taken as representative:

The sun is the heart of the planets. What is meant by "the heart of the planets"? The sun is situated in the center and does not move. Around it revolves first Mercury, then Venus, then Earth, then Mars, . . . then Jupiter, then . . . Thus it is said that the sun is the heart of the planets.

Does the earth too revolve around the sun? Indeed it does. How is it, then, that the sun . . . each day comes up in the east and goes down in the west? This is because of the earth's own movement. The earth orbits the sun; it also rotates on its own axis. The orbital movement is what produces winter and summer [that is, seasonal change]; the rotational movement is what produces day and night . . .

Do all of the planets rotate on their axes? Yes. Westerners, by telescopic observation of the planets, have discerned height variations [on the planetary surfaces] and this has enabled them to observe the rotational movement.[44]

Easily as important as the actual transmission of Western science was the spirit with which Wang T'ao went about it. In a long commentary appended to Wylie's *Hsi-kuo t'ien-hsüeh yüan-liu*, Wang took dead aim at the reigning shibboleths concerning Western learning and exploded them one by one. He begins by describing how Wylie's book came to be written:

When I was young I was fond of the writings of astronomers. I had my doubts, however, concerning the trustworthiness of astrological divination and portent theory, feeling that they were nothing but magic and superstition. On reaching the age of twenty, I traveled to Shanghai and got to know the Western scholar, Alexander Wylie. Whenever I had time left over from my editorial work, I would ply him with questions about Western matters. It was then, for the first time, that my knowledge of astronomy was filled out.

Around this time Li Shan-lan came and we pursued our studies together. One day I inquired about the number of Western astronomers there had been since ancient times. Wylie took out a book and showed it to me. As he recited its contents and drew explanatory diagrams with his fingers, I set down what he said with my brush. We finished in ten days. *Hsi-kuo t'ien-hsüeh yüan-liu* was, thus, produced . . . with great speed.

At the time a copy of Juan Yüan's *Ch'ou-jen chuan* [Biographies of astronomers and mathematicians] happened to be lying on the table.[45] Picking it up and examining it, I found that only seven of the persons [dealt with in Wylie's account] were included in the table of contents . . . Mr. Juan's [book] . . . is superficial and sketchy . . . He shows himself ignorant . . . of the fact that Western astronomy really originated in Greece and that around the beginning of the Spring and Autumn period there appeared [in that land] an outstanding man named Thales who not only knew that the earth was spherical . . . but also predicted a solar eclipse . . .

Such was the degree of precision which they [that is, the Westerners] attained three thousand years ago in their astronomical calculations. Those who subsequently carried on from these beginnings mastered the teachings that had been handed down and improved upon them. With the passage of time, their methods became increasingly refined and their calculations were modified until complete accuracy was reached. This is why the astronomers of today far excel those of antiquity . . .

Some persons, while granting the precision of the Westerners' astronomical learning, ask: How do we know that it did not originate in China and later spread to them? In China when Emperor Shun divided up governmental functions, orders were issued to Hsi and Ho [officials in charge of the calendar] and respectfully obeyed. In that period we were already able to calculate the revolutions of the sun and moon and to intercalate, while the Western countries were still without any calendar at all. Further evidence [of the Chinese origin of Western astronomy] is the fact that algebra is [commonly identified by the Westerners themselves] as "the method from the East" (*Tung-lai fa*).

Alas, [Wang rejoined], how does this differ from stealing another man's praise and appropriating it as one's own? Although it is true that Western astronomy began only in late Chou times, the advances it has gone through, generation after generation down to the present day, are readily ascertainable. Its superiority over that of China is due to the close attention that the Westerners have paid it and to the precision of their measuring instruments. As for their designation [of algebra] as "the method from the East," this merely points to the land of Arabia east of Europe. It does not refer to China.

Other persons say: The Westerners' astronomy is indeed beyond reproach, and their machines and tools, which through the use of water- and fire-power accomplish twice as much with half the effort, are truly excellent. Yet [in terms of the distinction between] the physical realm, which is called *ch'i*, and the metaphysical realm, which is called *tao*, the mastery of the Westerners is confined entirely to the former. Their religious writings are absurd and irrelevant and openly take issue with Confucianism. Their notions of heaven and hell are lifted from Buddhism and their doctrine of loving others as oneself is a plagiarization of the similar [tenet found] in Mo-tzu. In the realm of the ordinary they don't approach the simplicity of the Confucians, while in the realm of the abstruse they cannot compare with the mysteries of the Buddhists. Indeed, there is not a single thing [in their religion] that one can accept.

[Such critics, Wang rejoined], disregard the fact that Western scholars have been unremitting in their investigation of the laws of human nature (*hsing-li*). The rulers and peoples created by the Lord on High (Shang-ti) have appeared everywhere. The customs of each may diverge and there may be differences among the institutions of the various countries. But in terms of the laws that govern people's minds, all are the same. As has been said, "The East has its sages, and in mind and principle they are one; the West has its sages, and in mind and principle they are one." Although differences exist between East and West, their paths and spirits are truly the same. Wherefore the *Chung-yung* long ago depicted the sagely man in these clear terms: "Wherever ships and carriages reach, wherever the labor of man penetrates, wherever the heavens overshadow and the earth sustains, wherever the sun and moon shine, and wherever frosts and dew fall, all who have blood and breath honor and love him."[46] Alas! What a small thing astronomy is when ranged against perfection of this order.[47]

Without abandoning his vision of a Confucian-patented future—indeed the consummate sage eulogized in the *Chung-yung* was thought by many Chinese scholars to be none other than Confucius—Wang T'ao, in this commentary, clearly established his cosmopolitan credentials. By the time the commentary was written (1889), numbers of educated Chinese had long since accepted the usefulness of modern science. But, as the value and importance attached to science increased, there was a proportional growth in the need to de-Westernize it. For, as long as science was merely useful, it had not much mattered whether it was Western or Chinese, but once it began to be viewed as fundamental, the question of its origins became a problem.

To cope with this problem, many Westernizers of the late nineteenth century (including Feng Kuei-fen, Hsüeh Fu-ch'eng, Ch'en Chih, Liang Ch'i-ch'ao, and K'ang Yu-wei) took refuge in the ingenious theory that Western learning had originated in ancient China, from which it followed that it was not really "Western" at all. This exercise in intellectual gymnastics had the political virtue of disarming the opposition. It had the psychological merit of enabling Chinese to assimilate "Western" learning without any attendant feelings of cultural inferiority or national shame. Finally, by encouraging a revival of antiquity, it harmonized with one of the most deepseated of Chinese cultural predilections.

The two pieces of evidence most frequently adduced in support of the "Chinese origin" theory were, according to Ch'üan Han-sheng, the great antiquity of algebra in China (reflected, it was argued, in its designation by Westerners as "the method from the East") and certain sections of the *Mo-tzu* (fifth to fourth centuries B.C.), in which matters pertaining to science and technology came under discussion.[48]

Wang T'ao's assault on the Chinese origin theory was devastating in its completeness. Wang laid bare the shallowness and inadequacy of Juan Yüan's work. He rejected out-of-hand the thesis that Western algebra originally came from China; and, by linking Thales (who flourished two centuries prior to Mo-tzu) with the founding of Western astronomy, he demolished the *Mo-tzu* argument too—at least by implication. Most important, and logically consistent with his belief that not all of learning was Chinese in origin, Wang refused to accept the parochial proposition that China's culture was the only culture, historically, to have seriously concerned itself with *tao*. The whole point of the *Chung-yung* passage was that *tao* belonged to humanity. Sageness was a universal quality which *all* peoples, Western as well as Eastern, had the capacity to generate and cherish. In fact, it was precisely this capacity, natural to men everywhere, that gave to the human enterprise its underlying unity.

The Shanghai Polytechnic Institute and Reading Room. After more than two decades of exile in Hong Kong, Wang T'ao in the spring of 1884 again took up permanent residence in Shanghai. Although fifty-five years of age and as prone as ever to hypochondria, Wang appears to have been in reasonably good health, and he continued to carry on a full schedule of activity. He took occasional pleasure trips to Soochow and Hangchow and in the winter of 1888-1889 visited North China for the first time at the invitation of Shantung governor Chang Yüeh. (According to one writer, Wang's trip north was partly a ruse to get away from his nagging wife. Wang's special fondness for wine and women had continued, even as he got on in years, and his wife, to keep him from visiting the brothels, regularly dispatched an old servant to accompany him on his evening outings. As soon as it got past 10 o'clock, the servant would dutifully whisper the time in Wang's ear and urge his master to return home.)[49] After returning from Shantung, Wang founded his own publishing house, the T'ao-yüan shu-chü, reviving a project which in 1886 he had been forced to abandon for lack of funds.[50] Throughout the 1880's he contributed frequently to *Shen-pao*, which remained under the editorial direction of Ch'ien Cheng. In Shanghai he also resumed his associations with foreigners, notably Alexander Wylie and John Fryer.

Fryer, a prolific translator and energetic promoter of Western scientific and technical knowledge among the Chinese, invited Wang in 1886 to serve as curator of the Shanghai Polytechnic Institute and Reading Room (sometimes known as the Chinese Polytechnic Institution and Reading Room). Wang's experience and talents were perfectly suited to the position and, as it meant extra income, he accepted. The Polytechnic Institute, described by Biggerstaff as an "interesting, though not too successful, effort of well-disposed foreigners and progressive Chinese to bring Western scientific and technological knowledge to China,"[51] had begun operation in 1876 under joint Sino-Western control. Initially, its activities were confined to making available reading matter on scientific and technological subjects and to exhibiting models and specimens of Western manufactured items. Financial difficulties and poor attendance at the reading room led in 1885 to a reorganization of the Institute's governing committee and an extension of its activities. Before the year was out, elementary instruction in English, mathematics, geography, and other basic subjects was commenced, and in 1886 a "Chinese Prize Essay Scheme" was inaugurated for the purpose of inducing "the Chinese *literati* to investigate the various departments of Western knowledge with the view to their application in the Middle Kingdom."[52] Eventually a public lecture series was also instituted.

By all accounts, the most successful venture of the Polytechnic Institute was the prize essay competition. The idea for the competition came from Fryer, who served as the organization's secretary until his departure from China in 1896. The man who made the competition work, however, was Wang T'ao. Each quarter a prominent Chinese official was invited to devise a suitable question, to agree to criticize and rank the submitted essays, and to contribute at least part of the prize money. Three major and ten minor prizes were then awarded and the names of the winners announced in the Chinese press. The newspapers also provided space for the winning essays and at the end of each year, from 1886 to 1893, the essays of the twelve principal prize winners for that year, along with the judging officials' comments, were reprinted in book form and placed on sale.

During the first four years, the number of essayists in each contest ranged between twenty-six and eighty-one, most of them literati from Kiangsu and adjoining provinces. Examples of the topics which Li Hung-chang, Cheng Kuan-ying, and other officials asked them to write on follow: "What ought China at the present time to regard as of foremost importance in her endeavor to improve wealth and power?" "Compare early Chinese writings on science with Aristotle, Bacon, Darwin, and Spencer." "How can Chinese tea compete with Indian tea in the world market against unfair marketing practices?" "Since the hundred and ten years that have gone by, most of the countries in Europe have instituted for themselves each an Upper and a Lower House of Parliament . . . These institutions resemble very nearly the ideal of our ancient Sage-Emperors . . . nowadays, there is a complaint that 'those in power hold aloof, far away, from the common people; hence the latter find it impossible to bring their wants to their Sovereign's personal notice.' In view of this state of affairs it has often been mooted that China should inaugurate a Parliament, for the purpose of bringing the people into closer relationship with the Throne . . ."[53]

The editorial page of the *North-China Herald* judged some of the winning essays to be "of a very high order" and praised the undertaking in general as "a most powerful lever in the hands of the Polytechnic Institution for the enlightenment of China."[54] A large measure of the responsibility for this success must be granted to Wang T'ao. Without Wang's wide-ranging bureaucratic connections, it is doubtful whether the active interest of high officials could have been aroused. In addition to handling all of the correspondence with these officials, Wang took part in the evaluation of the essays, edited them for publication, wrote prefaces for each of the annual volumes, and saw these through publication.[55] For his services, Wang received "the warmest thanks" of the Institute's managing committee and (in 1897) a terse but telling epitaph from the pen of Fryer: "The prize-essay scheme has not been carried on with the same energy as formerly through the illness and death of Mr. Wang T'ao."[56]

Wang's contribution to the Polytechnic Institute was not restricted to running the prize essay competition. He helped to attract students to the Institute's classes, solicited funds from interested officials (such as Sheng Hsüan-huai), recruited instructors, and served on the committee of overseers. Wang's ultimate goal in all of this was educational and patriotic. He hoped, through the Polytechnic Institute's activities, to help generate a store of scientific and technical talent that would be of future use to the country.[57]

How useful was the Institute in fact? Relative to the prevailing level of production of technical talent in China, it must, one supposes, be counted as a qualified success. The Tsungli Yamen, in its famous memorial of May 18, 1887, urging modification of the government examinations to enable candidates to be tested in mathematics, observed that the Shanghai Polytechnic Institute was training a full 50 per cent of the country's mathematical talent.[58] What the Yamen failed to note, however, was the small number of students enrolled in the Institute's classes and the elementary level of the instruction offered. Certainly, relative to China's needs, it is hard to escape the conclusion that the Institute's contribution was negligible. More important by far was the role it played in encouraging Chinese appreciation of the validity and importance of modern science. Yet even here, it would appear, the Institute's impact was local and ephemeral. Most of the people reached were situated in the region around Shanghai, and after the mid-1890's other and more effective agencies for the stimulation of Chinese scientific interest came into being.

As Wang T'ao himself seemed to imply, in the examination reform proposals discussed earlier in this chapter, the problem of the acceptance of modern scientific and mathematical learning was as much social as intellectual. As long as such learning remained outside of the regular educational curriculum, peripheral to the dominant intellectual concerns of China's scholars and socially useless, a dozen Polytechnic Institutes would not significantly alter the balance. Once science and mathematics became standard fare, on the other hand, a single Polytechnic Institute was bound to be superfluous. Small-scale, privately-sponsored ventures of this sort were thus destined, one way or another, to encounter frustration in the society of late nineteenth-century China. Their best and only hope was to play some part, however insubstantial, in preparing the way for their own supersession.

7

ECONOMIC REFORM

In light of the fact that the Chinese economy prior to the twentieth century was overwhelmingly agrarian (or agriculture-related),[1] it may seem strange that Wang T'ao's economic thinking should be almost totally preoccupied with nonagricultural matters: transportation, mining, manufacture, and, above all, commerce. Historians in China today explain this by identifying Wang (along with other early reformers) as a progressive intellectual of the landlord class whose historic function was to enunciate the economic demands of the rising Chinese bourgeoisie.[2] The trouble with this explanation, in my view, is that it does not explain anything. Leaving aside the question of what Wang's class affiliations in fact were, the bone which unfailingly catches in the throat of the non-Marxist historian is the assumption that people's ideas and actions are invariably the reflection of class interests. *Reductio ad absurdum*: human beings are transformed into marionettes and history becomes a grand puppet show.

To reject the *exclusive* dominion of class interests over human motivation is not, of course, to deny the influence of such interests altogether. The problem is to delineate, with greater precision, the causal connection between the two. The argument can be made, for example, that the newspapers with which Wang

T'ao was associated in Hong Kong and Shanghai were all capitalistic enterprises (concerned with profit-making), that the readerships of these newspapers were composed largely of people involved in commerce, and that consequently it was good business not only to devote considerable space to commercial news but to have an editorial policy that promoted the interests of the commercial sector. This argument makes perfectly good sense. But all it tells us, in the end, is that it was probably in Wang T'ao's interest to advance the cause of commerce and of economic modernization. It does *not* tell us that he did this *because* it was in his interest.

It is pertinent, in this connection, to point out that Hsüeh Fu-ch'eng, Ma Chien-chung, and a host of other reformers who had only indirect affiliations with the world of commerce advanced proposals for economic modernization that were very similar to the proposals made by such people as Wang T'ao and Cheng Kuan-ying who were directly engaged in commerce-related activities. This would seem to suggest that factors other than immediate class interest carried some weight. In Wang T'ao's case it is not hard to identify these factors. First, Wang was committed to change in general, which in this context meant development of the nonagricultural sectors of the economy. Second, although the Chinese economy as a whole was agrarian, that part of it with which Wang in his adult years was most familiar was not. Hong Kong and Shanghai, after the middle of the nineteenth century, grew into bustling modern metropolises having little in common with the economic life of the Chinese hinterland, and it was natural for Wang to take this modern sector as his point of departure.

Third, and most germane, the overriding goal of Wang T'ao's reform thought, from the 1860's on, was to increase the wealth and power of China. Under the circumstances, nothing could have been more reasonable than to emphasize the benefits of manufacture and overseas commerce, for it was precisely in these areas—not agriculture—that the economies of the world's strongest nations (England, France) differed most visibly from China's. Wang recognized that the development of commerce and manufacture would benefit Chinese businessmen as well—and he viewed this as an added argument in its favor. But the primary argument turned on what such development would do for China.

The preoccupation with wealth (*fu*) and power (*ch'iang*), enshrined in the slogan "enrich the state and strengthen its military power" (*fu-kuo ch'iang-ping*), was a Legalist contribution to Chinese political thought and represented a distinct alternative to the customary Confucian emphasis on frugal government and popular welfare. There was, however, a less orthodox strain of Confucian political economy, which maintained that the goals of wealth and power were quite compatible with ultimate Confucian values.[3] This line of reasoning began to be used with growing frequency in the 1870's and 1880's, as Confucian civilization came under intensive attack from the West and increasing numbers of Chinese became convinced that the Chinese state would have to be greatly strengthened if the values they cherished were to be rescued from history's graveyard.

Wang T'ao's progress toward a wholehearted commitment to the goals of wealth and power was gradual. As early as 1859, in the very process of attacking the view that China's wealth and power could be augmented by expansion of foreign commerce and adoption of Western technology, Wang seemed to imply that wealth and power as such were desirable goals.[4] The commitment soon became more explicit. In 1865 he wrote Li Hung-chang that the problem of getting the foreigners in hand was a two-sided one, involving the establishment of Chinese economic control (*wo li-ch'üan*) and the promotion of China's national dignity (*shu kuo-wei*). The latter object, he pointed out, hinged on the achievement of the former; economic power was the sure road to state power.[5] To his critics, at this stage, who charged that with a policy of wealth and power "the influence of Kuan Chung and Shang Yang would blaze forth while the Way of Confucius and Mencius would languish," Wang answered bluntly that China's military power had to be built up before the time-honored virtues of Confucianism could once again flourish.[6]

Wang T'ao's thinking on wealth and power was not systematic. But there are certain themes that crop up again and again. One such, already adumbrated in his letter to Li, was the assumption that a powerful China depended on the prior establishment of a wealthy China.[7] Increasingly, as time went on, Wang addressed himself to the problems embraced by what today would be called "economic modernization." He was especially fascinated by the case of England which, though only a small island nation, was wealthier and stronger than any other country.[8] Although on occasion he maintained that England's wealth and power derived principally from her coal and iron reserves,[9] more often he expressed the view that English commerce was the decisive ingredient.[10] In any case, the important thing is that Wang T'ao perceived the many-sided character of Western economic strength. He saw that mining, manufacture, trade, monetary policy, banking, communications, and transportation were components of a single interdependent process, and that if China was to realize her vast economic potential she would have to attend to all of them.[11]

The fact that Wang T'ao's proposals for economic reform were advanced with the interests of the state uppermost in mind inevitably led to a strong emphasis on the power implications of economic change. It must not be thought, however, that Wang was therefore indifferent to the benefits of such change to the private sector. Wang was no longer straitjacketed by the static economic thinking of the past, which held that an increase in state wealth automatically entailed a decrease in the wealth of the people. He understood that in a growing economy *both* the state *and* the people could be enriched simultaneously.

TRANSPORTATION AND COMMUNICATIONS

Nowhere is this dual concern seen more clearly than in Wang's proposals for the modernization of China's transportation and communications facilities. It is hard for people nowadays to appreciate the range of emotions that greeted the advent of the steamship, the railroad, and the telegraph in the last century. For modern Westerners, hell-bent on conquering the world and the future, the novelty of these discoveries, their speed, and their enormous power potential were cause for exhilaration.[12] But for most Chinese, the same discoveries heralded not an expanding world but a contracting one, a future more to be feared than welcomed. It was a mark of Wang T'ao's modernity that, like his Western contemporaries, he responded affirmatively to the recent revolution in communications, seeing in it (from an early date) the technological basis for global unification.[13]

The transition from premodern to modern was least abrupt in the case of the steamship (a familiar means of conveyance outfitted with a new source of power) and perhaps this is one reason (though others readily come to mind) for the relatively low level of Chinese resistance to its introduction. Tseng Kuo-fan had urged the construction of steamships as early as 1861. And Wang T'ao, even in his most militantly anti-Western phase, favored Chinese adoption of the steamship for coastal policing and defense. In opposing its use in the interior, moreover, Wang based his argument not on fear or blind hostility but on the ostensibly practical consideration that China's inland harbors were not wide enough to accommodate steam-powered vessels.[14] This was in 1859. Before long, Wang's position on the utility of steamships broadened considerably. He continued to lay stress on their military value, arguing that China's traditional warships should be entirely replaced by steam-driven vessels and that there should be a special section of the military examinations devoted to steamship operation.[15]

Other themes, however, gained in prominence. One, with protonationalistic overtones, was the theme of self-reliance. From a very early point, Wang urged that China manufacture her own steamships and not depend on purchasing them from abroad. Part of the reason for this was purely economic. But Wang also noted that Western shipbuilding technology was constantly advancing, the prized products of today being abandoned tomorrow. Clearly, in these circumstances, there was the danger that the ships China bought from the West would be obsolete models; only by building her modern vessels herself could she be sure of staying abreast of the very latest developments in technology.[16] A parallel concern was expressed in Wang's criticism of the practice of relying on Westerners to build and operate China's steamships. Not only was this more expensive (Western salaries being much higher than Chinese), but it was also risky. In the event of war between China and the foreign powers, the Western pilots and engineers might decide to clear out, leaving China in the lurch. It was essential, therefore, for China to develop her own talent as quickly as possible, even if it meant sending technicians abroad for their training.[17]

Wang T'ao's incipient nationalism was also apparent in his opposition to the operation of foreign steamers in the Chinese interior. Steam traffic on the Yangtze River had begun in the 1860's and for the first decade was dominated by the American-founded Shanghai Steam Navigation Company. Even after the establishment in 1872 of the Chinese government-sponsored China Merchants Steam Navigation Company, foreign steamers retained a sizable share of the Yangtze trade, and this share grew instead of diminishing over time. Against this background, Wang T'ao, in the late 1870's, wrote Tong King-sing (T'ang T'ing-shu), the manager of the China Merchants outfit, urging the expansion of Chinese steamer activity in the interior. Wang reminded Tong that the operation of foreign steamships in Chinese rivers was a gross infringement of Chinese prerogative—something the Westerners would never tolerate in their own countries. He called for the training of far greater numbers of native pilots, so that China eventually could establish complete control over steam traffic in the interior.[18]

Wang saw, in the annual shipment of tribute grain from Kiangsu and Chekiang to Peking, another opportunity for the development of Chinese steam transport. For many centuries tribute grain had been conveyed north principally via the Grand Canal. During the turmoil of the mid-nineteenth century, however, the canal system had become inoperative, and for some years the grain had been sent by the coastal route in sandjunks. With the restoration of order in the eastern provinces in the late 1860's, many Chinese officials (including Tseng Kuo-fan) called for the re-establishment of the canal transport system. Powerful vested interests were involved and, although the argument was framed in terms of the multiple dangers of sea transport, the fact is a lot of people stood to lose a lot of money if the canal system fell into permanent disuse.

Wang viewed this argument as, at best, shortsighted, at worst, utter nonsense. Under the old system, he observed, the costs of maintaining the Grand Canal and keeping the grain junks in good repair constituted a net loss. In contrast, the proposed alternative of sending the grain by sea in steamers, although requiring a heavy initial outlay, would eventually pay for itself and even generate new wealth. Furthermore, it would have military and commercial side benefits which were absent in the traditional system. Wang suggested that the problem of protecting the grain cargoes could be handled by assigning a fixed number of troops to each carrier. When the grain shipments were completed, some of the steamers could then serve as a coast patrol, strengthening China's maritime defenses and also providing much-needed training for her modern navy. The ships that were not sent out on patrol could be leased to private companies for commercial shipments, all freight revenues being funneled to a central office for strict accounting. Income left after operating expenses had been met could be used for the maintenance of the fleet and the construction of additional ships. The state would thus be enriched, but at no cost to the people.[19]

A final refrain in Wang's discussions of steam transport was his belief that private Chinese individuals (*min-chien*) should be licensed to establish steamship firms for operation in the interior.[20] Steam transport was not only safe and speedy, but also highly profitable. And it distressed Wang that the profits should be monopolized, on the one hand, by private foreign firms, and on the other, by the Chinese government-backed China Merchants concern. Wang does not make it clear whether his primary motive in this was to promote private Chinese as against official Chinese interests or Chinese interests in general as against foreign interests. Certainly, the two themes were not, in any case, incompatible, and both seem to have bulked large in his mind.

In contrast with the steamship, the railroad encountered great opposition in nineteenth-century China. As late as 1880 there was not a mile of track in the entire country and fifteen years hence the total trackage was still under three hundred miles. The reasons for this resistance were many. Railroads were expensive to construct and maintain. The fear was widespread (as it had been in the West) that trains would throw people out of work. The usual problems pertaining to land use and right of way (not encountered, by the way, in the case of steam navigation routes) were greatly exacerbated in China by the high population density. There were many Chinese, also, who feared that the erection of a network of railroads would make the empire more vulnerable to foreign military penetration. The level of native resistance, for these and other reasons, was so high that when the British in 1876 completed an unauthorized pilot railway between Shanghai and Wusung, the Chinese government promptly purchased the line and had it destroyed.[21]

Wang T'ao's advocacy of railroad construction can be dated to his sojourn in Europe, if not earlier. Wang was dazzled by his maiden experiences with rail travel and predicted in a letter home that before a century was out the whole of China would be crisscrossed by railroads.[22] After returning to Hong Kong, Wang wrote repeatedly of the military and economic advantages of the railroad. The former had been demonstrated during the Franco-Prussian War, when the Germans used trains to transport troops, supplies, weapons, ammunition, and mail.[23] The commercial benefits were equally great, though less from passenger service than from the shipment of goods.[24] So important had the railroad become, Wang noted, that Europeans had taken to measuring a country's wealth and power by the extent of its railroad system.[25]

Wang knew that the Americans and Europeans were anxious to get Chinese permission to construct railway lines and he warned that if China did not take the initiative herself, she would be outrivaled by foreign companies in much the same way as had already happened in the steamship field.[26] Another expression of Wang's protonationalism was the emphasis he placed on the integrative function of railroads. Railroads had the potential not only for facilitating interregional trade, but also for transforming the vast expanse of China into a single military entity, such that if trouble were suddenly to break out in one part of the empire troops could be transferred there from other parts within a matter of days.[27]

The integrative value of the telegraph was even more manifest. With the Japanese lying in wait to the southeast and the Russians threatening from the northwest, it was urgent, Wang felt, that the different parts of China develop the capacity to communicate with each other instantaneously. Then, when there was an emergency in one locality, the entire province could be aroused to action, and when trouble broke out in one province, the whole empire could respond with alarm. To convey the notion of a single organism, all of whose parts were interconnected and immediately responsive to each other's needs, Wang used the metaphor, famous in Chinese military literature, of the snake of Ch'ang-shan. As a specific example of what he had in mind, he pointed to the problem of China's coastal defense. China had a very long coastline to protect with a limited number of modern warships. Without the telegraph, much of this coastline would, at any given moment, be vulnerable to enemy attack. But with the telegraph, the degree of vulnerability would be substantially narrowed.[28]

Although Wang T'ao favored the creation of a telegraph system in China principally for its military value, he was well aware of the nonmilitary benefits of high-speed communication. While in London in the late 1860's he had visited the central telegraph office and seen with his own eyes the abundant use made of it by ordinary citizens. He also praised the telegraph for its facilitation of international and transoceanic communication, especially between home governments and their diplomatic representatives abroad. When Wang got wind of the United States's plan to lay a telegraph cable across the Pacific, connecting California and Shanghai, he applauded the Americans for their initiative and foresight and lamented the fact that, in this field as in so many others, China lagged way behind the West.[29]

MINING

As Wang T'ao saw it, the problem of making China wealthy had two dimensions. It entailed, on the one hand, preventing the seepage of Chinese "profit" (*li*) abroad, and on the other hand, the exploitation of China's natural riches. Naturally, the two were not always separable. When Chinese arsenals were forced to rely on imported iron, as was partly the case, there was expenditure of capital abroad which, presumably, an increase in home production would obviate.[30]

Mining had, of course, existed in China since very ancient times, and during the T'ung-chih Restoration, according to Mary Wright, there was less resistance to it than to any other form of economic development.[31] This statement, however, has only relative validity. For, both during and after the restoration period, modern mining on a large scale was widely resisted by Chinese peasants, gentry, and officials. The key words were "modern" and "large scale." Mining by machine, it was feared, would throw people out of work, while extensive exploitation of the earth's riches, apart from upsetting the balance of cosmic forces known in Chinese as *feng-shui*, would divert people from their primary occupation, agriculture.

In dealing with arguments such as these, Wang T'ao displayed one of the most characteristic shortcomings of reformers: the inability to comprehend and really take seriously social inertia. Wang was endlessly facile in exposing the unreasonableness of those who opposed change, but he seemed to assume that if only their opposition could be intellectually dissolved, the rest would follow in due course. An elitist at heart, he pitched his argument to the rational facade of the conservative defense and never developed a strategy for coping with its irrational underpinnings.

Thus, Wang was on solid ground in insisting that the development of modern mining, far from generating unemployment, would actually create a net increase in employment opportunities.[32] But how did one go about selling this to working people who had no conception of economic growth? He was probably equally correct in surmising that the disruptive effects of mining operations during the Ming dynasty had been occasioned not by mining as such, but by its mismanagement.[33] But could one guarantee that the new mining enterprises would be free of dishonest and incompetent management? And what about *feng-*

shui? It was well and good for Wang to dismiss *feng-shui* as rank superstition.[34] But for the ordinary Chinese peasant, uneasy over the possibility that tampering with the earth's surface contours might create cosmic disharmonies and invite misfortune, the belief in *feng-shui* happened to be one of the deepest sources of opposition to mining (and, incidentally, to the construction of railway lines as well).[35]

So much for Wang's treatment of the opposition. What about the case in favor of mining development? In an age of steam transport, railways, and machine industry, Wang maintained, coal and iron were the chief foundations of wealth and power, surpassing gold and silver in preciousness.[36] In fact, the growing shortage of coal and iron in Europe was, in his judgment, one of the principal motives behind the renewal of Western colonial activity in the 1870's.[37]

The reports of Western geologists, such as Baron von Richthofen, had concluded that China was rich in mineral resources and that her coal beds, in particular, in addition to being of high quality, were twenty times more abundant than Europe's.[38] If she were to exploit these natural riches, there would be a number of distinct benefits, according to Wang. First, and most general, the extraction of wealth from nature was a way of increasing state revenues without raising taxes.[39] Second, by using raw materials originating in China, the costs of manufacturing armaments, ships, and machinery would be lowered.[40] Third, there were profits to be derived from the sale of coal to Westerners in China. (This, Wang noted, would clearly be in the Westerners' interests, as they would no longer have to pay the freight charges for shipping their coal in from abroad.[41]) Finally, as already mentioned, the expansion of mining activity would create new jobs, thereby contributing directly to the welfare of the population.

If the advantages of mining enterprise were so obvious, why was resistance to it so strong? One answer to this, of course, is that the advantages were not obvious at all to those vast numbers of Chinese who, as late as the turn of the century, were still not committed to the goal of economic development. China could have all the coal in the world, as Wang himself put it, and it would be of little avail if she continued "to place curbs on herself."[42] Another answer is that as modern Chinese mining enterprise did begin to develop in the 1880's and 1890's, it was so beset by financial and managerial problems that potential investors often shied away from involvement.[43] Mining, in brief, suffered from the same syndrome of difficulties that plagued other fields of early modern enterprise in China.

TECHNOLOGY AND MACHINE-POWERED INDUSTRY

Although Chinese resistance was the main reason for the failure of modern mining to develop more rapidly, the technological gap between China and the West was an important contributory factor. Western technology and technicians could be borrowed, as indeed they were. But proceeding in this way presented very real liabilities. It was costly. It placed China in a position of dependence upon the foreigner. It tended to increase, instead of lowering, native resistance to change. And it postponed the day when Chinese would become independent producers of new technology.

The last was especially important. It took no great perspicacity in the nineteenth century to discern the relationship between Western power and Western technology. What escaped the notice of many Chinese observers for the longest time was the dynamic, developmental nature of the latter. This lapse is not surprising, when one considers the threat such an insight posed to the whole *t'i-yung* justification for limited change. In a context of technological stasis, the borrower of technology can pull abreast of the producer without having to undergo major social transformation. But when the producer is constantly improving his technological base, the borrower is faced with the difficult choice of continuing indefinitely as a borrower, at the risk of perennially lagging behind, or becoming a producer himself and experiencing changes that reach far beyond the realm of technology.

Wang T'ao perceived this dilemma and accepted the logic of his choice. The concept of continuous technological innovation had been brought home to him in a very personal way when, on visiting an exhibition of foreign weaponry in Edinburgh (in the late 1860's), he discovered to his horror that the manual on firearms he had coauthored only a few years before (1863) was already dated.[44] Seeing European technological growth, at least in the military field, as an outgrowth of interstate rivalry,[45] Wang warned his countrymen against thinking that Europeans would rest on past accomplishments. Instead, he insisted, each nation would strive continually to improve on what it already had, inventing newer and better models. The lesson for China was clear: If she contented herself with mere borrowing, by the time a technique had been mastered it would already be obsolete. The only way for her to compete with the West effectively was to go beyond imitation and invent things herself.[46]

It would be too much to argue that Wang T'ao anticipated all of the implications of his position. However, he was well aware of the need to establish facilities for technical training and a system of incentives for the encouragement of invention. Also, although Wang's earlier discussions of technology tended to emphasize its military importance, with the passage of time the economic ramifications of technological advance—especially in the manufacturing field—loomed larger and larger in his thinking.

As far back as the late 1860's, Wang T'ao had recommended the introduction of machine power into *all* areas of Chinese manufacture.[47] His main focus, nevertheless, was consistently on the textile industry, which he regarded as second only to modern mining as a source of new wealth. In this field, as in others, the supreme advantage of mechanization was that it saved work and increased production. Since machine-driven reels and looms could match the output of one hundred men working by hand, he wrote Li Hung-chang in 1865, if every ten families were equipped with a modern reel and loom, each family would make a profit equal to that of ten families under the old system.[48]

In his discussions of textile production, Wang was especially sensitive to the implications for Sino-foreign commerce. Operating in part on the mercantilist assumption that whatever profit foreign traders made was at the expense of the Chinese, he feared the detrimental effects of the import trade in textiles and believed that the way for China to halt the drainage of profits abroad was through the manufacture of her own piece goods. Because of lower labor and transport costs, he reasoned, textiles made in China would undersell those imported from abroad and drive them from the market. At the same time there was the added inducement of expanded employment opportunities for Chinese.[49]

Competition with foreign imports was only one reason for encouraging native manufacture. Another was to enable China to get back her traditional export markets and acquire new ones. Wang noted the recent inroads that had been made by Japan and India into the export trades in silk, tea, and porcelain. The writing on the wall was clear. If China wanted to recover her position of preeminence in these fields, she could ill afford to rest on her laurels. Instead, she must develop new manufacturing techniques and become, in general, more attuned to the tastes, standards, and needs of foreigners. The same held true for the development of new markets. If Americans could export their dairy products all over the world and India's cavalry units could be supplied with horses from as far away as Australia, did it make sense for China, with her abundant livestock resources, to continue to neglect the entire field of animal husbandry? To Wang, it clearly did not. And he applied the same logic in other fields, citing the conspicuous success of the Japanese as evidence of the harvest to be reaped from assimilating Western methods of manufacture and adapting home production to foreign demand.[50]

FOREIGN COMMERCE AND ECONOMIC NATIONALISM

The most striking thing in Wang T'ao's advocacy of modern manufacture was the incessant, almost obsessive, preoccupation with the economic competition of the West. It seemed as though China had to run just in order to keep from falling behind; if she stood still, she would succumb before the forward momentum of Western economic penetration. Whether such fears were exaggerated is a legitimate question, and one to which Western economic historians are increasingly addressing themselves. For us, the important thing is that Wang had these fears and that they influenced, in a decisive way, his perception of the problem of economic development.

The point is sharpened somewhat when we ask the question:

development for what? A country can settle on a course of economic growth for a variety of reasons. Development may take place more or less spontaneously, as a result of capitalist enterprise. Or, as has been more common in the twentieth century, it may be undertaken by the state for social welfare or power-political ends. Now we have already seen that, in Wang T'ao's mind, the primary purpose of Chinese economic modernization was to increase national wealth and thereby lay the basis for enhanced state power. This does not mean, however, that private profit-making was spurned by Wang. The Stalinist developmental model and the traditional Chinese "model," it is true, both posit a fundamental contradiction between public and private (especially commercial) profit and assume that the latter can be increased only at the expense of the former. But when Wang T'ao and other Chinese reformers of the nineteenth century looked at the contemporary West, they discovered a set of circumstances that neither of these models explained very adequately. The key feature of their discovery, uniquely visible in the treaty ports of China, was the existence of an intimate alliance between commercial wealth and state power, the former financing the latter, the latter providing protection to the former.

Robert L. Reynolds, writing of early modern Europe, articulates this unusual aspect of the Western experience:

It was a great asset to the Europeans in commerce that European governments put their whole strength behind mercantile enterprise, and considered the devising of ways and means for making their merchants richer and stronger a valid activity. The most powerful foreign states with which European merchants came in contact may have been equal to the Europeans in warfare, but none of them was so helpful in the promotion of trade and of the merchant class . . . Modern governments which foster trade are following a pattern established by the strong states of Europe some six or seven hundred years ago. Those European governments had a theory that if their merchants were strong and rich, the governments themselves would carry greater weight in war and diplomacy.[51]

There was no question in Wang T'ao's mind that this was

precisely the theory on which European governments (especially that of Great Britain) operated. Statements like the following are encountered repeatedly in Wang's writings: "The basic principle on which the English nation is founded is commerce. Wherever [Englishmen] go, their commercial power (*shang-li*) is backed by military power (*ping-li*). Merchants took the lead in the opening up of the American continent and the gradual occupation of India. The East India Company was formed by merchants. And merchants were an essential element in the seizure of India and the establishment of intercourse with China. Is not [England's] reliance on the collective energy and intelligence of her subjects (*ch'ün-ts'e ch'ün-li*) great?"[5][2]

There was a time when Chinese would have been incredulous at the prospect of a nation sending its armies half way around the world in order to advance the interests of a small community of traders. After the jolt of the Opium War, however, the level of incredulity rapidly dropped and in time a few individuals, taking their cue from the European example, began to ask hard questions concerning the position of the merchant in Chinese society, the importance of commerce in the economy, and the overall relationship between commercial expansion and state power.

In the traditional Chinese formulation, agriculture was pictured as the primary source of national wealth—the foundation (*pen*)— while commerce was viewed as secondary in importance—a by-product or offshoot (*mo*) of the agrarian sector. Aside from reflecting (quite accurately) the fundamentally agrarian nature of the premodern Chinese economy, this formulation expressed a value preference: agriculture was good, commerce bad. The value preference was derived partly from Confucian disparagement of profit-making and partly from the state's dependence upon land tax revenues. For, if one accepted the premise that the only sector of the economy which actually produced wealth was the agrarian sector and the further premise that the economy as a whole was nongrowing, the conclusion was inescapable that the official and commercial sectors were competitors for a more or less fixed supply of surplus agricultural production.

Despite this negative mythology, there was a great deal of

commercial activity in pre-Opium War China and over the centuries a market structure evolved which, for a premodern economy, was second to none in scope and complexity. Chinese commerce, nevertheless, was marked by certain characteristics which seriously impaired its development, as compared with modern Western commerce. First, to the extent that the state bothered with commerce at all, it was for the purpose of regulating and taxing, rather than protecting and promoting it. Second, of the major Chinese social classes, the merchant ranked lowest, at least in terms of the ideology of the ruling scholar-official stratum and probably in many cases in reality as well. Third, the overwhelming preponderance of Chinese trade was domestic; as late as 1913 China's foreign trade per capita was probably smaller than that of any other country.[53] Fourth, the Chinese market structure was basically an extension of the rural economy, commodities traded being mostly products of agriculture and handicraft. Fifth, premodern transportation and communications (very costly both in money and in time), inadequate credit and banking facilities, and the chaotic condition of Chinese currency hampered the growth of an integrated national market at home and—though there were political and cultural reasons for this as well—effectively prevented Chinese merchants from cracking the foreign monopoly of the import-export trade with Europe and the United States.

In all of these areas, Wang T'ao was a vigorous proponent of change. For the stubborn traditionalists, who insisted that agriculture should be emphasized and commerce de-emphasized because that was how it had always been, and who were appalled lest the development of commerce lead to an abandonment of the "foundation," Wang barely concealed his scorn:

Alas, look at their discussions even of agricultural matters. Do they ever think in terms of the particular products of a locality or discriminate among different seeds and plants or bring wastelands under cultivation or initiate water control projects or deepen irrigation ditches or drain off flood waters or prepare for droughts or direct the peasants to work hard in the fields, providing them with supervision and instruction? All they know is to survey their lands and make levies, press for taxes and collect rents, and plague the people by setting over them cruel officials who act toward the peasantry as tigers and wolves. They [honor] only the name [of agriculture], not the substance. Their talk is big, but [in their conduct] they are shameless. This is truly a universal defect of today's literati.[54]

As Wang saw it, the problem with most literati, quite apart from their hypocrisy, was that they insisted on treating a brand new situation as though it were not new at all. The ill effects of foreign commerce (which Wang thought were considerable) could not be dealt with by pretending they did not exist. They had to be met head-on. To this end, Wang, like his friend Cheng Kuan-ying (but uninfluenced by Cheng),[55] took a stand which had many of the earmarks of economic nationalism. Wang knew that, if the vehicle for the West's intrusion was superior military power, its primary motive was material gain. China could not, in the foreseeable future, rival the West militarily. But she could take steps to compete in the economic realm. And if, through such competition, she could make it increasingly less profitable for the Westerners to stay in China, perhaps some day they would part. This mode of reasoning, curiously reminiscent of Lenin's program for combating imperialism, was first used by Wang in the 1860's. In his last years, when he was contributing regularly to the influential reform-oriented missionary periodical, *Wan-kuo kung-pao*, it formed his principal line of attack.

The basic premise on which Wang and many other Chinese operated, in the closing decades of the nineteenth century, was that any profit made by foreigners in China was a profit denied the Chinese themselves and constituted a drain of wealth from the country.[56] The problem, therefore, was how to recover, maintain, or acquire control over sources of profit that had been, or were in danger of being, wrested from China by the West (and later Japan). In other circumstances, a partial solution to this problem might have been to raise the tariffs on foreign imports. The treaties, however, deprived China of her freedom in this area, the tariff rate on most items being fixed at 5 per cent. Wang T'ao, although galled by these restrictions on China's tariff autonomy,[57] was sensible enough to see that as long as China remained weak, she was unlikely to succeed in persuading the foreigners to surrender an advantage they already enjoyed. If the drainage of Chinese wealth was to be stopped, therefore, a different kind of approach was called for—an approach that was not contingent on the altruism of the Western powers.

The gist of Wang's solution was for China to cease being passive and to begin taking more initiative in her economic activities, cutting into the West's profit-making capacity at every conceivable juncture.[58] The formation of Chinese steamship companies should be encouraged to compete with foreign firms in the interior carrying trade. Modern mining should be developed so that China could herself supply the needs both of Western shipping and of Chinese industry. Instead of importing woolen and cotton goods from the West, China should establish her own mechanized textile industries. And she should do the same in other areas of manufacture. Wang, at one point, was even willing to countenance an increase in the native production of opium in order to force down the price of imported opium and reduce foreign profits.[59]

It was, above all, in the field of commerce—particularly foreign commerce—that Wang felt the need for change. For it was here that the West seemed most vulnerable to Chinese competition. Thus, Wang wrote Ting Jih-ch'ang in 1875: "If [China] were one day to divest [Great Britain] of the profits she makes from foreign trade, the market for her coal and iron, machinery, textiles, and manufactured articles would contract and large numbers of workers and merchants would surely lose their jobs. Faced with unrest at home and with no help forthcoming from abroad, it would only be a matter of time before India gained its independence. [England] might snap like a mad dog and struggle like a hemmed-in beast. But it would be to no avail."[60]

The proto-Leninist analysis revealed in these lines became fairly ubiquitous among Chinese reformers during the next decade or two, suggesting an important reason for Lenin's enormous appeal in the twentieth century. The Leninist conclusion, however, was that the foreign economic stranglehold had to be broken (presumably by political means) *before* native capitalism could gain a lease on life. Wang T'ao argued just the reverse: that to bring an end to foreign commercial penetration, Chinese commerce must be transformed and energized.

Two themes stand out in Wang's discussions of this subject. One, first adumbrated in 1862, was his contention that Chinese merchants, instead of being the passive recipients of foreign trade, must learn to carry it overseas themselves, using Chinese-built vessels, insured by Chinese insurance companies. Although Chinese traders had traditionally played an important role in the intra-Asian carrying trade, rarely had they ventured farther afield. As long as the volume of long-distance commerce was low, this did not matter very much. But with the expansion of Sino-Western trade, beginning in the eighteenth century, an increasingly important place was created for such subsidiary operations as ship construction, shipping, insurance, and banking. Each of these fields constituted a golden opportunity for profit-making, and each, by Chinese default, was virtually monopolized by the West. Wang T'ao wanted China to challenge this monopoly.[61] There was nothing in international law, he inserted at one point, to prevent a country from carrying its own overseas trade; also, when Chinese merchants began importing commodities into European countries, there was no reason why they should pay an import tariff greater than 5 per cent ad valorem, as prescribed in the treaties.[62]

As Chinese involvement in all phases of the importing and exporting process increased, there would be indirect benefits as well. More jobs would be created for Chinese workmen, skilled and unskilled. In crisis situations, the government would be able to call upon Chinese merchants overseas to serve in various official capacities and also to make contributions of needed supplies (the merchants, of course, to be generously rewarded after termination of the crisis).[63] On the noneconomic side, increased activity of Chinese of standing abroad would provide the government with a more intimate picture of conditions in the West and equip it to make more intelligent decisions in matters affecting Sino-Western relations. The establishment of Chinese steamship and insurance companies with world-wide activities would also serve to augment

China's national prestige and influence, much as the old East India Company had done for Great Britain.[64]

Increased Chinese mercantile involvement overseas, however, would require the active support of the Chinese government. Which brings us to Wang T'ao's other major theme: the need for fundamental change in the Chinese official attitude toward commerce. There was an essential distinction, Wang insisted, between *wu-ts'ai*—devoting oneself to wealth—and *li-ts'ai*—managing wealth. "Devoting oneself to wealth" was a private matter, having reference to the self; but "managing wealth" was a public matter and had reference to the nation. Flaying the fat from the people in order to enrich oneself and developing the sources of wealth in order to benefit the people—the two were as different as night and day. And it was the first only—not the second—that the Classics condemned.[65]

The implications of a shift in government policy in this area were articulated by Wang at least as early as 1865. In his letter of that year to Li Hung-chang, he wrote: "Western governments both regulate and assist their merchants. Consequently, the profits [of the merchants] are immense and the revenues [of the government] are ample. We let our merchants go their own way, occasionally even curbing them and making extortionate demands on them, with the result that both the government and the merchants experience financial loss. Today, the sure way for us to recover economic control (*li-ch'üan*) is for this pattern to be completely reversed. Then, could our country fail to become strong and our people wealthy?"[66]

In short, Wang hoped that the government would replace its traditional negativism—or at best indifference—toward commerce with a policy of active concern and energetic promotion. To this end, he favored the use of paper money and the establishment of official banks.[67] He also wanted the government to cooperate with merchants in the setting up of new companies, though he warned that the merchants must have complete control over all matters, so that the officials did not "contend with them for the profits."[68] Wang was most vocal on the subject of likin abolition.

The likin (*li-chin*) was a multiple tax on internal commerce instituted in the early 1850's to help finance the government campaigns against the Taiping and Nien rebels. Long after these rebellions had been put down, however, the tax continued to be collected, much to the chagrin of foreign merchants, who seemed convinced that it was the chief barrier to expanded trade. Wang T'ao's opposition to the likin might appear to be a simple reflection of the foreign viewpoint, confirming the image of him as an "imperialist running dog." Closer examination, however, suggests a somewhat more complex picture. Wang agreed that the likin impost was an obstacle to trade. Also, since the tax was ultimately passed on to the consumer in the form of higher commodity prices, he saw it as being harmful to the welfare of the people (*min-sheng*). There were two questions, however, that had to be answered: First, to what extent did the tax meet a legitimate revenue need? And second, was it the best way to meet this need? Wang's answer to the first question dictated his response to the second. By his estimate, only 20 to 30 per cent of the amount collected was used for bona fide official purposes, the rest being siphoned off by bureaucratic peculation. This was why the post of likin collector was so much in demand among expectant officials. And it was good reason, Wang thought, for seeking alternative sources of provincial government revenue. Raising the tax on opium and levying vice taxes on foreign liquor and cigars were possibilities. Or, perhaps, a way could be found to revive the old poll tax without causing undue distress to the populace. Or—and this was the solution eventually favored by Wang—the Chinese government could propose to the foreign powers that the tariff on all imports and exports be increased to 20 per cent, in return for complete elimination of the likin impost.[69] The foreigners were not in the habit of giving things away, Wang reasoned, but maybe one could bargain with them.

By the early 1890's, Wang T'ao, detecting the need for a more explicit governmental commitment to the promotion of commerce, proposed that a Bureau of Commerce (*shang-chü*) be established for this purpose, comparable to the Ministries of Commerce in Western countries. The bureau would be charged with collecting and collating information, developing China's economic resources, and devising ways to keep Chinese wealth from flowing abroad and to attract foreign wealth to China. After all, foreign trade was a fine thing, Wang observed, as long as one did not lose by it. Yet, this was precisely what was happening to China. While world trade in silk prospered as never before, Chinese profits from silk steadily declined. Why? Because Chinese commerce remained stuck in the old grooves, adhering to outdated ways, as if nothing had changed in the world. A Bureau of Commerce would help to reverse this pattern. Wang also thought it would be a good idea for the government to establish special schools of commerce and technology, so that Chinese merchants, before engaging in trade abroad, could be given training in mathematics, geography, and foreign languages.[70]

Why, Wang T'ao asked in one of his last pieces of writing, did China's economic achievement not match that of the West? His answer was revealing: "For the simple reason that those above do not regard this as a matter of vital importance. If someone with great power were to take the first step and the officials were to provide their support, our customs and conventions could surely be changed, and within a decade or so many Western merchants would have their profits snatched from them by Chinese."[71]

A similar note was sounded in one of Wang's major editorials on reform ("Pien-fa"), dating from the late 1870's or early 1880's. After calling for sweeping changes ("from trunk to branch, from inside to outside, from great to small"), he cautioned: "But the most important point is that the government above should exercise its power to change customs and mores, while the people below should be gradually absorbed into the new environment and adjusted to it without their knowing it."[72]

What is principally significant about both of these statements is the undiluted expression of Wang T'ao's paternalism. Not just in the economic field, but in all fields, Wang expected, as a matter of course, that the initiative for reform would come from the state. Now there was nothing surprising or unusual in this. Paternalism has been rampant among reformers in modern China. But it did pose a problem. Wang T'ao knew, as well as anyone, that it was unrealistic to expect the Chinese government, in its existing condition, to play the role of reformer. If there was to be meaningful change in China's economic life, therefore, her political life also would have to be transformed.

8

POLITICAL REFORM

Wang T'ao's critique of Chinese government and political life was in some respects the most radical part of his reform program. It is disconcerting at first, therefore, to discover the degree to which his thinking tied into, and drew inspiration from, ancient political models and images. For a person whose ties to the old culture were still strong, such an approach was bound to be attractive. It was a central feature, moreover, of the reform-oriented "statecraft" (*ching-shih*) tradition. But was it intellectually legitimate? The answer, I think, is yes. For one thing, the models Wang harked back to were very much in the nature of ideal types, resisting confinement in a specific time (antiquity) or space (China). Wang had strong proprietary feelings about honest government and government responsive to people's needs, as well as a way of expressing such ideals that made them seem distinctively Chinese. But the fact is, there was little that was either Chinese or traditional about them. Ideals of this sort were more akin to universals, timeless verities to which political thinkers of all ages and countries could without embarrassment declare their allegiance.

A second, and closely related, factor facilitating Wang's habitual appeal to ancient Chinese prototypes was their vagueness and imprecision. There was a line from the *Shu-ching*, for example, which he cited with great frequency: "The people are a country's foundation; when the foundation is secure the country will be at peace" (*min wei pang pen, pen ku pang ning*). Divorced from context, the meaning of this dictum is far from self-evident. We are told, to be sure, that a country's stability depends on the condition of its populace. But what has to be done to make the population "secure" is not spelled out. Nor is it clear, from the description of the people as a country's "foundation," whether they are to be thought of as instrumentalities or as ends.[1]

A third (and more substantive) basis for Wang T'ao's justification of change in terms of an idealized vision of ancient Chinese political life was the devolutionary strain in his view of history. Wang, along with many others, believed that the condition of Chinese government had grown steadily worse since Ch'in times. To call for a revival of pre-Ch'in political behavior, therefore, was not necessarily to countenance reaction; it could just as well signify a commitment to sweeping reform. By the same token, when Wang T'ao praised Western governments for embodying "the spirit of the Three Dynasties," it was not the ritual implication of Chinese precedent that was noteworthy, but the willingness—anything but ritual—to acknowledge fulfillment in contemporary Western society of the most cherished Chinese political ideals. Since Wang refused to make the same claims for his own society, such praise signaled the sharpest possible break with old-style Chinese ethnocentrism.

PRESCRIPTIONS FOR GOOD GOVERNMENT

Wang T'ao's intense preoccupation with government—or what he called *chih-min* (lit. "the governance of the people")—can be traced to the beginnings of his adult career. As we have seen, however, the context of his concern changed significantly over the years. Up to about the middle of the 1860's the outstanding political problem facing the Ch'ing dynasty was popular rebellion. It was only after, one by one, the major insurrections had been quelled that the focus of Chinese political attention gradually shifted to the problem of national weakness. This changing context naturally affected Wang T'ao's ordering of governmental priorities. However, his definition of the principal shortcomings of Chinese government changed surprisingly little. These may be grouped, somewhat inadequately, under two headings: irrationality and unresponsiveness. As we discuss these shortcomings, it is well to bear in mind that for Wang they were so closely interrelated as to be inseparable.

Toward a more rational government. Wang T'ao's lexicon did not contain a word for "rational," but it seems to me that this word comes as close as any to describing one sort of measuring rod used by him in the evaluation of Chinese governmental practices. Collectively considered, these practices had taken on more and more of a baroque quality through the ages. Cumbersome, wasteful, excessively rigid, and full of incongruities, they fell far short of answering to the needs of government in Wang T'ao's day, and it was from this perspective that Wang passed judgment upon them.

Many of the practices denounced by Wang in the 1870's and after were ones which he had already singled out for criticism back in the Taiping days (see Chapter 2). Some of them, however, had worsened in the intervening period, and Wang's criticisms became correspondingly more vehement. An example was the custom of selling offices in order to augment imperial revenues. We now know that as of 1840 29 per cent of all local officials between the fourth and seventh ranks (which included taotais, prefects, and chou and hsien magistrates) had obtained their positions through purchase. By 1871 the figure had risen to 51 per cent, and it was still as high as 49 per cent in 1895.[2] Wang T'ao was not aware of these exact figures, but he knew how widespread the practice of buying official posts had become, and he was horrified by the potential consequences for good government. When such lucrative jobs as that of likin collector were assigned to office-purchasers, as was not uncommon, the traffic in official posts took on all the attributes of trading in the market-place. Compared to this, even the examination system, with all its failings, was, in Wang's view, a decided improvement. Wang proposed that the practice of selling official posts be abolished without delay and that alternative sources of revenue be tapped to make up for the loss.[3]

One possibility in this connection, desirable on other grounds as well, was to eliminate from the bureaucracy all persons who performed no essential function. Aside from the financial savings that would accrue from such a course, there would be a net gain in governmental efficiency. Wang took note, for example, of the problem that existed in those provinces in which a governor-general and a governor shared overlapping jurisdictions. When the views of these two powerful officials happened to coincide, everything was fine. But when they clashed, authority was fragmented and the smooth conduct of governmental affairs was impaired. The office of governor-general had not always been permanent in character. Originally it had been established by the Ming court for the purpose of commanding troops in the provinces, and as soon as a region became pacified, it was promptly discontinued. Wang recommended that, excepting the provinces of Chihli, Szechwan, and Kansu (which, because they had no governors, were already free of jurisdictional conflict), the office of governor-general, on becoming vacant, be eliminated, thus restoring the simpler system that had been current in Ming times.[4]

Wang did not insist on this point (that is, elimination of the governor-generalship). The important thing was that government be made less cumbrous, more effective, more streamlined. To this end, he opposed the common practice of assigning more than one post to a single official and argued strenuously (as he had in 1862) for longer terms of office at all levels of the bureaucracy.[5] More significant still, he advanced the idea (new to him) that the welter of laws and regulations that cluttered up Chinese administrative processes were a source of multiple evils and needed to be radically reduced in number. Wang's most extensive discussion of this notion was in an editorial entitled "Shang-chien" (In praise of simplicity), dating probably from the 1870's:

From the Han down to the present some two thousand years have passed, during which time the deceitfulness of man's nature has become extreme and mores have deteriorated greatly. The statutes and regulations are numerous and complex; litigation is troublesome. The laws are more intricate than the threads of a net, and official documents outnumber the pebbles on a beach. [Officials] regularly appeal to established precedents and base themselves on outworn statutes, causing people to be at a loss for what to do. The reports sent up from the provinces make a fine show of learning, but not one in a hundred has any substance to it. Add to this the maze of laws and regulations pertaining to the Six Boards and the confusion is complete. What people don't realize is that all this does is make it easier for the clerks to tamper with documents, engage in peculation, and twist the facts to suit their private ends . . .

Formerly, when Han Kao-tsu entered the Pass [in modern Shensi] he granted the elders of the region a law code consisting of only three statutes . . . Can it be said, then, that the governance of the empire depends upon having a multitude of laws and statutes? Will this prevent abuses and put an end to wrongdoing? In the present day, the officials and the people both suffer from the complexity [of the laws]. It is essential, therefore, that they be simplified.[6]

There is more than a faint echo here of Huang Tsung-hsi's distinction between "lawful laws" and "unlawful laws"—the simple laws of the Three Dynasties, which existed for the sake of the people, and the "comprehensive and detailed" laws of later periods, which were promulgated for the sake of one family (the ruling house) and constituted "the very source of disorder." Now Confucian scholars had always been somewhat mistrustful of positive law and assumed, as a matter of course, that the more laws a society needed, the more degenerate it must be. Wang T'ao, however, was not against laws as such (any more than Huang Tsung-hsi had been). What he opposed was their unchecked and needless proliferation. As Huang had put it: "If one measure is adopted, there are immediate fears of its being abused or evaded, and so another measure must be adopted to guard against abuses or evasions."[7]

This proliferation of laws and regulations, coupled with the enormous importance attached to precedent in the Chinese administrative process, placed a high premium on legal expertise and knowledge of local conditions. Since, with few exceptions, the only persons who possessed such knowledge and expertise were the yamen and board clerks, who in the T'ung-chih period were estimated to number over one million, the clerks were in a strategic position to manipulate the entire system to their advantage. This brought untold harm to the population. Also, because the clerks had a vested interest in precisely those aspects of the system that were most cumbersome and irrational, it formed a powerful check on reform. Wang T'ao saw this clearly: "What shall we do to eliminate the red tape [encumbering] the laws and regulations, while carrying out their basic intent? For this to be accomplished, a clean sweep must first be made of those in the empire who are now referred to as clerks."[8]

In a letter of 1870-1871 to Ting Jih-ch'ang, Wang took a closer look at the whole problem of clerical abuse:

The clerks are the ones who assist the officials in governing, and [the evil] of tampering with documents for illegal purposes is half owing to them. Because the clerks are not responsible and because, also, they are of base character and reputation, it is fitting that they should care only for what is of profit to them . . . While the occupant of an official post may be changed several times in the course of a year, clerks remain [in their positions] permanently. While officials dwell in deep seclusion [within their yamens], clerks circulate daily among the populace. Under the circumstances, it is inevitable that the clerks should take advantage of the officials and conceal things from them. For, to entrust people who are of low social standing with responsibilities proper to people of the highest station is an impossibility.[9]

Since most of the paperwork in the Chinese bureaucracy was performed by clerks, the clerical function as such could not be dispensed with. It was possible, on the other hand, to demand that those who performed this function be of higher moral and intellectual fiber. And this was the position Wang took. Specifically, he proposed that clerical jobs be filled, henceforth, by bona fide scholars (shih-jen), who after a period of probation would either be promoted to magistrate or discharged.[10] What Wang was asking for, in effect, was a massive extension of the formal governmental apparatus. This was a radical solution. (Feng Kuei-fen had put forward a similar one in his *Chiao-pin-lu k'ang-i*.) It rested on the premise that, as Mary Wright phrased it, "a Confucian state could control [the clerks] only by giving them status in the Confucian hierarchy, thus making them subject to its indoctrination and controls."[1][1]

Toward a more responsive government. Just as the "subbureaucracy" of clerks inhibited the development of a healthy relationship between the people and the officials, the officials themselves—the bureaucracy proper—formed an impenetrable barrier to effective communication between the populace and the throne. The emperor was so isolated and removed from the people that it was all but impossible for him to familiarize himself with popular problems and respond to popular needs. And the officials were, in this respect, like nothing so much as little emperors. Far from showing concern for the welfare of the people, they exploited them mercilessly, in reply to which the people, losing all confidence in the government, grew increasingly apathetic, alienated, and disloyal. This was a problem which Wang T'ao (perhaps under the influence of Ku Yen-wu) had already dwelt on in the early 1860's (see Chapter 2). In the closing decades of the century, it formed the central thread of his political critique.

Wang delineated the problem graphically in an important editorial of the late 1870's entitled "Chung-min" (The importance of the people):

Up to and through the Three Dynasties the monarch and the people were close and the world was well-governed. After the Three Dynasties the monarch and the people grew farther and farther apart, whereupon the quality of government declined. Starting with Ch'in, the practice of honoring the monarch and debasing the subject became institutionalized. Since then the court has been unapproachable and cut off from popular opinion. The people view the monarch as if looking up at the heavens; the palace gate is so far away that no one can knock at it. [The people] may suffer and grieve, but they cannot make their sufferings known. They may cry out in anguish, but their voices will not be heard. When calamity strikes or there is a poor harvest, edict after edict is handed down ordering assistance, either through remission of taxes or the distribution of relief funds. The officials, however, regard such orders as mere *pro forma* documents, while the clerks nibble away [at the funds set aside for relief] . . .

The monarch stands erect and impassive at court, honored above all men; the officials go forth to govern the people, and they too are universally honored. Regarding themselves as the designated representatives of the court, [they say to the people]: "You must follow our orders and heed our instructions; if you do not obey we can have you executed. What harm can you do to us?" The only thing they know how to do is squander the people's wealth and sap the people's strength. There is no form of exploitation that is beneath them. And when their purses are stuffed, they fly off with the wind. Not a one is there who is capable of acting sincerely on the people's behalf.

Now the original reason for providing officials was to govern the people. But today it is only to harm the people. No longer does one hear of officials being appointed for the protection of the people; one only hears of the people being fleeced for the benefit of the officials. Out of over a thousand [officials] there are perhaps one or two who are able to empathize with the people . . . Alas! They fail to see that even the lowliest of the people should not be offended against, that even the stupidest of the people should not be deceived.[1 2]

Wang T'ao, in this editorial, clearly has not abandoned his paternalism. Indeed, farther on he makes it quite explicit: "When the people are to the officials as sons and younger brothers are to fathers and elder brothers, good government will prevail all over."[1 3] Taking their cue from this, Communist historians, while praising Wang for elevating the importance of the people, have criticized him for being insufficiently democratic: "He was able only to talk about 'the governance of the people' (*chih-min*); he was unable to talk about 'government by the people' (*min-chih*)."[1 4] The trouble with such crisp dichotomizations is that they are too exclusive and inflexible to take the measure of Wang's political position accurately. It is true that Wang never became an advocate of "popular rights." But the fact that popular rule repelled him did not make him a friend of autocracy. Between the two extremes there was an important middle ground, and it was here that Wang took his stand.

Wang, moreover, had a fair amount of company. As Kwang-Ching Liu has pointed out, "the desire for greater communication between the literati and the throne and for the amelioration of autocracy" was a persistent theme in nineteenth-century Chinese political thought.[15] Persistent, but not static. In its initial formulations, the criticism of despotism was made independent of Western influence. (Certainly this was so in the cases of Pao Shih-ch'en, Kung Tzu-chen, and the early Wang T'ao; it may also have been true of the criticisms voiced later on by Tseng Kuo-fan and Feng Kuei-fen.[16]) After about 1870, however, the discussion began to be shaped in a pronounced way by the example of the West, leading to increased interest in and eventually advocacy of parliamentary government.

Wang T'ao's contributions to this gathering assault on autocracy were along several lines. One, prominently displayed in the editorial just cited and reiterated by him at almost every opportunity, centered on the theme of the breakdown of communication among different levels of the political hierarchy. The huge social and psychological distance that separated the emperor from his officials, and the officials from the people, had produced something worse than inefficiency, in Wang's view. It had thoroughly dehumanized the operations of government. By a process of immunization familiar enough to people in modern societies, the rulers (the wealthy and powerful), by virtue of their being far removed from the ruled (the poor and powerless), had become insensitive to the latter's needs and difficulties. Not directly witnessing popular suffering, it was all too easy for them to become part of the impersonal machinery that generated this suffering. And in the end, to paraphrase Wang T'ao, instead of the government existing for the benefit of the people, the people existed for the benefit of the government.

What was to be done to correct this situation? Since, in the last analysis, the problem of distance resolved itself into one of authority, the emperor having a monopoly of authority from the standpoint of the officials, and the officials being all-powerful in the eyes of the common people, the obvious solution was to press for a redistribution of authority at both levels. As regards the first level (comprising the throne and the bureaucracy), Wang boldly criticized a number of measures that Chinese emperors had availed themselves of (especially in Ming and Ch'ing times) for the purpose of increasing their effective power vis-à-vis officialdom. He also called for a radical reversal of this process: "At the center, the authority of the Son of Heaven should be entrusted to a chancellor,[17] the chancellor sharing it with the Six Boards. In the provinces, the authority of the Son of Heaven should be entrusted to the governors-general and governors, the governors-general and governors sharing it with the magistrates. Terms of office should, in all cases, be extended and each official should bear full responsibility for his post. [The throne for its part] should repose trust [in its officials] and not harbor suspicions toward them, though they be situated far away."[18]

Wang paid particular attention to the appointment-making power of the governors-general and governors, believing this to be their single most important function. He asked that it be broadened and strengthened. He also urged that in the exercise of this power, ability be given precedence over seniority, in order to guarantee that only the most qualified persons were chosen for the magisterial post.[19] For, if the governors-general and governors were the key executive officials at the provincial level, the magistrates were the ones whose administrative responsibilities brought them into closest contact with the population. It was, therefore, on the quality of this last group of officials, more than any other, that good government depended.

Even a supermagistrate, though, in order to do some good for the people in his jurisdiction, needed time. The imperial fear was that if a magistrate remained at the same post for a prolonged period he might develop strong local attachments and cease to represent effectively the interests of the throne. Wang T'ao's rejoinder to this was that if a magistrate knew he was not going to be at his post for more than a brief spell, he would have neither the opportunity nor the motivation to do a decent job: "They take up their duties in the morning and are removed by evening. The instructions issued at dawn are changed before sundown. [Official posts] are looked upon virtually as wayside inns. By what means, then, are the officials and the people to develop a close relationship? How can an area be governed in an orderly fashion?"[20]

As for the other side of the problem of good government—the quality of the magistrate himself—Wang T'ao was very explicit. The most important qualification of a successful magistrate was that he be responsive to popular sentiment (*min-ch'ing*). This meant providing the people with the means to make their views felt. But, more than that, it meant letting oneself, as an official, be guided by these views. As Wang put it in one of his letters: "In the governance of the people, the essential thing is, in leading the people, to follow their interests, and in communicating with the people, to comply with their wishes."[21] Or, again, in "Chung-min": "He who is good at ruling gives first importance to finding out what is troubling the people and to ascertaining the people's views. When the people regard something as inconvenient, he does not insist upon it; when the people regard something as impracticable, he does not force it upon them."[22]

If the object of good government was to benefit the people, should not the people know better than anyone else whether this object was being fulfilled? Wang T'ao's reply to this question was in the affirmative. And consistent with his response, he suggested, on at least one occasion, that the people ought perhaps to have a part in the selection of those who governed them. "The decision as to how able an official is, and whether he should be advanced or demoted," Wang wrote in a letter of 1884, "should be based on the assessment of his character and conduct registered by public opinion (*yü-lun chih mei-o shih-fei*)." Further along in the same letter, Wang proposed a mechanism for recruiting official talent that was suggestive of—and very possibly influenced by—Western elective procedures. Under the prevailing system of recommendation, he observed, the initiative came from above; furthermore, those recommended were generally men who had already served in an official capacity. "It is my view that the power of recommendation ought to start from below and proceed upwards, [people] being chosen by public opinion and scrutinized by public discussion. Let the best persons in each village and district be brought forward by public recommendation (*kung-chü*). Those who are recommended *by the most people* should be presented to the authorities, who can then give employment to the ones of their choice. The [power] of recommendation will thus have been made public."[2] [3]

GOOD GOVERNMENT: THE WESTERN EXAMPLE

The desire to bring Chinese government closer to the people, to make it more reflective of their interests and wishes, and to subject it to some form of popular restraint inevitably led Wang T'ao to a consideration of the alternatives offered by government in the West. The availability of a non-Chinese point of reference, and Wang's readiness to use it, marked a fresh departure in the tradition of Chinese criticism of autocracy. Although, to the best of my knowledge, Wang never *expressly* advocated a parliamentary system for China, there are numerous indications that he would have favored such a step. Wang repeatedly stated his preference for a system of government in which there was a sharing of power between the monarch and the people. Moreover, he was unstinting in his praise of the parliamentary institution's operation in Europe. In "Chung-min," he compared the three major systems of Western government in the following terms:

In monarchical government (*chün-chu*), one man rules above while the myriad officials and the populace scurry about below. When [the monarch] issues orders they must be carried out; when he speaks no one contradicts him. In popular government (*min-chu*), matters of national import are brought before the parliament (*i-yüan*). If the majority approve [a course of action] it is carried out; if they do not approve it is stopped. The president is armed only with executive powers. In [the system] of joint rule by the monarch and the people (*chün-min kung-chu*), when the court is faced with important governmental decisions pertaining to war, law, ceremonies and music, rewards and punishments, and the like, it must assemble the people in the upper and lower houses of parliament. If the monarch approves [a course of action], but the people do not, it cannot be carried out. If the people approve, but the monarch does not, again, it cannot be carried out. Only when the monarch and the people are in agreement can [a measure] be promulgated far and near.

It is maintained by some that if a monarch is to be ruler, the throne will have to be occupied by a monarch possessing the qualities of a Yao or a Shun for prolonged peace and good government to prevail, while if the people are to be the rulers, laws and regulations will be numerous and confusing, and unity of purpose will be difficult to come by, ultimately resulting in a proliferation of evils. Only when the monarch and the people share in governing (*chün-min kung-chih*) and there is communication between above and below can the sufferings of the people be made known above and the kindnesses of the monarch be extended to those below. In the close accord that obtains between the ruler and his subjects [under this arrangement], the lingering spirit of the Three Dynasties and before in China may still be discerned.[24]

What Wang was looking for was a system of government in which, to use his own phrasing, "the monarch is master above and the people are master below" (*chün chu yü shang erh min chu yü hsia*).[25] The nearest thing to this, in his day, was the parliamentary institution in the West. Wang commented on this institution in his history of France:

Since the National Assembly (*kuo-hui*) is established as a public body, not a private one, the people all submit to it. It is like this in all the countries of Europe ... Under such a [system], those above and those below are at peace with one another and the monarch and his subjects share in the governing (*chün-ch'en kung-chih*). Things can go on for a long time, without getting to the point where people suffer from tyrannical administration and popular support is lost through the avarice and cruelty [of the officials]. For the members of both the upper and the lower assemblies are chosen entirely by the public (*kung-chü*), and from the time they first put themselves forward [as candidates], they must display fairness and rectitude in order to win. If, [moreover, after becoming members], they should at some point do something that is improper, in flagrant violation of public sentiment and not in accord with popular opinion, the same people who elected them can also remove them. Thus, even if they are inclined to turn a deaf ear to people's criticisms, there are definite bounds to their misconduct. The institutions established in China during the Three Dynasties and before had this very same spirit. Each time that I get to this point in my study of European history, unfailingly my gaze is drawn far back to the age of the Yellow Emperor, Shen Nung, Shun, and Yü, and I sigh over how close [the Europeans] are to the ancients.[26]

Although this comment comes on the heels of a fairly systematic description of the workings of parliamentary government in
the Third Republic, the object of Wang's praise is the parliamentary institution in general, not its specifically French incarnation.
(This explains Wang's use of the term *chün*, or monarch.) In point
of fact, Wang held French political skill and achievement in rather
low esteem. It was Great Britain that took all the honors
here—even in the unlikely field of colonial government. The
reason, Wang tells us, why France tended to lose her colonies as
quickly as she gained them was that her way of governing people
was wrong. To found a colony might be a military matter, but to
keep it one had to know how to deal with people. The French,
unfortunately, had never learned this lesson. Having no compassion for the people under their rule, they used them as beasts and
trampled upon them as grass under foot. Even if the natives were
stupid, how could the desire for revenge not be awakened in their
breasts? French colonial rule was, therefore, constantly threatened
by native revolt.[27]

The British, by contrast, were masterful colonizers, the secret of
their success being that their colonial subjects were treated
according to the same high standards that were applied at home.
Hong Kong flourished under British rule because it was well
governed. The primitive islanders of Tahiti, on coming under the
civilizing influence of the first British missionaries, responded by
converting to Protestantism in large numbers. The people of
post-Sepoy India did not rise up against their foreign overlords
because the British governed with compassion and dispensed huge
sums of relief money whenever there was a food shortage.[28] And
so on. For all Wang T'ao's instinctive proto-Leninism when it was
a matter of foreign pressure on China, when it came to British
colonialism around the world, his guard dropped. It dropped so
far, in fact, that when he heard that there were elements in
England who favored the dismantling of the British empire
because of the tremendous financial drain it posed, Wang T'ao
denounced this viewpoint as "superficial" and sided unhesitatingly
with the proponents of empire.[29]

How is this unexpected softness toward British imperialism to be explained, or can it only be explained away? The answer, like the question, is mixed. It would be hard to deny that Wang T'ao's outlook, over the years, had become subject to a certain amount of Anglification. He had lived, ever since 1849, in places that were partly or entirely under British rule (Hong Kong, the International Settlement of Shanghai, Scotland). A major part of his working life had been spent in the employ of British missionaries. And back in the early sixties, British intervention on his behalf had very possibly saved his life. It would be surprising, under the circumstances, if Wang did not, to some extent, see the world through British eyes.

But there were other, less personal, grounds, too, for Wang T'ao's charitable attitude toward British imperialism. One of the most important of these was the part played by imperial Britain as a brake upon Russian expansion in the Far East. In global strategic terms, British imperialism was less an enemy than a friend, and Wang T'ao, on any number of occasions, had called upon the British to join China (and Japan) in a defensive alliance against the Russian menace.[30]

Still, anyone who peruses nineteenth-century Chinese materials covering foreign relations will be struck by the relative mildness of the indictment of Great Britain. As the foreign power chiefly responsible for the Opium War, initiating a century of Chinese humiliation, and as the country with by far the largest economic stake in the Ch'ing empire, England, from a Marxist-Leninist perspective, clearly represented the vanguard of Western imperialism. Yet contemporary Chinese—and here Wang T'ao was typical—stubbornly refused to be as upset by British economic aggression as they were by French religio-cultural aggression or the territorial hunger of Russia and Japan. England, for all her sins, was seldom singled out as the devil *ne plus ultra*.

This was especially true in the case of reform-minded Chinese. To characterize such persons as "Anglophiles" would be excessive: they did not condone England's past record in China; nor were they free of apprehension over her designs for the future.[31] They did, nevertheless, almost without exception, admire England enormously.

Part of the basis for this admiration was an idealized vision of British political and social conditions. British public servants, Wang T'ao wrote in his "Chi Ying-kuo cheng-chih" (Note on British government), were chosen by "recommendation and election" (*chien-chü*), and their good conduct and character had to be certified by a majority of the people of their native place before they could win office. Once in office, moreover, their treatment of the people was benevolent and just: "the officials never dare to use severe punishments, heavy fines, or tyrannical and excessive taxation. Nor dare they accept any bribery . . . or squeeze the blood and flesh of myriads of people in order to fill up their own pockets." The English people, for their part, were mostly public-spirited and law-abiding. Those who were suspected of violating the law were given a fair trial and, if convicted, were placed in a prison system the likes of which China had not seen since the Three Dynasties.

Important state matters, Wang went on, had to be discussed and approved by both houses of Parliament before action could be taken, and in questions of war and peace the whole nation was sounded out, to see where the majority of the people stood. "Therefore, the army is not mobilized in a precipitate manner, [and when the nation does go to war] there is strong popular support."

In praise of another aspect of the British political system, the monarchy, Wang indirectly censured the kindred Chinese institution: "The expenditure of the British ruler is a constantly fixed amount for every year; he does not dare to eat myriads of delicacies. His palaces are all very simple; he does not care for extravagance, and he has never had separate mansions and distant palaces linked with one another over scores of li. The king has only one queen, and besides her there is no concubine, and there has never been a multitude of three thousand beautiful women in the harem."

In the field of social welfare, too, the Chinese government got low marks in comparison with the British. Although the British people were taxed much more heavily than the Chinese, they bore it without resentment because the benefits they received were proportionally greater. Public works and charitable institutions were financed by the state. Government funds were provided for the support of widows, orphans, and old people, and efforts were made to find employment for the handicapped. The healthy quality of British society was not entirely owing to the government, according to Wang. The country's economic vitality (and consequent low rate of unemployment) and the cleansing influence of weekly religious worship were other contributing factors. British government, nevertheless, received the lion's share of the credit, and Wang was quick to liken it to Chinese government in the Golden Age of remote antiquity.[32]

If the benevolent character of England's government was one reason for Wang T'ao's high opinion of that country's political system, it was not the only reason. Nor, I would venture, was it the most important. At least as crucial to Wang and other Chinese reformers was the bearing of British political life on Britain's national power. In his "Chi Ying-kuo cheng-chih" Wang observed:

Commentators confine themselves to applauding the training of England's navy, the arrangement of her military affairs, the excellence of her firearms, and the pre-eminence of her armored ships of war as sufficient evidence of her power; the abundance of her industry, her quantities of coal and iron, and the geographical spread of her commerce as sufficient evidence of her wealth. They then proceed to regard these things as the groundwork of the nation, not realizing that these are but the external aspects (mo) of wealth and power, not the essential core (pen). The real strength of England lies in the fact that there is a sympathetic understanding between the governing and the governed, a close relationship between the ruler and the people.[33]

The fostering of a consolidated national spirit was of such paramount importance to Wang that, after spending the greater part of his adult life championing the introduction of Western learning and methods—sometimes making this an explicit precondition for the attainment of wealth and power[34]—we find him remarking in 1893: "If [Chinese leaders] truly desire to achieve wealth and power, they can succeed irrespective of whether they apply Chinese methods (Chung-fa) or Western methods. The primary thing is for the governing and the governed to be of one mind and united strength, the efforts of all devoted to realization of this objective."[35]

PRESCRIPTIONS FOR NATIONAL POWER

In addressing himself to the issue of national power, Wang T'ao gave full weight to purely military factors. He was a tireless advocate of improved training methods, a more realistic system of military examinations, better pay, the streamlining of China's army, the creation of a modern naval force, construction of an extensive network of defense installations, adoption of the most advanced military technology, and the rest.[36] At the same time, there are indications that Wang predicated China's military strengthening upon her economic development (see Chapter 7). Furthermore, Wang makes it abundantly clear that, in his scheme of things, the "management of military affairs" (*chih-ping*) as well as the development of the economy were both of secondary importance, as compared to the "governance of the people" (*chih-min*).[37] It was the latter that formed, to use his own phrase, the true "groundwork of the nation."

Although, as we have seen, there were other reformers in nineteenth-century China who felt that closer communication between ruler and subject would lead to better government, Wang T'ao was one of the first to argue that better government would result in a stronger nation. Wang was struck, in particular, by the sense of public-spiritedness and devotion to the common interest that he discerned in Western societies. He appreciated the role played by physical unification in Prussia's victory over France in 1870-1871,[38] but what really stirred him was the intangible force impelling German merchants in such faraway places as Jakarta and India to volunteer funds for the war effort.[39] It was this same quality, too, that excited his admiration in connection with France's prompt payment of her war indemnity: "How could she do it so quickly? Was it not levied entirely upon the people? The joy with which the people paid up, the pleasure which they took in performing their obligation, when it came to safeguarding the nation, is clear. In this matter the sentiments of the whole population were as one."[40]

The willingness of the German and French peoples to support their governments, in these instances, was ultimately an expression of confidence. Wang T'ao understood this very well. "Of all the great evils in the world," he wrote in 1893, "the greatest is when the people lack confidence in their rulers. Imagine the [Chinese] government today issuing a proclamation, saying: 'The state is now launching a large program of public works and would like to borrow ten million [taels] from the people, repayment guaranteed in ten years. You people, forward funds without delay.' Would anyone really respond? Yet, when a foreign bank issues share-certificates, people rush in droves [to buy them up] ... Alas! The people lack confidence in their own government, but they have confidence in foreigners."[41]

Since the people lacked confidence in their rulers, they could not be counted on to support them in time of crisis. China had the largest population in the world. But it remained a mere collection of individuals—"a heap of loose sand," to borrow one of Sun Yat-sen's favorite metaphors—instead of fusing into a single organism, a nation. Why was this so? Where was the sense of common interest, the spirit of national solidarity, so conspicuous in Western countries?

The comparison with the West was new. But the question, in one form or another, had been nagging Wang T'ao for a long time. Way back in the period of the Anglo-French military expeditions and the embroilment over Canton, in the late 1850's, Wang had chided China's governors-general and governors for their propensity to "see the gain or loss of the lone province of Kwangtung as having no relationship to the vital interests of the court, and the question of whether the court should resist the barbarians as having no relationship to the fortunes of the provinces."[42] Wang took up the same theme, a few years later, in the context of the Taiping Rebellion, this time, however, prescribing a cure for the malady, through selective revival of the political traditions of China's "feudal" age. The cohesiveness of the "feudal" system, he argued with seeming incongruity, lay in its diffusion of power, for when the throne shared its power and territory with influential families throughout the empire, the latter had a more palpable interest in the fate of the dynasty and were more apt to equate its survival with their own (see Chapter 2).

The incongruity was, of course, only seeming. In underscoring the connection between power-sharing and interest-community, Wang had, in fact, identified one of the prime sources of strength in any political system. Put in more homely terms, the greater the stake people have in a system, the harder they will fight to defend it. For *their* interests and the government's interests being indistinguishable, a threat to the government will be perceived by them as a threat to themselves.

The counterpart to greater sharing of power, on the part of the government, was greater participation and involvement, on the part of the people. This had ramifications in a number of fields. It implied a better-informed population, through the development of the daily newspaper and the spread of educational opportunity. In the sphere of economics, as we saw in the last chapter, it meant removal of restrictions on mercantile activity and encouraging merchants to venture into uncharted areas. It also entailed government sharing with the people of benefits derived from such new enterprises as mining, manufacture, railway and steamship construction, and the like.[43]

In the military realm, Wang was greatly impressed with the Western practice of "not distinguishing between soldiers and civilians" (*ping-min pu-fen*). Since all able-bodied men were regarded as potential soldiers or militiamen (*min-ping*), even a small country like England was able to maintain a sizable armed force. More important still was the great determination and morale of the militiamen, owing to the fact that they were called upon to fight in defense of their own homes and families. Wang T'ao proposed that the "nation-in-arms" concept be introduced in every city, town, and village of China. Sons and younger brothers would then be protecting fathers and elder brothers, and since the militia would train together with the regular troops, the latter would be less inclined to mistreat the people.[44]

For Wang T'ao, the most important application of the concept of popular participation was in the political field proper. The implications for national strength were drawn by him most explicitly in a letter written in late 1880, when China seemed to be on the verge of war with Russia:

The fact that the countries of Europe, though no match for China in territory and population, are able to have their way throughout the empire is attributable to the unanimity of sentiment prevailing between ruler and ruled and to the sharing of governmental power between the sovereign and the people. The fact that the Chinese people, though more numerous than the people of any other country, are nevertheless treated with contempt by powerful neighbors and ruthless enemies stems from the failure of communication between ruler and ruled and the distance separating the sovereign and the people. On top all power is lodged in the hands of one man, while below the common people are unable to participate in the formulation of policies. If the system of the Western nations prevailed in China, the entire population would rise up and come to China's defense.[45]

Elsewhere, Wang T'ao specifically identified parliamentary government as the means by which Western countries attained unanimity of sentiment between ruler and people:

Since every governmental matter, major or minor, must be deliberated upon by the parliament before action can be taken, there is no tyranny and oppression at home and they are able to safeguard [their position] abroad; in ordinary times they engage energetically in trade and business, while in time of crisis they go all out in support of the public interest ... No different when they have gone far across the seas than they are within the confines of their own borders, they remain mindful of the sentiments binding a ruler and his people (*chün-min chih hsin*) and always aspire to advance their countries' fortunes.[46]

Again, we see the intimate connection that existed in Wang T'ao's mind between good government and national power. Wang was a great admirer of parliamentary government. Yet, as intimated in the piece just cited, it was not out of any profound commitment to democracy or liberal values that he found this form of government praiseworthy. He found it praiseworthy because it fostered the solidarity of ruler and ruled that he believed to be the taproot of Western strength. This pattern of reasoning was commonly encountered in the arguments for constitutionalism advanced by Japanese in the 1870's. Later on it became familiar in China also, as people like Yen Fu stressed the integral relationship between individual freedom and national power in the West.

Was this a gross misunderstanding of the noblest features of the Western political tradition? A failure of transcultural communication grounded in plain ignorance? Not really. Benjamin Schwartz has argued, in Yen Fu's case, that it was more a difference of perspective, a different problem context that caused Yen to discern in Western thought new logical connections. New, but not untenable.[47] I would make the same claim for Wang T'ao. Wang was not versed in Western thought. But had he been, I suspect it would have made little difference. What was crucially important was the Chinese problem context out of which Wang and Yen operated. The central issue, for both men, was not how to justify maximal individual liberty, as an end in itself or as a means to the fullest possible development of the individual personality. Rather, it was how best to generate Chinese national strength. The Western issue of the individual versus the state was not for export. The Chinese issue was China versus the West.

WANG T'AO AND EARLY CHINESE NATIONALISM

In this book I have drawn attention to several facets of Wang T'ao's thinking that seem to me to signal an early expression of Chinese nationalism. One such facet, discussed in Chapter 3 and elsewhere, was Wang's abandonment of the old *t'ien-hsia* outlook (China qua world) and his acceptance of a more relativistic view of China's place in the world (China qua nation, China qua one version of civilization among several possible versions). Along with this shift in world view came a new stress on competition and rivalry among national units, seen most clearly in Wang's use of the Spring and Autumn and Warring States metaphors to characterize European interstate relations (Chapter 4) and in the vigorously competitive outlook he adopted in economic matters (Chapter 7). The accent on competition fed directly into Wang's emphatic commitment to wealth and power—a facet of incipient nationalism which he shared with growing numbers of Chinese after 1870. Wealth and power were by definition relative goals, measurable only within a comparative—and hence competitive—frame of reference. Their attainment, Wang T'ao was convinced, hinged most decisively on the creation of a new kind of relationship between the Chinese people and their leaders—a relationship marked, above all, by a sense of common interest and identity.

Politically, this translated into a sense of nationhood. Kuo Sung-tao had once expressed amazement at the palpable lack of indignation felt by his countrymen against the Western importation of opium.[48] To Liang Ch'i-ch'ao, some decades later, "it seemed as though the Chinese could look with equanimity on foreign invasion."[49] One could, in fact, generalize that the humiliations inflicted on China a hundred years ago seem to have been experienced more vividly in the twentieth century than at the time of infliction. An awareness of nationhood had to develop before infringements on national sovereignty could awaken a sense of shame.

In this area, as in so many others, Wang T'ao stood at some distance from his contemporaries. During the early part of his career, his antagonism to the West had been more or less unqualified. This phase, however, did not last very long, and as Wang's education in things Western proceeded, he became at once more discriminating in his resentments and more sensitive to the specific issue of national sovereignty and control. This sensitivity was frequently expressed in response to tangible humiliations or infringements on Chinese sovereignty. Thus, outraged at the inhumanity of the coolie traffic centering at Macao, Wang proposed detailed measures for ending it and urged that the Tsungli Yamen negotiate with Portugal for the return of Macao to Chinese jurisdiction.[50] Wang was also adamant in opposing the treaty restrictions on China's tariff autonomy, as we have seen. And he was one of the first to call for the abolition of extraterritoriality, a practice which, he said, impinged directly on the "authority of the nation" (*kuo-chia chih ch'üan*) and was to be found only in China, Japan, and Turkey—not among the Europeans themselves.[5 1]

In the final analysis, though, Wang T'ao realized that all proposals for reducing foreign control and reasserting Chinese sovereignty would amount to nothing unless China's leaders adopted a new way of thinking. "The fact," he wrote in 1880, "that nowadays powerful neighbors and ruthless enemies continually eye us from all sides is actually a blessing for China and not a misfortune. This is just the thing we need to stimulate our determination to forge ahead . . . For if we can become ashamed at not being as good as the Western nations (*ch'ih pu jo Hsi-kuo*), it may yet be possible for us to do something about it."[5 2] Sixteen years later, in his preface to Young J. Allen's book on the Sino-Japanese War, Wang again voiced the hope that the sense of shame, aroused now by her humiliating defeat at the hands of tiny Japan, would awaken China to the need for fundamental change.[5 3]

Wang T'ao was no rabid nationalist. A rabid, uncompromising nationalist would never praise British imperialism as benign imperialism, in contrast to the more malignant strain carried by France. Nor would he be likely to write, as Wang did in 1892, an essay in honor of Columbus, to mark China's contribution to the fourth centennial celebrations of the discovery of America.[5 4] Wang T'ao's nationalism was a cosmopolitan, openminded nationalism— as, in a sense, it had to be. For, in moving toward a nationalistic outlook, Wang was responding not just to the West, but also to other Chinese responses to the West. Virulent, unyielding hostility to the West, in Wang's day, was the special mark of the ultraconservative, the man who rejected reform and modernization outright. As long as ultraconservatism remained a powerful force, it was imperative that anyone committed to modernization separate himself decisively from the ultraconservative stance. Only when all-out resistance to change atrophied, as it did in the twentieth century, would Chinese nationalism inherit its venom.

I have referred to Wang T'ao's outlook as incipient or protonationalism. It may be helpful, at this point, to clarify my use of these terms. There is little difficulty in distinguishing Wang's attitude from the kind of antiforeignism generally exhibited by educated Chinese in the second half of the nineteenth century. This antiforeignism sprang from an overriding sense of cultural superiority. Its characteristic mode of expression was contempt, and it stood opposed to virtually all forms of Western influence. Wang T'ao, in sharp contrast, was generous enough to concede that there were important respects—not just guns and ships—in which China was visibly inferior to the West. The dominant feeling this recognition left him with was shame, not contempt. Indeed, it was the desire to eradicate the sources of this shame that impelled Wang to become a persuasive advocate of limited "Westerniza-tion." For it was not Western influence that Wang opposed, but Western control.[55] He understood that China would have to accept something of Western culture before she could ever rid herself of the West.

Although many antiforeign Chinese communicated their con-tempt for the West by icy indifference, there was another variety of xenophobe in the nineteenth century who was of a much more militant cast. Bellicose by nature and ever ready in a crisis to sound the call to arms, his ultraconservatism was distinguished by an almost mystical faith in the capacity of an aroused Chinese people to overcome the barbarian and his tricky weapons. Benja-min Schwartz has aptly described this current of thought as "muscular Confucianism."[56] Despite its ultraconservative orienta-tion, there seems to be a considerable community of spirit between it and some of the more righteously pugnacious speci-mens of Chinese Communist writing.

The difference between this type of xenophobe and Wang T'ao was not just a matter of style. Wang, although quick to raise his voice against any incursions on Chinese sovereignty, had a healthy respect for Western power and, like Kuo Sung-tao, invariably counseled moderation and reliance on diplomacy in situations where war with the West threatened.[57] Furthermore, while it is true that Wang T'ao attached great importance to popular spirit and determination, he saw such qualities as essential preconditions for Chinese modernization. This was a far cry from the position of his more militantly xenophobic peers, who were convinced that as long as the minds of the people were steadfast China could dispense with modernization altogether.

Clearly Wang T'ao left mere antiforeignism way behind. But did he become a modern nationalist in the fullest sense of the word? This question is harder to answer. If mature nationalism requires a conscious rejection of the whole of "tradition," Wang would certainly not qualify. But neither would Sun Yat-sen, Chiang Kai-shek, or a host of other twentieth-century figures who are generally regarded as nationalists. Schwartz discards this rather inflexible formula and substitutes a more reasonable one based on relative priorities. "Where the commitment to the preservation and advancement of the societal entity known as the nation takes priority over the commitment to all other values and beliefs," he tells us, "where other values and beliefs are judged in terms of their relevance to this end rather than vice versa, nationalism in a precise sense is already on the scene."[58]

Does Wang T'ao qualify by this definition? Almost. It has been said of Wang that, for all his independence of mind, his thought followed the same basic pattern as that of Feng Kuei-fen and Chang Chih-tung; that is, like them, he championed the introduction of Western learning less because he prized it for its own sake than because he believed it necessary for the preservation of ultimate Chinese values.[59] Parts of Wang's writings support this assessment; substantial parts do not. We are left, in any case, with the rubbery problem of identifying the Chinese values that for Wang T'ao were ultimate. If these values were at bottom Confucian, it would perhaps be fair to group Wang with Feng and Chang. But if Wang's primary commitment was to the advancement of the Chinese nation, if the goals of wealth and power had become ends for him instead of means, it would bring him much closer to nationalism in Schwartz's sense.

The trouble with Schwartz's definition, for our purposes, is that it refers to the end point of a process, the point at which a new commitment has been consciously articulated and nationalism "in a precise sense" has emerged. Wang T'ao, clearly, had not reached such a point. Wang never faced the problem of priorities head-on and certainly he was not prepared to loudly proclaim: "My flag, with or without Confucianism." Wang was, on the other hand, deeply engaged in the process of value reorientation. While others were maintaining that China must adopt new means to preserve an old faith, Wang T'ao, unobtrusively, maybe even unconsciously, suggested that the faith itself had to be altered to ensure the survival of China. Wang's conception of Confucius as a potential reformer was part of this reappraisal. Equally important was his de-Sinification of *tao*, expressed in the conviction that *tao* was the common property of civilized men all over.[60] However one chooses to assess the validity of these changes, in terms of the objective fate of Confucianism, there is no question that, in Wang T'ao's mind, they removed the grounds for conflict between a powerful China and a Confucian China: a *truly* Confucian China would be a powerful China too. In this admittedly subjective sense, Wang came about as near as one could come in modern Chinese history to being that most improbable of hybrids, a Confucian nationalist.

PART IV. LITTORAL AND HINTERLAND

IN MODERN CHINESE HISTORY

PROLOGUE

The decision to study the life and thinking of a man like Wang T'ao deserves explicit justification. Some would maintain that a life—any life—is significant just because it happened. Human existence justifies itself. In a rigorously individual-centered historical approach, I suppose this would be true. But where we are principally concerned, as I am in this book, with the history of a country, something else is necessary. My main interest is less in Wang T'ao than in what Wang T'ao tells me about modern China. If Wang is not instructive in this larger-than-Wang sense, his life, for my purposes, is reduced in importance.

One of the ways in which a life may acquire larger meaning is through influence on other lives. The range of variation here is of course great, stretching from the individual who influences events only incrementally all the way to the man—a Jesus or a Mao— whose life (presumably) changes the course of history. The case for the latter has to be built with extreme caution, as it involves the sticky methodological problem—ultimately intractable—of determining what would have been different had the "great man" never lived. We may *presume* that modern Chinese history would have run a different course had Mao Tse-tung not been a part of it.

But we cannot prove this. Nor can we determine how different it would have been.

A difficulty of another sort arises in the case of the individual whose influence on history is incremental. Here the problem is one of visibility. It is perfectly plausible to argue that, within limits set by the physical environment (biological, geographical, and so forth), history is neither more nor less than the sum total of individual influences. Social classes do not have positions on issues. Political parties do not formulate decisions. Institutions do not act. It is the individuals comprising these larger groupings who are the ultimate makers of events. The individual role, however, is not always accessible to the public eye, and even when it is, it is often so imperceptible that it cannot be "tracked." Historical change takes place. We know that influence has been exerted. But we are unable to follow the process.

We are unable, that is, to reconstruct the process by which one life influences another and the sum total of individual lives translates into collective historical experience. Faced with this difficulty, many historians still find it profitable, in their quest for insight into the aggregate experience, to study the life of a single individual. This individual need not be a person of great influence. Indeed, his influence—whatever its extent—may have been quite invisible. The only requirement, really, is that his biographical development focus on problems or embody patterns which, in some fashion, are discernible in other individuals as well. In this way, even though his role as a *maker* of history may have been small, his value as an *experiencer* of history becomes potentially great.

Wang T'ao is a case in point. Scholars judge Wang to have been a probable influence upon the thinking of Sun Yat-sen, K'ang Yu-wei, Cheng Kuan-ying, Wu T'ing-fang, and others. Yet, I have not taken pains to trace this influence, because I am convinced that, if (like laboratory scientists) we could isolate Wang out from modern Chinese history, not very much would be changed. It is not, in other words, for his actual shaping of the larger picture that Wang T'ao is important to the historian. His importance lies in his capacity, as an individual human being with thoughts and feelings, to throw light on this picture, to articulate what it was like to be part of it.

Building on this premise, my point of departure in the first three sections of this book has been essentially biographical. That is, I have sought, through detailed exploration of Wang T'ao's life and mind, to illuminate processes of change which many Chinese (albeit each in his own way) experienced in the last century. In Part IV, I should like to try a somewhat different approach, known more and more commonly among historians as prosopography or collective biography.* [1] As just suggested, Wang T'ao, for all his individuality, was not unique. There were other people in the China of his day who were, in important respects, like him. And if, by studying these people as a group, we can define the characteristics they held in common, insights which Wang T'ao's life alone might offer only in a very tentative way may be placed on a more solid footing.

One of the great, unworked themes in modern Chinese history has been the polarity between littoral and hinterland. This polarity can probably be traced to the sixteenth century, if not earlier. (Which is one reason why I use the term "littoral" instead of "treaty port"; another reason is that Hong Kong, while becoming an important part of the littoral culture, was not a treaty port.) The historic event that lay behind the creation of the littoral-hinterland polarity was the emergence, from about 1500 on, of a maritime civilization of global embrace. As inhabitants of the southeastern littoral of China became more and more deeply involved in this new civilization, their identification with the culture of the Chinese hinterland progressively weakened.[2]

The contrast between littoral and hinterland became increasingly pronounced after 1842, as Western beachheads were established, first, on the China coast, and later, along the Yangtze. In and around these beachheads, a culture grew up which was more commercial than agricultural in its economic foundations, more modern than traditional in its administrative and social arrange-

---

*This final part of the book is tentative and exploratory in nature, as much a beginning as an ending. I hope to develop the ideas presented more fully in the future.

ments, more Western (Christian) than Chinese (Confucian) in its intellectual bearing, and more outward- than inward-looking in its general global orientation and involvement. The center of gravity of Chinese civilization remained firmly planted in the hinterland. But, with the passage of time, the littoral became increasingly important as a stimulus to hinterland change—a "starter" in the bacteriological sense—and some of the foremost actors in modern Chinese history were products of the new coastal-riverine culture.

In probing the significance of these individuals and their interaction with representatives of the hinterland culture, I find it helpful to postulate a general framework for the analysis of cultural change. Sweeping cultural change, as a rule, takes place in two phases. The first phase belongs to the pioneers. These are the individuals who, through their writings and their activities, transform what was once totally strange into something a little less strange, gradually desensitizing people to the newness of the new, making it less conspicuous, more palatable. At some point, the culture then moves into a second phase, in which broad acceptance is given to changes that a short time before would have been acceptable only on the acculturated fringes. This stage is dominated by the legitimizers—people who have been converted to the need for deep-seated change but who insist, all the while, that such change be accompanied by some form of indigenous validation.

In the context of modern Chinese history, this two-phase process assumes the form of a succession of littoral assaults upon the hinterland, followed in each instance by hinterland attempts to legitimize the assaults through Sinicization. The first assault was the Taiping Rebellion. In the course of being Sinicized,[3] however, the Taipings lost their original innovating spirit. They began to look less like Christian revolutionaries and more like traditional Chinese rebels. It was different in the case of the second assault, that of the pioneer reformers (defined here as those reformers, or reform-minded modernizers, who were active or first achieved prominence prior to 1890). The legitimation of this assault was carried out, initially, by the self-strengthening officials and, later on, by the hinterland reformers of the 1890's, reaching a peak in the Reform Movement of 1898. The leader of that movement, K'ang Yu-wei, was successful insofar as he preserved the reform impetus of the littoral while justifying it in hinterland (Confucian) terms. Where K'ang failed was in the realm of execution. The final assault from the littoral was Sun Yat-sen's revolutionary movement. Its legitimizing phase, successful both in conception and in execution, was dominated by the figure of Mao Tse-tung.

So formulated, this sequence of assaults and legitimations is overly schematic and probably misleading. I would not want to suggest, for example, that all pioneer reformers and revolutionaries were products of the littoral or that the hinterland was the only possible source of legitimation. Nor do I wish to convey an idea of innovation and legitimation as totally severable processes or of K'ang Yu-wei and Mao Tse-tung as mere legitimizers of change, unimportant as innovators.*

The qualifications one can think of are endless. And yet the broad picture still stands. We have, in modern Chinese history, two largely separate and distinct cultural environments evolving side by side. Although to a high degree self-contained, these two environments interacted in strategic ways, each performing essential functions over time. In the nineteenth century, and for a while in the twentieth, the littoral assumed primary responsibility for the pioneering of change, the hinterland for its validation. Moreover, as long as neither could do what the other did (or at least not as well), this symbiotic relationship between the two cultures persisted. But once the hinterland, in addition to legitimizing change, also became the principal locus of innovation, the littoral atrophied. Shanghai and Canton, in the second half of the twentieth century, are still there, and they will always be "littoral" in a geographical and economic sense. Culturally, however, they have been absorbed into a new Chinese hinterland.

*The whole question of radicalism in this context is intriguing. Who was the more radical: K'ang Yu-wei or Yung Wing? Mao Tse-tung or Sun Yat-sen? My choices, unhesitatingly, are K'ang and Mao, not because they were "newer" than Yung and Sun (see my discussion of the ambiguity of the label "new" in the Prologue to Part I), but because they spearheaded important attempts to integrate change with tradition (the primary mechanism for doing this, in each instance, being the identification and reinterpretation of traditions which, although authentically Chinese, had strongly unorthodox affiliations). Perhaps one can generalize that the more acculturated one became in modern China, the less chance one had to generate radical change. For acculturation, in making a person newer, also made him more remote from the native scene.

9

THE PIONEER REFORMERS

AND THE LITTORAL

Littoral and hinterland, as cultural types, represent endpoles of a continuum. If one were to locate on this continuum the three leading figures in the modern Chinese revolution, Mao Tse-tung would appear on the hinterland end, Sun Yat-sen on the littoral end, and Chiang Kai-shek somewhere in between. Mao and Sun come pretty close to being classic articulations of their respective types; Chiang is a composite, partaking of both hinterland and littoral characteristics.

The pioneer reformers break down into comparable subtypes, though as a group their center of gravity tends to be farther over on the littoral end of the continuum.[1] On the extreme littoral we find such individuals as Yung Wing, Ho Kai, Tong King-sing, and Wu T'ing-fang—the first two completely deracinated, the last two substantially so. Next we have a group of reformers whose ties to the littoral were strong but who could also boast of a solid background in Chinese learning and culture. In this category would be placed people like Wang T'ao, Cheng Kuan-ying, Ma Chien-chung, and Ma Liang. Finally, there was a minority of pioneer reformers who, although they had significant contacts with the littoral or with the West directly (or with the West indirectly through the agency of Japan), were in basic respects products of the Chinese hinterland. Feng Kuei-fen, Hsüeh Fu-ch'eng, Huang Tsun-hsien, and Kuo Sung-tao were outstanding examples of this type.

Although there were other pioneer reformers besides the twelve above, scholars would probably agree that, add or subtract a name or two, these include most of the important ones. Using their careers as case material, I should like, in this final chapter, to try to define the specific ways in which their reformism was conditioned by the littoral and, on a somewhat more general plane, the role played by the littoral as an agent of change in nineteenth-century China. For purposes of analysis, the pioneer reformers will be divided into two subgroups: those whose primary involvement (at least as adults) was with the littoral (the first eight men) and those whose main identification was with the hinterland (the last four).

PIONEER REFORMERS OF THE LITTORAL

Yung Wing (Jung Hung, 1828-1912). A native of Hsiang-shan hsien, Kwangtung, Yung as a boy received a thoroughly Christian education, first at a school operated by the wife of the Prussian missionary, Karl Gützlaff, and later (1841-1847) at the Morrison Education Society school in Macao and Hong Kong. The head teacher at the Morrison school was an American missionary, Samuel R. Brown,[2] and when Brown returned to the United States in 1847 he took Yung and two fellow students with him.[3] After studying for several years at Monson Academy in Monson, Massachusetts, Yung entered Yale. He received his degree in 1854, becoming the first Chinese graduate of an American university.

In the same year, Yung Wing, now a naturalized American citizen, returned to China, where for the next decade he worked at a variety of jobs (secretary to Peter Parker, interpreter-translator, tea merchant) in Canton, Hong Kong, and Shanghai. In 1864 he again went to the United States, commissioned by Tseng Kuo-fan to buy machinery for what was to become the Kiangnan Arsenal. As reward for his efforts, Yung in 1867 was made an official of the fourth rank.

Yung Wing is best known for his initiation and promotion of a project to educate Chinese youths in the United States. With the support of Tseng, Li Hung-chang, and Ting Jih-ch'ang, the project got under way in 1872, with Yung as assistant commissioner. By the time this pathbreaking educational venture was terminated (1881)—a casualty partly of conservative anxiety over the excessive Americanization of the students and partly, it would appear, of Chinese bureaucratic infighting—over a hundred Chinese had received substantial training in a variety of technical areas.

While in America supervising the educational mission, Yung Wing was named associate minister to Washington and in 1878 took part in the opening of the first Chinese legation in the United States. At some point (possibly while still at the Morrison school) he became a convert to Christianity and in 1875 he married an American woman. After a brief spell in China in the early 1880's, Yung settled down in Hartford. In 1895, however, he returned once more to his native land, at Chang Chih-tung's invitation. During the next few years he was an active supporter of the reform movement and also became involved in several new modernizing schemes. None of these bore fruit, though, and in 1902 Yung went back to America.[4]

Ho Kai (Ho Ch'i, 1859-1914). Ho Kai, a native of Nan-hai hsien, Kwangtung, was the son of Ho Fu-t'ang (Ho Chin-shan), a businessman and former preacher affiliated with the Hong Kong branch of the London Missionary Society (LMS). After preparatory education at the Government Central School in Hong Kong, Ho continued his studies in Great Britain at Aberdeen University, St. Thomas' Medical and Surgical College, and Lincoln's Inn. Returning to Hong Kong in 1882, with degrees in both law and medicine and an English wife (Alice Walkden), Ho embarked on a long and distinguished career as barrister, public official, teacher, philanthropist, and reformer.

The most important of Ho's philanthropic endeavors was the founding of the Alice Memorial Hospital (completed in 1887), an institution providing free care for Chinese patients. Named after Ho's deceased wife and, according to one source, largely funded with the inheritance she left him, the hospital was administered and controlled (on Ho's own stipulation) by the LMS. Ho was also the moving force behind the establishment of the College of

Medicine for Chinese in Hong Kong, which was attached to the hospital and served as the nucleus of the University of Hong Kong. Ho Kai taught physiology and medical jurisprudence at the College, where he had as one of his more promising students the future revolutionary, Sun Yat-sen.

The British colony's most prominent Chinese resident, Ho Kai served three terms on the Hong Kong Legislative Council (1890-1914) and took part in many other civic activities. In recognition of his services, he received from the British government the coveted honor of being named Companion of the Order of St. Michael and St. George and in 1912 was knighted.

Ho Kai's career as a political reformer in the larger Chinese context was launched in 1887 with an attack on the self-strengthening movement which, in one scholar's view, was so trenchant that "it stands as a symbolic turning point in the reform movement."[5] Ho's essays on reform were all written in collaboration with Hu Li-yüan.[6] Their principal themes were the importance of developing Chinese commerce and the need for basic governmental changes, including the introduction of some form of parliamentary system.[7]

Tong King-sing (T'ang Ching-hsing, T'ang T'ing-shu, Tong Chik, T'ang Chieh, 1832-1892). Born in Hsiang-shan hsien, Kwangtung, Tong, like his lifelong friend Yung Wing, was early immersed in a Christian environment at the Morrison Education Society school. After studying at the school for six years (1842-1848), he was enrolled in another missionary institution in Hong Kong. During the early and middle 1850's Tong, having acquired an excellent command of English, became an interpreter for the Hong Kong government. In 1858 he took up duties as interpreter and clerk with the Shanghai Maritime Customs. He also found time to publish (1862) a Chinese-English phrase book to assist Cantonese merchants in their transactions with foreigners. From 1863 to 1873 Tong was Shanghai comprador for the British firm of Jardine, Matheson, and Company. While serving in this capacity, he engaged in numerous investment activities of his own and in 1872 was elected a director of Jardine's China Coast Steam Navigation Company.

Tong King-sing's intimate knowledge of the shipping business attracted the notice of Li Hung-chang, and soon after the China Merchants Steam Navigation Company was formed Li invited Tong to serve as its manager (1873-1884). Tong was also the principal organizer of the Kaiping Mining Company and served as the company's director from 1877 until his death in 1892. In 1874 Tong and Yung Wing founded *Hui-pao*, one of the earliest Chinese-owned newspapers. Tong thus had a leading hand in a number of China's pioneering modern-style enterprises. His knowledge of the West was extended by a tour of Europe in 1883, and he was much admired by the foreigners of the day for his ability, integrity, and determination to see China modernize along Western lines.[8]

Wu T'ing-fang (Ng Choy, 1842-1922). Although born in Singapore, Wu's ancestral home was Hsin-hui, Kwangtung, and his merchant father moved the family back to China when Wu was only three years old. Growing up in a suburb of Canton, Wu's early education was in the traditional Chinese curriculum. Finding this uninspiring, however, he began to study English at a mission hall near his home and six months later (at the age of thirteen) entered St. Paul's College in Hong Kong. Although St. Paul's had been founded by the Church Missionary Society some years earlier as a theological college, its curriculum had become quite secularized and during his four years at the school Wu was able to concentrate on English, mathematics, and natural science.

From 1859, the year of his graduation, until 1874, Wu worked as a translator at the Hong Kong Police Court. In 1860 he helped found the *Chung-ngoi san-po (Chung-wai hsin-pao)*, the first Chinese-language daily, and for some time thereafter shouldered the paper's editorial responsibilities. In the early 1870's Wu took part in the establishment of at least two other Chinese-language newspapers, including (as we have seen) Wang T'ao's *Tsun-wan yat-po*.

In 1874 Wu T'ing-fang went to London to study law. Three years later, after becoming China's first barrister, he returned to Hong Kong to launch what soon turned into a highly successful legal career. The governor of the colony appointed Wu to the post of acting magistrate and, in 1880, to membership on the Legislative Council—both firsts for Chinese in Hong Kong.

The great turning point in Wu T'ing-fang's career came in 1882 when he left Hong Kong to join Li Hung-chang's staff. In the fourteen years that Wu spent working under Li, he tried with little success to push the governor-general in the direction of major institutional reform. Wu's principal contributions to Li's operations were in the fields of law, diplomacy, and railway management. He assisted in the negotiations terminating the Sino-French and Sino-Japanese Wars and in 1887 was appointed director of the China Railway Company, which was charged with the construction of a rail line between Tientsin and T'ang-ku. Wu became the manager of the line upon its completion.

The autonomous phase of Wu T'ing-fang's public career began in 1897 with his appointment as minister to the United States, Spain, and Peru. After his recall in 1902 Wu became an active promoter of legal reform. When the court in Peking refused to consider sweeping changes in Chinese criminal procedures, however, he resigned his post as vice-president of the Board of Punishments. Although he served once again as minister to Washington (1907-1909), by the end of his term Wu's disillusionment with the Ch'ing had become complete and the Wuchang revolt found him solidly in the revolutionary camp. During the first decade of the Republic Wu was a close follower of Sun Yat-sen and held a number of major offices.

As a reformer, Wu T'ing-fang was a consistent champion of political liberalism combined with cultural conservatism. He was also a bug on physical fitness and wrote a book entitled *Yen-shou hsin-fa* (New methods for extending life). In his later years Wu was known to Westerners as a baptized Christian and there is some reason to believe that he entered the church as a youth. The sources, however, do not speak clearly on this point, and all we can say with certainty is that Wu's connections with Christianity were close. His wife, who was the sister of Ho Kai, was a devout Christian all her life.[9]

Cheng Kuan-ying (1842-1923). Born in Hsiang-shan hsien, Kwangtung, Cheng came from a family of moderate means. His father was a schoolteacher and his early education was geared to the examinations. At the age of seventeen, having failed to acquire the *hsiu-ts'ai* degree, he moved to Shanghai to enter trade. In

Shanghai he studied English with an uncle and later with John Fryer. For many years beginning in 1860 Cheng worked as a comprador for two leading British firms, Dent and Company and Butterfield and Swire. Cheng's fund-raising activities in connection with famine relief in Shansi in 1878-1879 brought him to the attention of Li Hung-chang, who asked him to inaugurate the first Chinese-owned cotton mill, the Shanghai Cotton Cloth Mill. Li also made Cheng a manager of the Shanghai branch of the China Merchants Company in 1882. Cheng left the company two years later, but rejoined it in 1892 and was elected in 1907 to its first board of directors. Over the years Cheng also served as manager of several other *kuan-tu shang-pan* enterprises, including the Imperial Telegraph Administration, the Hanyang Ironworks, and the Kwangtung section of the Canton-Hankow railroad. Like Tong King-sing, Cheng acquired official rank by purchase, eventually becoming a taotai.

Better educated and more intellectually-disposed than most compradors, Cheng Kuan-ying was an avid reader of missionary literature on reform, and the humanitarian sentiments pervading his own writings were very likely of Christian provenance. Cheng's essays on reform, emphasizing institutional change and commercial development, were initially published (probably in 1880) under the title *I-yen* (Easy words). A much larger and more famous work, *Sheng-shih wei-yen* (Warnings to a prosperous age), first appeared around 1893 and so impressed the Kuang-hsü Emperor that he ordered it reprinted for official distribution.[10]

Ma Chien-chung (1844-1900). A native of Tan-t'u hsien, Kiangsu, Ma Chien-chung was born into a scholarly Catholic family which traced its intellectual descent to the great Sung scholar, Ma Tuan-lin, and its religious heritage to the days of Ricci. Although his formal education was carried on in Jesuit schools in Shanghai (where he acquired an early mastery of French, Greek, and Latin), he also received a solid grounding in the Chinese classical tradition. In 1877 Li Hung-chang, having learned of Ma's talents, sent him to France along with a group of students studying ship construction. While in Paris, Ma studied government and international law at the École Libre des Sciences Politiques. In 1878 he became the first

Chinese to receive the baccalaureate and in the following year he was awarded the licentiate by the Faculté de Droit of the Université de Paris.

Back in China, in the early 1880's, Ma Chien-chung quickly became one of the principal foreign affairs experts on Li Hung-chang's staff, performing such a varied assortment of tasks that Cordier dubbed him "un véritable Maître Jacques." In 1881-1882 Ma undertook diplomatic missions for Li in India and Korea. From 1884 to 1891 he served as assistant manager of the China Merchants Company. He went with Li to Shimonoseki in 1895 and also on his trip around the world the following year. The last period of Ma's life was spent in the preparation of his influential grammatical study, *Ma-shih wen-t'ung* (Mr. Ma's grammar; 1904), described by a modern linguist as "the first Chinese grammar in the Western sense of the word."[1 1]

Ma Liang (Ma Hsiang-po, 1840-1939). The elder brother of Ma Chien-chung, Ma Liang was the more religious of the two. After completing his theological studies and probation, he became a Jesuit priest in 1870; however, six years later, as a result of conflicts with his superiors, he returned to lay life. During the 1870's Ma served as principal of the Jesuit College of Ignatius in Shanghai, where he had studied as a boy. Around this time, he also developed a serious interest in Western science and mathematics and did some translation work.

After leaving the priesthood, Ma Liang began the second of his many careers—this one as an adviser on technological, financial, and diplomatic matters to prominent officials. In the late 1870's he served for a time as director of a machine factory in Shantung; at the request of Li Hung-chang he also looked into that province's mining affairs. In Tokyo in 1882, as counselor of the Chinese legation, Ma met Itō Hirobumi and began to study Japanese. Before long, however, Li Hung-chang sent him to Korea to help the Korean government reform its administration and army. After his brother's assignment to the China Merchants Company, Ma Liang served the company in a number of capacities, including that of auditor. At the invitation of Governor Liu Ming-ch'uan, he then went to Taiwan, where in 1886 he advanced a plan for the island's development through foreign financial assistance. After returning to the mainland, he was sent by Li Hung-chang to the United States to negotiate a loan. The Ch'ing government, however, blocked both the loan and the Taiwan development project.

From 1887, the year of his arrival back in China, until 1896, Ma Liang concentrated on the study of science. His only significant official role during this period appears to have been a stint as Chinese consul at Nagasaki in 1892. In 1896 he became associated with Liang Ch'i-ch'ao, whose rise to prominence was in part owing to Ma and his brother. Shortly after the turn of the century Ma Liang was instrumental in the founding of Aurora Academy (later Aurora University) and, with Yen Fu, Fu-tan Academy, and served for a time as principal at both schools. Ma's active involvement in Chinese educational, political, and religious affairs extended well into the twentieth century.[1][2]

COMMON CAREER PATTERNS AND WORLD OUTLOOKS

"Had he been born as a member of the governing class in Japan," Hu Shih once wrote of Wang T'ao, "he could have easily made himself an Ito, an Okubo, an Okuma, or at least a Saigo."[1][3] Hu's two-edged remark, praising Wang and damning the society that was unable to use him, serves as a fitting characterization of the littoral reformers in general and the plight in which they found themselves in nineteenth-century China. All of these men were extraordinarily gifted, yet none was able to convert his abilities into power and influence in the Chinese context. Quite to the contrary, it seems that the closer they got to the sources of power, the more circumscribed they became as reformers. Power and innovation, in the late Ch'ing, were like fire and water.[1][4]

Although the backgrounds, experiences, and outlooks of the reformers in our sample diverge in particulars, on a more general plane they exhibit a high degree of uniformity. Most striking, perhaps, is the presence in each instance of an uninhibited willingness to innovate, to pioneer, to do the unconventional thing. Half of the group received degrees from foreign universities and of the remaining four all but Cheng Kuan-ying visited the West for extended periods before 1890. With the partial exception of Wang T'ao, all had a speaking knowledge of a European tongue, and at least six (Ho Kai, Yung Wing, Wu T'ing-fang, Tong King-sing, and the two Mas) could read one or more Western languages fluently.[15] Moreover, the occupations the littoral reformers engaged in at one time or another—journalism, law, the priesthood, modern enterprise, diplomatic service abroad—were, for the most part, unheard-of in China prior to the Opium War. Indeed, it would scarcely be an exaggeration to say that the career patterns of these men evoked the China of the 1920's and 1930's more than that of the nineteenth century.

One exception to this was the multiple careerism of the littoral reformers, which contrasted with the growing tendency toward occupational specialization exhibited by Western-educated Chinese of the twentieth century. As in most frontier-like situations, there was an acute shortage of certain kinds of human resources in nineteenth-century China. People who had these resources were, therefore, called upon to play a much wider assortment of roles than would have been the case in a more highly developed context. This tendency was especially pronounced in a society where innovation was not accepted as a positive value. In such a society, modern expertise was defined more as a mental state—a matter of outlook—than as a product of specialized training, and the mere fact of being "modern-spirited" was often enough to qualify one for the gamut of modernizing tasks.

To be "modern-spirited" in the nineteenth century meant (in the sense in which I am using it) to be aware of the unprecedented character of the situation confronting China and receptive to the idea of fundamental change ("modernization") as the only way to respond to this situation effectively. All of the littoral reformers were modern-spirited in this sense. They were tireless promoters, to a man, of the blessings of Western technology. Ma Liang, Yung Wing, Cheng Kuan-ying, and Wang T'ao championed education in modern science. Wu T'ing-fang and Ho Kai were prominent advocates of legal reform. Cheng Kuan-ying, Ho Kai, Wang T'ao, and Wu T'ing-fang evinced an early enthusiasm for representative political institutions. And practically all of the littoral reformers were actively involved in the establishment of China's modern press.[16]

Implicit in the idea of fundamental change was a new vision of

China's relationship to the rest of the world. The new world view shared by the reformers of the littoral had no place for outworn assumptions of Chinese superiority and self-sufficiency. Instead, it was predicated on earnest respect for Western civilization and a newfound willingness to see the civilization of China substantially transformed. The two most characteristic expressions of this new world view were an enthusiastic appreciation of the benefits to be derived from foreign commerce and, on the political side, a growing acceptance of nationalistic premises. Insofar as its two focal points were trade and nationalism, it seems like a mirror image of the contemporary Western world view, and to some extent no doubt it was. In one basic respect, however, it was not. The emerging world view of modern China incorporated, from the outset, a strong undercurrent of resentment and outrage—the sense, sometimes muted, of a score to be settled with the West.

Traditionally, as pointed out in a previous chapter, Chinese had tended to regard agriculture as primary and commerce as secondary. Foreign commerce, in particular, had been viewed as unimportant, since in the official image China already had everything she needed. This image may have been warranted prior to the Opium War era. But by the latter half of the nineteenth century, the economic encroachment of the maritime West had begun to challenge the older conception of China's needs and a new conception, shaped mainly by national power considerations, began to take hold. The reformers of the littoral were in the forefront of this development. Indeed, they were so prominently identified with it that Chinese Communist historians have defined Cheng Kuan-ying, Ma Chien-chung, Ho Kai, and Yung Wing, as well as Wang T'ao, in terms of their articulation of the economic demands of the nascent Chinese bourgeoisie.[17]

I have already examined, in Wang T'ao's case, the presumed implication that these men favored economic, and more specifically commercial, development because they stood to benefit from it personally, their class interests propelling them in this direction. This may or may not have been so. What seems more important to me is the fact that almost all of the littoral reformers identified commercial interests with national interests and were convinced that the surest way to increase China's wealth, relative to that of the West, was to outcompete Western commerce. To this end, Wang T'ao, Ho Kai, and Cheng Kuan-ying, in particular, called for greater protection and encouragement of commerce on the part of the Chinese government, higher social status for merchants, and a much more energetic Chinese role in the overseas carrying trade and all its subsidiary operations.[18]

It is significant that early Chinese formulations of a rationale for economic modernization should have been dictated by considerations more of national strength than of popular welfare (though the latter, too, had a place, especially in the proposals of Cheng Kuan-ying). To the reformers of the 1870's and 1880's, the goals of wealth and power were inseparable. And among those who talked of Sino-foreign economic competition, there was the strongest predisposition to think also in terms of political rivalry with the Western nations. Viewed in this light, it is not surprising that the reformers of the littoral were among the first generation of modern Chinese to begin the transition to nationalism.

Sometimes this was revealed in their actions. One thinks of Tong King-sing's engaging in modern enterprise in order to compete with the foreigners,[19] or Yung Wing's investigation and scathing indictment of the conditions of Chinese coolie labor in Peru (1873),[20] or the prominent part later taken by Cheng Kuan-ying in the boycott movement of 1905, protesting the discriminatory features of American immigration policy,[21] or Wu T'ing-fang's negotiation in 1899 of a Sino-Mexican treaty in which China for the first time secured most-favored-nation status,[22] or the youthful Ma Liang's announcement, on turning down an offer of employment with the French consulate, that his knowledge of French would be placed at the service of his own country.[23]

The incipient nationalism of the littoral reformers was also expressed in their writings, where certain themes cropped up with great frequency. One such was the articulation of an acute sense of shame, long before the Sino-Japanese War made such feelings fashionable.[24] Another was the overriding concern with wealth and power. Still another, displayed most conspicuously in the essays of Cheng Kuan-ying, Wang T'ao, and Ho Kai, was the notion that the key to national strength lay in a close, trusting relationship between ruler and people—a relationship all three men regarded as being encouraged, in the West, by representative political institutions.[25]

The only thing left was to supply the phenomenon here described with a label. One of the first Chinese reformers to do so was Cheng Kuan-ying, who some time prior to 1892 wrote: "The reason why China is poor and weak whereas the West is rich and strong lies in their different social customs—the familism (*chia-tsu chu-i*) of China and the nationalism (*kuo-chia chu-i*) of the West."[26] Cheng, incidentally, also identified in this statement one of the great barriers to the emergence of nationalism in modern China: the centering of loyalties and attachments upon proximate, tangible institutions, such as family, clan, and village, rather than upon remote abstractions like the state.

THE HONG KONG-SHANGHAI CORRIDOR

The reformers of the littoral, in their career patterns and world outlooks, diverged sharply from their Chinese contemporaries. How is this divergence to be explained? Aside from their exposure to Christian influences, which will be touched on later, the reformers' biographies reveal a number of common features. Most conspicuous, perhaps, were their geographical origins and the geographical loci of their educational and occupational careers. All eight men were born near, and spent considerable parts of their lives in, one or the other of the two primary zones of Western penetration in nineteenth-century China: the Canton-Hong Kong-Macao zone and the Shanghai zone.* Their careers, moreover, bespeak an extraordinary degree of back-and-forth movement between the two zones, so great that one is tempted to describe a Hong Kong-Shanghai corridor. Wang T'ao, as we have already seen, worked in Shanghai during the 1850's, spent most of the period from 1862 to 1884 in Hong Kong, and then moved back to

---

*Two exceptions to the first part of this statement must be noted. Shanghai was not yet a zone of Western penetration at the time of Wang T'ao's birth (1828) or Ma Liang's (1840). Moreover, in Wang's case, exposure to Western influence was nil prior to his first visit to Shanghai at age nineteen. This may explain the fact that Wang was in some ways the least acculturated of the littoral reformers.

Shanghai. Conversely, Cheng Kuan-ying, Tong King-sing, and Yung Wing, although born and partially educated in the Canton-Hong Kong-Macao zone, spent substantial portions of their adult careers in Shanghai.

The essential point, of course, is not the matter of movement per se—a phenomenon that was even more routine on the foreign side—but the degree to which Hong Kong and Shanghai represented interchangeable parts of a highly cohesive, self-contained littoral environment. It was the common cultural and institutional character of the two zones, in the final analysis, that made physical movement between them natural.

The consequences for the littoral reformers of having spent much of their lives in these two zones were several. The most obvious, reinforced by their years abroad, was the simple fact of intensive, day-to-day exposure to Westerners, Western institutions, Western ways of doing things, and Western cultural and material influences. Inevitably, such exposure forced a different slant on the world and unlocked the door to a host of fresh possibilities. Shanghai and Hong Kong provided microcosms of the modernization process at work.

And yet, as urban environments, these two cities were neither unequivocally modern nor altogether Western. Both might better be described as intellectual and cultural frontiers, outposts of intercultural collision where parochial (traditional) commitments were subjected to constant challenge. Rhoads Murphey's characterization of Shanghai will do for Hong Kong as well: "Shanghai was a place where two civilizations met and where neither prevailed. To the foreigners, it was out of bounds, beyond the knowledge or supervision of their own culture, where each man was a law unto himself . . . Morality was irrelevant or meaningless . . . For the Chinese, Shanghai was equally off limits. Those who had chosen this new kind of life . . . were by that choice cut off from traditional China and from the sanctions which it imposed."[27] Shanghai and Hong Kong thus offered a distinctive moral environment, one in which the social and psychological pressures that worked against innovation in the hinterland were, in large measure, neutralized.

Living in Shanghai and Hong Kong also had an immediate

bearing on certain specific attitudes of the littoral reformers. The importance they attached to commercial competition with the West was one. This attitude derived not only from personal economic interest but also from a direct assessment of foreign fears. Wang T'ao, for example, wrote Ting Jih-ch'ang in 1875 that the British were all in favor of China's adopting a policy of self-strengthening, as this would reduce the Russian threat and enhance the regional stability necessary for the conduct of trade. "What they dread," he went on, "is not our military power but our commercial power, for they are afraid that our country will use its commercial power to contend with them for mastery. Formerly, when the arsenal was established at Shanghai and the shipyard was built at Foochow . . . , they had no misgivings whatever. But as soon as the China Merchants Steam Navigation Company was formed, everyone got all excited. This was only a first small step in the development of our commercial power, yet already they were starting to get apprehensive."[28]

Developments in Hong Kong in the 1870's and 1880's seemed to bear out Wang's observation. While British and other non-Chinese merchants had once dominated the colony's business, by 1881 seventeen of the twenty largest firms had come into Chinese hands. This steady growth of Chinese commercial interests was often accomplished at the expense of Westerners in the colony. British businessmen, already frustrated over the unexpectedly poor showing of the China market, began to feel threatened by their native rivals, growing so jittery by the mid-1880's that Hong Kong became rife with rumors of a "Chinese takeover."[29]

The colonial atmosphere of Hong Kong and Shanghai also made a direct contribution to the feelings of shame and inferiority that were so crucial to the emerging nationalism of the littoral reformers. This worked in two quite distinct ways. First, there was the personal shame generated by collaboration with the enemy. All of the littoral reformers, after all, had been connected at one time or another with foreign institutions (missionary societies, commercial firms, government organs, Christian schools). Insofar as they lived and worked with people who benefited directly from Western imperialism, they too, in some sense, became beneficiaries of this imperialism—"collaborateurs" in the French sense.[30] Such collaboration, from the standpoint of the hinterland Chinese, was the ultimate form of "sell-out"—its practitioners were labeled *Han-chien* or "Chinese traitors"—and since few collaborators were so emancipated as to be entirely impervious to hinterland norms, feelings of shame inevitably developed. Nationalism, by restoring dignity and self-respect, provided the perfect antidote to such feelings.

In colonial (Hong Kong) and semicolonial (Shanghai) societies shame was also directly aroused by the attitudes of the colonizer. If colonial society was amoral in one of its sides, it was hyper-moral in another. Linda Shin has argued convincingly that the idealism, dogmatism, and hypocrisy that characterized middle-class Victorian society in England were often redoubled in intensity in colonial settings. Thus, among the British residents of Hong Kong, the unrelenting quest for social respectability gave rise to extreme snobbery and the erection of rigid social barriers, leading in turn to the almost complete exclusion of Chinese from the colony's social and political institutions. Exclusion, of course, was only a polite form of discrimination; Yung Wing, Wang T'ao, and Cheng Kuan-ying catalogued some of the less polite variants that were rampant in their day in Shanghai.[31] (Another variant, this one noncolonial, was the revocation of Yung Wing's American citizenship, after the passage of the exclusion laws.[32]) The line between hypermorality and amorality was thus a fine one. In both Shanghai and Hong Kong, moreover, the injury of racial discrimination was constantly abetted by the insult of the foreign penchant for glorifying Western civilization and power, while denigrating the cultural traditions of China. Individual shame and national shame, in such a context, became indistinguishable and feelings of personal hurt, insecurity, and inferiority served as a rich spawning ground for nationalistic passions.[33]

ACCESS TO THE HINTERLAND:
LI HUNG-CHANG AND THE LITTORAL REFORMERS

Although in the twentieth century the distance between the hinterland and the littoral cultures narrowed appreciably, in the nineteenth century it was enormous. In fact, it was not until the founding of the T'ung-meng hui (Revolutionary alliance) in 1905 that a true son of the littoral, Sun Yat-sen, succeeded in bridging the gap more or less on littoral terms. Prior to this, it had been bridged, if at all, only on terms set by the hinterland culture, with the consequence that much of the innovating potential of the littoral was vitiated. This, in a nutshell, was the dilemma faced by the littoral reformers. If they were to exert influence beyond the confines of the littoral, they had to gain access to the hinterland power structure. But since this power structure was largely informed by traditional values, goals, and operating procedures, in becoming part of it they risked the dilution, if not nullification, of their impact as innovators.

For people who were closely identified with the littoral, the primary access points to the hinterland power structure in the nineteenth century were those high officials who had wide-ranging responsibilities in the foreign affairs area—people like Tseng Kuo-fan, Ting Jih-ch'ang, Chang Chih-tung, Liu K'un-i, and, above all, Li Hung-chang. As Chinese officials went, these were relatively open-minded men. Overcoming their own prejudices and the scruples of the hinterland in general, they were willing to associate with the acculturated men of the littoral and even to make room for them on their staffs. They needed foreign expertise badly, and prior to the turn of the century the littoral was almost the only source of supply of this scarce commodity.[34] The men of the littoral, for their part, in going to work for such officials, acquired the prestige and status of the hinterland, but paid for it dearly in their freedom. As members of the Chinese bureaucracy, they had to play by the rules in order to succeed. Frustrated in their efforts to introduce comprehensive reform, the best they could hope for was to serve as instruments of limited, "defensive"[35] modernization.

The period during which most of the pioneer reformers of the littoral were in their prime coincided roughly with the quarter-century of Li Hung-chang's domination of Chinese foreign relations and modernization efforts (ca. 1870-1895). The frequency with which Li served as their principal point of hinterland access is, nonetheless, extraordinary. Five of them—Wu T'ing-fang, Cheng Kuan-ying, Tong King-sing, Ma Liang, and Ma Chien-chung—were members of Li's personal retinue for varying lengths of time. A sixth, Yung Wing, performed a number of special missions under Li's direct authority. A seventh, Wang T'ao, apparently was invited to serve on Li's staff but declined,[36] and the last and youngest, Ho Kai, worked for a spell under Li's protégé, Sheng Hsüan-huai.[37]

The frustrations met by those reformers of the littoral who chose to work in the bureaucracy are easily documented. Yung Wing's problems with the educational mission to America have already been noted. Wu T'ing-fang, according to a recent study, was forced to discard or modify his hopes for significant reform during the fourteen years he spent in Li Hung-chang's employ and was so distressed that he thought of resigning on several occasions.[38] Ma Liang, who did resign, years later described a revealing incident that took place during the period of his service with Li. While passing through Hong Kong in 1885, Ma observed that the great development of British commerce since the colony's founding had been harmful both to Cantonese and to non-British foreign trading interests. It occurred to him that this situation might be rectified by transforming Kowloon, which lay opposite Hong Kong, into a major port of trade and connecting it by rail to Canton. Since Ma did not know the then governor-general of Kwangtung and Kwangsi, Chang Chih-tung, he asked a person from Chang's home place to deliver the proposal to him. Chang read Ma's memorandum and praised it warmly, but did nothing more about it. On returning to Tientsin, Ma broached his plan to Li Hung-chang. Li, too, thought it was an excellent idea, but he was unwilling to sponsor it himself, insisting that the initiative must come from Chang Chih-tung. "Thus," Ma concluded, "my plan evaporated into thin air!"[39]

Wang T'ao and Ho Kai either had more foresight or less patience. Wang, over the years, corresponded freely with the members of Li's entourage and certainly hoped to influence Li in this roundabout fashion.[40] But he never accepted an official post. Ho Kai, after much persuasion by Wu T'ing-fang, consented to join

Sheng Hsüan-huai's staff in 1896. His aversion for the corruption and inefficiency of official life was so strong, however, that he left his new post within a matter of weeks and hastened back to Hong Kong, more convinced than ever that reform within the Ch'ing bureaucracy was an impossibility.[4][1]

Was it a disaster for Chinese modernization that the littoral's main access point to the hinterland in the seventies, eighties, and early nineties happened to be Li Hung-chang? Or was it the system that was principally at fault? I find it hard to avoid the conclusion that it was the system. My suspicion is that Li was not personally receptive to radical innovation.[4][2] Even if he were, however, it would not have been possible for him to promote such innovation and still amass the power he amassed. Li's political genius enabled him to reach the pinnacle of Chinese bureaucratic power. But in mastering the system, he also became its creature. Tong King-sing is said to have remarked of his relationship with Li: "The viceroy leads, but I am the man that pushes."[4][3] The only thing to be added to this is that there were real limits to how far Li could be pushed without threatening his political position, and Li knew these limits better than anyone.

REFORMERS, REBELS, AND REVOLUTIONARIES OF THE LITTORAL

Although operating within the confines of the hinterland was hard on the littoral reformers, it was short of crippling. For the hinterland, to them, was very much like a penitentiary without walls, which they could enter or leave at will. An analogous freedom of movement existed with respect to the ideological commitment to reform. This, too, could be left behind with relative ease if the prospects for modernization through some alternative means, such as rebellion or revolution, seemed more promising. The shared experience of the littoral, in such circumstances, turned out to be far more important than commitment to a particular approach to change.

A significant aspect of this shared cultural background was Christianity. In the case of the Taiping Rebellion, the only rebel movement of the nineteenth century with (partial) littoral origins and pretensions to being a modernizing force, the Christian connection has been widely noted.[44] The influence of Christianity on the pioneer reformers, on the other hand, has been completely overlooked. Certainly, if one takes the nineteenth century as a whole, it is undeniable that the vast majority of reformers were neither Christian nor Christianity-inspired (though more than a few were strongly influenced by missionary writings on secular topics). If, however, we train our sights upon the *pioneer* phase of Chinese reformism, we discover a significant number of reformers (all affiliated with the littoral) who, at one time or another, were more than casually exposed to Christian influences. Of the eight littoral reformers dealt with in this chapter, six, as boys, attended mission schools. Two worked closely with missionaries during portions of their adult careers. And at least five were, at some stage in their lives, bona fide practicing Christians. Christianity, for these individuals, was an important dimension of the overall experience of acculturation. It helped them to wrench free from the old culture. And, while it appears not to have inspired their specific reform ideas, it was clearly instrumental in enabling them to pioneer a reformist approach.[45]

Almost as neglected as the influence of Christianity on Chinese reform has been the place it held in the life of the early revolutionary movement. Sun Yat-sen's baptism in Hong Kong in 1884 is, of course, common knowledge. But it is not commonly appreciated that most of the leaders of the Hong Kong Hsing-Chung hui, the inner circle of budding revolutionaries in the Canton-Hong Kong area at the turn of the century, were also Christians. These included—and this is only a partial listing—Lu Hao-tung, Sun's boyhood friend; Cheng Shih-liang, a fellow medical student, also a Triad, who alerted Sun to the revolutionary potential of the secret societies; Ch'en Shao-pai, Sun's top lieutenant for the better part of a decade and the editor of the first Chinese newspaper to openly advocate revolution; Tse Tsan-tai (Hsieh Tsuan-t'ai), an overseas Chinese from Australia; Tso Tou-shan, the proprietor of a religious bookshop in Canton which served as an important revolutionary hideout in 1895; Shih Chien-ju a gentry-revolutionary; and Wang Chih-fu and Ou Feng-ch'ih, two Chinese pastors.[46] Most if not all of these men were products of missionary educational institutions, one of which, Canton Christian College (later to become Lingnan University), is described by Harold Schiffrin as having "played a pivotal role in the early years of the revolutionary movement."[47] According to Schiffrin, the leadership in both the Canton plot of 1895 and the Canton phase of the Waichow uprising of 1900 was predominantly Protestant. Christians, moreover, accounted for some 30 per cent of the insurgents in the Waichow campaign as a whole. Small wonder if, in the train of these events, nervous Chinese officials imagined they were witnessing a resurrection of the Taiping movement.[48]

The fluid quality that marked interaction among reformers, rebels, and revolutionaries of the littoral was apparent both at the intellectual and personal levels. The modernization proposals of the Taiping leader, Hung Jen-kan, for example, bore a close similarity to those of some of the littoral reformers.[49] Two of the latter, moreover, were personally acquainted with Hung, Yung Wing having become friendly with him in Hong Kong in 1856 and Wang T'ao having come to know him in Shanghai two years earlier. It is significant, given these connections, that after Hung joined the rebels in 1859, Yung and Wang, separately, made journeys into rebel territory, talked with rebel leaders, and submitted proposals designed to further the Taiping cause. Although these overtures came to nought, they signaled the willingness of both men to contemplate a nonreformist approach to Chinese modernization.[50]

Even more revealing was the ease with which, later on, the littoral reformers crossed the divide between reform and revolution. Here, the main point of contact was Sun Yat-sen. Sun, of course, had had a brief career himself as a reformer. During his reformist years he had been directly influenced by his medical school mentor, Ho Kai, and probably also by the writings of Cheng Kuan-ying and Wang T'ao. The climax of this phase of Sun's career came in 1894, with his abortive attempt (aided, it will be recalled, by Wang T'ao) to present a reform petition to Li Hung-chang. Li was preoccupied at the time by more pressing matters—war with Japan was in the offing—and henceforth Sun became a committed revolutionary.[51]

Henceforth, also, the flow of traffic accelerated, as one littoral reformer after another (of those that lived)[52] became converts to—or at least involved in—the revolutionary cause. The first to take this step was Ho Kai, who as early as March 1895 joined in the deliberations of the Hsing-Chung hui high command and secretly assisted them in their revolutionary plotting.[53] Cheng Kuan-ying was also in contact with Sun's men at this time, though the part (if any) he played in the Canton plot is unclear.[54] Between 1900 and 1902 Yung Wing appears to have given his support to a number of projected uprisings against the government, and he was regarded by the revolutionaries as a prime candidate for a top governmental post in the event that they should be successful.[55] When they finally did succeed, in 1911, Yung was too old to accept Sun Yat-sen's invitation to participate in the new government. However, Ma Liang and Wu T'ing-fang, both of whom were strongly committed to republican ideals, did accept official positions, the latter achieving prominence from the outset as the revolutionaries' chief representative at the negotiations that culminated in the Manchu abdication.[56]

While the littoral was a better place to make revolution than the hinterland, it was far from ideal. Foreign officials, like their Chinese counterparts, placed a high premium on law and order, and more than a few revolutionary plots were broken up by the foreign constabularies of Hong Kong and Shanghai. This helps to explain the undercover nature of Ho Kai's involvement with the Hsing-Chung hui and, perhaps also, the obscurity of the revolutionary connections of Cheng Kuan-ying and Yung Wing. All of these men, after all, were prominent figures in the Sino-foreign world of the littoral, with positions and reputations to look after and protect.

The littoral, on the other hand, was enormously important in facilitating the transition from reformer to revolutionary. Littoral revolutionaries, like Sun Yat-sen, and littoral reformers, like Ho Kai and Yung Wing, could speak to one another—actually (since so many of them hailed from the Canton area) as well as figuratively.

They had common social and geographical backgrounds, common religious affiliations, common educational experiences, common world outlooks. And, in the final analysis, these shared traits made them much closer to each other, measured in social and cultural terms, than either was to his ideological opposite number in the hinterland.

PIONEER REFORMERS OF THE HINTERLAND

The sociocultural distance separating littoral and hinterland during the initial phase of the revolutionary movement is well known. Sun Yat-sen's closest associates were drawn almost entirely from the littoral, especially from the Canton-Hong Kong-Macao zone; his contacts with hinterland revolutionaries did not become significant until the formation of the T'ung-meng hui in 1905. A similar pattern was displayed among the early reformers. True, people like Cheng Kuan-ying, Wu T'ing-fang, and Tong King-sing had ample contact with reform-minded members of the official community—the so-called "self-strengtheners"—and they acquired a certain amount of status in the process. It was never enough, however. Their acculturation had gone too far to permit full respectability, and prior to the 1890's the open admiration they felt for the pioneer reformers of the hinterland was seldom if ever reciprocated.[5][7]

To what extent does the fact that a number of pioneer reformers were principally identified with the hinterland upset the proposition that the littoral was crucial as a stimulus to innovation in nineteenth-century China? Not as much as one might think. A brief look at the careers of four early hinterland reformers suggests that, here too, contact with the littoral—or with the West or Japan—had an important stimulative value.

Feng Kuei-fen (1809-1874). A leading scholar, teacher, official adviser, and reformer in the "statecraft" (*ching-shih*) tradition, Feng was born in Soochow, Kiangsu. After taking the *chin-shih* degree in 1840, he worked for a number of years in the Hanlin Academy. Following the example of his fellow provincial, Ku Yen-wu (1613-1682), whom he greatly admired, Feng's scholarly interests were very broad, ranging over such diverse subjects as philology (his specialty was the *Shuo-wen*), mathematics, administrative problems, and foreign affairs. After the Taiping occupation of Nanking, Feng helped to organize the defense of Soochow. However, the rebel assault on this city in 1860 caused him, together with numbers of other Soochow scholars and officials, to seek out the relative security of Shanghai. It was in Shanghai, around 1860, that Feng's best-known work on reform, *Chiao-pin-lu k'ang-i* (Straightforward words from the Chiao-pin studio), was composed (the preface is dated 1861). A number of Li Hung-chang's ventures, including the establishment in Shanghai in 1863 of a school for the study of Western languages and sciences, were undertaken as a direct result of Feng Kuei-fen's prodding. Feng also advised Li for a time in the middle sixties, before taking on (in 1869) the chief editorship of the Soochow prefectural gazetteer.[58]

Kuo Sung-tao (1818-1891). A native of Hsiang-yin, Hunan, Kuo was strongly influenced in his classical training by the unorthodox early Ch'ing thinker, Wang Fu-chih (1619-1692), also from Hunan province. On becoming a *chin-shih* in 1847, Kuo was appointed to the Hanlin Academy. Later he gained more practical experience under Tseng Kuo-fan in the campaigning against the Taipings. After serving in a number of other official positions, including that of acting governor of Kwangtung (1863-1866), Kuo in 1877 became the first Chinese minister to be stationed in a Western country (England). As a diplomat, Kuo Sung-tao worked closely with and was heavily dependent upon Li Hung-chang, in whose secretariat he had briefly served in 1862. Although the foreign affairs stands of the two men were close, however, Kuo's ideas on reform were far more radical than Li's, and the latter "was unable, perhaps . . . unwilling, to exert his power on Kuo's behalf to any great extent."[59] The furor aroused by the journals Kuo kept in Europe was so intense that, on his return to China (in late 1878), he avoided the customary trip to Peking and proceeded directly to Hunan. Here, in forced early retirement, Kuo continued to feed ideas to Li Hung-chang through his correspondence.[60]

Hsüeh Fu-ch'eng (1838-1894). Another of China's pioneer diplomatic envoys, Hsüeh was born in Wu-hsi, Kiangsu, the son of a district magistrate. Although, as a mere *hsiu-ts'ai*, he never achieved high rank in the bureaucracy, he served for many years on the secretarial staffs of Tseng Kuo-fan (1865-1872) and Li Hung-chang (1875-1884) and was an influential writer on matters pertaining to reform and modernization. Hsüeh's first important collection of essays on reform, *Ch'ou-yang ch'u-i* (Simple proposals regarding foreign affairs), was submitted to Li Hung-chang in 1879. Even prior to this date, moreover, he had earned a reputation for himself in the foreign affairs field. A memorial written by him in 1875 is said to have been instrumental in persuading the Chinese government to agree to the stationing of envoys abroad. Hsüeh also played a significant part in the drafting of the Chefoo Convention of 1876, and two years later he was recommended for (and declined) a position on the staff of China's new minister to Germany. The capstone of Hsüeh Fu-ch'eng's career came with his appointment as minister to England, France, Italy, and Belgium in 1889. Hsüeh's experience in Europe lasted for more than four years (1890-1894) and the diaries he kept during this period brought him considerable acclaim as a reformer.[61]

Huang Tsun-hsien (1848-1905). Well known as a poet, reformer, and diplomat, Huang was born into a Hakka family in Chia-ying-chou, Kwangtung. In his early twenties he visited Hong Kong (1870) and was impressed by the colony's municipal government (as would be K'ang Yu-wei nine years later). His exposure to the culture of the littoral was extended in 1875 by trips to two northern treaty ports, Tientsin and Chefoo. Huang became a *chü-jen* in 1876 and the following year was appointed counselor to the Chinese legation in Tokyo. During the six years that he spent in Japan (1877-1882), he learned some Japanese (how much is not certain), met many Japanese scholars, and became a strong admirer of Meiji achievements in the sphere of modernization. Huang's *Jih-pen tsa-shih shih* (Poems about Japan) was published by the Tsungli Yamen in 1879, and his *Jih-pen kuo-chih* (History of Japan), completed in 1887 and first printed in 1890, became a primary source of information on Japan for the reformers of the 1890's, being read by the Kuang-hsü Emperor himself in 1898.

Huang Tsun-hsien's diplomatic career took him to San Francisco (where he served as consul-general, 1882-1885), London (where he was legation counselor during the first year of Hsüeh Fu-ch'eng's ministership), and Singapore (where he was consul general from 1891 to 1894). After returning to China in 1894, he held a number of provincial posts and became a prominent leader of the reform movement in Hunan. Although the reformist phase of his career was cut short by the coup d'état of September 1898, Huang's poetry, which was innovative in style and emotionally patriotic in content, served as a continuing inspiration to Chinese in the twentieth century.[62]

The ideas advanced by the pioneer reformers of the hinterland were, on the whole, strikingly similar to those put forward by the littoral reformers. Feng Kuei-fen, Kuo Sung-tao, Hsüeh Fu-ch'eng, and Huang Tsun-hsien (although to different degrees) all displayed openmindedness in their attitudes toward the West and, explicitly or implicitly, accepted the West as a model for Chinese emulation. Their respect for the West, moreover, went well beyond "ships and guns." Even Feng Kuei-fen, the earliest of the four, although convinced that it was only in the realms of science and technology that China could actually *learn* from the West, nonetheless recognized Western superiority in the use of human resources, in the exploitation of the soil (economic), and in the ease with which ruler and ruled were able to communicate (political).[63]

Kuo Sung-tao, Hsüeh Fu-ch'eng, and Huang Tsun-hsien went a good bit farther than this. Kuo, after discovering in London the political-economic institutional basis for Western military superiority, became sharply critical of the narrow military focus of Chinese self-strengthening efforts. Reserving special praise for British economic policies, railway development, parliamentary government, and law, he was struck, above all, by the capacity of Western institutions to foster a relationship of sympathy and trust between the government and the people.[64] Hsüeh Fu-ch'eng was equally impressed with the institutional organization of the West and, in addition to advancing a host of proposals in the realm of economic modernization, urged China to ready herself for major institutional changes.[65] Huang Tsun-hsien, who in the 1890's became a close friend and intellectual mentor of Liang Ch'i-ch'ao, was another advocate of institutional reform, more daring perhaps than either Kuo Sung-tao or Hsüeh Fu-ch'eng in the degree of change he was prepared to accept.[66]

As in the case of the reformers of the littoral, the general receptivity to change of the early hinterland reformers was accompanied by visible stirrings in the direction of nationalism. This was expressed in diverse ways. Feng Kuei-fen, viewing China's defeat in the *Arrow* War as the "greatest outrage since creation," urged upon his fellow countrymen the development of a sense of shame, which he saw as a psychological precondition for Chinese self-strengthening.[67] Kuo Sung-tao, through his insistence upon the autonomy of Western history and the greatness of Western civilization, relativized the history and civilization of China, thereby creating an intellectual framework for nationalism.[68] Focusing on a more specific issue, Hsüeh Fu-ch'eng, as early as 1879, urged that China seek treaty revision so that extraterritoriality might be eliminated and the tariff on imports raised. No less alert than Kuo Sung-tao to the economic foundations of power, Hsüeh deplored the drain of wealth from China to Europe and suggested, as a remedy, a more active role for Chinese merchants in foreign commerce.[69] The protonationalism of Huang Tsun-hsien was revealed both in his poetry and in his moving accounts of the heroes of the late Tokugawa and early Meiji periods whose determined efforts to arouse the Japanese people to the need for reform were consciously emulated by the reformers of the 1890's in China.[70]

Given the closeness of the reform programs of the hinterland and littoral reformers (at least insofar as they represented responses to the Western challenge),[71] what is it about the former group of men that warrants their being classified as "hinterland"? For one thing, although the careers of the hinterland reformers were by no means totally lacking in innovativeness (three having played pioneer diplomatic roles), the range of career innovation was far narrower than in the case of the reformers of the littoral. With the partial exception of Feng Kuei-fen, all were officials by vocation and became interested in and concerned with the West in the course of their official duties. By contrast, those reformers of the littoral who joined the bureaucracy did so only after they had undergone a considerable process of acculturation and had made their marks in other occupational pursuits. It may be added, in this connection, that the hinterland reformers were all degree-holders, three of the four having gone beyond the *hsiu-ts'ai*, whereas none of the littoral reformers made it past the *hsiu-ts'ai* and only one of them (Wang T'ao) got that far.

The contrast may be pressed further. Not one of the pioneer reformers of the hinterland seems to have gained control over a Western language. None, moreover, attended foreign schools or universities, took up employment with foreigners (quite the reverse, Kuo Sung-tao had foreigners, among them Halliday Macartney, working for him), or became converts to the foreign religion. The hinterland reformers, in short, although exposed to the intellectual and visual impact of the littoral, were in no sense products of the special cultural milieu generated there. They were observers of, rather than participants in, this milieu. The attack leveled by the gentry of Hunan against Kuo Sung-tao owed its sting precisely to the fact that Kuo was one of them. Had Kuo been a Yung Wing or a Ho Kai, he would have been ignored.

THE LITTORAL AND CHANGE IN
NINETEENTH-CENTURY CHINA

The experience of the pioneer reformers of the hinterland, nevertheless, seems to support the contention that in nineteenth-century China exposure of some kind to the culture of the littoral was critically important in paving the way for far-reaching change. Such exposure did not have to take the form of actual residence in the littoral (though it happened to in Feng Kuei-fen's case). It could also come about through travel there (Huang Tsun-hsien's visits in the first half of the 1870's to Hong Kong, Tientsin, and Chefoo), involvement in regions where the Western-influenced Taipings were active (Hsüeh Fu-ch'eng and Feng Kuei-fen were both driven from their Kiangsu homes by the rebels and Kuo Sung-tao campaigned against them), close connections with officials (like Li Hung-chang and Tseng Kuo-fan) who were heavily engaged in foreign affairs, service as officials in primary zones of Western penetration (Kuo Sung-tao in Canton in the mid-sixties), early life experience in or near such zones (Feng Kuei-fen and Hsüeh Fu-ch'eng in Kiangsu, Huang Tsun-hsien in Kwangtung), and so forth.

In emphasizing the variety of opportunities available to the hinterland reformers for contact with the littoral, I do not mean to make light of the shaping influence actual residence abroad had on the reform ideas and attitudes of people like Huang Tsun-hsien, Kuo Sung-tao, and Hsüeh Fu-ch'eng. Still, it is my strong belief that the initial "shock" of exposure to Western culture was experienced by these men in China, before they ever ventured abroad. Indeed, it may be presumed that the relative success of their adjustment to this shock was a major reason for their being sent abroad in the first place.

This poses a very difficult question: Why is it that a tiny handful of hinterland Chinese between 1860 and 1890 responded with imagination and boldness to the stimulus of the Western intrusion, while the vast majority did not? In approaching this question, it is helpful to keep in mind, first, that, in the littoral also, only a small minority of Chinese became *actively* committed to modernization and reform (although, in proportional terms, it was a much larger minority than in the hinterland and, in any case, represented but a small fraction of those in the littoral who were conditioned by experience to give *passive* acceptance to the new), and second, that some Chinese with direct experience of life in the West (a Liu Hsi-hung,[72] for example), instead of turning into apostles of change, actually became more confirmed than ever in their hinterland prejudices. What all this suggests is that, however necessary the littoral may have been as a stimulus to change in nineteenth-century China, it did not suffice. The pressures (and attractions) of the littoral operated within a context comprised of a rich array of cultural (Chinese) and transcultural (human) factors, and it was this total context that ultimately determined who would be receptive to change and who not.

The general proposition is unimpeachable. It is when we get

down to cases that things become complicated. The problem, reduced to its simplest terms, is to explain why some people, when exposed to a stimulus, react in a certain way, while others, when exposed to the same stimulus, react in other ways or not at all. In the case of the pioneer reformers (littoral and hinterland both), a basic distinction may be drawn, at the outset, between those who were immersed in the littoral from an early age, as a result of circumstances beyond their control, and those whose contact with the littoral came later (biographically speaking), was less profoundly acculturative, and was a matter (at least partly) of conscious choice. I am not primarily concerned with the former group (which embraces the six littoral reformers educated under missionary auspices), for the problem with them is less one of accounting for receptivity to innovation—I presume that most Chinese youths who experienced mission school educations were more or less sympathetic to change—than of explaining the prominence that they, in particular, attained as innovators.

In terms of the problem addressed here, it is the second group (consisting of Wang T'ao, Cheng Kuan-ying, and the four hinterland reformers) that is of paramount interest. All of these men were reared in hinterland environments and were trained as youths in the classical Confucian heritage. Yet, unlike countless thousands of other educated Chinese, they did not become prisoners of this heritage, tightly chained to a parochial Chinese past. Instead, under the stimuli of Western cultural influence and the political and economic challenges (real or imagined) that the Western presence posed, they launched a process of cultural self-reassessment which, in one guise or another, has continued in China right up to the present day.

Although accidental factors (such as being in the right place at the right time) always play a role in history, they can never constitute sufficient explanations of why certain men behave in certain ways. Substantive factors must also be taken into consideration, especially when the problem is to account for innovative behavior in a sociocultural setting in which the pressures against innovation are strong. H.G. Barnett, in his monumental study, *Innovation: The Basis of Cultural Change*, observes that, to understand a given individual's reaction to something new, three kinds of variables must be examined: the intrinsic nature of the new thing or idea ("novelty characteristics and values"), the persuasive power of those who advocate it ("advocate assets"), and the life situation of the individual reactor ("biographical determinants"). In analyzing the last of these variables, he suggests four categories of individuals who, in any cultural context, are most likely to be receptive to innovation: the dissident, the indifferent, the disaffected, and the resentful.[73]

Although Barnett's analysis presupposes that all three of his variables will be operative in any concrete instance, their relative weighting may vary considerably. Certainly, in the case of the second group of Chinese reformers noted above (those whose first significant contact with the littoral came in adulthood), it was the "biographical determinant" that was of primary importance. To argue that Feng Kuei-fen and Kuo Sung-tao—the earliest-born and therefore the most intriguing—were estranged from Confucian culture would be patently absurd. It is clear, nevertheless, that both men were influenced by intellectual countercurrents within this culture that made them dissatisfied with aspects of the status quo. Feng Kuei-fen, although viewed by Mary Wright as in many respects the very embodiment of Restoration Confucianism, has been described in more recent scholarship as a proponent of radical institutional change at the local level (where he applied the ideas of his philosophical mentor Ku Yen-wu) as well as a man for whom the ideal of wealth and power had already become an accepted value by 1860-1861, if not before.[74] Kuo Sung-tao, as we have seen, identified strongly in his early training with Wang Fu-chih (who was one of the few thinkers in premodern China to enunciate anything resembling a theory of progress), and it has been suggested that Wang's philosophy may have conditioned Kuo's own receptivity to change.[75]

Although, in these particular instances, the initial commitment to change appears to have been nourished by indigenous philosophical influences, it might just as well have been stimulated by career disappointment (as in Wang T'ao's failure to pass the chü-jen examination), personality idiosyncrasy, or some other factor. The important point is that there existed in pre-Opium War China a number of individuals who, for one reason or another, were dissatisfied with facets of their society and believed in the possibility of its betterment. Inclined in the direction of reform before ever being exposed to influences from the West, they were in a unique position, once the Western challenge materialized, to appraise it flexibly, to see it as part opportunity and not all disaster.

Feng Kuei-fen and Kuo Sung-tao have great historical significance. They have long been recognized as "early responders" to the "Western impact." But only now are scholars beginning to ask why. Why *them*? Even the most rudimentary broaching of this question—and certainly that is all I would claim for what I have attempted here—reveals that the Chinese culture which came into growing contact with Western civilization in the nineteenth century was anything but inert. Alive with tensions, contradictions, and problems of all kinds, it was perfectly capable of generating, from within itself, the impulse to change. This is not to say that the littoral was not of vital importance to people like Feng and Kuo. It is the nature of its importance that requires redefinition. The littoral, in their case, did not *create* the impulse to change. Rather, by generating new problems, thrusting old problems into a new perceptual framework, and supplying for the solution of problems—old and new—a radically different repository of ideas and technologies, the littoral transformed the context within which the indigenous impulse to change operated.

In the case of those pioneer reformers who either were born later or underwent extensive acculturation, the role of the littoral was more fundamental still. Six of these men—the Ma brothers, Ho Kai, Yung Wing, Wu T'ing-fang, and Tong King-sing—derived their commitments to change, as well as many of their specific reformist goals, directly from Western example and instruction. And at least three of the remaining four, upon reaching impasses in their hinterland careers, found in the littoral opportunities for achievement and success that, in previous eras of Chinese history, had not existed.[76]

With the growing impact of the littoral as a stimulus to change in the post-rebellion years, the role of the hinterland also shifted. Increasingly overshadowed (although never eliminated) as a *source* of change, its primary function, in the total change process, became more and more one of legitimation.* K'ang Yu-wei's use of New Text Confucianism to make Western-inspired change acceptable was perhaps the most dramatic instance of this phenomenon. But just as significant, ultimately, was the almost complete domination of the reform activity of the 1890's and 1900's by certified products of the hinterland culture. Reform, at last, had become respectable. The only trouble was that it was too late. And before it could really be tried, the Chinese empire fell apart.

*I refer specifically to the nineteenth and early twentieth centuries. By the middle of the twentieth century, as already noted, the center of innovation had passed back to the Chinese heartland.

NOTES, BIBLIOGRAPHY,

GLOSSARY, AND INDEX

ABBREVIATIONS USED IN NOTES

CT	Wang T'ao, *T'ao-yüan ch'ih-tu*
CTHC	Wang T'ao, *T'ao-yüan ch'ih-tu hsü-ch'ao*
FKCL	Wang T'ao, *Fa-kuo chih-lüeh*
PFCC	Wang T'ao, *P'u-Fa chan-chi* (1895 ed., unless otherwise noted)
WKKP	*Wan-kuo kung-pao*
WLWP	Wang T'ao, *T'ao-yüan wen-lu wai-pien*
WYYT	Wang T'ao, *Weng-yu yü-t'an*
HF	Hsien-feng reign, 1851-1861

NOTES

PART I

PROLOGUE

1. All references to the meeting between Wang T'ao and Sun Yat-sen ultimately derive from Ch'en Shao-pai's oral account, *Hsing-Chung-hui ko-ming shih-yao*, in Ch'ai Te-keng et al., eds., *Hsin-hai ko-ming* (Shanghai, 1957), I, 28. Ch'en says that the two met at the home of Cheng Kuan-ying, who was from the same hsien in Kwangtung as Sun and was a long-time friend of Wang T'ao. I am grateful to Harold Schiffrin for elaborating on the circumstances of this meeting in a letter of November 20, 1964, to the author. See also his book, *Sun Yat-sen and the Origins of the Chinese Revolution* (Berkeley, 1968), p. 38.

2. Ibid., p. 27.

3. Some sources give a much earlier date for Wang's death. But the evidence supporting the 1897 date is overwhelming. A number of works (including an edition of Wang's *WLWP* and several books by other reformers) were printed under Wang T'ao's name in 1897. A postface by Wang is found in two 1897 editions of Feng Kuei-fen's *Chiao-pin-lu k'ang-i*, one of them published by Wang himself. John Fryer, one of Wang's foreign colleagues, in a report on the activities of the Chinese Polytechnic Institution from February 11, 1896, to July 1, 1897, states: "The prize-essay scheme has not been carried on with the same energy as formerly through the illness and death of Mr. Wang T'ao" (*North-China Herald and Supreme Court and Consular Gazette*, July 16, 1897, p. 128). Ts'ai Erh-k'ang, a Chinese friend and associate, in his *Chu-t'ieh-an tu-shu ying-shih sui-pi*, says that Wang died in the 4th month of the 23rd year of Kuang-hsü (May 2-30, 1897). Although I

have not seen Ts'ai's work (it may exist in manuscript form only), it is cited in two independent studies of Wang T'ao: Wu Ching-shan, "Wang T'ao shih-chi k'ao-lüeh," in *Shang-hai yen-chiu tzu-liao* (Shanghai, 1936), p. 686; Hsieh Wu-liang, "Wang T'ao—Ch'ing-mo pien-fa-lun chih shou-ch'uang-che chi Chung-kuo pao-tao wen-hsüeh chih hsien-ch'ü-che," *Chiao-hsüeh yü yen-chiu*, March 1958, p. 39. See also T'an Cheng-pi, comp., *Chung-kuo wen-hsüeh-chia ta tz'u-tien* (Shanghai, 1934), pp. 1713-1714.

4. Frederic Wakeman, Jr., "High Ch'ing: 1683-1839," in James B. Crowley, ed., *Modern East Asia: Essays in Interpretation* (New York, 1970), pp. 1-27.

5. The phrase is Albert Craig's. See his "Introduction: Perspectives on Personality in Japanese History," in Albert M. Craig and Donald H. Shively, eds., *Personality in Japanese History* (Berkeley, 1970), p. 10 .

1. THE EARLY YEARS IN KIANGSU

1. *WLWP*, 11:16b-17. The most complete chronology of Wang T'ao's life is found in Wu Ching-shan, pp. 679-686. In English, see Arthur W. Hummel, ed., *Eminent Chinese of the Ch'ing Period* (Washington, 1943, 1944), II, 836-839.

2. Wang T'ao, *Man-yu sui-lu*, in Wang Hsi-ch'i, comp., *Hsiao-fang-hu-chai yü-ti ts'ung-ch'ao* (Taipei, 1962), LXII, 9806-9807.

3. *WLWP*, 11:21.

4. *WLWP*, 11:9b-10, 21; Wang T'ao, *Man-yu sui-lu*, p. 9807.

5. *WLWP*, 11:16b. The examining official was Chang Fei. Chang, later governor of Kiangsi, was killed in 1862 by Moslem rebels in Shensi. Wang T'ao, lamenting the fact that he was too young at the time to become friendly with Chang Fei, later expressed his appreciation for the encouragement Chang gave him. See *WYYT*, 1:1.

6. Wang T'ao, *Man-yu sui-lu*, pp. 9808-9809; Wu Ching-shan, p. 680. On teaching as a career, see Chung-li Chang, *The Income of the Chinese Gentry* (Seattle, 1962), pp. 89-109.

7. *CT*, 1:18-20b. The eight-legged essay style is described in John K. Fairbank, Edwin O. Reischauer, and Albert Craig, *East Asia: The Modern Transformation* (Boston, 1965), p. 122.

8. See David Nivison, "Protest against Conventions and Conventions of Protest," in Arthur Wright, ed., *The Confucian Persuasion* (Stanford, 1960), pp. 177-201.

9. *WLWP*, 11:17. See also Wang's preface (1889) to *CTHC*, pp. 1a-b.

10. See his letters (of 1848-1849) to Yang Yin-ch'uan, in *CT*, 1:18b-20b, 22; also his letter of ca. 1851, *CT*, 2:8-9; also his letter to Yang Yin-ch'uan (ca. 1858), *CT*, 3:9b-11. From 1848 on Wang periodically took the "annual" examinations in the prefectural capital. But this was merely to retain his status as a *hsiu-ts'ai*. See Wang T'ao, *Heng-hua-kuan shih-lu* (Tokyo, 1881), 1:21b-22; Wang T'ao, "Ying-juan tsa-chi" (unpublished diary), HF 3/2/7 (March 16, 1853); Wu Ching-shan, p. 681; *CT*, 3:2.

11. *Man-yu sui-lu*, pp. 9809-9810, as translated in H. McAleavy, *Wang T'ao: The Life and Writings of a Displaced Person* (London, 1953), p. 4.

12. "Ch'un-jih Hu-shang kan-shih" (Reactions to Shanghai in the spring), in *Heng-kua-kuan shih-lu*, 1:19b-20; see also Wang T'ao, *Ying-juan tsa-chih*, (1875), 5:10b-11.

13. *WLWP*, 7:29a-b. Wang's preoccupation with dreams at this time is also indicated in the brief poem, "Chi-meng" (On dreams), in *Heng-hua-kuan shih-lu*, 1:23b.

14. Hummel, II, 836; Wu Ching-shan, p. 680.

15. McAleavy, p. 5; *CT*, 2:1-2, 2b-3; *Ying-juan tsa-chih*, 1:7a-b.

16. *WLWP*, 11:22-23; letter to Yang Yin-ch'uan, *CT*, 2:4a-b; "Pei ch'iu ch'ü" (Autumn lament), *Heng-hua-kuan shih-lu*, 2:5-6b; McAleavy, p. 5.

17. Letter to Yang Yin-ch'uan (ca. 1850), *CT*, 2:2.

18. Letter to Yang Yin-ch'uan, *CT*, 2:11. See also Wang's letter to Chou T'eng-hu (1859), *CT*, 4:6a-b.

19. *Man-yu sui-lu*, p. 9809, as translated in McAleavy, p. 4.

20. Letter to Ying Lung-t'ien (ca. 1858), *CT*, 3:8b.

21. The diaries are in the library of the Institute of History and Philology, Academia Sinica, Taiwan. I am grateful to Lo Hsiang-lin for informing me of their whereabouts and to Wang Erh-min for having had them transcribed for me in triplicate. A copy has been deposited with the Harvard-Yenching Library. None of the diaries, of which there are six, is paginated. Their titles and dates are as follows: "T'iao-hua-lu jih-chih," June 11-22, 1849; "Ming-hsiang-liao jih-chi" (alternate title: "Ying-juan tsa-chi"), July 17-October 12, 1852; "Ying-juan tsa-chi," October 13, 1852-April 17, 1853; "Hu-ch'eng wen-chien lu," July-September 1853; "Ying-juan jih-chih," April 18, 1853-January 29, 1854; "Heng-hua-kuan jih-chi," September 22, 1854-May 4, 1855.

22. "Ming-hsiang-liao jih-chi," HF 2/7/6 (August 20, 1852), 2/8/18 (October 1, 1852), 2/8/26 (October 9, 1852).

23. "Ying-juan tsa-chi," HF 2/9/18 (October 30, 1852), 2/10/24 (December 5, 1852).

24. "Ying-juan jih-chih," HF 3/4/27 (June 3, 1853), 3/7/middle (mid-August 1853).

25. "Heng-hua-kuan jih-chi," HF 5/1/17 (March 5, 1855), 5/3/11 (April 26, 1855).

26. T'an Cheng-pi, pp. 1713-1714; Hummel; II, 836; *WYYT*, 1:13.

27. *WYYT*, 1:12-13, 13a-b, 2:8b-9b; Wang T'ao, *Ying-juan tsa-chih*, 4:15a-b. Muirhead's book was a composite translation of two English works. See Alexander Wylie, *Memorials of Protestant Missionaries to the Chinese* (Taipei, 1967), p. 169. In Chiang's preface to his own history of England he was very critical of British governmental institutions. The preface and the biographies of Washington and Caesar are included in his *Hsiao-ku-t'ang wen-chi* (Shanghai, 1868), 5:2b-7b, 7:2b-5.

28. *North-China Herald*, September 18, 1891, p. 394. The essay which prompted the exchange of letters was a discussion of the Hart memorandum and is found in *Huang-ch'ao ching-shih-wen hsü-pien*, comp. Ko Shih-chün (Taipei, 1964), II, 815-818. See also Chiang Tun-fu, 3:15-22b.

29. Hummel, I, 479-480. For a more detailed biography of Li, see Li Yen,

Chung suan-shih lun-ts'ung (Peking, 1955), IV, 331-361. On Li's relationship with Wang T'ao, see Wang P'ing, *Hsi-fang li-suan-hsüeh chih shu-ju* (Taipei, 1966), pp. 155-159.

30. W.A.P. Martin, *A Cycle of Cathay, or China, South and North, with Personal Reminiscences* (New York, 1896), pp. 368-370.

31. Kung Ch'eng is not mentioned in Wang's diaries. We may assume, therefore, that he and Wang became friends after 1855 (the year the diaries cease). There is a biography of Kung Tzu-chen in Hummel, I, 431-434.

32. McAleavy, pp. 9-10, translated from Wang T'ao, *Sung-pin so-hua* (Shanghai, 1934), pp. 82-83.

33. *Ying-juan tsa-chih*, 5:3b-4.

34. McAleavy, pp. 10-12.

35. "Hu-ch'eng wen-chien lu," HF 3/6 (July 6-August 4, 1853).

36. "Heng-hua-kuan jih-chi," 4/8/24 (October 15, 1854), 4/8/26 (October 17, 1854), 4/8/27 (October 18, 1854), 4/8/28 (October 19, 1854), 5/2/1 (March 18, 1855), 5/2/15 (April 1, 1855).

37. *The Report of the Directors to the Sixty-First General Meeting of the Missionary Society, Usually Called the London Missionary Society, on Thursday, May 10th, 1855* (London, 1855), p. 53. Wang is identified here as Wang-lan-King (that is, Wang Lan-ch'ing), his courtesy name at the time.

38. In discussing the missionary influence on Wang, McAleavy, having seen only published sources, states (p. 21): "Certainly, his mind never received the slightest tincture of Christianity."

39. The printed version of this letter is in *WLWP*, 8:3-5. The manuscript version is reproduced in Lindsay Ride's "Biographical Note," prefacing the 1960 Hong Kong edition of *The Chinese Classics*, p. 16. Another example of this kind of distortion is contained in the *published* account of the trip Wang took with Medhurst and Muirhead in October 1854. In this account Wang makes no reference to preaching or to the distribution of religious literature. See *Man-yu sui-lu*, pp. 9810-9811.

40. See, for example, *Ying-juan tsa-chih*, 6:11a-b.

41. See, for example, *WLWP*, 3:2b-6b.

42. Technically, the designation "Delegates' Version" applied only to the New Testament. But because the Old Testament was done along the same lines and was stylistically uniform with the New Testament translation, the same designation was commonly extended to the whole Bible. See *Records of the General Conference of the Protestant Missionaries of China Held at Shanghai, May 7-20, 1890* (Shanghai, 1890), pp. 51-52; Alexander Wylie, "The Bible in China," in his *Chinese Researches* (Shanghai, 1897), pp. 103-104; Eric M. North, *The Book of a Thousand Tongues* (New York and London, 1938), p. 85; William Canton, *A History of the British and Foreign Bible Society* (London, 1904-1910), II, 396-399; Henry Otis Dwight, *The Centennial History of the American Bible Society* (New York, 1916), pp. 242-244.

43. Wylie, "The Bible in China," pp. 103-104.

44. R. Wardlaw Thompson, *Griffith John: The Story of Fifty Years in*

China (New York, 1906), p. 431; Kenneth Scott Latourette, *A History of Christian Missions in China* (London, 1929), pp. 263, 266.

45. *Records . . . 1890*, p. 52. See also Muirhead's appraisal, in Thompson, p. 431.

46. Wylie, *Memorials of Protestant Missionaries to the Chinese*, p. 35.

47. Joseph Edkins, in a letter of October 3, 1855, states that at that time there were two *hsiu-ts'ai* in the Shanghai branch of the church, "one of whom was a principal assistant in the translation of the Scriptures." The reference is clearly to Wang T'ao. See *The Missionary Magazine and Chronicle* 20:68 (1856).

48. *The Report of the Directors to the Sixtieth General Meeting of the Missionary Society, Usually Called the London Missionary Society, on Thursday, May 11th, 1854* (London, 1854), p. 63.

49. *The Report . . . 1855*, p. 53.

50. Thompson, pp. 47-49.

51. Arthur F. Wright, "The Study of Chinese Civilization," *The Journal of the History of Ideas* 21:233-255 (1960); Mark Mancall, "The Persistence of Tradition in Chinese Foreign Policy," *The Annals of the American Academy of Political and Social Science* 349:16-19 (September 1963).

52. Wang has a brief biography of Chou in *Ying-juan tsa-chih*, 4:24b-25.

53. *CT*, 3:3b.

54. Wang bases himself here, apparently, on the critique of British government made by Chiang Tun-fu. See *Hsiao-ku-t'ang wen-chi*, 7:2b-5.

55. The same idea, in essence, is expressed by Wang in a later essay, found in *WLWP*, 5:18b-19b.

56. *CT*, 4:4b-12b. See also Leong Sow-theng, "Wang T'ao and the Movement for Self-Strengthening and Reform in the Late Ch'ing Period," *Papers on China* 17:109-112 (1963). Ideas similar to those expressed in the letter to Chou reappear in an essay written about the same time and found in *WLWP*, 6:12-14b.

57. Hummel, I, 479; Li Yen, IV, 343, 348.

58. *CT*, 4:12b-19.

59. *CT*, 4:19-22b. Wang made some of the same points in a letter written later in the same year to the bibliophile, Yü Sung-nien. He was particularly critical of the dynasty's resort to force in June 1859, which he felt may have achieved its immediate aims but bode no good for the future. See *CT*, 5:1-3b.

60. *CT*, 4:6, 20.

2. THE AMBIGUITIES OF REBELLION: WANG T'AO AND THE TAIPINGS

1. See Franz Michael, in collaboration with Chung-li Chang, *The Taiping Rebellion: History and Documents* (Seattle, 1966-1971), I, 216 (Map 15); Mary C. Wright, *The Last Stand of Chinese Conservatism: The T'ung-chih Restoration, 1862-1874* (Stanford, 1957), p. 98.

2. Ping-ti Ho, *Studies on the Population of China, 1368-1953* (Cambridge, Mass., 1959), pp. 238-239.

3. Ibid., p. 242.

4. Roughly half of *WYYT* is concerned with the rebellion; there are several lengthy accounts of it in *WLWP*. See also Lo Erh-kang, "Wang T'ao shou-ch'ao Hsieh Chieh-ho 'Chin-ling kuei-chia chi-shih-lüeh' chih fa-hsien," *Ta-kung pao*, April 22, 1937; Chien Yu-wen, " 'Ch'ang-mao chuang-yüan' Wang T'ao pa," *I-ching* No. 33:45 (July 5, 1937). For more on Wang's Taiping writings, see below, Chap. 5, n. 7.

5. "Ying-juan jih-chih," HF 3/9 (October 3-31, 1853); *Ying-juan tsa-chih*, 5:13b. For an account of the Small Sword Society's activities and organization, see "Hu-ch'eng wen-chien lu," HF 3/7 (August 5-September 2, 1853).

6. Rhoads Murphey, *Shanghai: Key to Modern China* (Cambridge, Mass., 1953), p. 10.

7. "Heng-hua-kuan jih-chi," HF 5/1/2 (February 18, 1855); *CT*, 2:17b-18b; *Ying-juan tsa-chih*, 3:3a-b. Wang describes in some detail the destruction caused in the process of recovering the Chinese city from the rebels.

8. *CT*, 2:17b-19, 5:11-12b. For a bitter critique of contemporary officialdom in general and the Shanghai yamen clerks in particular, see "Ming-hsiang-liao jih-chi," HF 2/8/16 (September 29, 1852), 2/8/19 (October 2, 1852).

9. It reached 500,000 in 1864. See Murphey, *Shanghai*, p. 10.

10. *Ying-juan tsa-chih*, 6:7a-b.

11. He claimed that the reason for his nonparticipation was his fear that if anything happened to him there would be no one to look after his mother. See *CT*, 2:21a-b.

12. *WLWP*, 11:17-18; Wu Ching-shan, p. 682. On the role of gentry refugees in organizing militia defense in the Shanghai area, see Stanley Spector, *Li Hung-chang and the Huai Army: A Study in Nineteenth-Century Chinese Regionalism* (Seattle, 1964), pp. 29 ff.

13. *CT*, 5:12b-23.

14. *CT*, 5:21b-22.

15. *CT*, 6:1-7.

16. *CT*, 6:7-10. On the dating of this letter see Wu Ching-shan, p. 682; *WLWP*, 9:11. Both sources indicate that Tseng's army was quartered in Anking at the time Wang wrote the letter. Anking was not retaken by government forces until September 1861.

17. *WLWP*, 7:8b-10b.

18. *WLWP*, 7:10b-13.

19. For the dates of Wang's departure from and return to Shanghai (the importance of which will soon be seen), see *WLWP*, 11:10, and Wang's letter (of ca. 1864) to James Legge, *CT*, 6:16. The circumstances of the composition of "I-t'an" are recounted in *WLWP*, 12:15a-b, 33a-b. Only thirteen of the forty-four parts were published by Wang, first in his newspaper, *Hsün-huan jih-pao*, in 1874, and later in *WLWP*, 12:15-33b.

20. *WLWP*, 12:31b-33.

21. *WLWP*, 12:19-20b, 20b-21b, 21b-24.

22. *WLWP*, 12:30b-31.

23. *WLWP*, 12:29b-30b, 30b-31b. On the *yen-lu*, see Lloyd Eastman, *Throne and Mandarins: China's Search for a Policy During the Sino-French Controversy, 1880-1885* (Cambridge, Mass., 1967), pp. 20-21, 190-193.

24. *WLWP*, 12:29a-b.

25. *WLWP*, 12:17-19. Whether Wang really viewed the grand secretaries as chancellors or was using this as a cover to enable him to advocate restoration of an abolished post is not clear. In this connection, see also *WLWP*, 6:28-30.

26. *WLWP*, 12:27-28b.

27. *WLWP*, 12:24-25b, 25b-27.

28. *WLWP*, 12:15b-17.

29. *CT*, 7:17b. For a brief discussion of Huang, along with translated excerpts from *Ming-i tai-fang lu*, see Wm. T. de Bary et al., eds., *Sources of Chinese Tradition* (New York, 1961), pp. 585-597. A more extended analysis of Huang's political thought is found in de Bary's "Chinese Despotism and the Confucian Ideal: A Seventeenth-Century View," in John K. Fairbank, ed., *Chinese Thought and Institutions* (Chicago, 1957), pp. 163-203. See also Wolfgang Franke, *The Reform and Abolition of the Traditional Chinese Examination System* (Cambridge, Mass., 1963), pp. 20-21.

30. This characterization of the traditionalist is Myron Weiner's. See his "Introduction," in Myron Weiner, ed., *Modernization: The Dynamics of Growth* (New York, 1966), p. 7.

31. The details concerning the capture of the letter are taken from Kuo T'ing-i, *T'ai-p'ing t'ien-kuo shih-shih jih-chih* (Taipei, 1963), p. 855.

32. Ibid., pp. 845-846; Hummel, I, 461.

33. A full translation of the Huang Wan letter may be found in Michael, III, 1052-1063. There is a photoreproduction of the original letter in *T'ai-p'ing t'ien-kuo wen-shu* (Peiping, 1933), unpaginated. The full Chinese text is also included in Hsieh Hsing-yao, "Wang T'ao shang-shu T'ai-p'ing t'ien-kuo shih-chi k'ao," in his *T'ai-p'ing t'ien-kuo shih-shih lun-ts'ung* (Shanghai, 1935), pp. 189-197. See also Hsiang Ta et al., comps., *T'ai-p'ing t'ien-kuo* (Shanghai, 1957), II, 766-772.

34. Hsieh Hsing-yao, "Wang T'ao shang-shu . . . shih-chi k'ao," p. 186; Shang Yen-liu, *T'ai-p'ing t'ien-kuo k'o-chü k'ao-shih chi-lüeh* (Shanghai, 1962), p. 89; Hsieh Hsing-yao, "Kuan-yü 'Shang-hai tsai T'ai-p'ing t'ien-kuo shih-tai' ti shih-liao," in Li Ting-i et al., comps., *Chung-kuo chin-tai-shih lun-ts'ung* (Taipei, 1956), Ser. 1, IV, 184-185.

35. *Ta-Ch'ing Mu-tsung-i (T'ung-chih) huang-ti shih-lu* (Taipei, 1964), I, 573 (23:29b-30 in original ed.). See also Ch'en Ch'i-yüan, *Yung-hsien-chai pi-chi* (Shanghai, 1925), 12:5a-b; Masuda Wataru, "Ō Tō ni tsuite," *Jimbun kenkyū* 14.7:98 (August 1963).

36. See Bruce's two communications to the Tsungli Yamen, dated September 13 and September 24, 1862, in *Wen-hsien ts'ung-pien* (Peiping, 1930-1943), Ser. 20, pp. 1-4b. Since the courtesy name used in the original letter was identical with one of the courtesy names then being used by Wang (see n. 42 below), the authorities on finding the letter probably suspected Wang immediately. Further evidence of this is a letter from Li Hung-chang to Tseng Kuo-fan, dated T'ung-chih 1/3/15 (April 13, 1862), in which Li

identifies the letter has having been written by a *hsiu-ts'ai* from Hsin-yang. The fact that the author was from Hsin-yang (Wang T'ao's hsien too) is nowhere indicated in the letter proper. See Li Hung-chang, *Li Wen-chung-kung ch'üan-chi* (Taipei, 1962), IV, 8.

37. For the length of time Wang spent in the consulate, see "Nan-hsing" (The trip south), *Heng-hua-kuan shih-lu*, 3:13; the date of his departure from Shanghai is given in a letter to Yang Yin-ch'uan, *CT*, 6:11.

38. Michael, I, 156-157.

39. That is, if we except an oral admission allegedly made by Wang years later to his friend Huang Tsun-hsien. See Cheng Hsien, "Huang Kung-tu—Wu-hsü wei-hsin yün-tung ti ling-hsiu," *I-ching* No. 10:21 (1936); Ch'ien Chung-lien, *Huang Kung-tu hsien-sheng nien-p'u*, in Huang Tsun-hsien, *Jen-ching-lu shih-ts'ao chien-chu* (Shanghai, 1957), p. 28.

40. *CT*, 6:16a-b. See also *WLWP*, 11:18; "Shu-ai" (Setting forth my grief), *Heng-hua-kuan shih-lu*, 3:14a-b; "Nan-hsing," ibid., pp. 12-14.

41. Wu Ching-shan, pp. 671-676.

42. Hsieh Hsing-yao, "Wang T'ao shang-shu . . . shih-chi k'ao," p. 199; Lo Erh-kang, "Shang T'ai-p'ing-chün shu ti Huang Wan k'ao," *Kuo-hsüeh chi-k'an* 4.2:124-128 (June 1934); Lo Erh-kang, "Huang Wan k'ao," in his *T'ai-p'ing t'ien-kuo shih chi-tsai ting-miu chi* (Peking, 1955), pp. 112-115 (this is a considerably reworked version of the preceding article by Lo); Shang Yen-liu, pp. 84-86.

In his autobiography, Wang claims that he was given the name Li-pin at birth and changed it to Han (courtesy name, Lan-chin) after passing the *hsiu-ts'ai* examination (*WLWP*, 11:16b). At no point in his published writings does he admit to ever having had the courtesy name Lan-ch'ing (Wu Ching-shan, pp. 689-691, lists all of the names for Wang that can be derived from his published works). We know, however, from the seals accompanying Wang's diary manuscripts and from the *hsiu-ts'ai* lists for Wang's hsien, that Wang Li-pin's courtesy name was Lan-ch'ing (Lo Erh-kang, "Shang T'ai-p'ing-chün," p. 126). Furthermore, it is clear from a contemporary diary that, as late as the summer of 1861, Wang was still known by this courtesy name. See Ch'en Nai-ch'ien, comp., *Yang-hu Chao Hui-fu nien-p'u*, in *T'ai-p'ing t'ien-kuo*, VIII, 746.

Lo Erh-kang further conjectures that Wang's original given name may have been Wan ("Shang T'ai-p'ing-chün," p. 128). See also Ch'en Chen-kuo, " 'Ch'ang-mao chuang-yüan' Wang T'ao," *I-ching* No. 33:41 (July 5, 1937).

Wang T'ao, for what it is worth, wrote a short note on the *Li-sao* in which he revealed a strong emotional identification with the tragic fate of the poem's reputed author, Ch'ü Yüan. Whenever he read the poem as a youth, Wang claims, he wept so hard he could not finish it. *WLWP*, 10:4b-5.

43. Lo Erh-kang, "Shang T'ai-p'ing-chün," pp. 128-147; Lo Erh-kang, "Huang Wan k'ao," pp. 115-135; Hsieh Hsing-yao, "Wang T'ao shang-shu . . . shih-chi k'ao," pp. 197-203.

44. Hu Shih, "Pa kuan ts'ang Wang T'ao shou-kao ch'i ts'e," *Kuo-li Pei-p'ing t'u-shu-kuan kuan-k'an* 8.3:1-5 (May-June 1934); Chien Yu-wen,

" 'Ch'ang-mao chuang-yüan' Wang T'ao pa," p. 44; Chien Yu-wen, "Kuan-yü Wang T'ao," *Ta-feng* 58:1785 (December 1939).

45. *CT*, 6:10b; Ch'en Ch'i-yüan, 12:5; McAleavy, pp. 16-17.

46. Lo Erh-kang, "Shang T'ai-p'ing-chün," pp. 142-143.

47. Bruce's communication of September 13, 1862, in *Wen-hsien ts'ung-pien*, Ser. 20, p. 2; Hummel, II, 836; Lo Erh-kang, "Huang Wan k'ao," pp. 127-128, 136-139. That Wang had remarried as early as 1852 is noted in "Ying-juan tsa-chi," HF 2/9/21 (November 2, 1852).

48. Lo Erh-kang, "Huang Wan k'ao," pp. 136-139. Among the proposals submitted by Wang to the Shanghai authorities in the fall of 1860 was one recommending the use of Western officers to lead Chinese troops into battle (*CT*, 5:16a-b). Wu Hsü, who was the recipient of this proposal, had an important hand in the founding of the Ever Victorious Army (Michael, I, 171). Wang Chih-ch'un, in his *Ko-kuo t'ung-shang shih-mo chi* (1895), 16:1, affirms that Wu was influenced by Wang T'ao's advice. Wang T'ao himself, in a profile of Henry Burgevine, maintains that the establishment of the Ever Victorious Army (of which Burgevine was for a time commander) was in direct response to his proposal (see *WYYT*, 2:12b-13b). See also Masuda, pp. 98-99. The view that the Huang Wan letter was written with British interests in mind is also advanced by Teng Ssu-yü in his *Historiography of the Taiping Rebellion* (Cambridge, Mass., 1962), p. 66.

49. Shang Yen-liu, pp. 86-87.

50. Accounts of his career can be found in Hummel, I, 367-369; So Kwan-wai and Eugene P. Boardman (with the assistance of Ch'iu P'ing), "Hung Jen-kan, Taiping Prime Minister, 1859-1864," *Harvard Journal of Asiatic Studies* 20.1-2:262-294 (June 1957); Michael, I, 134-168; Y.C. Teng, "The Failure of Hung Jen-kan's Foreign Policy," *Journal of Asian Studies* 28:125-138 (November 1968); Jen Yu-wen (Chien Yu-wen), *The Taiping Revolutionary Movement* (New Haven, 1973), pp. 351-376 et passim.

51. *The Missionary Magazine and Chronicle* 24:277 (1860); see also ibid., p. 296. So Kwan-wai and Eugene Boardman (p. 269) say that Hung studied at "a Shanghai missionary school."

52. "Heng-hua-kuan jih-chi," HF 4/9/8 (October 29, 1854). This is the only reference in the diary to a person named Hung.

53. Quoted in So Kwan-wai and Eugene Boardman, pp. 269-270.

54. *The Missionary Magazine and Chronicle* 24:271-278 (1860).

55. Letters from Edkins, July 30, 1860, and John, August 16, 1860, ibid., pp. 298-302. Translations of the letters from Hung and Li, inviting the missionaries to Soochow, are in Michael, III, 1111-1116.

56. The quote is from Edkins's description of the Nanking trip, "Narrative of a Visit to Nanking," in Jane Edkins, *Chinese Scenes and People* (London, 1863), p. 266. Wang T'ao's name is not mentioned in the narrative. But Hu Shih discovered, among some of Wang's manuscripts in the Palace Museum, a stray page of diary, dated HF 11/2/1 (March 11, 1861), in which Wang states: "The English missionary, Joseph Edkins, asked me to accompany him on a trip to Nanking. I couldn't decline." See Hu Shih, "Pa kuan-ts'ang," pp. 1-5.

Hsieh Wu-liang, p. 39, asserts that Wang T'ao stayed in Nanking for almost a year. I have found no evidence to corroborate this.

57. Muirhead was another who came away from a visit to Nanking early in 1861 impressed by the religious level of the rebels. See his letter of February 9, 1861, in *The Missionary Magazine and Chronicle* 25:198-209 (1861). Some of the LMS missionaries were outspoken in their opposition to British entry into the war on the government side. For a strong defense of British neutrality, see James Legge's letter of July 11, 1862, ibid., 26:283-288 (1862).

58. Helen M. Lynd, "Clues to Identity," in Hendrik M. Ruitenbeek, ed., *Varieties of Modern Social Theory* (New York, 1963), p. 19.

59. Murphey, *Shanghai*, p. 8. For further discussion, see Chap. 9 below.

60. Robert K. Merton, "Social Structure and Anomie," in Ruitenbeek, p. 389.

3. THE YEARS IN EXILE: HONG KONG AND EUROPE

1. It is generally agreed that Wang never really sat for the Taiping examinations. Although most scholars believe the nickname "Ch'ang-mao chuang-yüan" to have been given him by friends, it may have been devised by Wang himself. See Shang Yen-liu, p. 92; Hsieh Hsing-yao, "Wang T'ao shang-shu . . . shih-chi k'ao," p. 198; Ch'en Chen-kuo, p. 43; Chien Yu-wen, " 'Ch'ang-mao chuang-yüan' Wang T'ao pa," pp. 44-45; Chien Yu-wen, "Kuan-yü Wang T'ao," p. 1785; Hsieh Wu-liang, p. 38.

2. Hsieh Hsing-yao, "Wang T'ao shang-shu . . . shih-chi k'ao," pp. 203-204.

3. *CT*, 6:11-18; *Man-yu sui-lu*, pp. 9813-9814; McAleavy, pp. 18-20.

4. Lindsay Ride, "Biographical Note," p. 1.

5. *CTHC*, 5:3.

6. *WLWP*, 8:4b; *Man-yu sui-lu*, p. 9815.

7. *CT*, 1:8b.

8. *WLWP*, 8:4.

9. *The Chinese Classics*, III, viii.

10. See, for example, *The Chinese Classics*, IV, 167 (Prolegomena), 9, 13, 14, 22, 30, 35, 43, 45, 61, 66, 77, 92, 106, 115, 161-162, 210, 259, 412, 430, 459, 499, 508, 526, 542, 580, 616, 639; V, 4 (Prolegomena), 10, 97, 134, 302, 833; *The Li Kî* [*Li chi*], in F. Max Müller, ed., *The Sacred Books of the East* (Oxford, 1885), XXVII, 97, 168, 171, 202, 227, 245, 277, 285, 287, 299-300, 310.

11. The original manuscripts of Wang's collected commentaries on the *Shih-ching* ("Mao-shih chi-shih," 30 chüan), the *Li chi* ("Li-chi chi-shih"), and the *I-ching* ("Chou-i chi-shih") are in the New York Public Library. The last-named, unlike the others, is very brief. Wang also did a lengthy compilation of commentaries on the *Ch'un-ch'iu* and *Tso-chuan* ("Ch'un-ch'iu Tso-shih-chuan chi-shih," 60 chüan). This and other of Wang's unpublished writings on the classics are described by him in his *T'ao-yüan chu-shu tsung-mu* (Shanghai, 1889), pp. 4-6.

12. *The Chinese Classics*, IV, 176 (Prolegomena). Wang's letter accom-

panying the presentation of "Mao-shih chi-shih" to Legge (ca. 1864) is in *CT*, 6:15b-17. He claims to have spent about ten months on this compilation. For Legge's appraisals of Wang's other compilations, see *The Chinese Classics*, V, 145-146 (Prolegomena); *The Lî Kî*, XXVII, xii.

13. Quoted in Helen E. Legge, *James Legge: Missionary and Scholar* (London, 1905), p. 43.

14. Legge's second invitation to Wang T'ao is referred to in *CT*, 10:12b-13. Engaged at the time in the translation of one of the most difficult of Chinese texts, Legge must have felt Wang's absence keenly.

15. *The Chinese Classics*, V, 146 (Prolegomena).

16. Shinjō Shinzō, *Tung-yang t'ien-wen-hsüeh shih yen-chiu*, tr. Shen Chün (Shanghai, 1933), pp. 326-327, 367. See also Tseng Tz'u-liang's introduction to a reprint of three of Wang's treatises under the composite title, *Ch'un-ch'iu li-hsüeh san-chung* (Peking, 1959). Tseng seeks to minimize the influence of Chalmers on Wang, supporting his view with three lengthy and technical letters written by Wang to Chalmers in which the differences of viewpoint between the two men are set forth (see ibid., pp. 112-134). Wang himself, although critical of Chalmers's complete downgrading of traditional Chinese mathematical knowledge, recognized that without Western astronomy and mathematics the chronology of the Spring and Autumn period could never have been set straight. See *WYYT*, 3:3b-4; *Man-yu sui-lu*, p. 9847; letter to Stanislas Julien (ca. 1868), *CT*, 7:21. See also the "Appendix on the Astronomy of the Ancient Chinese" by Chalmers in *The Chinese Classics*, III, 90-104 (Prolegomena); and the evaluation of Chalmers's work in Léopold de Saussure, *Les origines de l'astronomie chinoise* (Taipei, 1967), pp. 390-393, 422-430.

17. Joseph Levenson developed some of these thoughts more fully in his *Liang Ch'i-ch'ao and the Mind of Modern China* (Cambridge, Mass., 1965), pp. 109-113.

18. Wylie, *Memorials of Protestant Missionaries to the Chinese*, pp. 37-38, 281.

19. Ibid., pp. 190-191. See esp. Edkins's *Chinese Buddhism: A Volume of Sketches, Historical, Descriptive, and Critical* (London, 1880).

20. For an appraisal, see Howard Levy's introduction to the second edition (New York, 1964).

21. *The Chinese Classics*, V, 51 (Prolegomena). See also Edkins, *Chinese Buddhism*, p. 397; Paul A. Cohen, *China and Christianity: The Missionary Movement and the Growth of Chinese Antiforeignism, 1860-1870* (Cambridge, Mass., 1963), pp. 79-80.

22. On Wong Shing, see Chap. 9, n. 3 below.

23. The title of the work was *Huo-ch'i lüeh-shuo*. The edition used here is in 1 ts'e (Hong Kong, 1881). The occasion for its compilation was Li Hung-chang's ordering of Ting Jih-ch'ang to return from Kwangtung to Kiangsu to supervise the manufacture of ammunition and firearms. The book's immediate purpose was to enable Chinese to begin to produce modern weapons themselves, so that they would be less dependent on Western purchases. Copies were presented to Li and Ting. See Wang's initial preface,

dated August 24-September 2, 1863 (reproduced in *WLWP*, 8:9-11); Hummel, II, 721; *CT*, 7:10a-b, 13. Wang claims that one Chinese commander, Fang Yao, distributed 200 copies of the book to his subordinate officers (*T'ao-yüan chu-shu tsung-mu*, p. 3).

24. Apparently Wong Shing. A number of Wang's letters were written on behalf of friends. In every instance, however, the thinking is clearly Wang's (as well, presumably, as the friend's) and therefore I have not hesitated to treat these letters as Wang's own. (It is, of course, doubtful whether Wang would have selected these letters for publication if they did not reflect his own ideas.)

25. *CT*, 7:2b-3.

26. *CT*, 7:1-10b.

27. *Man-yu sui-lu*, pp. 9816-9822.

28. Ibid., p. 9822.

29. Ibid., pp. 9823-9830.

30. Ibid., p. 9838.

31. Ibid., pp. 9831, 9845.

32. Ibid., pp. 9830-9831.

33. Ibid., p. 9840.

34. Ibid., pp. 9840-9844.

35. Ibid., pp. 9846-9850.

36. See the poems in *Heng-hua-kuan shih-lu*, 4:7b-10.

37. *Man-yu sui-lu*, pp. 9850-9856.

38. *CT*, 8:4b; letter from E.D. Grinstead of the British Museum to author, March 6, 1967.

39. *Man-yu sui-lu*, p. 9825. Wang's diary has the meeting with Julien taking place in 1868, but it is clear from other sources that it was not until Wang's return trip through Paris that the two men actually met. See *CT*, 7:18-21b; *FKCL*, 7:16b. The biography of Julien is in *WLWP*, 11:26b-28.

40. *Man-yu sui-lu*, p. 9841; see also *WLWP*, 11:18b.

41. The original editions of the three short story collections published by Wang were: *Tun-k'u lan-yen* (1875); *Sung-yin man-lu* (Shanghai, 1887); and *Sung-pin so-hua* (Shanghai, 1887). All three collections appeared in many additions. *Tun-k'u lan-yen* was so popular that a pirated edition was issued in Kiangsi under the title *Hsien-t'an hsiao-hsia lu* (Idle tales for a summer vacation). The stories in *Sung-yin man-lu* and *Sung-pin so-hua* appeared originally in the mid-1880's in the illustrated Shanghai magazine, *Hua-pao*. Some editions of *Sung-yin man-lu* were entitled *Hou Liao-chai chih-i* (Supplement to *Liao-chai chih-i*). A punctuated edition of *Sung-pin so-hua* came out in Shanghai in 1934; another punctuated edition appeared in the same year under the title *T'ao-yüan pi-chi* (The notebooks of Wang T'ao). Wang T'ao discussed the background of each of the three collections in *T'ao-yüan chu-shu tsung-mu*, pp. 2b-3, 10. There is a translation of one of Wang's stories in McAleavy, pp. 29-36.

42. *CT*, 7:18-21b; *FKCL*, preface, pp. 1b, 3a-b.

43. So it is said at least. See Ch'en Chen-kuo, p. 42; Wu Ching-shan, p. 683; *WLWP*, 9:11a-b, 11:18b-19.

44. Roswell S. Britton, *The Chinese Periodical Press, 1800-1912* (Taipei,

1966), p. 42; see also Frank H.H. King, ed., and Prescott Clarke, *A Research Guide to China-Coast Newspapers, 1822-1911* (Cambridge, Mass., 1965), p. 27.

45. Ko Kung-chen, *Chung-kuo pao-hsüeh shih* (Peking, 1955), p. 74; Ch'en Chih-lan, "Pen-pao ch'uang-tsao i-lai," in *Hua-tzu jih-pao ch'i-shih-i chou-nien chi-nien-k'an* (unpaginated) (Hong Kong, 1934); Tseng Hsü-pai, comp., *Chung-kuo hsin-wen shih* (Taipei, 1966), I, 145. Britton (p. 46) and King and Clarke (pp. 28, 61) apparently err in giving 1872 as the year the *Hua-tzu jih-pao* was first published.

46. On Ho Kai, see Chap. 9, n. 7 below. On Yung Wing, see Chap. 9, n. 4 below. Wang T'ao knew Yung Wing, though it is not certain how well. Ch'en Chen-kuo (p. 42) says that they were intimate friends, but Ch'en is often unreliable. Yung makes no mention of Wang in his autobiography. Wang did, however, write a congratulatory note on the occasion of Yung's establishment of a public school in his native village (see *WLWP*, 8:7b-9). On Wu T'ing-fang, see Chap. 9, n. 9 below. While Wu was still in England studying for the bar, Wang T'ao, in a letter to Ting Jih-ch'ang (ca. 1875), recommended him, as well as Chang Tsung-liang and Ch'en Yen, for government positions. *CT*, 9:17; see also Wang's letter to Tong King-sing (ca. 1876), *CT*, 9:22a-b. During the years that Wu T'ing-fang served on Li Hung-chang's staff, as Li's legal adviser and foreign affairs deputy, he and Wang frequently exchanged letters. Wang also was well acquainted with Tong King-sing, one of the most prominent compradors of the late nineteenth century and for eleven years (1873-1884) director of the China Merchants Steam Navigation Company (see *CT*, 9:20b-22b, 11:1b-4). On Tong, see Chap. 9, n. 8 below.

47. Ko Kung-chen, p. 119; Britton, p. 42; Yüan Ch'ang-ch'ao, *Chung-kuo pao-yeh hsiao-shih* (Hong Kong, 1957), pp. 29-30; Liu Yüeh-sheng, comp., *Hsiang-kang Chi-tu-chiao-hui shih* (Hong Kong, 1941), pp. 155-156. Details on the sale of the press may be found in the LMS Archives, South China: Box 7 (1870-1874). The purchasers, represented by a Mr. Chun-a-yin (very possibly Ch'en Yen), also wanted to lease the premises on which the printing plant was located. The missionaries, however, would consent to this only "if they would bind themselves not to work on Sundays and to allow no unchristian or antichristian articles to appear in their paper." The Chinese would not submit to these conditions and in the upshot the equipment was moved to a new location. Letter of E.J. Eitel to J. Mullens, January 28, 1873.

48. Hummel, II, 838. The paper was known in English as the "Universal Circulating Herald." Some writers (for example, Britton) give 1873 as the year in which *Tsun-wan yat-po* began publication. The confusion apparently stems from the fact that the paper's first issue appeared on the 17th day of the 11th month of T'ung-chih 12. The conventional equivalent of T'ung-chih 12 in the Western calendar is 1873. But in this case the date falls late enough in the lunar year to bring it over to January of 1874. See *Hsün-huan jih-pao liu-shih chou-nien chi-nien t'e-k'an* (Hong Kong, 1932), p. 13.

49. Britton, pp. 42-43; Ko Kung-chen, p. 119; *Hsün-huan jih-pao liu-shih chou-nien chi-nien t'e-k'an*, p. 13.

50. One other Chinese-operated daily, *Chao-wen hsin-pao*, preceded *Tsun-wan yat-po* by a few months, but it did not last. See Ko Kung-chen, p. 119.

51. Ibid., p. 119; *Hsün-huan jih-pao liu-shih chou-nien chi-nien t'e-k'an*, p. 14; Britton, pp. 64, 67, 69. Ch'ien Cheng, a Chekiang *hsiu-ts'ai*, married Wang T'ao's eldest daughter in 1868 while Wang was still in Scotland. From Wang's many letters to him and Ch'ien's prefaces and postfaces to Wang's works (for example, *PFCC* and *WYYT*), it is clear that the two men had a deep affection for one another. Hung Shih-wei's personal relationship with Wang is less well documented. See Hung's preface (1875) to *Tun-k'u lan-yen* (1880 ed.).

52. On Hu Li-yüan, see Chap. 9, n. 6 below.

53. Britton, p. 43; Ko Kung-chen, pp. 119-120; *Hsün-huan jih-pao liu-shih chou-nien chi-nien t'e-k'an*, p. 13. A reproduction of an 1874 issue of *Tsun-wan yat-po* appears ibid., pp. 15-18. The only copies of the paper from the nineteenth century that I have been able to examine personally (and possibly these are the only ones extant) are some 1874 issues located at the British Museum.

54. *WLWP*, 7:21-22b; *FKCL*, 18:18b-19b, 21:28b-29b.

55. *WLWP*, 2:27b.

56. Ko Kung-chen, pp. 104-105; letter to Ting Jih-ch'ang (ca. 1870-1871), *CT*, 8:11b; letter to Li Chao-t'ang (ca. 1874-1875), *CT*, 9:15b-16; letter to Fang Yao (ca. 1884-1885), *CTHC*, 4:16b-17. Wang also proposed publication of an annual volume of official correspondence concerning Sino-foreign relations. Western governments, he noted, in issuing instructions to their envoys abroad, had to rely exclusively on the communications of these selfsame envoys. In the Margary affair, there was some suspicion that the demands made by the British negotiators exceeded the instructions of the Foreign Office. If China had had a Western-language publication in which the relevant documentation could have been included for distribution in England, an aroused British public might have been able to soften British demands somewhat. See Wang's letter to Tong King-sing (ca. 1876), *CT*, 9:21b-22b.

57. *WLWP*, 7:21b; *FKCL*, 21:28b-29b; letter to Li Chao-t'ang (ca. 1874-1875), *CT*, 9:15b-16. For Liang Ch'i-ch'ao's views on the political role of the press see Britton, pp. 86-90.

58. Letter to Tong King-sing (ca. 1876), *CT*, 9:20b-21; letter to Yü Ch'ien-chih (ca. 1876), *CT*, 10:5b; letter to Yang Yin-ch'uan (ca. 1876), *CT*, 10:6-7. In these letters Wang discusses his "work in progress."

59. Wang T'ao's trip to Japan and his associations with Japanese men of letters are dealt with in Chap. 4.

60. *Shen-pao* (often transliterated *Shun Pao*) was founded in 1872 by the British businessman, Frederick Major. It was highly successful, partly owing to its unexcelled news service, partly because of the high-quality editorial direction provided by such men as Ch'ien Cheng, Wang T'ao, and Huang Hsieh-hsüan (editor-in-chief from 1896 to 1905), and partly because Major "had the judgment to efface his own connection and let his Chinese editors produce an essentially Chinese paper." *Shen-pao*, prior to the 1890's, was one of the few Chinese-language papers—*Tsun-wan yat-po* was another—that was willing to criticize the Chinese government. By 1895 it had a circulation of

15,000. In 1907 it was bought out by Chinese and henceforth remained under Chinese ownership. See Britton, pp. 63-70, 81.

61. *Wan-kuo kung-pao* was an outgrowth of *Chiao-hui hsin-pao* (Church news), a weekly miscellany devoted to religion, science, and news, and started by the American Protestant missionary, Young J. Allen, in Shanghai in 1868. In 1875 the name was changed to *Wan-kuo kung-pao* (with the English title "The Globe Magazine") and the magazine's coverage was expanded to include information on all aspects of Western life and culture. Suspended in 1883, owing to lack of funds, *Wan-kuo kung-pao* resumed publication in 1889 as a monthly (with the new English title "Review of the Times") and in the 1890's became an influential stimulus to Chinese reform thought. Besides Allen himself, regular missionary contributors included Alexander Williamson, Calvin Mateer, Timothy Richard, William Muirhead, Joseph Edkins, and Gilbert Reid.

Wang T'ao was closely associated with Young Allen in the 1890's. Between September 1890 and December 1893, one or two pieces by him (some of them reprinted from *WLWP* or *Shen-pao*) appeared in each monthly issue of *Wan-kuo kung-pao* save one. Wang was one of the Chinese judges of an essay contest sponsored by the magazine in 1895 (see *WKKP* No. 74:29 [March 1895]). Allen, moreover, thought highly enough of Wang to invite him to write a preface for his influential work on the Sino-Japanese War. See *Chung-Tung chan-chi pen-mo* (Shanghai, 1897), prefatory matter, pp. 4a-b. The preface (dated April 13-22, 1896) was reprinted in *WKKP* No. 89:5b-7 (June 1896).

62. Britton, pp. 41, 86; Lin Yutang, *A History of the Press and Public Opinion in China* (Chicago, 1936), p. 79; Hung Shen, "*Shen-pao* tsung-pien-tsuan 'Ch'ang-mao chuang-yüan' Wang T'ao k'ao-cheng," *Wen-hsüeh* 2.6:1040-1042 (June 1934).

63. Lü Shih-ch'iang, "Wang T'ao p'ing-chuan," *Shu ho jen* No. 61:480 (July 1, 1967).

64. *Records . . . 1890*, p. 264. On Wang's association with Allen see n. 61 above.

65. See, for example, Hu Shih, *The Chinese Renaissance* (Chicago, 1934), pp. 11-12.

66. *WLWP*, 11:20a-b. See also Wang's two poems, "K'u wang-nü T'iao-hsien" (A lament for my deceased daughter T'iao-hsien) and "Shuai-tsung" (The decline of my family line), *Heng-hua-kuan shih-lu*, 4:14b-15, 16a-b.

67. *CT*, 9:9b-10.

68. It would appear, from the account of Wang T'ao's Japanese friend, Oka Senjin (Oka Shikamon), that Wang began to smoke opium some time before 1884. It is not clear whether Wang ever became addicted. See Oka's *Kuan-kuang chi-yu* (Tokyo, 1886), 1:5; also Sanetō Keishū, "Ō Tō no raiyū to Nihon bunjin," in his *Kindai Nisshi bunka ron* (Tokyo, 1941), pp. 57, 98. After his trip to Japan, Wang T'ao was criticized in some quarters for his unrestrained interest in women. Oka came to his friend's defense, arguing that it was natural for a man as troubled as Wang to find outlets of this sort. See

Oka's postface to Wang's Japan diary in Oka Senjin, *Ts'ang-ming-shan-fang wen ch'u-chi* (Tokyo, 1920), 6:4b; also Sanetō, pp. 88-89.

I would not want to suggest, of course, that Wang's hedonistic life-style was a consequence exclusively of his misfortunes. When he was nearly sixty years old, Wang wrote John Fryer: "All my life I have been rather a Bohemian, fond of song and girls and wine, and even to-day I am always in the gardens and other resorts here in Shanghai. This has always seemed to me a perfectly normal recreation and not the sort of thing a man has to hide from other people." McAleavy, p. 26, as translated from *CTHC*, 6:21. See also Wang's preface to a collection of writings he compiled about women of pleasure, *Yen-shih ts'ung-ch'ao* (1878).

PART II

PROLOGUE

1. This career pattern became increasingly common in the late Ch'ing. See Chap. 9 below; also Benjamin Schwartz, *In Search of Wealth and Power: Yen Fu and the West* (Cambridge, Mass., 1964), pp. 25-26, 32.

2. *Insight and Responsibility* (New York, 1964), p. 96.

3. *The Dynamics of Modernization: A Study in Comparative History* (New York, 1966), p. 54.

4. VIRTUE AND POWER IN THE CONTEMPORARY WORLD

1. The best discussion of the evolving tension between "ideology" and "realism" in China's traditional relations with foreign countries is found in Wang Gungwu, "Early Ming Relations with Southeast Asia: A Background Essay," in John K. Fairbank, ed., *The Chinese World Order: Traditional China's Foreign Relations* (Cambridge, Mass., 1968), pp. 34-62.

2. *PFCC*, 19:15b-16. For other examples of comparisons between late Chou and contemporary European interstate politics, see *PFCC*, 17:28a-b, 20:36b; *WLWP*, 4:6, 24, 26b, 27b-29b, 5:13, 8:27-28b; *CT*, 11:11; *CTHC*, 4:15b.

3. See, for example, the treaty of September 26, 1815, which set up the Holy Alliance and in which the signatories (the kings of Austria, Prussia, and Russia) refer to themselves as "members of one and the same Christian nation" called upon by Providence to govern "three branches of the One family." In E. Hertslet, ed., *The Map of Europe by Treaty* (London, 1875-1891), I, 318.

4. See Richard L. Walker, *The Multi-State System of Ancient China* (Hamden, Conn., 1953).

5. Wang was not alone. According to him, the analogy with the late Chou had first been used by Chang Ssu-kuei in his preface (1864) to W.A.P. Martin's translation of Henry Wheaton's *Elements of International Law (Wan-kuo kung-fa)*. See Fuse Chisoku, "Ō Shi-sen no Fusō yūki," in his *Yūki ni arawaretaru Meiji jidai no Nisshi ōrai*, in *Tōa kenkyū kōza* No. 84:26-27 (December 1938); also Immanuel C.Y. Hsü, *China's Entrance into the Family of Nations: The Diplomatic Phase, 1858-1880* (Cambridge, Mass., 1960), pp.

134-135. The analogy was used by many other Chinese as well in the latter decades of the nineteenth century. See, for example, Kuo Sung-tao, in David Hamilton, "Kuo Sung-tao: A Maverick Confucian," *Papers on China* 15:12 (1961). A critique of the analogy was provided by Ho Shu-ling, "Lun chin chih shih-chü yü Chan-kuo ta i," in *Huang-ch'ao ching-shih-wen hsin-pien*, comp. Mai Chung-hua (Taipei, 1965), I, 124-126. Ho listed eight discrepancies between the Warring States period and the contemporary world.

6. Walker, p. 99.

7. *CT*, 9:12b. See also *WLWP*, 6:6b-7b; *PFCC*, 5:1b.

8. *WLWP*, 6:1.

9. *WLWP*, 2:3. For another example of Wang's position that before a country could make effective use of international law it had to become wealthy and powerful see *WLWP*, 2:5b. For a Communist assessment of Wang's views on international law see Wang Wei-ch'eng, "Wang T'ao ti ssu-hsiang," in *Chung-kuo chin-tai ssu-hsiang shih lun-wen chi* (Shanghai, 1958), pp. 43-44.

10. *WLWP*, 5:7b-9. Compare Wang's position on international law and treaties with that of Fukuzawa Yukichi (as of 1878): "A few cannons are worth more than a hundred volumes of international law. A case of ammunition is of more use than innumerable treaties of friendship." As quoted in Carmen Blacker, *The Japanese Enlightenment: A Study of the Writings of Fukuzawa Yukichi* (Cambridge, 1964), p. 129.

11. A prominent exception was Li Hung-chang. For a pioneering analysis of Chinese images of Russia toward the end of the Ch'ing, see Don Price, "The Chinese Intelligentsia's Image of Russia, 1896-1911," Harvard University, Ph. D. dissertation, 1967.

12. Letters to Cheng Tsao-ju (ca. 1879-1880), *CT*, 12:1-2, 26-27b; *WYYT*, 4:9b.

13. See, for example, *CT*, 12:1-2, 26-27b; *CTHC*, 4:15a-b; *WLWP*, 8:27-28b.

14. See, for example, *PFCC*, 19:15b-16; *CT*, 11:11, 12:2, 18b; *CTHC*, 1:15b; *WLWP*, 4:6, 24, 27b-29, 8:27-28b. For a much more elaborate statement of the Ch'in-Russia analogy, see Ch'en Chih (Yao-lin-kuan-chu), "O-jen kuo-shih k'u-lei ch'iang Ch'in lun," *Shih-wu pao*, Vol. 18, Kuang-hsü 23/1/21 (February 22, 1897); reprinted in *Huang-ch'ao ching-shih-wen hsin-pien*, II, 293-295. Ch'en Chih, after propounding an explicitly cyclical view of history, details ten parallels between Ch'in and Russia and enjoins his fellow countrymen not to repeat the mistakes of the Warring States period.

15. See T.A. Hsia, "Demons of Paradise: The Chinese Images of Russia," *The Annals of the American Academy of Political and Social Science* 349:28 (September 1963).

16. Wang Shu-huai, *Wai-jen yü wu-hsü pien-fa* (Taipei, 1965), pp. 140 ff.

17. The anti-Russian bias of Wang's Japanese friends is also pertinent here. See, for example, the excerpt from one of Oka Senjin's writings in *WLWP*, 10:9b-11; Sanetō, p. 98; Wang T'ao, *Fu-sang yu-chi*, in *Hsiao-fang-hu-chai yü-ti ts'ung-ch'ao*, LII, 8068.

18. *WLWP*, 11:21b; Wu Ching-shan, p. 687.

19. *WYYT*, 4:2b-3, 7a-b.

20. *WYYT*, 4:3a-b, 5:6a-b.

21. "Ko-lun-pu ch'uan-tsan," *WKKP* No. 42:11b (July 1892).

22. Wang's work on the Franco-Prussian War, *P'u-Fa chan-chi*, was reprinted in Japan in 1878 by the Army Ministry and again in 1887 (Osaka). As documentation in his polemic against the Japanese claim that the Ryūkyū Islands formerly belonged to Japan, Wang cited the famous Japanese historical work, *Dai Nihon shi* (History of great Japan). In *Fa-kuo chih-lüeh* (General history of France) he made extensive use of recent Japanese histories of France (see Chap. 5).

23. See Chap. 1. The events of Wang T'ao's stay in Japan were recorded by him in *Fu-sang yu-chi* (A record of travels in Japan). A detailed study of the trip is provided in Sanetō, pp. 52-100, and a more summary account in Fuse, pp. 22-34.

24. Masuda, pp. 91-92. Kurimoto Joun, the son of a doctor, had been a retainer of some standing in the last years of the Tokugawa and in 1867 was commissioned by the *bakufu* to go to France in order to strengthen Franco-Japanese ties. Thus, as Masuda stresses, his assessment of *P'u-Fa chan-chi* was based on a personal knowledge of the French scene on the eve of the outbreak of the Franco-Prussian conflict. Kurimoto became chief editor of the *Hōchi shimbun* in 1874. He also played a prominent part in the formation of other early Meiji newspapers and appears to have been especially well-known for his drama criticism. See Marius B. Jansen, *Sakamoto Ryōma and the Meiji Restoration* (Princeton, 1961), pp. 318-319, 407; *Japan Biographical Encyclopedia and Who's Who* (Tokyo, 1958), pp. 738-739; Komiya Toyotaka, comp. and ed., *Japanese Music and Drama in the Meiji Era*, tr. Edward G. Seidensticker and Donald Keene (Tokyo, 1956), p. 319; Sanetō, pp. 62-63, 74, 85, 91.

25. Sanetō, pp. 61-63. On Wang's illness, see *CT*, 12:19b; *CTHC*, 1:9b-10, 13-14, 20b, 2:11b; *WLWP*, 9:7, 11:19b.

26. A strong *jōi* advocate during the *bakumatsu* period, Sada in 1862 had led a band of troops to Edo in an attempt to overthrow the shogunate, for which action he was imprisoned by his clan. In 1870 Sada went to Korea where he tried, without success, to act as Japan's properly delegated representative. After the Meiji government's decision not to invade Korea, he continued to write articles advocating a strong policy toward that country, believing that Korea was necessary to Japan for both historical and geopolitical reasons. Sada's belletristic interests were manifested in his founding of a "club" for the housing of fine works of literature and in his compilation of an anthology of Meiji prose and poetry (*Meiji shibun*), a copy of which he presented to Wang T'ao. His brisk nature was evidenced in an incident that occurred in the course of a banquet he was giving in Wang T'ao's honor. So many people were pestering Wang for specimens of his calligraphy that Sada abruptly tore up the paper and threw away the writing brushes. See Sanetō, pp. 62, 67, 68, 70, 72, 92-93; Marius B. Jansen, *The Japanese and Sun Yat-sen* (Cambridge, Mass., 1954), pp. 23-24; *Japan Biographical Encyclopedia and Who's Who*, p. 1263; Fuse, p. 27.

27. Shigeno, an ex-samurai from Satsuma, was involved in the negotiations that followed the British bombardment of Kagoshima in 1863. After the Restoration, he served first in the Ministry of Education and then in the Office of Historiography. In 1881 he was appointed deputy chief editor of the reorganized College of Historiography, from which base he became "the actual director of the government's historiographical undertakings." Shigeno's influence on the development of modern historical studies in Japan took two directions: (1) the disengagement of historical inquiry from political and moral factors and (2) the fusion of Western historical methods with those of the *k'ao-cheng* school. See Jiro Numata, "Shigeno Yasutsugu and the Modern Tokyo Tradition of Historical Writing," in W.G. Beasley and E.G. Pulleyblank, eds., *Historians of China and Japan* (London, 1961), pp. 264-287 (the quotation from p. 269). See also Sanetō, pp. 61-64, 68-71, 75, 77, 85-86, 90; *Japan Biographical Encyclopedia and Who's Who*, p. 1387.

28. Oka, who was widely known by his *hao*, Shikamon (or Rokumon), compiled a book on France which was one of the principal sources for Wang T'ao's history of that country. He also wrote a strongly royalist account of the Meiji Restoration. Katayama Sen, who went on to become a leading Asian Communist, studied at Oka's school (the Oka juku) in the early 1880's and soon became "the favorite of his teacher." Hyman Kublin, *Asian Revolutionary: The Life of Sen Katayama* (Princeton, 1964), pp. 36-38, 41, 45. Oka was one of Wang T'ao's strongest Japanese admirers. His grandiloquent praise of Wang's work on the Franco-Prussian War (in a colophon to *Fu-sang yu-chi*) speaks for itself: "When *P'u-Fa chan-chi* was introduced in Japan its readers became aware for the first time of Mr. Wang Tzu-ch'üan [Wang T'ao] and recognized that, having shaken a generation out of its paralysis with his fine penetrating writing, Wang was truly one of the great men of the age." *Ts'ang-ming-shan-fang wen ch'u-chi*, 6:4; Sanetō, pp. 61-62. See also ibid., pp. 63, 68-69, 71-72, 77, 86, 88-89, 97-99; Marius B. Jansen, "Japanese Views of China During the Meiji Period," in Albert Feuerwerker, Rhoads Murphey, and Mary C. Wright, eds., *Approaches to Modern Chinese History* (Berkeley, 1967), pp. 174-175. Wang reciprocated in full his friend's admiration. See WLWP, 10:7-9b, 9b-11; CTHC, 1:23b. For a particularly moving expression of the depth of his feeling for Oka, see Wang's comment in his friend's *Ts'ang-ming-shan-fang wen ch'u-chi*, 4:8b-9.

29. Also known by his original given name, Masanao, Nakamura in the early 1870's helped to found a number of important societies, the most famous of which was the Meirokusha (Sixth year of Meiji society). During its brief lifespan, the Meirokusha, under the intellectual guidance of Fukuzawa Yukichi, spread Western ideas through lectures and the publication of a magazine (*Meiroku zasshi*). On Nakamura's relationship with Wang T'ao, see Sanetō, pp. 63, 80, 85-86; a brief sketch of his career is in *Japan Biographical Encyclopedia and Who's Who*, p. 996.

30. On his departure from Tokyo, Wang was supplied with Ho Ju-chang's personal carriage for the trip to the railroad station. Sanetō, p. 75; see also ibid., pp. 67-68, 70, 74. Although Huang Tsun-hsien had an active diplomatic career which took him to posts in London, Singapore, and San Francisco, as

well as Tokyo (see Chap. 9 below), he was probably better known in China for his fine poetry. When Wang T'ao was about to leave Japan, Huang showed him the manuscript of a group of poems he had written describing the customs and mores of the Japanese. Wang felt that the poems were very important and persuaded Huang to permit him to publish them. After his return to Hong Kong, he discovered that the collection had already been published by the Tsungli Yamen. But, wanting Huang's poems to receive the widest possible reading, he went ahead and printed them anyway (in 1880). See *WLWP*, 9:5b-7b; Sanetō, p. 61; Ch'ien Chung-lien, p. 29; Chou Tso-jen, *"Jih-pen tsa-shih shih,"* *I-ching* No. 3:3-5 (1936). For an allusion to Wang T'ao in one of Huang's poems, see Huang Tsun-hsien, pp. 198-199. On the relationship between the two men, see Ch'ien Chung-lien, p. 28; Wang T'ao's letters to Huang, *CT*, 12:11-12, 18-19b.

Other Chinese friends made by Wang T'ao in Japan are named by him in a letter to Sheng Hsüan-huai (1879-1880), *CT*, 11:11b-12b.

31. Sanetō, pp. 64-65. Sanetō, who has read widely in the Japan diaries of visiting Chinese in the Meiji period, makes a point of the uniqueness of Wang T'ao's behavior in Japan.

32. Ibid., p. 86.

33. In addition to those already mentioned, some of the more prominent of the friends made by Wang in Japan were: Fujita Mokichi (1852-1892), one of Fukuzawa's disciples and an editor of the *Hōchi shimbun*; Hoshino Tsune (1839-1917), a historian; Iwaya Ichiroku (1834-1905), one of the great calligraphers of the Meiji era; Komaki Masanari (1843-1922), a leading Japanese scholar of the Chinese classics; Mishima Chūshū (1826-1915), another leading classical scholar and teacher; Washizu Kidō (1825-1882), a scholar and senior secretary in the Ministry of Justice.

34. An example was the visit to China of Oka Senjin in 1884. See Oka's letter to Wang announcing his forthcoming trip, in *Ts'ang-ming-fang-shan wen ch'u-chi*, 4:18-19. Wang T'ao's name appears frequently in Oka's travel diary, *Kuan-kuang chi-yu*. On the diary, see Jansen, "Japanese Views of China During the Meiji Period," pp. 174-175. Wang's postface to Oka's diary was printed in *Shen-pao*, May 22, 1887, p. 1 (in the 40-volume Taipei reprint of 1965, it appears in Vol. XL, p. 27757). See also his letter to Oka (mid-1880's), *CTHC*, 6:7. For a selection of Wang's other prefaces and postfaces to Japanese works see *WLWP*, 9:9b-11, 12-15b, 10:5-7, 11:2b-5b, 15b-16.

35. *CT*, 12:12-13, 21b-22b. Wang was personally acquainted with at least three founders of the Kōa kai: Nagaoka Moriyoshi (1843-1906), Watanabe Kōki (1848-1901), and Sone Toshitora (1847-1910). See *CT*, 12:12-13; Sanetō, pp. 80, 84. On Sone see below in text.

36. There is a brief biography of Sone in Kuzuu Yoshihisa, *Tōa senkaku shishi kiden* (Tokyo, 1933), III, 316-317; see also Jansen, *The Japanese and Sun Yat-sen*, pp. 65, 241n16.

37. Similar qualities evoked paeans of praise from Wang for the early Japanese radical, Yoshida Shōin (*FKCL*, 14:14-15).

38. The heart of the plan called for the restoration of the Ryūkyūan king's authority over the two southernmost islands of the Ryūkyū chain. See Wang's

letters to Wu T'ing-fang (summer, 1883) and Sheng Hsüan-huai (summer, 1883), *CTHC*, 2:11b-12b, 14-15b.

39. Sone's book, entitled *Fa-Yüeh chiao-ping chi*, was published in Tokyo in 1886. A facsimile edition was produced in Taipei in 1971. Wang T'ao helped edit the book and also wrote a long preface (June 2, 1884) to it, found on pp. 22-30 of the facsimile edition and in *WLWP*, 11:2b-5b.

40. For a typical statement of Wang's feelings in this vein, see his letter to Oka Senjin (spring, 1880), *CT*, 12:12-13; for Oka's similar view, as noted by Wang, see *WLWP*, 10:11.

41. *WLWP*, 5:22b-23b. See also his letter (on a friend's behalf) to Li Chao-t'ang (ca. 1874-1875), *CT*, 9:11b-12.

42. *WLWP*, 5:23b-25b, 25b-31, 6:1-3, 3-5. The first two of the above editorials are reproduced in *Hsiao-fang-hu-chai yü-ti ts'ung-ch'ao*, LI, 7851-7856.

43. *WLWP*, 6:3-5. See also *WLWP*, 5:9-11b; letter to Cheng Tsao-ju (ca. 1879-1880), *CT*, 11:18b-20.

44. See letter to Ting Jih-ch'ang (1879), *CT*, 11:7b-9; letter to Ho Ching (1879-1880), *CT*, 11:15-17; letter to Oka Senjin (spring, 1880), *CT*, 12:12-13; letter to Cheng Tsao-ju (1880), *CT*, 12:21b-22b; letter to Cheng Tsao-ju (1880), *CT*, 12:26-27b; letter to Cheng Tsao-ju (ca. 1881), *CTHC*, 1:4b-5b; letter to Ting Jih-ch'ang (late 1881), *CTHC*, 1:6b-7b; letter to Cheng Tsao-ju (1881-1882), *CTHC*, 1:16a-b; letter to unidentified Japanese (1884), *CTHC*, 1:22-23b; *WLWP*, 4:21-23, 23-25.

45. *WLWP*, 10:7.

46. *WYYT*, 2:4b-6, 4:3b-4.

47. *WLWP*, 2:10a-b; preface to Young J. Allen's *Chung-Tung chan-chi pen-mo*, p. 4b (see also *WKKP* No. 89:6b); letter to Li Hung-chang (1865), *CT*, 7:3b; "Lun i hsing chih-tsao i kuang mao-i," *WKKP* No. 45:3b-4 (October 1892).

48. Wo-jen (1804-1871) was an arch-conservative who vehemently opposed the introduction of Western learning. His objections to the latter are summarized in Ssu-yü Teng and John K. Fairbank, *China's Response to the West: A Documentary Survey, 1839-1923* (Cambridge, Mass., 1954), pp. 76-77. See also Hao Chang, "The Anti-Foreignist Role of Wo-jen (1804-1871)," *Papers on China* 14:1-29 (1960).

49. *WLWP*, 5:10-11.

50. For criticisms of Japanese modernization as being superficial see *WLWP*, 10:7b; letter to Fang Ming-shan (ca. 1879-1880), *CT*, 11:10b-11; letter to Ma Chien-chung (ca. 1882-1883), *CTHC*, 1:21.

51. Letter to Fang Ming-shan (ca. 1879-1880), *CT*, 11:10b-11.

52. *WLWP*, 5:10, 10:7b-8; letter to Cheng Tsao-ju (ca. 1881), *CTHC*, 1:4b-5; letter to Ting Jih-ch'ang (ca. 1881), *CTHC*, 1:6b; letter to Fang Ming-shan (ca. 1881), *CTHC*, 1:8; letter to Ma Chien-chung (ca. 1882-1883), *CTHC*, 1:21; letter to Li Hsiao-ch'ih (early 1880's), *CTHC*, 2:8.

53. *WLWP*, 10:8; letter to Fang Ming-shan (ca. 1879-1880), *CT*, 11:10b-11; letter to Cheng Tsao-ju (ca. 1881), *CTHC*, 1:4b-5; letter to Li Hsiao-ch'ih (early 1880's), *CTHC*, 2:8a-b.

54. There are few sources for Wang's reactions to the Sino-Japanese War. The best is his preface to Allen's *Chung-Tung chan-chi pen-mo.* The preface was reprinted in *WKKP* No. 89:5b-7 (June 1896). See also Wang's preface (ca. 1895) to *Ko-chih shu-yüan k'o-i* (1893), pp. 1a-b.

55. See, for example, *WLWP,* 1:23b, 2:13b-14, 21-25, 25-26b, 26b-29, 3:1-2.

56. Wang's writings, particularly after 1870, teem with references to wealth and power (*fu-ch'iang*) as China's proper goals. His thinking in this area is further delineated in Chaps. 7-8 below.

57. *WLWP,* 2:25. Wang's view that consuls, without military backing, would be of little service, was reiterated by him in *WLWP,* 3:8b-10. In light of the fact that, in so many of his writings, Wang supported the establishment of consulates abroad, it seems reasonable to conclude that, in the present pieces, he was arguing less *against* consulates than *for* self-strengthening.

5. HEAVEN AND MAN IN THE MAKING OF HISTORY

1. John T. Marcus, "Time and the Sense of History: West and East," *Comparative Studies in Society and History* 3:134 (1960-1961). See also Burton Watson, *Ssu-ma Ch'ien: Grand Historian of China* (New York, 1958), pp. 133, 141, 143; Mircea Eliade, *Cosmos and History: The Myth of the Eternal Return* (New York, 1959), esp. pp. 87-90. There were a few Chinese thinkers in the traditional era, such as Wang Fu-chih, who did enunciate theories of progress. But, Joseph Needham notwithstanding, these were highly atypical. Needham's commendable eagerness to demolish old stereotypes gets a bit out of hand in the following statement: "The apocalyptic, almost the messianic, often the evolutionary and (in its own way) the progressive, certainly the temporally linear, these elements were always there [in Chinese culture], spontaneously and independently developing since the time of the Shang kingdom, and in spite of all that the Chinese found out or imagined about cycles, celestial or terrestrial, *these were the elements that dominated the thought of the Confucian scholars and Taoist peasant-farmers.* Strange as it may seem to those who still think in terms of the 'timeless Orient,' on the whole *China was a culture more of the Irano-Judaeo-Christian type than the Indo-Hellenic"* (emphasis supplied). *Time and Eastern Man: The Henry Myers Lecture 1964* (Glasgow, 1965), p. 52. Yang Lien-sheng, while affirming the general rule that the Chinese extolled the past over the present, points out certain exceptions and argues that these exceptions constituted a conception of "progress" of sorts. See his "Ch'ao-tai chien ti pi-sai," in *Ch'ing-chu Li Chi hsien-sheng ch'i-shih-sui lun-wen chi* (Taipei, 1965), I, 139-148.

2. Blacker, pp. 158-159. Another possibility was to extend the time limit of the cycles and view all of history since the "golden age" as part of the downward swing of one long cycle. See Derk Bodde, "Harmony and Conflict in Chinese Philosophy," in Arthur F. Wright, ed., *Studies in Chinese Thought* (Chicago, 1953), pp. 27, 30-31, 36.

3. E.G. Pulleyblank, "Chinese Historical Criticism: Liu Chih-chi and Ssu-ma Kuang," in Beasley and Pulleyblank, p. 145.

4. The classic statement of this theory is found in Chia I's "The Faults of Ch'in." See de Bary, *Sources of Chinese Tradition*, pp. 166-168; also Watson, p. 149.

5. Bodde, p. 21.

6. For a discussion of the respective roles of *t'ien* and *jen* as causative agents in history, see Lien-sheng Yang, "Toward a Study of Dynastic Configurations in Chinese History," in his *Studies in Chinese Institutional History* (Cambridge, Mass., 1963), pp. 12-17. See also Watson, p. 144 ff.

7. And, significantly, about the Taipings, who presented the other major challenge of the age. Wang's numerous short pieces on the Taipings, written mostly in the 1850's and 1860's, were never brought together in book form. They consisted of several synoptic accounts of the history of the movement (often focusing on battles), essays on strategy for dealing with the rebels, short discussions of Taiping customs, and a few dozen vignettes of government and rebel leaders. Wang's most thoughtful and comprehensive diagnosis of the causes of the rebellion is found in the "I-t'an" essays, discussed in Chap. 2; see also *WLWP*, 6:14b-24b.

Wang's sketches of leading participants were done in the usual manner of Chinese "biographies." The rebels were portrayed as crafty, power-hungry, ruthless, cowardly; the imperialists, as courageous, loyal, talented, upright. Dead imperialists were martyrs to the cause; dead rebels, as the following pronouncement on the death of Shih Ta-k'ai suggests, died because they had rebelled: "Shih came from a well-to-do family. Unlike other rebels, he was not forced by straitened circumstances to rebel. His own death and the extermination of his family were, therefore, self-inflicted and he does not deserve to be pitied." *WYYT*, 6:14; see also *WYYT*, 6:10-11.

8. *T'ao-yüan chu-shu tsung-mu*, pp. 8a-b. See also Wang's letter to Ting Jih-ch'ang (ca. 1864-1865), *CT*, 7:16b; Wang Wei-ch'eng, p. 40; the preface to Wang T'ao, comp., *Hsi-hsüeh chi-ts'un liu-chung* (Shanghai, 1889-1890). In Wang T'ao's autobiography, dated 1880, he says that "Ssu-ming pu-ch'eng" was only 36 chapters in length. Unless this is an error, the presumption must be that the bulk of the work was compiled in the 1880's. See *WLWP*, 11:21b.

9. *T'ao-yüan chu-shu tsung-mu*, pp. 10a-b.

10. I have examined three editions of *P'u-Fa chan-chi:* the original 14-chüan edition (Hong Kong) of 1873 (Hoover Library, Stanford); the 20-chüan edition (Shanghai) of 1886 (in the John Fryer collection, Berkeley); and the 20-chüan edition (Shanghai) of 1895 (Harvard-Yenching Library). The 1886 and 1895 editions are the same. The original edition was reprinted by the Japanese Army Ministry in 1878; a second Japanese version was put out in Osaka in 1887. A 4-chüan abridgement was published in Hong Kong in 1898 by Li Kuang-t'ing. I have used the 1895 edition, unless otherwise noted.

As to the time of writing of the various parts, Wang states that the first 12 chüan of the original edition were completed in August 1871, chüan 13-14 being added on in 1873, just prior to publication. In the 20-chüan edition, most the new material deals with events of the years 1873 and 1874. See *fan-li* (Directions to reader), *PFCC*, pp. 2b-3; letters to Sheng Hsüan-huai and Wu T'ing-fang (ca. 1886), *CTHC*, 5:7, 9.

The first 12 chüan of *P'u-Fa chan-chi* were widely circulated in manuscript form, thus enabling Tseng Kuo-fan, who died in 1872, to see this part of the work. See Ch'en Kuei-shih's preface to the 1873 edition (reprinted, without Ch'en's name, in *WLWP*, 8:21-24); also *WLWP*, 9:11a-b; letter to Yü Yün-mei (ca. 1871), *CT*, 8:16a-b.

For Chinese praise of *P'u-Fa chan-chi*, see Lo Hsiang-lin, *Hsiang-kang yü Chung-Hsi wen-hua chih chiao-liu* (Hong Kong, 1961), pp. 63-64, and the prefaces to the 1873 edition. For laudatory Japanese comment, see Masuda, pp. 91-92; Sanetō, pp. 61-62.

11. For Wang's own evaluation of the works of Wei and Hsü, see his letter to Ting Jih-ch'ang (1870), *CT*, 8:8a-b.

12. Wang constantly berated his contemporaries for not appreciating this. See, for example, *WLWP*, 5:14b-16b.

13. McAleavy, p. 25.

14. *PFCC*, first preface, p. 2b (also in *WLWP*, 8:15b); *PFCC*, second preface (also in *WLWP*, 8:17b-21).

15. *PFCC*, first preface, p. 4 (also in *WLWP*, 8:17a-b).

16. *PFCC*, first preface, p. 4 (also in *WLWP*, 8:17).

17. See Cohen, *China and Christianity*, pp. 229-261.

18. *PFCC*, first preface, pp. 4a-b (also in *WLWP*, 8:17a-b); *PFCC*, 20:36.

19. See his letter to Ting Jih-ch'ang (1870), *CT*, 8:8b-9.

20. See, for example, *PFCC*, 1:24b-25b, 3:18, 6:16, 15:13-14. German patriotism, in particular the active identification of all classes with the nation's war goals, also left Wang deeply impressed. Although Wang did not explicitly designate Prussia as a model for China to follow in her own quest for power, other Chinese, later on, did. See, for example, Cheng Kuan-ying, *Sheng-shih wei-yen tseng-ting hsin-pien* (Taipei, 1965), I, 112.

21. *PFCC*, second preface, p. 7b (also in *WLWP*, 8:20). For a similar Japanese viewpoint, see Donald H. Shively, "Nishimura Shigeki: A Confucian View of Modernization," in Marius B. Jansen, ed., *Changing Japanese Attitudes Toward Modernization* (Princeton, 1965), p. 223n.

22. *PFCC*, first preface, p. 2b (also in *WLWP*, 8:16). See also *PFCC*, 6:16. The application of the Ch'in symbol to France in this instance marked an exception to Wang's general tendency to reserve it for Russia.

23. *PFCC*, 2:16b-20; see also *PFCC*, 4:24b-25b.

24. *PFCC*, 14:7b-13b, 20:36.

25. *PFCC*, 6:20b-21b.

26. *PFCC*, 2:20b. Compare this with Fukuzawa Yukichi's interpretation of the outcome of the war (Blacker, p. 96).

27. *FKCL*, preface, pp. 1a-b; letter to Ting (1870), *CT*, 8:8b-9. Wang then proceeded to do the histories of Russia and the United States alluded to earlier in this chapter.

28. The earliest printed version of the original preface is in *WLWP*, 8:12-14. It is undated and has the title "*Fa-kuo t'u-shuo hsü*" (Preface to *Fa-kuo t'u-shuo*). A dated version of the same preface appears in *FKCL*, with the title "*Fa-kuo chih-lüeh yüan-hsü*" (Original preface to *Fa-kuo chih-lüeh*). To complicate matters further, in his autobiography Wang says that he wrote

a book entitled *Fa-chih* (A gazetteer of France) in eight chapters. This presumably refers to the eight *new* chapters written by him in 1870. See *WLWP*, 11:21b.

Wang also included a second preface (*hsü-yen*) in *FKCL*, but it is not dated (see n. 29 below). That *FKCL* was largely written in the 1880's is clear from the sources Wang claims to have used. The two most important of these were Japanese: Oka Senjin's *Fa-lan-hsi chih* (Gazetteer of France) and Okamoto Kansuke's *Wan-kuo shih-chi* (An account of world history). Wang appears to have discovered the latter work during his visit to Japan. Since Okamoto's preface is dated 1879, the very earliest Wang could have used the book was after his return to China late in 1879. The date of publication of Oka's book is harder to pin down. I have not been able to locate a copy of it. The two Japanese biographies of Oka that I have seen mention the book but do not say when it was written. Wang T'ao, on the other hand, refers to it in his Japan diary, so it could not have come out later than 1879. See *Fu-sang yu-chi*, p. 8068; Kuzuu Yoshihisa, III, 177-178; Nakajima Masao, ed., *Taishi kaiko roku* (Tokyo, 1936), II, 421-425.

29. Wang never relinquished his commitment to the cyclical view of history. It is strongly reiterated in his second preface (*hsü-yen*) to *FKCL* (p. 1b), which though undated can clearly be assigned, on the basis of internal evidence, to the 1880's.

30. *FKCL*, original preface, pp. 1b-2 (also in *WLWP*, 8:13).

31. Karl Marx, *The Eighteenth Brumaire of Louis Bonaparte*, in Lewis S. Feuer, ed., *Basic Writings on Politics and Philosophy: Karl Marx and Friedrich Engels* (Garden City, 1959), p. 320.

32. *FKCL*, second preface, pp. 3a-b. According to Wang Gungwu (p. 38), the "histories of Sung, Liao, Chin, Yuan, and Ming compiled between 1297 and 1739 . . . left the chapters on 'foreign countries' (*wai-kuo*) with hardly any comment."

33. *FKCL*, *fan-li* (Directions to reader), p. 1b.

34. On the works of Oka and Okamoto see n. 28 above. If the 1873 number (which I have seen) is any indication, *Hsi-kuo chin-shih hui-pien* appears to have consisted of translated excerpts from the Western press.

` 35. The "i-shih" in Wang's sobriquet refers specifically to historical facts omitted from the standard dynastic histories (*cheng-shih*). See Morohashi Tetsuji, comp., *Dai Kan-Wa jiten* (Tokyo, 1955-1960), XI, 98.

36. These are essentially the same three differences noted by Wang in his letter of 1859 to Chou T'eng-hu (discussed in Chap. 1).

37. *FKCL*, 3:27-28b. See also *FKCL*, 9:28.

38. Wang's antimissionary views are spelled out in *WLWP*, 3:2b-6b.

39. *FKCL*, 4:25-26b.

40. *FKCL*, 5:32b-33.

41. *FKCL*, 5:33a-b.

42. *Ko-ming*, meaning "to deprive a dynasty of its mandate to rule," was an ancient Chinese compound. But it did not acquire the modern force of "revolution," apparently, until the mid-1890's. In China, that is. The Japanese had begun to use it in its modern sense quite a bit earlier. See

Schiffrin, pp. 99-100; also Joseph R. Levenson, *Confucian China and Its Modern Fate* (Berkeley, 1958-1965), II, 119-128.

43. See Wang's critical account of the Paris Commune, *PFCC*, 16:4-20b.

44. For an example of this reasoning see *FKCL*, 21:19.

45. *FKCL*, 17:35b-37. For similar praise of English penal practices see *WLWP*, 4:17b.

46. *Hsi-kuo t'ien-hsüeh yüan-liu*, another of the treatises published at this time (in *Hsi-hsüeh chi-ts'un liu-chung*, ts'e 1), also embodied a historical approach. But its actual author was Alexander Wylie, one of Wang T'ao's missionary associates in Shanghai in the 1850's. Wang's part was confined to converting Wylie's oral account into readable literary Chinese. See *Hsi-kuo t'ien-hsüeh yüan-liu*, pp. 27b-28.

47. Here, as elsewhere in *Hsi-hsüeh yüan-shih k'ao*, the accuracy of Wang's dating leaves much to be desired. The solar eclipse, the prediction of which gained Thales fame in his own day, took place on May 28, 585 B.C.

48. *Hsi-hsüeh yüan-shih k'ao*, in *Hsi-hsüeh chi-ts'un liu-chung*, ts'e 2, pp. 4, 5, 11, 22b, 35.

49. See Ch'üan Han-sheng, "Ch'ing-mo ti 'Hsi-hsüeh yüan ch'u Chung-kuo' shuo," in Li Ting-i et al., eds., *Chung-kuo chin-tai-shih lun-ts'ung*, Ser. 1 (Taipei, 1956), V, 216-258. That Wang T'ao had not always been immune to the belief that Western learning originated in China is plain from his "Yüan-hsüeh" (The origins of learning), *WLWP*, 1:2b-3b. But this appears to have been one of his earlier editorials and the position represented in it was completely abandoned by Wang in later years.

50. *WYYT*, 5:2a-b.

51. *Hsi-kuo t'ien-hsüeh yüan-liu*, p. 29. Wang states here (in a comment on Wylie's text) that algebra first came from Arabia. Elsewhere (*Man-yu sui-lu*, p. 9848; *FKCL*, 17:11) he says that the sciences of calculation originated in India and gradually diffused westward. See also *WLWP*, 7:22b-24, where Wang suggests that other features of Western culture, such as Christianity, also had their origin in India.

52. *Hsi-hsüeh yüan-shih k'ao*, pp. 7a-b.

53. *WLWP*, 5:18b-19b. Many of the same themes are found in *WLWP*, 5:16b-18. See also *CTHC*, 3:9.

54. *PFCC*, second preface, pp. 5-8b (also in *WLWP*, 8:17b-21). See also *WLWP*, 3:17b-19.

55. See, for example, *PFCC*, second preface, pp. 5-8b (also in *WLWP*, 8:17b-21); *WLWP*, 3:17b-19, 4:10, 5:6, 13-14b, 16. Wang's attitude toward war was well within the mainstream of traditional Chinese thought on the subject (see Bodde, pp. 51-52).

56. *PFCC*, second preface, p. 5 (also in *WLWP*, 8:17b); *WLWP*, 3:17b.

57. *PFCC*, second preface, pp. 7b-8 (also in *WLWP*, 8:20a-b).

58. In one of his editorials Wang gives, as examples of recent European wars fought for unjust purposes, the Crimean War and Prussia's successive conquests of Denmark, Austria, and France; he compares these to the essentially just "wars" of the Ch'ing government against the rebels. Note that in this context Prussia in her war with France is judged to have acted

unjustly. See *WLWP*, 3:17b-19. For a sampling of Wang's critical attitude toward Western (and Japanese) expansionist activities in Asia see *WLWP*, 5:14b-16b (the West in general), 6:1-3 (Japan and the Ryūkyū Islands), 6:7b-9 (France and Annam); *CT*, 9:16, 11:20a-b, 12:1-3b; *CTHC*, 2:9b-10b, 4:15a-b.

59. Wang discusses some of the differences between the Western and earlier foreign intrusions in *CTHC*, 3:7b-8. See also *WLWP*, 7:17a-b.

60. *WLWP*, 1:10, 12b, 5:17.

61. *WLWP*, 1:13. See also *WLWP*, 1:10, 11:13b. The last item (Wang's colophon to Cheng Kuan-ying's *I-yen*) is also found in Cheng Kuan-ying, *Sheng-shih wei-yen tseng-ting hsin-pien*, II, 1295-1296. One of Wang's earliest statements in support of sweeping technological change is found in an essay written by him in England in the late 1860's (see *WLWP*, 7:17b-18b).

62. Aside from *Hsi-hsüeh yüan-shih k'ao* (discussed above in text), see *WLWP*, 5:16b-18.

63. There was even a cyclical side to Wang's *ta-t'ung* thinking. "It is a fixed principle of the world," he wrote in 1892, "that the multitude of different things derived from one source and will return to one source. Five thousand years ago, the entire globe proceeded from a state of unity to one of differentiation. Five thousand years later the entire globe is proceeding from a state of differentiation to one of unity. The ship and the wheel invented by the Sages will bring together the people of all continents and make them into one family, one nation." "Ko-lun-pu ch'uan-tsan," p. 11b. Wang's vision of a unified future world appeared in his writings with growing frequency from the late 1860's. The earliest references are in *WLWP*, 7:18b; *Man-yu sui-lu*, pp. 9830-9831. For later references, see *PFCC*, second preface, pp. 6a-b, 8 (also in *WLWP*, 8:19, 20b-21); *WLWP*, 1:2a-b, 11b, 12b, 2:1b, 4:23b-24, 5:16b-18, 6:9b, 7:23b-24, 10:3b-4b, 11:13; *CT*, 7:17b-18; *CTHC*, 3:1, 8; *Hsi-kuo t'ien-hsüeh yüan-liu*, p. 29b; *FKCL*, 17:15b-16; "Ko-lun-pu ch'uan-tsan," pp. 11-12b. See also Leong Sow-theng, pp. 121-125.

Chinese Communist analyses of Wang's *ta-t'ung* thought are in Wu Yen-nan, "Shih lun Wang T'ao ti kai-liang-chu-i ssu-hsiang," *Shih-hsüeh yüeh-k'an* No. 4:18 (April 1958); Wang Wei-ch'eng, pp. 49-50.

64. *WLWP*, 6:9b; see also *WLWP*, 1:11b; *FKCL*, 17:16; *Man-yu sui-lu*, pp. 9830-9831.

65. Quoted in Spencer J. Palmer, *Korea and Christianity: The Problem of Identification with Tradition* (Seoul, 1967), pp. 22-23.

66. Among Wang T'ao's missionary acquaintances, Joseph Edkins documented his conviction that there was "one origin to language and religion" (*North-China Herald*, January 12, 1894, p. 54) in two books: *China's Place in Philology: An Attempt to Show That the Languages of Europe and Asia Have Common Origin* (London, 1871) and *The Early Spread of Religious Ideas Especially in the Far East* (London, 1894). John Chalmers wrote *The Origins of the Chinese: An Attempt to Trace the Connection of the Chinese with Western Nations in Their Religion, Superstitions, Arts, Language, and Traditions* (Hong Kong, 1866). Timothy Richard, after exhaustive study of comparative religion, concluded that the similarities which he detected

between Christianity and Mahayana Buddhism resulted not from borrowing but from common origin; see Paul A. Cohen, "Missionary Approaches: Hudson Taylor and Timothy Richard," *Papers on China* 11:51 (1957).

67. *WLWP*, 5:7b.

68. *WLWP*, 5:18.

69. Draft letter to the authorities (mid-1880's), *CTHC*, 3:8b.

70. *WLWP*, 1:1; *FKCL*, 17:16.

71. *WLWP*, 1:1; *FKCL*, 17:16.

72. See, for example, *Man-yu sui-lu*, pp. 9830-9831; *WLWP*, 1:2; *Hsi-kuo t'ien-hsüeh yüan-liu*, p. 29b.

73. Condorcet considered the human race to be capable of "indefinite perfectability" in all of its aspects (moral, intellectual, and the like). His view of progress, if one may speak metaphorically, was a vertical one; Wang T'ao's was horizontal. See Antoine-Nicolas de Condorcet, *Sketch for a Historical Picture of the Progress of the Human Mind*, tr. June Barraclough (New York, 1955), pp. 173-202.

74. *Man-yu sui-lu*, p. 9830; *WLWP*, 1:1, 11, 6:9b-10, 7:23b.

PART III

PROLOGUE

1. *China: The People's Middle Kingdom and the U.S.A.* (Cambridge, Mass., 1967), p. 104.

2. *WLWP*, 7:19a-b.

3. It appears in *WLWP*, 7:15b-19.

4. A similar theme is pursued in *WLWP*, 5:16b.

5. The *I-ching* formula was widely quoted by nineteenth-century protagonists of reform. Its meaning, according to Yang Lien-sheng, is similar to Kroeber's "exhaustion of possibilities." "Ch'ao-tai chien ti pi-sai," p. 146.

6. Two influential books which advance this hypothesis, either explicitly or implicitly, are Wright, *The Last Stand of Chinese Conservatism*, and Levenson, *Confucian China and Its Modern Fate*.

7. "Reform and Revolution in China's Political Modernization," in Mary C. Wright, ed., *China in Revolution: The First Phase, 1900-1913* (New Haven, 1968), p. 83 (italics in original).

8. Referring to Japanese political modernization, Robert E. Ward says: "While the complete modern political synthesis may date only from the 1860's and 1870's, basic elements of that synthesis . . . have histories that go back from one and a half to five or six centuries beyond that. This substantially alters the traditional time perspective on the political modernization of Japan. It is seen in these terms not as a process that has taken place in the single century that has intervened since the Restoration but as a cumulative product of two and a half to six or seven centuries of gradual preparation, the last century of which was characterized by a greatly increased pace and scope of political change." See the "Epilogue" in Robert E. Ward, ed., *Political Development in Modern Japan* (Princeton, 1968), p. 580; see also Gasster, p. 84.

9. See Paul A. Cohen, "Ch'ing China: Confrontation with the West, 1850-1900," in Crowley, *Modern East Asia: Essays in Interpretation*, pp. 48-49. In his stimulating essay, *The Dynamics of Modernization: A Study in Comparative History*, Cyril E. Black, adopting a worldwide perspective, argues for the existence of seven distinct patterns of political modernization. Significantly, he views China and Japan as belonging to the same pattern (along with Russia, Iran, Turkey, Afghanistan, Ethiopia, and Thailand).

10. Patriotic twentieth-century Chinese, in an effort to emancipate modern Chinese history from the grip of the Western impact, have argued that the seeds of capitalism and modern science were planted in China from the late Ming on—prior to the full onslaught of the West. Even if this is granted, however, it pales in significance compared to developments in Tokugawa Japan. For a critique of the view that modern scientific thought emerged independently in the early Ch'ing, see Levenson, *Confucian China and Its Modern Fate*, I, 3-14.

11. Wright, *The Last Stand of Chinese Conservatism*, p. 274.

12. The evolution of Wang's justifications for change is discussed in Leong Sow-theng, pp. 118 ff.

13. *WLWP*, 1:10; see also *WLWP*, 1:12b, 5:17.

14. *WLWP*, 1:10, 13, 11:13b.

6. EDUCATIONAL REFORM

1. On the emergence of a modern public opinion at the turn of the century, see Akira Iriye, "Public Opinion and Foreign Policy: The Case of Late Ch'ing China," Feuerwerker et al., *Approaches to Modern Chinese History*, pp. 216-238; Mary C. Wright, "Introduction: The Rising Tide of Change," in Wright, *China in Revolution: The First Phase, 1900-1913*, pp. 30-32.

2. Traditionally, of course, the literati had been much better known for their power to frustrate change than for their ability—or inclination—to promote it. Literati resistance to change was frequently voiced through the vehicle of *ch'ing-i* or "pure discussion." See Cohen, "Ch'ing China: Confrontation with the West, 1850-1900," pp. 49-52; Eastman, *Throne and Mandarins*, pp. 16-29.

3. Both quoted in John W. Gardner, *Excellence: Can We Be Equal and Excellent Too?* (New York, 1962), pp. 33-34.

4. *The Last Stand of Chinese Conservatism*, p. 68.

5. As cited ibid.

6. As cited ibid., p. 69.

7. Gardner, p. 43.

8. *The Last Stand of Chinese Conservatism*, p. 68.

9. Ibid., pp. 68-69.

10. Schwartz, pp. 15-16.

11. *CT*, 7:5.

12. *CT*, 11:21.

13. *WLWP*, 8:24-25.

14. *WLWP*, 10:21b.

15. "Lun so t'an yang-wu chung nan tso-yen ch'i-hsing," *WKKP* No. 59:5b

(December 1893). See also Wang's "Chiu-shih ch'u-i," first part, *WKKP* No. 43:12-13b (August 1892); and his "Lun i te-jen i li-ts'ai," *WKKP* No. 46:7b-9 (November 1892).

16. See, for example, "Lun i te-jen i li-ts'ai," p. 7b; also Wang's explanation of China's defeat in the Sino-Japanese War, as revealed in his preface (ca. 1895) to *Ko-chih shu-yüan k'o-i* (1893), pp. 1a-b.

17. "Ch'ü hsüeh-hsiao chi-pi i hsing jen-ts'ai lun," in Ch'en Chung-i, comp., *Huang-ch'ao ching-shih-wen san-pien* (Taipei, 1965), II, 39; also in Cheng Kuan-ying, *Sheng-shih wei-yen* (Shang-hai shu-chü ed., 1896), 1:3. Although this essay is undated, I estimate it to have been written between ca. 1885 and ca. 1892. The connection between men of ability and national wealth and power is also made by Wang in *CTHC*, 2:9b, 3:2-6; "Lun i te-jen i li-ts'ai," pp. 7b-9; preface (October 5, 1888) to *Ko-chih shu-yüan k'o-i* (1887), p. 1.

18. See, for example, *WLWP*, 2:7a-b.

19. *WLWP*, 2:10b-11. See also *WLWP*, 4:4b-6b, 8:28b-29b; "Lun i te-jen i li-ts'ai," pp. 7b-9.

20. For example, "Lun i te-jen i li-ts'ai," pp. 7b-9; "Lun ch'u-shih hsü ch'iu chen-ts'ai," *WKKP* No. 58:5b-6b (November 1893).

21. *CTHC*, 3:7a-b.

22. Gardner, p. 3.

23. The expression is used in Chung-li Chang, *The Chinese Gentry: Studies on Their Role in Nineteenth-Century Chinese Society* (Seattle, 1955), pp. 166, 197-202.

24. Letters of ca. 1848 to Yang Yin-ch'uan, *CT*, 1:18-20b; see Chap. 1 above.

25. *WLWP*, 12:24-25b; see Chap. 2 above.

26. *CT*, 7:6a-b. In the early 1890's Wang again took issue with the system of recommendation as then practiced. The proper purpose of recommendation, in his view, was to make available to the government the services of gifted people who were unknown and, for one reason or another, had been unable to enter the government via the normal channel. When high officials recommended relatives and friends, or subordinates already in the government, this purpose was frustrated. Furthermore, the danger of officials forming cliques was heightened. Wang suggested, as an alternative procedure, that prospective officials be recommended *from below*. The local officials could then try them out and, if they proved effective, present them to the higher officials. See "Lun i te-jen i li-ts'ai," p. 8.

27. *WLWP*, 3:21b-22. Emphasis supplied.

28. As reprinted in *WKKP* No. 43:12-13 (August 1892). Wang's proposal was far more radical than the reform of 1887, which instituted a separate examination for specialists in mathematics. These specialists (only three of whom, beyond the fixed quota, were permitted to pass) had to take the regular examinations as well. In contrast with Wang's proposal, however, those who took the regular examinations were not required to take the examination in mathematics (see Franke, p. 31).

29. See also, in this connection, Wang's preface (May 1892) to *Ko-chih shu-yüan k'o-i* (1890), pp. 1a-b.

30. See, for example, *FKCL*, 17:8-13b.

31. "Ch'ü hsüeh-hsiao chi-pi i hsing jen-ts'ai lun," pp. 39-41.

32. *WLWP*, 2:8b-9.

33. *WLWP*, 2:4b-5. See also Wang's preface (October 5, 1888) to *Ko-chih shu-yüan k'o-i* (1887), p. 1.

34. See, for example, Gardner, passim; C. Arnold Anderson, "The Modernization of Education," in Weiner, pp. 68-80; Franke, pp. 69-70; Ronald Dore, *Education in Tokugawa Japan* (Berkeley, 1965), pp. 33-67.

35. *WLWP*, 1:23b, 2:7-8b, 18b, 3:12-14; *WYYT*, 3:3; letter to authorities (ca. 1884-1885), *CTHC*, 3:11a-b; letter to Sheng Hsüan-huai (late 1880's), *CTHC*, 5:13b.

36. "Lun i hsing chih-tsao i kuang mao-i," p. 2b; letter to the authorities (ca. 1884-1885), *CTHC*, 3:12a-b.

37. "Lun Ch'uan-tung she-li yang-wu hsüeh-shu," *WKKP* No. 47:9b-11b (December 1892).

38. *WLWP*, 8:7b-9.

39. *WLWP*, 8:5-7b.

40. "Chiu-shih ch'u-i," first part, p. 12b (reprinted from *Shen-pao*). Wang T'ao's sensitivity to the problem of female subjugation in China was expressed on a number of occasions. In an early editorial, "Yüan-jen" (The origins of man), he criticized the practice of concubinage and made a forceful defense of monogamous marriage, judging it to be the only basis for a harmonious, well-ordered society. *WLWP*, 1:3b-5b. Wang also wrote a preface for the 1888 edition of *Ching-hua yüan*, a famous early nineteenth-century novel which satirized the double standard between the sexes and was critical of the neglect of female education and the evils of footbinding and concubinage. Hummel, I, 473. Wang's stand on female education was applauded by Young Allen. *Records . . . 1890*, p. 264 (Allen refers to Wang as Wong-tao).

41. *WYYT*, 2:6a-b, 7-8b, 9b-10b.

42. *WYYT*, 3:6a-b, 5:1b, 2b-5b.

43. Wang describes their contents briefly in *T'ao-yüan chu-shu tsung-mu*, pp. 7-8.

44. *Hsi-hsüeh t'u-shuo*, in Wang T'ao, *Hsi-hsüeh chi-ts'un liu-chung*, ts'e 1, pp. 2b-3b.

45. First published in 1799 in 46 chüan, Juan Yüan's (1764-1849) highly regarded collection contained biographies and summaries of the works of 280 astronomers and mathematicians, including 37 Europeans. Hummel, I, 402.

46. The translation of the *Chung-yung* passage is from Wing-tsit Chan, tr. and comp., *A Source Book in Chinese Philosophy* (Princeton, 1963), p. 112.

47. *Hsi-kuo t'ien-hsüeh yüan-liu*, pp. 27b-29b.

48. Ch'üan Han-sheng, pp. 216-217.

49. Hung Shen, pp. 1043-1044; see also McAleavy, p. 27.

50. Letters to Sheng Hsüan-huai and Wu T'ing-fang (ca. 1886), *CTHC*, 5:7, 8b-9. Wang asked Sheng and Wu (both of whom were on Li Hung-chang's staff at the time) to help sell his works in Tientsin, so that the proceeds could be applied to the publication of his other writings.

51. Knight Biggerstaff, "Shanghai Polytechnic Institution and Reading Room: An Attempt to Introduce Western Science and Technology to the Chinese," *Pacific Historical Review* 25.2:127 (May 1956).

52. Ibid., p. 141. See also Adrian Arthur Bennett, *John Fryer: The Introduction of Western Science and Technology into Nineteenth-Century China* (Cambridge, Mass., 1967), Chap. 3.

53. Biggerstaff, pp. 141-142; Bennett, pp. 56-57; *North-China Herald*, May 27, 1892, p. 701; ibid., March 22, 1894, pp. 435-436. For other examples, see Wang's preface (December 12, 1892) to *Ko-chih shu-yüan k'o-i* (1891), p. 1b; also his preface (ca. 1895) to ibid. (1893), p. 1.

54. *North-China Herald*, May 27, 1892, p. 701; see also ibid., April 14, 1893, pp. 513-514.

55. Ibid., July 20, 1889, p. 85; Bennett, p. 57. (Wang is referred to in these sources as Wang Tsz-ching or Wang-tsz-ching.) The annual volumes were published under the title *Ko-chih shu-yüan k'o-i* (The Polytechnic Institute prize essays). A full set may be found in the Fryer collection at Berkeley. An editorial in the *North-China Herald* characterized the preface to the third volume in the following language: "Wang writes as the apostle of a new faith to a people by no means convinced that all this enthusiasm for isms and museums is not a flouting of the ever-sacred doctrines of the Holy Man. Talent, he observes, 'is not confined to one corner of the world.'" November 1, 1889, p. 536.

56. Ibid., July 20, 1889, p. 85; ibid., July 16, 1897, p. 128. See also Biggerstaff, p. 143.

57. Letters to Shao Yu-lien (ca. 1886), Sheng Hsüan-huai (ca. 1887), *CTHC*, 5:3a-b, 10b, 13b-14; *North-China Herald*, August 15, 1890, p. 196. According to Biggerstaff (p. 134), the most notable contributors of funds to the Polytechnic Institute were Li Hung-chang, Shen Pao-chen, and Feng Chün-kuang.

58. Biggerstaff, p. 149.

7. ECONOMIC REFORM

1. Albert Feuerwerker, *The Chinese Economy, ca. 1870-1911* (Ann Arbor, 1969), p. 1.

2. Mou An-shih, *Yang-wu yün-tung* (Shanghai, 1961), p. 84; T'ang Chih-chün, *Wu-hsü pien-fa shih lun-ts'ung* (Wuhan, 1957), pp. 55-66; Shih Chün, Jen Chi-yü, and Chu Po-k'un, comps., *Chung-kuo chin-tai ssu-hsiang shih chiang-shou t'i-kang* (Peking, 1957), pp. 53-56; Wang Wei-ch'eng, pp. 47-49; Hu Sheng, *Imperialism and Chinese Politics* (Peking, 1955), pp. 106-107.

3. See Schwartz, esp. Chap. 2.

4. See Chap. 1 above. Other early allusions to the goals of wealth and power may be found in Wang's letter to Kiangsu Governor Hsü Yu-jen (ca. 1859-1860), *CT*, 4:19b-20b; *WLWP*, 12:31b-33.

5. *CT*, 7:7b-8b.

6. Letter to Ting Jih-ch'ang (ca. 1870-1871), *CT*, 8:15b-16.

7. *WLWP*, 2:14-16b, 3:22, 4:25; "Lun i hsing chih-tsao i kuang mao-i,"

pp. 3a-b; "Lun Chung-kuo mei-t'ieh chih fu Mei-kuo chin-yin chih fu," *WKKP* No. 57:9 (October 1893).

8. See, for example, *WYYT*, 3:5-6.

9. *WYYT*, 3:5-6; *WLWP*, 3:22; "Lun Chung-kuo mei-t'ieh chih fu Mei-kuo chin-yin chih fu," p. 9; *CT*, 8:10b-11.

10. *WLWP*, 4:19; *FKCL*, 16:18b; Alexander Wylie (Wei-lieh-ya-li) and Wang T'ao, *Hua-Ying t'ung-shang shih-lüeh*, in *Hsi-hsüeh chi-ts'un liu-chung*, ts'e 2, p. 15b; *CT*, 9:19.

11. See, for example, *WLWP*, 2:14-16b, 3:22, 10:22-32; "Lun i hsing chih-tsao i kuang mao-i," pp. 2b-4.

12. Werner Sombart judged the four "life-values" of modern man to be speed, size, novelty, and power. See his *The Quintessence of Capitalism*, tr. M. Epstein (New York, 1915), pp. 176-180.

13. *WLWP*, 4:23b-24, 7:18a-b.

14. Letter to Chou T'eng-hu (1859), *CT*, 4:7b-8.

15. *WLWP*, 2:18a-b, 3:12-14, 16-17b, 7:5a-b; letter to Li Hung-chang (1865), *CT*, 7:9.

16. *WLWP*, 2:18a-b, 3:12-14, 7:5a-b; letter to the authorities (ca. 1884-1885), *CTHC*, 3:10b.

17. *WLWP*, 1:23b, 3:12-14; letter to Ting Jih-ch'ang (1875), *CT*, 9:18a-b.

18. *CT*, 11:3b-4.

19. *WYYT*, 3:2-3. Although the China Merchants Steam Navigation Company was financed in part by a government subsidy for carrying tribute grain by sea, the Grand Canal was not completely displaced until 1901.

20. *WLWP*, 2:13b, 15b-16, 3:22b.

21. A memorial of 1881, presenting the case against railroads, in some detail, is summarized in Chi-ming Hou, *Foreign Investment and Economic Development in China, 1840-1937* (Cambridge, Mass., 1965), pp. 242-243.

22. *CT*, 7:18; *Man-yu sui-lu*, p. 9823; *WLWP*, 7:18.

23. *PFCC*, 5:10b, 7:1. See also *WLWP*, 3:21b-23b, 25b-27b; *FKCL*, 17:27b-30; *CTHC*, 3:13, 4:16b; *Man-yu sui-lu*, p. 9840.

24. *WLWP*, 2:16, 3:25b-27b; *FKCL*, 17:27b-30; *CTHC*, 4:16b; *Man-yu sui-lu*, p. 9840.

25. *FKCL*, 17:27b-30.

26. *WLWP*, 3:25b-27b; *CT*, 8:11.

27. See esp. *WLWP*, 2:16, 3:22.

28. *WLWP*, 3:14-15b.

29. *FKCL*, 17:30-31b; *WLWP*, 3:23. In his discussions of the telegraph, Wang overlooked its very considerable impact on world banking and trade.

30. Draft letter to authorities (ca. late 1884), *CTHC*, 3:5.

31. *The Last Stand of Chinese Conservatism*, p. 183.

32. *WLWP*, 2:16a-b, 10:31b-32; letter to Ting Jih-ch'ang (ca. 1870-1871), *CT*, 8:10b-11. Wang suggested, specifically, that mining be developed in the overcrowded provinces of Kwangtung and Fukien in order to create more jobs and keep the inhabitants of these provinces from having to go abroad to seek work. *WLWP*, 1:24b-25.

33. *WLWP*, 2:16, 10:23b-24b; *WYYT*, 3:5-6.

34. *WLWP*, 10:24.

35. Railway lines and tunnels presented a special problem, as bad influences were believed to travel more easily along straight lines. Samuel Couling, *The Encyclopaedia Sinica* (Shanghai, 1917), I, 175.

36. *WLWP*, 2:14b, 10:23b-24b, 31b-32; "Lun Chung-kuo mei-t'ieh chih fu Mei-kuo chin-yin chih fu," pp. 8-9; "Lun so t'an yang-wu chung nan tso-yen ch'i-hsing," p. 5b; letter to Ting Jih-ch'ang (ca. 1870-1871), *CT*, 8:10b-11; draft letter to authorities (ca. 1884-1885), *CTHC*, 3:12b-13b; *WYYT*, 3:5-6.

37. *WLWP*, 5:16a-b.

38. *WLWP*, 2:15, 10:23b-24b; "Lun Chung-kuo mei-t'ieh chih fu Mei-kuo chin-yin chih fu," pp. 8-9; *WYYT*, 3:5-6.

39. *WLWP*, 2:21, 10:23b-24b; draft letter to authorities (ca. 1884-1885), *CTHC*, 3:13a-b.

40. *WLWP*, 2:14b-15, 10:31b-32; letter to Ting Jih-ch'ang (ca. 1870-1871), *CT*, 8:10b-11; draft letter to authorities (ca. late 1884), *CTHC*, 3:5; draft letter to authorities (ca. 1884-1885), *CTHC*, 3:12b-13b; *WYYT*, 3:5-6.

41. *WLWP*, 2:14b-15b, 10:31b-32. Wang was quite right in this respect. Foreign steamers operating in Chinese waters found native coal either too expensive or poor in quality. Large quantities therefore had to be imported each year, often from places as far away as the United States and Britain. See Chi-ming Hou, pp. 65-66.

42. *WYYT*, 3:5b.

43. Wang discusses some of the difficulties encountered by modern mining companies in his "Lun Chung-kuo mei-t'ieh chih fu Mei-kuo chin-yin chih fu," p. 8.

44. *Huo-ch'i lüeh-shuo*, later preface (*hou-hsü*) (1871) (reprinted in *WLWP*, 8:11-12). In his writings after 1871, Wang made frequent reference to the process of ongoing technological innovation in the West. See, for example, *WLWP*, 3:16-17b, 5:16a-b; *PFCC*, later preface (*hou-hsü*) (1871) (also in *WLWP*, 8:18b-19b); *Huo-ch'i lüeh-shuo*, later colophon (*hou-pa*) (1880) (also in *WLWP*, 10:2); letter to Ting Jih-ch'ang (1875), *CT*, 9:17b-18.

45. *WLWP*, 5:16a-b; *PFCC*, later preface (1871) (also in *WLWP*, 8:18b-19b).

46. *Huo-ch'i lüeh-shuo*, later preface (1871) (also in *WLWP*, 8:11-12); *Huo-ch'i lüeh-shuo*, later colophon (1880) (also in *WLWP*, 10:2).

47. *WLWP*, 7:18.

48. *CT*, 7:8b. See also Wang's letter to Ting Jih-ch'ang (ca. 1870-1871), *CT*, 8:10b-11.

49. *WLWP*, 2:15b, 4:20b; "Lun i hsing chih-tsao i kuang mao-i," pp. 2b-4. In one of his articles, Wang voiced concern over the threat posed by imported cotton cloth to Chinese handicraft production. See "Lun i she shang-chü i wang shang-wu," *WKKP* No. 49:6b (February 1893).

50. "Lun i hsing chih-tsao i kuang mao-i," pp. 2b-4.

51. *Europe Emerges: Transition Toward an Industrial World-Wide Society, 600-1750* (Madison, 1961), pp. 418-419.

52. *Hsi-hsüeh chi-ts'un liu-chung*, preface, p. 2b. See also *WLWP*, 2:25a-b,

10:23, 27; *Hua-Ying t'ung-shang shih-lüeh,* p. 15b; letter to Li Hung-chang (1865), *CT,* 7:8b; "Lun i she shang-chü i wang shang-wu," p. 7.

53. Feuerwerker, *The Chinese Economy,* p. 56; Rhoads Murphey, *The Treaty Ports and China's Modernization: What Went Wrong?* (Ann Arbor, 1970), pp. 46-47.

54. *WLWP,* 2:14a-b.

55. Wang's first knowledge of Cheng's work came in the 1870's (1871 at the earliest), when Cheng sent Wang the manuscript of *I-yen* (Easy words) for his criticism. The germs of Wang's economic nationalism, however, had already been enunciated in his letter of 1865 to Li Hung-chang (see below in text). On Wang's relationship to *I-yen* (which appears to have been first published in 1880), see the excellent article by Ichiko Chūzō: "Tei Kannō no Ekigen ni tsuite," in *Wada hakushi koki kinen Tōyōshi ronsō* (Tokyo, 1960), pp. 107-115. The economic thought in *I-yen* is discussed in Liu Kuang-ching, "Cheng Kuan-ying *I-yen*: Kuang-hsü ch'u-nien chih pien-fa ssu-hsiang," Part I, *Ch'ing-hua hsüeh-pao,* N.S., 8.1-2:398-410 (422-425 for English summary) (August 1970). Cheng's fully developed views are presented in *Sheng-shih wei-yen tseng-ting hsin-pien,* II, 753-766. See Chap. 9, n. 10 below.

56. This thesis, known as the "drain effect," has been elaborated by modern economists. See Chi-ming Hou, pp. 93-94, 131, 254.

57. See his "Li-chüan pi lun," in *Huang-ch'ao ching-shih-wen san-pien,* I, 739; letter to Tong King-sing (ca. late 1870's), *CT,* 11:2-3; *WLWP,* 3:28b.

58. Wang T'ao's perception of the problem—and his solution—call to mind the circumstances in early Meiji Japan. Faced with an excess of imports over exports, and a resulting drain of specie, the Japanese, like the Chinese, were prevented by treaty from dealing with the problem by raising tariffs. One of the major aims of early Meiji industrial policy, therefore, was to promote production of manufactured goods which could compete with foreign imports and drive them from the domestic market. See Thomas C. Smith, *Political Change and Industrial Development in Japan: Government Enterprise, 1868-1880* (Stanford, 1955), p. 26.

59. Letter to Li Hung-chang (1865), *CT,* 7:10. Wang, at other points, urged the adoption of a variety of measures aimed at prohibiting opium-smoking. See *WLWP,* 2:11b, 4:12-14b, 12:13-15; "Chiu-shih ch'u-i," first part, pp. 12-13b; *WYYT,* 3:11a-b; letter to Ting Jih-ch'ang (ca. 1870-1871), *CT,* 8:10a-b.

60. *CT,* 9:20. The increasing effectiveness of the rivalry which Chinese merchants offered their foreign counterparts is documented by Yen-p'ing Hao in his *The Comprador in Nineteenth-Century China: Bridge between East and West* (Cambridge, Mass., 1970), pp. 117-120. Carrying Wang T'ao's argument a step further, John A. Hobson wrote (in 1902): "It is at least conceivable that China might so turn the tables upon the Western industrial nations, and, either by adopting their capital and organizers, or as is more probable, by substituting her own, might flood their markets with her cheaper manufactures, and refusing their imports in exchange might take her payments in liens upon their capital, reversing the earlier process of investment until she gradually obtained financial control over her quondam patrons and civil-

izers." Quoted in Akira Iriye, "Imperialism in Eastern Asia," in Crowley, *Modern East Asia: Essays in Interpretation*, p. 132.

61. The recommendations of people like Wang T'ao notwithstanding, Feuerwerker reports that, as late as the 1920's, the actual process of importing and exporting remained "almost completely" in foreign hands. *The Chinese Economy*, pp. 59-60.

62. "Lun i she shang-chü i wang shang-wu," pp. 7a-b. Wang's earliest advocacy (1862) of Chinese merchants going overseas themselves is in *WLWP*, 12:31b-32. See also *WLWP*, 2:18b-19, 25a-b, 4:2b-3, 10:23, 25b-27, 31b-32; *Hua-Ying t'ung-shang shih-lüeh*, p. 19; "Chiu-shih ch'u-i," second part, *WKKP*, No. 44:15b-16 (September 1892), letter to Li Hung-chang (1865), *CT*, 7:8b. Wang, initially, prescribed the same medicine (expanded overseas commerce) for Vietnam as a means of enabling that country to avoid being completely colonized by France. He soon reversed himself, however, despairing of the likelihood that the Vietnamese could do anything to save themselves. See *WLWP*, 6:5-9.

63. *WLWP*, 10:23; "Lun i she shang-chü i wang shang-wu," pp. 7a-b.

64. *WLWP*, 10:26b-27, 31b-32; "Lun i she shang-chü i wang shang-wu," pp. 7a-b.

65. "Lun i she shang-chü i wang shang-wu," p. 6.

66. *CT*, 7:8b. For similar themes, see *WLWP*, 2:18b-19, 10:31b-32.

67. Letter to Wu T'ing-fang (ca. 1885), *CTHC*, 4:5; *WLWP*, 2:18b.

68. *WLWP*, 10:25a-b, 27. In this connection, Wang often argued that the government, in its economic enterprises, should share the profits (or benefits) with the people (*yü min kung ch'i li*). See, for example, *WLWP*, 1:19, 20b-21.

69. *WLWP*, 2:13a-b; "Li-chüan pi lun," pp. 738-739. Whether Wang's apprehensions over the likin tax were warranted is, of course, another matter. Feuerwerker has this to say: "Compared to freight and handling markups of 15 to 100 percent, it appears unlikely that the common likin rate of two per cent at each tax station had more than a small effect on the total amount and direction of internal trade. The British . . . found it difficult to sell Lancashire cloth in the interior of China because domestic handicraft weaving offered effective competition. The marketing structure and size of China's domestic commerce were constrained not primarily by burdensome official exactions, but by the limitations of premodern transportation and communications." *The Chinese Economy*, pp. 47-50.

70. "Lun i she shang-chü i wang shang-wu," pp. 6-7b.

71. Ibid., p. 7.

72. *WLWP*, 1:14b; I have followed here the rendering in de Bary, *Sources of Chinese Tradition*, p. 720.

8. POLITICAL REFORM

1. Ambiguity—and the importance of context in removing it—is of course a staple of history everywhere. In nineteenth-century England, Charles Kingsley, reacting with horror to the inequities of the Industrial Revolution, drew on the Biblical injunction, "he that will not work, neither shall he eat,"

to justify a program of Christian Socialism. But it can easily be seen how a Social Darwinist, mesmerized by the doctrine of the survival of the fittest, might use the same words to sanctify rejection of even the most minimal welfare state. See Crane Brinton, *English Political Thought in the Nineteenth Century* (Cambridge, Mass., 1954), p. 124.

2. Kwang-Ching Liu, "Nineteenth-Century China: The Disintegration of the Old Order and the Impact of the West," in Ping-ti Ho and Tang Tsou, eds., *China in Crisis* (Chicago, 1968), I, 114-115.

3. *WLWP*, 2:19-21 (also in *Huang-ch'ao ching-shih-wen san-pien*, I, 464-466). See also *WLWP*, 2:17b-18, 3:10b; letter to Ting Jih-ch'ang (ca. 1870-1871), *CT*, 8:13a-b.

4. *WLWP*, 2:11b-12.

5. *WLWP*, 2:17b; draft of letter to authorities (ca. late 1884), *CTHC*, 3:6b; letter to Wu T'ing-fang (ca. 1885), *CTHC*, 4:5.

6. *WLWP*, 2:16b-17.

7. De Bary, *Sources of Chinese Tradition*, pp. 591-592.

8. *WLWP*, 2:9; see also Wang's letter to Li Hung-chang (1865), *CT*, 7:5b-6.

9. *CT*, 8:13.

10. *CT*, 8:13a-b; see also *WLWP*, 2:9.

11. *The Last Stand of Chinese Conservatism*, p. 94.

12. *WLWP*, 1:22a-b.

13. *WLWP*, 1:22b. In the draft of a letter to the authorities (ca. late 1884), Wang's paternalistic preferences were stated even more literally: "If a district is treated as a family and the magistrate is to the people as parents are to their children; and if, by extension, the same is held to be true of prefects, taotais, governors, and governors-general, will not the people always be of service [to the officials]?" *CTHC*, 3:7. See also *WLWP*, 7:4a-b.

14. Wang Wei-ch'eng, p. 46.

15. "Nineteenth-Century China," p. 177.

16. Ibid., pp. 123-124, 177.

17. The office of chancellor or prime minister (*tsai-hsiang*), it will be recalled, had been abolished by the first emperor of the Ming in 1380. T'ai-tsu, at the time, warned his descendants never to restore the post and prescribed the death penalty for anyone who advocated doing so. The post never was restored in Ming times, and the Ch'ing followed suit. Since the prime ministership had traditionally been the focal point of strong power (thus countervailing the power of the throne) its abolition has often been taken as a sign of the increasingly despotic character of Chinese government in the last five hundred years of the imperial era. See Charles O. Hucker, *The Traditional Chinese State in Ming Times (1368-1644)* (Tucson, 1961), p. 53.

18. *WLWP*, 2:17a-b.

19. *WLWP*, 1:16, 2:17b; draft of letter to authorities (ca. late 1884), *CTHC*, 3:6b.

20. Draft of letter to authorities (ca. late 1884), *CTHC*, 3:6b.

21. *WLWP*, 10:21b.

22. *WLWP*, 1:22b.

23. Draft of letter to authorities, *CTHC*, 3:7. Emphasis supplied. A similar system of "recommendation" from below, also very possibly influenced by Western elective procedures, was suggested by Feng Kuei-fen around 1860. See Lü Shih-ch'iang, "Feng Kuei-fen ti cheng-chih ssu-hsiang," *Chung-hua wen-hua fu-hsing yüeh-k'an* 4.2: 1-2 (February 1971).

24. *WLWP*, 1:21b-22.

25. *WLWP*, 1:23.

26. *FKCL*, 16:27a-b.

27. *FKCL*, 24:19b-20b.

28. *WLWP*, 4:18b, 8:2-3; *WYYT*, 4:2a-b; *FKCL*, second preface, pp. 2b-3.

29. *WLWP*, 7:24-25b.

30. See Chap. 4, n. 44 above.

31. Wang T'ao, in spite of his high regard for England, continued to be suspicious concerning her long-term ambitions in Asia. See *WLWP*, 1:26, 5:6-7b; letter to a Vietnamese official (ca. 1880), *CT*, 11:20b-22.

32. *WLWP*, 4:16b-18b; some of the quoted excerpts from this editorial are based on the translation in Teng and Fairbank, *China's Response to the West*, p. 140. For more examples of Wang's high opinion of British government see *WLWP*, 1:23, 3:10-12, 10:21a-b.

33. *WLWP*, 4:17.

34. See, for example, *WLWP*, 4:25, 11:13; *CT*, 10:11b.

35. "Lun so t'an yang-wu chung nan tso-yen ch'i-hsing," p. 4b. See also ibid., p. 5b; "Lun i te-jen i li-ts'ai," p. 7b; *WLWP*, 3:8.

36. Wang's suggestions for military reform, although alluded to at many points in this study, did not seem to me to warrant separate treatment. Apart from the proposals of the Taiping period and such works as *P'u-Fa chan-chi* and *Huo-ch'i lüeh-shuo*, discussed in the text, the interested reader will want to consult the following items: *WLWP*, 1:23b, 2:4a-b, 5b-8b, 13b, 18a-b, 3:12-14, 16-17b, 22, 6:5, 11:7b-9b; "Ch'ü hsüeh-hsiao chi-pi i hsing jen-ts'ai lun," p. 41; *WYYT*, 3:2-3, 4:11b-12b; *FKCL*, 17:16-27b; "Chiu-shih ch'u-i," second part, pp. 14-15; "Yüeh Te-kuo Shih-hao ch'uan-ch'ang chang-ch'eng shu-hou," *WKKP* No. 51:3-4b (April 1893); "Lun hsün-yüeh p'ao-t'ai," *WKKP* No. 56:10b-11b (September 1893); *CT*, 7:8b-9, 8:14-15, 9:13b-15, 10:14b-15, 11:9-10, 12:16b-17b; *CTHC*, 3:2b-5, 9-12, 4:16a-b, 5:11-12, 13b-14.

37. On the priority of *chih-min* over *chih-ping*, see *FKCL*, second preface, pp. 2b-3; *WLWP*, 1:15b, 7:3b; *CT*, 10:12, 14b, 11:17.

38. "One has but to observe the war between France and Prussia," he wrote, "to know that one cannot rely only on firearms. Prussia's victory over France resulted from her ability to fuse north and south Germany into one nation." *PFCC*, 6:15b-16. See also *PFCC*, 1:24b-25b, 3:18, 15:13-14.

39. *PFCC*, 2:9b-12.

40. *FKCL*, 16:13b.

41. "Lun so t'an yang-wu chung nan tso-yen ch'i-hsing," p. 5b. In this connection, Ho Kai, alive to the dangers of foreign loans, complained (in 1887) that domestic borrowing was difficult in China because there was insufficient confidence in the government. Schiffrin, p. 26.

42. Letter to Kiangsu Governor Hsü Yu-jen (1859), *CT*, 4:13b-14.

43. See, for example, *WLWP*, 1:19, 20b-21, 3:22b.

44. *WLWP*, 1:18b-19.

45. Letter to Fang Ming-shan, *CT*, 12:25.

46. *WLWP*, 3:7b.

47. See esp. Chap. 12 of his *In Search of Wealth and Power.*

48. Hsiao Kung-ch'üan, *Chung-kuo cheng-chih ssu-hsiang shih* (Taipei, 1961), V, 684-685.

49. Levenson, *Liang Ch'i-ch'ao and the Mind of Modern China*, p. 111.

50. *WLWP*, 7:25b-27b, 10:27b-29b.

51. *WLWP*, 3:27b-29; letter to Ting Jih-ch'ang (ca. 1870-1871), *CT*, 8:12a-b.

52. Colophon to *I-yen*, in Cheng Kuan-ying, *Sheng-shih wei-yen tseng-ting hsin-pien*, II, 1297 (also in *WLWP*, 11:13b-14).

53. *Chung-Tung chan-chi pen-mo*, pp. 4a-b (also in *WKKP* No. 89:5b-7). The awakening of national shame is also a frequent theme in *Tzu-ch'iang-chai pao-fu hsing-kuo lun ch'u-pien* (Shanghai, 1897). Compiled by Wang T'ao on the eve of his death, this is a collection of essays on reform and related matters by Wang K'ang-nien, Liang Ch'i-ch'ao, Ch'en Ch'iu, Ch'en Chih, and others. Many of the essays first appeared in the periodical *Shih-wu pao* (The Chinese progress).

54. "Ko-lun-pu ch'uan-tsan."

55. This may be compared with Joseph Levenson's formulation: "A culturalism bars foreign ideas, but it may actually invite or not actively oppose foreign material force. Nationalism reverses these relations; it may admit foreign ideas, but it will blaze against foreign material incursions." *Liang Ch'i-ch'ao and the Mind of Modern China*, p. 110.

56. Schwartz, p. 15.

57. *CT*, 12:3b-4, 15b-16b, 16b-17, and postface (*shu-hou*); *CTHC*, 2:16-17b, 4:2-3b; *WLWP*, 3:21b-23b, 10:11-13, 12:12b-13. On Kuo see Hummel, I, 438.

58. Schwartz, p. 19.

59. Teng and Fairbank, *China's Response to the West*, p. 137. Whether it is fair to characterize Feng Kuei-fen in this manner is another question. See Chap. 9 below.

60. See Part III, Prologue, above.

PART IV

PROLOGUE

1. The approach is defined, and its advantages and limitations discussed, in Lawrence Stone, "Prosopography," *Daedalus: Journal of the American Academy of Arts and Sciences* Winter 1971:46-79. Although the term "prosopography" often implies large aggregates of people and the use of quantitative methods of investigation, there is no reason in theory why it can't be extended (as here) to the study of relatively small groups.

2. For suggestive remarks on this development see Frederic Wakeman, Jr.,

"The Opening of China," in Joseph R. Levenson, ed., *Modern China: An Interpretive Anthology* (New York, 1971), pp. 147-154.

3. The Sinicization of the Taipings is discussed in So Kwan-wai and Eugene Boardman, pp. 292-294.

9. THE PIONEER REFORMERS AND THE LITTORAL

1. This was less true of the initial phase (1895-1911) of the revolutionary movement. Although its most prominent spokesman was Sun Yat-sen, and its funding and much of its ideology were littoral in origin, large numbers of pioneer revolutionaries (like Huang Hsing) were products of the Chinese hinterland. See Chün-tu Hsüeh, *Huang Hsing and the Chinese Revolution* (Stanford, 1961); Mary Backus Rankin, "The Revolutionary Movement in Chekiang: A Study in the Tenacity of Tradition," in Wright, *China in Revolution*, pp. 319-361.

2. Brown's annual reports to the directors of the Society give a full picture of the school's curriculum as it developed over time. Brown detailed, in a number of these reports, the efforts made both in class and out to achieve the pupils' conversion to Christianity, which he viewed as being "the only perfectly satisfactory result of our labours." See, for example, the 3rd, 4th, 7th, and 8th annual reports, in *The Chinese Repository*, Vol. X, No. 10 (October 1841); Vol. XI, No. 10 (October 1842); Vol. XIV, No. 10 (October 1845); Vol. XV, No. 12 (December 1846).

3. The two fellow students, Wong Shing (Huang Sheng) and Wong Foon (Huang K'uan), may be classified as second-rung modernizers—men who performed significant pioneering functions but who never achieved real fame in nineteenth-century China. Both Wongs were Christians who in later life had close connections with the London Missionary Society. Wong Shing returned to China in 1848 because of ill health. After learning the printing trade, he was for some twenty years superintendent of the LMS press in Hong Kong (in which capacity he supervised the printing of Legge's *Chinese Classics*). In the early 1870's, it will be recalled, he helped Wang T'ao (with whom he had earlier collaborated in the production of a book on modern firearms) purchase the press's equipment and found the *Tsun-wan yat-po*. Wong Shing was the first Chinese to sit with Englishmen on a jury. In 1874 he returned to the United States with the Chinese education mission and was later appointed interpreter to the new Chinese legation in Washington. Wong's son, Wong Wing-sheung (Huang Yung-shang), was an early follower of Sun Yat-sen and took part in the formation of the Hong Kong Hsing-Chung hui. The Wong family, originally from Hsiang-shan hsien, Kwangtung, were related to Ho Kai. Britton, p. 45; Ch'en Hsüeh-lin, "Huang Sheng: Hsiang-kang Hua-jen t'i-ch'ang yang-wu shih-yeh chih hsien-ch'ü," *Ch'ung-chi hsüeh-pao* 3.2:226-231 (May 1964); Schiffrin, pp. 48-49; Wang T'ao, *Huo-ch'i lüeh-shuo*, first preface (reproduced in *WLWP*, 8:9-11).

Wong Foon (1828-1878), also a native of Hsiang-shan, after completion of his secondary school education, studied medicine at the University of Edinburgh, becoming the first Chinese doctor to be trained in the West. After getting his medical degree, he returned to China (1857) under the auspices of the LMS. For the next twenty years, Wong Foon practiced medicine in

Canton. Around 1860 he was appointed by Li Hung-chang as a medical adviser, but disliking administrative work he quit this position after six months. In 1863 Wong was named the Customs Medical Officer for Canton, a job he held until his death. For the last dozen years of his life (1866-1878) he taught medicine at the Canton Hospital Medical School, an Anglo-American missionary institution directed by Dr. John Kerr. K. Chimin Wong and Lien-teh Wu, *History of Chinese Medicine*, 2nd ed. (Shanghai, 1936), pp. 371-372, 391, 395, 405; William Warder Cadbury, *At the Point of a Lancet: One Hundred Years of the Canton Hospital, 1835-1935* (Shanghai, 1935), pp. 52, 116-117, 121-123, 127, 164, 175-176; Yung Wing, *My Life in China and America* (New York, 1909), pp. 32-33; Thomas E. La Fargue, *China's First Hundred* (Pullman, 1942), p. 21.

4. There is a biography of Yung Wing (under Jung Hung) in Hummel, I, 402-405. Yung's retrospective account of his life (*My Life in China and America*) must be used with caution, as it is self-serving and marred by inaccuracies. The most detailed scholarly account of Yung's career is in Lo Hsiang-lin, *Hsiang-kang yü Chung-Hsi wen-hua chih chiao-liu*, pp. 77-134. Two accounts which focus on Yung's educational mission are La Fargue; and Otake Fumio, "Shindai ni okeru Chūgoku no gaikoku ryūgakusei," in Hayashi Tomoharu, comp., *Kinsei Chūgoku kyōikushi kenkyū* (Tokyo, 1958), pp. 309-328. Yung's years in America are studied in Edmund H. Worthy, Jr., "Yung Wing in America," *Pacific Historical Review* 34:265-287 (August 1965).

5. Lloyd Eastman, "Political Reformism in China Before the Sino-Japanese War," *Journal of Asian Studies* 27.4:698 (August 1968).

6. Biographical information on Hu Li-yüan (ca. 1847-ca. 1916) is very sparse. Born into a merchant family from San-shui hsien, Kwangtung, he lived in Hong Kong from an early age. His educational background was both Chinese and Western. He competed unsuccessfully in the civil service examinations and was a graduate of Queen's College in Hong Kong. A prosperous merchant and a close friend of Ho Kai, Hu served for a while (1879-1881) on the translating staff of Wang T'ao's *Tsun-wan yat-po*. He visited Japan at the time of the Sino-Japanese War. See Lu T'ing-ch'ang, "Hu I-nan hsien-sheng shih-lüeh," in Hu Li-yüan, *Hu I-nan hsien-sheng ch'üan-chi* (1920), ts'e 1; *Hsün-huan jih-pao liu-shih chou-nien chi-nien t'e-kan*, p. 14; Jen Chi-yü, "Ho Ch'i Hu Li-yüan ti kai-liang-chu-i ssu-hsiang," in *Chung-kuo chin-tai ssu-hsiang-shih lun-wen chi*, p. 75.

7. Biographical material on Ho Kai is found in Schiffrin, pp. 20-26 and passim; Brian Harrison, ed., *University of Hong Kong: The First Fifty Years, 1911-1961* (Hong Kong, 1962), pp. 6, 11, 35; Arnold Wright, ed., *Twentieth-Century Impressions of Hong Kong, Shanghai, and Other Treaty Ports of China* (London, 1908), p. 109; Linda P. Shin, "China in Transition: The Role of Wu T'ing-fang (1842-1922)," Ph.D. dissertation, University of California (Los Angeles) (1970), pp. 131-134; Wu Hsing-lien, *Hsiang-kang Hua-jen ming-jen shih-lüeh* (Hong Kong, 1937), supplement, pp. 1-2; Lo Hsiang-lin, *Hsiang-kang yü Chung-Hsi wen-hua chih chiao-liu*, pp. 135-178; Lo Hsiang-lin, *Kuo-fu chih ta-hsüeh shih-tai* (Chungking, 1945), pp. 7-16.

The reform thought of Ho Kai and Hu Li-yüan is analyzed in Eastman,

"Political Reformism in China Before the Sino-Japanese War," pp. 695-710, passim; Hsiao Kung-ch'üan, VI, 795-803; Jen Chi-yü, "Ho Ch'i Hu Li-yüan ti kai-liang-chu-i ssu-hsiang," pp. 75-91; Onogawa Hidemi, "Ka Kei Ko Reien no shinsei rongi," in *Ishihama sensei koki kinen Tōyōgaku ronsō* (Osaka, 1958), pp. 121-133; Watanabe Tetsuhiro, "Ka Kei Ko Reien no shinseiron," in *Ritsumeikan bungaku* No. 11:939-955 (November 1961).

8. For biographical material and a detailed examination of the comprador phase of Tong's career, see Liu Kuang-ching, "T'ang T'ing-shu chih mai-pan shih-tai," *Ch'ing-hua hsüeh-pao*, N.S., 2.2:143-183 (June 1961). His involvement with the China Merchants Company and the Kaiping Mining Company is covered in Albert Feuerwerker, *China's Early Industrialization: Sheng Hsüan-huai (1844-1916) and Mandarin Enterprise* (Cambridge, Mass., 1958), pp. 110-111, and Ellsworth C. Carlson, *The Kaiping Mines (1877-1912)*, 2nd ed. (Cambridge, Mass., 1971), pp. 5-8, 31, 38, and passim. See also Kenneth Folsom, *Friends, Guests, and Colleagues: The Mu-fu System in the Late Ch'ing Period* (Berkeley, 1968), pp. 144-146; Hummel, II, 956; Yen-p'ing Hao, pp. 196, 199, and passim.

9. There is a biography of Wu T'ing-fang in Howard L. Boorman, ed., *Biographical Dictionary of Republican China* (New York, 1967-1971), III, 453-456. Linda Shin's study is much more complete and, in the case of discrepancies with the account in Boorman, I have accepted Shin as authoritative. (Boorman, for example, has Wu attending the British Central School in Hong Kong, rather than St. Paul's.) Dr. Shin, in a letter to the author, June 22, 1971, indicates that she thinks it likely that Wu was baptized even before going to Hong Kong to study at St. Paul's, though the evidence for this is circumstantial. See also Cyril Pearl's *Morrison of Peking* (Sydney, 1967), in which Wu is described (p. 234) as "a baptized Christian with two concubines."

10. Biographical information on Cheng may be found in Feuerwerker, *China's Early Industrialization*, pp. 116-117; Yen-p'ing Hao, pp. 186-187, 196-197, 201-206, and passim. His thought is studied in Liu Kuang-ching, "Cheng Kuan-ying I-yen," pp. 373-425; Wang Yung-k'ang, "Cheng Kuan-ying ch'i jen chi ch'i ssu-hsiang," *Shih-hsüeh yüeh-k'an* No. 1:34-40 (January 1958); Chou Fu-ch'eng, "Cheng Kuan-ying ti ssu-hsiang," in *Chung-kuo chin-tai ssu-hsiang shih lun-wen chi*, pp. 99-109. The various editions of Cheng's writings are unraveled in Ichiko, pp. 107-115.

11. Biographical information on Ma Chien-chung is extremely scattered. The sketch presented here is pieced together from the following sources: Henri Cordier, *Histoire des relations de la Chine avec les puissances occidentales, 1860-1902* (Paris, 1901-1902), II, 499-500; Spector, pp. 282-283; Y.C. Wang, *Chinese Intellectuals and the West, 1872-1949* (Chapel Hill, 1966), pp. 80-81; Folsom, pp. 139-140; Chang Jo-ku, *Ma Hsiang-po hsien-sheng nien-p'u* (Shanghai, 1939), passim; Li Chi, tr. and ed., "*A Provisional System of Grammar for Teaching Chinese*" with Introduction and Commentary (Berkeley, 1960), pp. 173-176. Two Chinese Communist studies of Ma's thought are Jen Ching-wu, "Ma Chien-chung tsai *Shih-k'o-chai chi-yen* li so piao-hsien ti ssu-hsiang," *Kuang-ming jih-pao*, November 14, 1953; and Jen

Chi-yü, "Ma Chien-chung ti ssu-hsiang," in *Chung-kuo chin-tai ssu-hsiang shih lun-wen chi*, pp. 66-74. Two treatises written by Ma in France in 1878 (one on diplomacy, the other on diplomatic service) are scrutinized in Banno Masataka, "Furansu ryūgaku jidai no Ma Kenchū," *Kokka gakkai zasshi* 84.5-6:1-37 (August 1971).

12. There is a biography of Ma Liang in Boorman, II, 470-473. Much interesting detail on his life is also furnished in Chang Jo-ku. Despite the fact that, by the end of the Ch'ing, Ma Liang was over seventy and could already look back upon an extremely active and unusual career, he has been completely overlooked by students of the late Ch'ing (Hummel, for example, has no mention of him). As an indication of how total the blackout has been, a respected scholar, some years ago, briefly described the modernizing activities of Ma Chien-chung's brother, one S.P. Ma, and confessed to being unable to provide fuller identification. (Ma was best known by his courtesy name, Hsiang-po, which in nineteenth-century English-language materials would probably have been transliterated Siang-po. Hence the S.P.) See Feuerwerker, *China's Early Industrialization*, pp. 142, 284n147.

13. *The Chinese Renaissance*, pp. 11-12.

14. Like most sweeping statements, this one can profit from qualification. The great self-strengthening officials of the latter half of the nineteenth century, although primarily important (in my view) as legitimizers of change, also engaged in a certain amount of innovative activity on their own. An interesting question raised by Jonathan Porter, in his book on Tseng Kuo-fan, is how much of this innovation was deliberate, how much, inadvertent. See *Tseng Kuo-fan's Private Bureaucracy* (Berkeley, 1972), pp. 16-17, 129-133.

15. Although Wang T'ao appears to have spoken some English, there is no evidence that he could read it. Cheng Kuan-ying, in Liu Kuang-ching's opinion, "probably did not learn enough English to read this language easily." "Cheng Kuan-ying *I-yen*," p. 418.

16. The journalistic achievements of Wang T'ao, Wu T'ing-fang, Tong King-sing, Ho Kai, and Yung Wing have already been noted (see also Chap. 3 above). Cheng Kuan-ying, possibly taking up a suggestion that had first been advanced by Wang T'ao around 1876, made an abortive effort at one point to launch a Western-language newspaper for the purpose of publicizing the Chinese side in Sino-Western disputes. See Wang's letter to Tong King-sing, *CT*, 9:21-22; Ko Kung-chen, p. 104; Cheng Kuan-ying, *Sheng-shih wei-yen hou-pien* (Taipei, 1969; original preface dated 1909), III, 1720-1723.

17. See Chap. 7, n. 2 above.

18. Cheng Kuan-ying's mature ideas on commerce may be found in *Sheng-shih wei-yen tseng-ting hsin-pien*, II, 677-802, esp. his essay "Shang-chan" (Commercial warfare) (pp. 753-766). See also Yen-p'ing Hao, pp. 204-205. For Cheng's earlier economic views, see Liu Kuang-ching, "Cheng Kuan-ying *I-yen*," pp. 398-410, 422-425. Wang T'ao's economic thought is dealt with in Chap. 7 above. Ho Kai's economic views are discussed in Onogawa, pp. 132-133; Watanabe, pp. 943-946.

19. Yen-p'ing Hao, p. 194.

20. Yung Wing, pp. 191-196.

21. Yen-p'ing Hao, pp. 205-206.

22. Boorman, III, 454.

23. Fang Hao, "Ma Hsiang-po hsien-sheng shih-lüeh," in Ma Liang, *Ma Hsiang-po hsien-sheng wen-chi* (Peiping, 1947), p. 2.

24. See Chap. 8 above; also Shin, p. 132.

25. See Chap. 8 above. Also Shin, pp. 133-134; Yen-p'ing Hao, p. 203; Cheng Kuan-ying, "I-yüan" (Parliaments), in his *Sheng-shih wei-yen tseng-ting hsin-pien*, I, 49-85.

26. Quoted in Yen-p'ing Hao, p. 205.

27. *Shanghai*, p. 8.

28. *CT*, 9:19b.

29. Shin, pp. 49-50. Foreign fear of the growth of Chinese commercial power in Hong Kong was the central theme of one of Wang T'ao's editorials. *WLWP*, 4:1-3. The stagnation of the China trade after 1873 and the growing tendency for it to pass into native hands were by no means confined to Hong Kong. See Nathan A. Pelcovits, *Old China Hands and the Foreign Office* (New York, 1948), pp. 103-104, 111-112, 132.

30. See Milton E. Osborne, *The French Presence in Cochinchina and Cambodia: Rule and Response (1859-1905)* (Ithaca, 1969), esp. Chap. 6.

31. Teng and Fairbank, *China's Response to the West*, pp. 115-116; *CT*, 4:6; Yung Wing, pp. 67-73.

32. Worthy, pp. 283-284.

33. Shin, pp. 132-133.

34. Folsom, pp. 95-96, and Porter, pp. 123-133, both make the point that the *mu-fu* system provided an institutional vehicle for the employment of unorthodox talent.

35. The term is used (although in a slightly different way) by Black, p. 71.

36. "Li Wen-chung-kung chih Wang T'ao" (Li Hung-chang's recognition of Wang T'ao), in Hsü K'o, comp., *Ch'ing-pai lei-ch'ao* (Shanghai, 1928), 30:28; Hung Shen, p. 1034.

37. Shin, pp. 229-230.

38. Ibid., p. 120.

39. Chang Jo-ku, pp. 154-161.

40. Members of Li's *mu-fu* with whom Wang maintained a regular correspondence included, among others, Wu T'ing-fang, Ma Chien-chung, Sheng Hsüan-huai, Tong King-sing, and Cheng Tsao-ju.

41. Shin, pp. 229-230.

42. Li's limitations as a reformer are discussed in Kwang-Ching Liu, "The Confucian as Patriot and Pragmatist: Li Hung-chang's Formative Years, 1823-1866," *Harvard Journal of Asiatic Studies* 30:7, 35, 44-45 (1970).

43. Folsom, p. 146.

44. The importance of Taiping Christianity is emphasized by Jen Yu-wen (Chien Yu-wen) in *The Taiping Revolutionary Movement*.

45. I have explored the Christian contribution to Chinese reformism more fully in "Littoral and Hinterland in Nineteenth-Century China: The 'Christian' Reformers," a paper prepared for the conference on missionaries held at Cuernavaca in January 1972.

46. Schiffrin, pp. 16, 19, 47-48, 52, 66, 89, 172-174. See also the biography of Ch'en Shao-pai in Boorman, I, 229-231. Schiffrin, pp. 16, 33, 89, et passim, gives Ou Feng-ch'ih's name as Ch'ü Feng-ch'ih. The character at issue, when used as a surname, is generally read "Ou." See Boorman, I, 230. Other Chinese Christians active in the early revolutionary movement are listed in Chien Yu-wen, "Kuang-tung wen-hua chih yen-chiu," in *Kuang-tung wen-wu* (Hong Kong, 1941), 8:12.

47. Schiffrin, p. 22.

48. Ibid., pp. 89-90, 228-229.

49. On Hung Jen-kan, see Chap. 2 above. Among Taiping leaders, Hung came the closest to being a classic littoral type. His ideas on Westernization were presented in a pamphlet of 1859 entitled *Tzu-cheng hsin-p'ien* (A new treatise on aids to administration) and addressed to Hung Hsiu-ch'üan. A summary may be found in So Kwan-wai and Eugene Boardman, pp. 284-291. There is a full translation in Michael, III, 748-777.

50. Wang T'ao's connection with Hung Jen-kan is discussed in Chap. 2 above. Yung Wing's relationship with Hung, his visit to the Taiping area, and his proposals to the rebels are described in Lo Hsiang-lin, *Hsiang-kang yü Chung-Hsi wen-hua chih chiao-liu*, pp. 80-82; Yung Wing, pp. 107-112. Masuda Wataru (pp. 99-100) argues that the seemingly "two-faced" behavior of Wang and Yung must be viewed in the context of the extraordinary political conditions prevailing at the time. Both men saw the West as the truly critical problem of the day and felt that the cessation of internal unrest was more urgent than who led in the accomplishment of this end. Masuda notes, in this connection, that Yung Wing (like Wang T'ao, although in reverse order) offered his advice first to Hung Jen-kan and then to Tseng Kuo-fan.

51. Schiffrin, pp. 20-38.

52. Tong King-sing died in 1892, Wang T'ao in 1897, and Ma Chien-chung in 1900. It is doubtful, in my mind, whether any of them had affiliations with the young revolutionary movement.

53. Schiffrin (pp. 70-82) describes Ho Kai's role and also (pp. 211-212) discusses his limitations as a revolutionary.

54. Ibid., pp. 65, 67.

55. Ibid., pp. 221, 239, 305; Lo Hsiang-lin, *Hsiang-kang yü Chung-Hsi wen-hua chih chiao-liu*, pp. 106-108.

56. Boorman, II, 472-473; III, 455-456.

57. Wang T'ao, for example, expressed publicly his high regard for three of the four early hinterland reformers dealt with in this chapter. He published (with his own preface) Huang Tsun-hsien's poems on Japan in 1880 (see Chap. 4, n. 30 above) and reprinted (with his own preface) Feng Kuei-fen's *Chiao-pin-lu k'ang-i* (Shanghai, 1897). Moreover, his newspaper, *Tsun-wan yat-po*, carried a laudatory two-part sketch of Kuo Sung-tao (reprinted in *WKKP* Vol. 13:82b-83, 92a-b [October 16, 1880 and October 23, 1880]). To the best of my knowledge, none of these reformers reciprocated Wang's esteem openly (although Huang Tsun-hsien and Wang had met and become friends in Tokyo in 1879).

Yen-p'ing Hao, discussing the parallel case of Cheng Kuan-ying, suggests (pp. 221-222) that modern Chinese—he uses the example of Mao Tse-tung—were reluctant to admit their intellectual indebtedness to compradors. See also Hao Chang, *Liang Ch'i-ch'ao and Intellectual Transition in China, 1890-1907* (Cambridge, Mass., 1971), p. 4. André Chih, citing the cases of Ma Liang and Ma Chien-chung, argues that it was virtually impossible for Christians to exercise significant influence in nineteenth-century China. See his *L'Occident "chrétien" vu par les Chinois vers la fin du XIXe siècle (1870-1900)* (Paris, 1962), p. 128.

58. The fullest English-language account of Feng's career is in Hummel, I, 241-243. For a recent—and revisionist—study of his thought, see Lü Shih-ch'iang, "Feng Kuei-fen," pp. 1-8.

59. Hamilton, p. 20.

60. Hummel, I, 438-439; Hamilton, pp. 1-29; Spector, pp. 279-281.

61. Hummel, I, 331-332; Immanuel Hsü, pp. 175-176; Teng and Fairbank, *China's Response to the West*, pp. 140-146; Kwang-Ching Liu, "Nineteenth-Century China," pp. 142-143; Spector, pp. 281-282.

62. Hummel, I, 350-351; Noriko Kamachi, "Huang Tsun-hsien (1848-1905): His Response to Meiji Japan and the West," Ph.D. dissertation, Harvard University, 1972.

63. Teng and Fairbank, *China's Response to the West*, pp. 50-55; Kwang-Ching Liu, "Nineteenth-Century China," pp. 127-128.

64. Hamilton, pp. 10-11.

65. Teng and Fairbank, *China's Response to the West*, pp. 117-118, 142-146; de Bary, *Sources of Chinese Tradition*, pp. 714-717.

66. Charlton M. Lewis, "The Reform Movement in Hunan (1896-1898)," *Papers on China* 15:70-71 (1961); Kamachi, passim. Huang's influence on Liang Ch'i-ch'ao is the focus of an article: Chang P'eng-yüan, "Huang Tsun-hsien ti cheng-chih ssu-hsiang chi ch'i tui Liang Ch'i-ch'ao ti ying-hsiang," *Chung-yang yen-chiu-yüan chin-tai-shih yen-chiu-so chi-k'an* 1:217-237 (1969). See also Gasster, pp. 70-72.

67. Kwang-Ching Liu, "Nineteenth Century China," p. 128; see also Teng and Fairbank, *China's Response to the West*, p. 54, where Feng attaches great importance to Chinese control over the manufacture, repair, and use of Chinese ships and weaponry. ("If we cannot manufacture, nor repair, nor use them, then they are still the weapons of others ... Eventually we must consider manufacturing, repairing, and using weapons by ourselves ... only thus can we play a leading role on the globe; and only thus shall we restore our original strength, and redeem ourselves from former humiliations.")

68. Hamilton, pp. 1, 12-14.

69. Kwang-Ching Liu, "Nineteenth-Century China," pp. 142-143; Spector, p. 282.

70. Richard C. Howard, "Japan's Role in the Reform Program of K'ang Yu-wei," in Lo Jung-pang, ed., *K'ang Yu-wei: A Biography and a Symposium* (Tucson, 1967), pp. 285, 304-305.

71. There was, of course, an entire side to the reform proposals of men like Feng Kuei-fen and Hsüeh Fu-ch'eng that was addressed to domestic problems and had little relationship to the West. This was true of Wang T'ao

and Cheng Kuan-ying as well. It was less characteristic, however, of the littoral reformers in general.

72. On Liu, see Immanuel Hsü, pp. 187-188.

73. H.G. Barnett, *Innovation: The Basis of Cultural Change* (New York, 1953), pp. 378-410.

74. Hao Chang, *Liang Ch'i-ch'ao*, p. 30; see also ibid., pp. 73-74. See also Lü Shih-ch'iang, "Feng Kuei-fen," passim.

75. Hamilton, pp. 3, 24-25.

76. Wang T'ao and Cheng Kuan-ying, as we have seen, opted for new, littoral-oriented careers only after failure in the examinations. Huang Tsun-hsien did not pass the *chü-jen* examination until 1876, when he was almost thirty years old. Disgusted with a system that provided so little opportunity for advancement, he rejected pursuit of the elusive *chin-shih* degree and embarked upon a career in diplomacy (see Chang P'eng-yüan, p. 218).

BIBLIOGRAPHY

Allen, Young J. (Lin-lo-chih 林樂知). *Chung-Tung chan-chi pen-mo* 中東戰紀本末 (A complete account of the Sino-Japanese war). Shanghai, 1897.

Anderson, C. Arnold. "The Modernization of Education," in Myron Weiner, ed., *Modernization: The Dynamics of Growth*. New York, Basic Books, 1966.

Banno Masataka 坂野正高. "Furansu ryūgaku jidai no Ma Kenchū" フランス留 學時代の馬建忠 (Ma Chien-chung in France), *Kokka gakkai zasshi* 國家學會 雜誌 (The journal of the Association of Political and Social Sciences) 84.5– 6: 1–37 (August 1971).

Barnett, H. G. *Innovation: The Basis of Cultural Change*. New York, McGraw-Hill, 1953.

Bennett, Adrian Arthur. *John Fryer: The Introduction of Western Science and Technology into Nineteenth-Century China*. Cambridge, Mass., East Asian Research Center, Harvard University, 1967.

Biggerstaff, Knight. "Shanghai Polytechnic Institution and Reading Room: An Attempt to Introduce Western Science and Technology to the Chinese," *Pacific Historical Review* 25.2: 127–149 (May 1956).

Black, C. E. *The Dynamics of Modernization: A Study in Comparative History*. New York, Harper and Row, 1966.

Blacker, Carmen. *The Japanese Enlightenment: A Study of the Writings of Fukuzawa Yukichi*. Cambridge, Cambridge University Press, 1964.

Bodde, Derk. "Harmony and Conflict in Chinese Philosophy," in Arthur F. Wright, ed., *Studies in Chinese Thought*. Chicago, University of Chicago Press, 1953.

Boorman, Howard L., ed. *Biographical Dictionary of Republican China*. 4 vols. New York, Columbia University Press, 1967–1971.

Brinton, Crane. *English Political Thought in the Nineteenth Century*. Cambridge, Mass., Harvard University Press, 1954.

Britton, Roswell S. *The Chinese Periodical Press 1800–1912*. Taipei, 1966.

Cadbury, William Warder. *At the Point of a Lancet: One Hundred Years of the Canton Hospital, 1835–1935*. Shanghai, 1935.

Canton, William. *A History of the British and Foreign Bible Society*. 5 vols. London, J. Murray, 1904–1910.

Carlson, Ellsworth C. *The Kaiping Mines (1877–1912)*. 2nd ed. Cambridge, Mass., East Asian Research Center, Harvard University, 1971.

Chalmers, John. *The Origins of the Chinese: An Attempt to Trace the Connection of the Chinese with Western Nations in Their Religion, Superstitions, Arts, Language, and Traditions*. Hong Kong, 1866.

———— "Appendix on the Astronomy of the Ancient Chinese," in James Legge, *The Chinese Classics*, III (Prolegomena).

Chan Wing-tsit, tr. and comp. *A Source Book in Chinese Philosophy*. Princeton, Princeton University Press, 1963.

Chang Chung-li. *The Chinese Gentry: Studies on Their Role in Nineteenth-Century Chinese Society*. Seattle, University of Washington Press, 1955.

———— *The Income of the Chinese Gentry*. Seattle, University of Washington Press, 1962.

Chang Hao. "The Anti-Foreignist Role of Wo-jen (1804–1871)," *Papers on China* 14: 1–29 (1960).

———— *Liang Ch'i-ch'ao and Intellectual Transition in China, 1890–1907*. Cambridge, Mass., Harvard University Press, 1971.

Chang Jo-ku 張若谷. *Ma Hsiang-po hsien-sheng nien-p'u* 馬相伯先生年譜 (Chronological biography of Mr. Ma Liang). Shanghai, 1939.

Chang P'eng-yüan 張朋園. "Huang Tsun-hsien ti cheng-chih ssu-hsiang chi ch'i tui Liang Ch'i-ch'ao ti ying-hsiang" 黃遵憲的政治思想及其對梁啟超的影響 (Huang Tsun-hsien's political thought and his influence on Liang Ch'i-ch'ao), *Chung-yang yen-chiu-yüan chin-tai-shih yen-chiu-so chi-k'an* 中央研究院近代史研究所集刊 (Bulletin of the Institute of Modern History, Academia Sinica) 1: 217–237 (1969).

Ch'en Chen-kuo 陳振國. " 'Ch'ang-mao chuang-yüan' Wang T'ao" 長毛狀元王韜 (Wang T'ao: "First-ranking metropolitan graduate of the long-haired rebels"), *I-ching* 逸經 (Uncanonical classics), no. 33: 41–44 (July 5, 1937).

Ch'en Ch'i-yüan 陳其元. *Yung-hsien-chai pi-chi* 庸閒齋筆記 (Miscellaneous notes from the Yung-hsien studio). 12 chüan. Shanghai, 1925.

Ch'en Chih 陳熾 (Yao-lin-kuan-chu 瑤林館主). "O-jen kuo-shih k'u-lei ch'iang Ch'in lun" 俄人國勢酷類強秦論 (On the great similarity between the national condition of Russia and that of mighty Ch'in), *Shih-wu pao* 時務報 (Chinese progress), vol. 18, Kuang-hsü 23/1/21 (February 22, 1897). Reprinted in *Huang-ch'ao ching-shih-wen hsin-pien* 皇朝經世文新編 (New collection of Ch'ing essays on statecraft), comp. Mai Chung-hua 麥仲華. 2 vols. Taipei, 1965. II, 293–295.

Ch'en Hsüeh-lin 陳學霖. "Huang Sheng: Hsiang-kang Hua-jen t'i-ch'ang yang-wu shih-yeh chih hsien-ch'ü" 黃勝香港華人提倡洋務事業之先驅 (Wong Shing: A distinguished Chinese of early Hong Kong), *Ch'ung-chi hsüeh-pao* 崇基學報 (The Chung Chi journal) 3.2: 226–231 (May 1964).

Ch'en Nai-ch'ien 陳乃乾, comp. *Yang-hu Chao Hui-fu nien-p'u* 陽湖趙惠甫年譜 (A chronological biography of Chao Lieh-wen of Yang-hu), in *T'ai-p'ing t'ien-kuo*, VIII, 727–762.

Ch'en Shao-pai 陳少白. *Hsing-Chung hui ko-ming shih-yao* 興中會革命史要 (Outline of the revolutionary history of the Hsing-Chung hui), in *Hsin-hai ko-ming* 辛亥革命 (The 1911 revolution). 8 vols. Shanghai, 1957. I, 21–75.

Cheng Hsien 正先. "Huang Kung-tu: Wu-hsü wei-hsin yün-tung ti ling-hsiu" 黃公度戊戌維新運動的領袖 (Huang Tsun-hsien: A leader of the 1898 reform movement), *I-ching*, no. 10: 16–21 (July 1936).

Cheng Kuan-ying 鄭觀應. *Sheng-shih wei-yen* 盛世危言 (Warnings to a prosperous age). 5 chüan. Shanghai, Shang-hai shu-chü 上海書局, 1896.

—— *Sheng-shih wei-yen tseng-ting hsin-pien* 盛世危言增訂新編 (Warnings to a prosperous age: Revised and expanded edition). 2 vols. Taipei, 1965.

—— *Sheng-shih wei-yen hou-pien* 盛世危言後編 (Warnings to a prosperous age: Second part). 3 vols. Taipei, 1969.

Chiang Tun-fu 蔣敦復. *Hsiao-ku-t'ang wen-chi* 嘯古堂文集 (Collected prose of Chiang Tun-fu). 8 chüan. Shanghai, 1868.

Chien Yu-wen 簡又文. " 'Ch'ang-mao chuang-yüan' Wang T'ao pa" 長毛狀元王韜跋 (Comment on "Wang T'ao: 'First-ranking metropolitan graduate of the long-haired rebels' "), *I-ching*, no. 33: 44–45 (July 1937).

—— "Kuan-yü Wang T'ao" 關於王韜 (Concerning Wang T'ao), *Ta-feng* 大風 (Typhoon magazine) 58: 1785 (December 1939).

—— "Kuang-tung wen-hua chih yen-chiu" 廣東文化之研究 (The study of Kwangtung culture), in *Kuang-tung wen-wu* 廣東文物 (The civilization of Kwangtung). 10 chüan. Hong Kong, 1941. 8: 2–35.

Ch'ien Chung-lien 錢仲聯. *Huang Kung-tu hsien-sheng nien-p'u* 黃公度先生年譜 (Chronological biography of Mr. Huang Tsun-hsien), in Huang Tsun-hsien, *Jen-ching-lu shih-ts'ao chien-chu*.

Chih, André. *L'Occident "chrétien" vu par les Chinois vers la fin du XIX* siècle (1870–1900)*. Paris, Presses Universitaires de France, 1962.

Chinese Repository, The. Canton, 1832–1851.

Ch'ing-pai lei-ch'ao 清稗類鈔 (A classified compilation of Ch'ing anecdotal material), comp. Hsü K'o 徐珂. 92 chüan. Shanghai, 1928.

Chou Fu-ch'eng 周輔成. "Cheng Kuan-ying ti ssu-hsiang" 鄭觀應的思想 (Cheng Kuan-ying's thought), in *Chung-kuo chin-tai ssu-hsiang shih lun-wen chi* 中國近代思想史論文集 (A collection of essays on the history of modern Chinese thought). Shanghai, 1958.

Chou Tso-jen 周作人. "*Jih-pen tsa-shih shih*" 日本雜事詩 (Poems on miscellaneous things Japanese), *I-ching*, no. 3: 3–5 (1936).

Chung-kuo chin-tai ssu-hsiang shih chiang-shou t'i-kang 中國近代思想史講授提綱 (A teaching outline for the history of modern Chinese thought), comp. Shih Chün 石峻, Jen Chi-yü 任繼愈, and Chu Po-k'un 朱伯崑. Peking, 1957.

Ch'üan Han-sheng 全漢昇. "Ch'ing-mo ti 'Hsi-hsüeh yüan ch'u Chung-kuo' shuo" 清末的西學源出中國說 (The late Ch'ing theory that "Western learning originated in China"), in Li Ting-i 李定一 et al., eds., *Chung-kuo chin-tai-shih lun-ts'ung* 中國近代史論叢 (Collection of essays on modern

Chinese history), 1st ser., vol. 5. Taipei, 1956.

Cohen, Paul A. "Missionary Approaches: Hudson Taylor and Timothy Richard," *Papers on China* 11: 29–62 (1957).

—— *China and Christianity: The Missionary Movement and the Growth of Chinese Antiforeignism, 1860–1870.* Cambridge, Mass., Harvard University Press, 1963.

—— "Ch'ing China: Confrontation with the West, 1850–1900," in James B. Crowley, ed., *Modern East Asia: Essays in Interpretation.* New York, Harcourt, Brace, and World, 1970.

—— "Littoral and Hinterland in Nineteenth-Century China: The 'Christian' Reformers," paper prepared for conference on missionaries, Cuernavaca, January 1972.

Condorcet, Antoine-Nicolas de. *Sketch for a Historical Picture of the Progress of the Human Mind,* tr. June Barraclough. New York, Noonday Press, 1955.

Cordier, Henri. *Histoire des relations de la Chine avec les puissances occidentales, 1860–1902.* 3 vols. Paris, Félix Alcan, 1901–1902.

Couling, Samuel. *The Encyclopaedia Sinica.* 2 vols. Shanghai, 1917.

Craig, Albert M. "Introduction: Perspectives on Personality in Japanese History," in Albert M. Craig and Donald H. Shively, eds., *Personality in Japanese History.* Berkeley, University of California Press, 1970.

de Bary, Wm. T. "Chinese Despotism and the Confucian Ideal: A Seventeenth-Century View," in John K. Fairbank, ed., *Chinese Thought and Institutions.* Chicago, University of Chicago Press, 1957.

—— et al., eds. *Sources of Chinese Tradition.* New York, Columbia University Press, 1961.

de Saussure, Léopold. *Les origines de l'astronomie chinoise.* Taipei, 1967.

Dore, Ronald. *Education in Tokugawa Japan.* Berkeley, University of California Press, 1965.

Dwight, Henry Otis. *The Centennial History of the American Bible Society.* New York, Macmillan, 1916.

Eastman, Lloyd. *Throne and Mandarins: China's Search for a Policy During the Sino-French Controversy, 1880–1885.* Cambridge, Mass., Harvard University Press, 1967.

—— "Political Reformism in China Before the Sino-Japanese War," *Journal of Asian Studies* 27.4: 695–710 (August 1968).

Edkins, Jane. *Chinese Scenes and People.* London, 1863.

Edkins, Joseph. *China's Place in Philology: An Attempt to Show That the Languages of Europe and Asia Have Common Origin.* London, 1871.

—— *Chinese Buddhism: A Volume of Sketches, Historical, Descriptive, and Critical.* London, 1880.

—— *The Early Spread of Religious Ideas Especially in the Far East.* London, 1894.

Eliade, Mircea. *Cosmos and History: The Myth of the Eternal Return.* New York, Harper and Row, 1959.

Erikson, Erik. *Insight and Responsibility.* New York, Norton, 1964.

Fairbank, John K. *China: The People's Middle Kingdom and the U.S.A.* Cambridge, Mass., Harvard University Press, 1967.

——, Edwin O. Reischauer, and Albert M. Craig. *East Asia: The Modern Transformation.* Boston, Houghton Mifflin, 1965.

Fang Hao 方豪. "Ma Hsiang-po hsien-sheng shih-lüeh" 馬相伯先生事略 (A sketch of Mr. Ma Liang), in Ma Liang, *Ma Hsiang-po hsien-sheng wen-chi*.

Feng Kuei-fen 馮桂芬. *Chiao-pin-lu k'ang-i* 校邠廬抗議 (Straightforward words from the Chiao-pin studio). Shanghai, Kuang-jen-t'ang 廣仁堂, 1897.

Feuerwerker, Albert. *China's Early Industrialization: Sheng Hsuan-huai (1844–1916) and Mandarin Enterprise*. Cambridge, Mass., Harvard University Press, 1958.

———— *The Chinese Economy, ca. 1870–1911*. Ann Arbor, Center for Chinese Studies, University of Michigan, 1969.

Folsom, Kenneth. *Friends, Guests, and Colleagues: The Mu-fu System in the Late Ch'ing Period*. Berkeley, University of California Press, 1968.

Franke, Wolfgang. *The Reform and Abolition of the Traditional Chinese Examination System*. Cambridge, Mass., East Asian Research Center, Harvard University, 1963.

Fuse Chisoku 布施知足. "Ō Shisen no Fusō yūki" 王紫詮の扶桑遊記 (Wang T'ao's diary of his trip to Japan), in his *Yūki ni arawaretaru Meiji jidai no Nisshi ōrai* 遊記に現はれたる明治時代の日支往來 (Sino-Japanese intercourse in the Meiji period as revealed in travel diaries), in *Tōa kenkyū kōza* 東亞研究講座 (Lectures on East Asian studies), no. 84: 22–34 (December 1938).

Gardner, John W. *Excellence: Can We Be Equal and Excellent Too?* New York, Harper and Row, 1962.

Gasster, Michael. "Reform and Revolution in China's Political Modernization," in Mary C. Wright, ed., *China in Revolution: The First Phase, 1900–1913*. New Haven, Yale University Press, 1968.

Hamilton, David. "Kuo Sung-tao: A Maverick Confucian," *Papers on China* 15: 1–29 (1961).

Hao Yen-p'ing. *The Comprador in Nineteenth-Century China: Bridge between East and West*. Cambridge, Mass., Harvard University Press, 1970.

Harrison, Brian, ed. *University of Hong Kong: The First Fifty Years, 1911–1961*. Hong Kong, Hong Kong University Press, 1962.

Hertslet, E., ed. *The Map of Europe by Treaty*. 4 vols. London, 1875–1891.

Ho Ping-ti. *Studies on the Population of China, 1368–1953*. Cambridge, Mass., Harvard University Press, 1959.

Ho Shu-ling 何樹齡. "Lun chin chih shih-chü yü Chan-kuo ta i" 論今之時局與戰國大異 (On the great differences between today's situation and that of the Warring States), in *Huang-ch'ao ching-shih-wen hsin-pien*. I, 124–126.

Hou Chi-ming. *Foreign Investment and Economic Development in China, 1840–1937*. Cambridge, Mass., Harvard University Press, 1965.

Howard, Richard C. "Japan's Role in the Reform Program of K'ang Yu-wei," in Lo Jung-pang, ed., *K'ang Yu-wei: A Biography and a Symposium*. Tucson, University of Arizona Press, 1967.

Hsi-kuo chin-shih hui-pien 西國近事彙編 (A classified compilation of recent Western events). 4 chüan. Shanghai, 1873.

Hsia, T. A. "Demons of Paradise: The Chinese Images of Russia," *The Annals of the American Academy of Political and Social Science* 349: 27–37 (September 1963).

Hsiao Kung-ch'üan 蕭公權. *Chung-kuo cheng-chih ssu-hsiang shih* 中國政治思想史 (A history of Chinese political thought). 6 vols. Taipei, 1961.

Hsieh Hsing-yao 謝興堯. "Wang T'ao shang-shu T'ai-p'ing t'ien-kuo shih-chi k'ao" 王韜上書太平天國事蹟考 (An inquiry into the matter of Wang T'ao's letter to the Taipings), in his *T'ai-p'ing t'ien-kuo shih-shih lun-ts'ung* 太平天國史事論叢 (Essays on Taiping history). Shanghai, 1935.

―――― "Kuan-yü 'Shang-hai tsai T'ai-p'ing t'ien-kuo shih-tai' ti shih-liao" 關於上海在太平天國時代的史料 (Concerning historical materials on "Shanghai in the Taiping period"), in Li Ting-i, *Chung-kuo chin-tai-shih lun-ts'ung*, 1st ser., vol. 4.

Hsieh Wu-liang 謝無量. "Wang T'ao: Ch'ing-mo pien-fa-lun chih shou-ch'uang-che chi Chung-kuo pao-tao wen-hsüeh chih hsien-ch'ü-che" 王韜清末變法論之首創者及中國報道文學之先驅者 (Wang T'ao: Originator of the concept of *pien-fa* in the late Ch'ing and pioneer in Chinese journalistic writing), *Chiao-hsüeh yü yen-chiu* 教學與研究 (Teaching and research), March 1958, pp. 37–42.

Hsü, Immanuel C. Y. *China's Entrance into the Family of Nations: The Diplomatic Phase, 1858–1880*. Cambridge, Mass., Harvard University Press, 1960.

Hsüeh Chün-tu. *Huang Hsing and the Chinese Revolution*. Stanford, Stanford University Press, 1961.

Hsün-huan jih-pao 循環日報 (Universal circulating herald). Hong Kong, 1874.

Hsün-huan jih-pao liu-shih chou-nien chi-nien t'e-k'an 循環日報六十週年紀念特刊 (Special volume commemorating the sixtieth anniversary of the *Tsun-wan yat-po*). Hong Kong, 1932.

Hu Sheng. *Imperialism and Chinese Politics*. Peking, 1955.

Hu Shih. *The Chinese Renaissance*. Chicago, University of Chicago Press, 1934.

Hu Shih 胡適. "Pa kuan ts'ang Wang T'ao shou-kao ch'i ts'e" 跋館藏王韜手稿七冊 (A note on the library's seven Wang T'ao manuscripts), *Kuo-li Pei-p'ing t'u-shu-kuan kuan-k'an* 國立北平圖書館館刊 (Bulletin of the National Library of Peiping) 8.3: 1–5 (May–June 1934).

Hua-tzu jih-pao ch'i-shih-i chou-nien chi-nien k'an 華字日報七十一週年紀念刊 (Volume commemorating the seventy-first anniversary of the *Hua-tzu jih-pao*). Hong Kong, 1934.

Huang-ch'ao ching-shih-wen hsü-pien 皇朝經世文續編 (Supplementary collection of Ch'ing essays on statecraft), comp. Ko Shih-chün 葛士濬. 2 vols. Taipei, 1964.

Huang Tsun-hsien 黄遵憲. *Jen-ching-lu shih-ts'ao chien-chu* 人境廬詩草箋註 (Annotated edition of Huang Tsun-hsien's collected poems). Shanghai, 1957.

Hucker, Charles O. *The Traditional Chinese State in Ming Times (1368–1644)*. Tucson, University of Arizona Press, 1961.

Hummel, Arthur W., ed. *Eminent Chinese of the Ch'ing Period*. 2 vols. Washington, United States Government Printing Office, 1943–1944.

Hung Shen 洪深. "*Shen-pao* tsung-pien-tsuan 'Ch'ang-mao chuang-yüan' Wang T'ao k'ao-cheng" 申報總編纂長毛狀元王韜考証 (An examination of the evidence on Wang T'ao, Editor-in-chief of *Shen-pao* and "First-ranking metropolitan graduate of the long-haired rebels"), *Wen-hsüeh* 文學 (Literature) 2.6: 1033–1045 (June 1934).

Ichiko Chūzō 市古宙三. "Tei Kannō no *Ekigen* ni tsuite" 鄭觀應の易言について (On Cheng Kuan-ying's *I-yen*), in *Wada hakushi koki kinen Tōyōshi ronsō* 和田博

士古稀記念東洋史論叢 (A collection of essays on Oriental history presented to Dr. Wada on the occasion of his seventieth birthday). Tokyo, 1960.

Iriye Akira. "Public Opinion and Foreign Policy: The Case of Late Ch'ing China," in Albert Feuerwerker, Rhoads Murphey, and Mary C. Wright, eds., *Approaches to Modern Chinese History*. Berkeley, University of California Press, 1967.

——— "Imperialism in Eastern Asia," in James B. Crowley, *Modern East Asia: Essays in Interpretation*.

Jansen, Marius B. *The Japanese and Sun Yat-sen*. Cambridge, Mass., Harvard University Press, 1954.

——— *Sakamoto Ryōma and the Meiji Restoration*. Princeton, Princeton University Press, 1961.

——— "Japanese Views of China During the Meiji Period," in Albert Feuerwerker et al., *Approaches to Modern Chinese History*.

Japan Biographical Encyclopedia and Who's Who. Tokyo, 1958.

Jen Chi-yü 任繼愈. "Ho Ch'i Hu Li-yüan ti kai-liang-chu-i ssu-hsiang" 何啟胡禮垣的改良主義思想 (The reformist thought of Ho Kai and Hu Li-yüan), in *Chung-kuo chin-tai ssu-hsiang shih lun-wen chi*.

——— "Ma Chien-chung ti ssu-hsiang" 馬建忠的思想 (Ma Chien-chung's thought), in *Chung-kuo chin-tai ssu-hsiang shih lun-wen chi*.

Jen Ching-wu 任靜吾. "Ma Chien-chung tsai *Shih-k'o-chai chi-yen* li so piao-hsien ti ssu-hsiang" 馬建忠在適可齋記言裡所表現的思想 (Ma Chien-chung's thought as displayed in *Shih-k'o-chai chi-yen*), *Kuang-ming jih-pao* 光明日報 (Kuang-ming daily), November 14, 1953.

Jen Yu-wen (Chien Yu-wen). *The Taiping Revolutionary Movement*. New Haven, Yale University Press, 1973.

Kamachi Noriko. "Huang Tsun-hsien (1848–1905): His Response to Meiji Japan and the West." Ph. D. dissertation, Harvard University, 1972.

King, Frank H. H., ed., and Prescott Clarke. *A Research Guide to China-Coast Newspapers, 1822–1911*. Cambridge, Mass., East Asian Research Center, Harvard University, 1965.

Ko-chih shu-yüan k'o-i 格致書院課藝 (The Polytechnic Institute prize essays). Shanghai, 1887–1895.

Ko Kung-chen 戈公振. *Chung-kuo pao-hsüeh shih* 中國報學史 (History of Chinese journalism). Peking, 1955.

Komiya Toyotaka, comp. and ed. *Japanese Music and Drama in the Meiji Era*, tr. Edward G. Seidensticker and Donald Keene. Tokyo, 1956.

Kublin, Hyman. *Asian Revolutionary: The Life of Sen Katayama*. Princeton, Princeton University Press, 1964.

Kuo T'ing-i 郭廷以. *T'ai-p'ing t'ien-kuo shih-shih jih-chih* 太平天國史事日誌 (A historical chronology of the Taiping kingdom). Taipei, 1963.

Kuzuu Yoshihisa 葛生能久. *Tōa senkaku shishi kiden* 東亞先覺志士記傳 (Stories and biographies of pioneer East Asian adventurers). 3 vols. Tokyo, 1933.

La Fargue, Thomas E. *China's First Hundred*. Pullman, State College of Washington, 1942.

Latourette, Kenneth Scott. *A History of Christian Missions in China*. London, Society for Promoting Christian Knowledge, 1929.

Legge, Helen E. *James Legge: Missionary and Scholar.* London, The Religious Tract Society, 1905.

Legge, James, tr. *The Lǐ Kǐ,* in F. Max Müller, ed., *The Sacred Books of the East,* vols. 27–28. Oxford, 1885.

———— tr. *The Chinese Classics.* 5 vols. Hong Kong, Hong Kong University Press, 1960.

Leong Sow-theng. "Wang T'ao and the Movement for Self-strengthening and Reform in the Late Ch'ing Period," *Papers on China* 17: 101–130 (1963).

Levenson, Joseph R. *Confucian China and Its Modern Fate.* 3 vols. Berkeley, University of California Press, 1958–1965.

———— *Liang Ch'i-ch'ao and the Mind of Modern China.* Cambridge, Mass., Harvard University Press, 1965.

Lewis, Charlton M. "The Reform Movement in Hunan (1896–1898)," *Papers on China* 15: 62–90 (1961).

Li Chi, tr. and ed. *"A Provisional System of Grammar for Teaching Chinese" with Introduction and Commentary.* Berkeley, Center for Chinese Studies, Institute of International Studies, University of California, 1960.

Li Hung-chang 李鴻章. *Li Wen-chung-kung ch'üan-chi* 李文忠公全集 (The collected works of Li Hung-chang). 7 vols. Taipei, 1962.

Li Yen 李儼. *Chung suan-shih lun-ts'ung* 中算史論叢 (Collected writings on the history of Chinese mathematics). 5 vols. Peking, 1955.

Lin Yutang. *A History of the Press and Public Opinion in China.* Chicago, University of Chicago Press, 1936.

Liu Kuang-ching 劉廣京. "T'ang T'ing-shu chih mai-pan shih-tai" 唐廷樞之買辦時代 (Tong King-sing: His comprador years), *Ch'ing-hua hsüeh-pao* 清華學報 (Tsing Hua journal of Chinese studies). New Series, 2.2: 143–183 (June 1961).

———— "Cheng Kuan-ying *I-yen*: Kuang-hsü ch'u-nien chih pien-fa ssu-hsiang" 鄭觀應易言光緒初年之變法思想 (Cheng Kuan-ying's *I-yen*: Reform proposals of the early Kuang-hsü period), part I, *Ch'ing-hua hsüeh-pao.* New Series, 8.1–2: 373–425 (August 1970).

Liu Kwang-Ching (Liu Kuang-ching). "Nineteenth-Century China: The Disintegration of the Old Order and the Impact of the West," in Ping-ti Ho and Tang Tsou, eds., *China in Crisis.* 2 vols. Chicago, University of Chicago Press, 1968.

———— "The Confucian as Patriot and Pragmatist: Li Hung-chang's Formative Years, 1823–1866," *Harvard Journal of Asiatic Studies* 30: 5–45 (1970).

Liu Yüeh-sheng 劉粤聲, comp. *Hsiang-kang Chi-tu-chiao-hui shih* 香港基督教會史 (A history of the Hong Kong Christian church). Hong Kong, 1941.

Lo Erh-kang 羅爾綱. "Shang T'ai-p'ing-chün shu ti Huang Wan k'ao" 上太平軍書的黃畹考 (An examination of the letter submitted by Huang Wan to the Taiping army), *Kuo-hsüeh chi-k'an* 國學季刊 (Journal of sinological studies) 4.2: 123–149 (June 1934).

———— "Wang T'ao shou-ch'ao Hsieh Chieh-ho 'Chin-ling kuei-chia chi-shih-lüeh' chih fa-hsien" 王韜手鈔謝介鶴金陵癸甲紀事略之發現 (The discovery of Wang T'ao's hand-written copy of Hsieh Chieh-ho's "General account of events in Nanking in the years 1853–1854"), *Ta-kung pao* 大公報, no. 178 (April 22, 1937).

—— "Huang Wan k'ao" 黃琬考 (An examination of Huang Wan), in his *T'ai-p'ing t'ien-kuo shih chi-tsai ting-miu chi* 太平天國史記載訂謬集 (Revised accounts of the history of the Taiping kingdom). Peking, 1955.

Lo Hsiang-lin 羅香林. *Kuo-fu chih ta-hsüeh shih-tai* 國父之大學時代 (Sun Yat-sen's university days). Chungking, 1945.

—— *Hsiang-kang yü Chung-Hsi wen-hua chih chiao-liu* 香港與中西文化之交流 (The role of Hong Kong in the cultural interchange between China and the West). Hong Kong, 1961.

London Missionary Society Archives. South China. Box 7 (1870–1874).

Lu T'ing-ch'ang 陸廷昌. "Hu I-nan hsien-sheng shih-lüeh" 胡翼南先生事略 (A sketch of Mr. Hu Li-yüan), in Hu Li-yüan 胡禮垣 *Hu I-nan hsien-sheng ch'üan-chi* 胡翼南先生全集 (The collected writings of Mr. Hu Li-yüan), ts'e 1. 1920.

Lü Shih-ch'iang 呂實強. "Wang T'ao p'ing-chuan" 王韜評傳 (An assessment of Wang T'ao), *Shu ho jen* 書和人 (Books and people), no. 61: 473–480 (July 1, 1967).

—— "Feng Kuei-fen ti cheng-chih ssu-hsiang" 馮桂芬的政治思想 (Feng Kuei-fen's political thought), *Chung-hua wen-hua fu-hsing yüeh-k'an* 中華文化復興月刊 (Chinese cultural renaissance monthly) 4.2: 1–8 (February 1971).

Lynd, Helen M. "Clues to Identity," in Hendrik M. Ruitenbeek, ed., *Varieties of Modern Social Theory*. New York, E. P. Dutton and Company, 1963.

Ma Liang 馬良. *Ma Hsiang-po hsien-sheng wen-chi* 馬相伯先生文集 (The collected writings of Mr. Ma Liang). Peiping, 1947.

Mancall, Mark. "The Persistence of Tradition in Chinese Foreign Policy," *The Annals of the American Academy of Political and Social Science* 349: 14–26 (September 1963).

Marcus, John T. "Time and the Sense of History: West and East," *Comparative Studies in Society and History* 3: 123–139 (1960–1961).

Martin, W. A. P. *A Cycle of Cathay, or China, South and North, with Personal Reminiscences*. New York, 1896.

Marx, Karl. *The Eighteenth Brumaire of Louis Bonaparte*, in Lewis S. Feuer, ed., *Basic Writings on Politics and Philosophy: Karl Marx and Friedrich Engels*. Garden City, Doubleday and Company, 1959.

Masuda Wataru 增田涉. "Ō Tō ni tsuite" 王韜について (On Wang T'ao), *Jimbun kenkyū* 人文研究 (Studies in the humanities) 14.7: 90–100 (August 1963).

McAleavy, Henry. *Wang T'ao: The Life and Writings of a Displaced Person*. London, The China Society, 1953.

Merton, Robert K. "Social Structure and Anomie," in Hendrik M. Ruitenbeek, ed., *Varieties of Modern Social Theory*.

Michael, Franz. *The Taiping Rebellion: History and Documents*. 3 vols. Seattle, University of Washington Press, 1966–1971.

Missionary Magazine and Chronicle, The. London, 1836–1866.

Morohashi Tetsuji 諸橋轍次, comp. *Dai Kan-Wa jiten* 大漢和辭典 (Encyclopedic Chinese-Japanese character dictionary). 13 vols. Tokyo, 1955–1960.

Mou An-shih 牟安世. *Yang-wu yün-tung* 洋務運動 (The foreign matters movement). Shanghai, 1961.

Murphey, Rhoads. *Shanghai: Key to Modern China*. Cambridge, Mass., Harvard University Press, 1953.

—— *The Treaty Ports and China's Modernization: What Went Wrong?* Ann Arbor, Center for Chinese Studies, University of Michigan, 1970.

Nakajima Masao 中島眞雄, ed. *Taishi kaiko roku* 對支回顧錄 (Reminiscences of China). 2 vols. Tokyo, 1936.

Needham, Joseph. *Time and Eastern Man: The Henry Myers Lecture 1964*. Glasgow, Royal Anthropological Institute of Great Britain and Ireland, 1965.

Nivison, David. "Protest against Conventions and Conventions of Protest," in Arthur Wright, ed., *The Confucian Persuasion*. Stanford, Stanford University Press, 1960.

North-China Herald and Supreme Court and Consular Gazette, The. Shanghai, 1889–1894, 1897.

North, Eric M. *The Book of a Thousand Tongues*. New York, Harper and Brothers, 1938.

Numata Jiro. "Shigeno Yasutsugu and the Modern Tokyo Tradition of Historical Writing," in W. G. Beasley and E. G. Pulleyblank, eds., *Historians of China and Japan*. London, Oxford University Press, 1961.

Oka Senjin 岡千仞. *Kuan-kuang chi-yu* 観光紀游 (A record of my travels). 10 chüan. Tokyo, 1886.

—— *Ts'ang-ming-shan-fang wen ch'u-chi* 藏名山房文初集 (The prose writings of Oka Senjin: First collection). 6 chüan. Tokyo, 1920.

Okamoto Kansuke 岡本監輔. *Wan-kuo shih-chi* 萬國史記 (An account of world history). 20 chüan. 1900.

Onogawa Hidemi 小野川秀美. "Ka Kei Ko Reien no shinsei rongi" 何啟胡禮垣の新政論議 (The *Hsin-cheng lun-i* of Ho Kai and Hu Li-yüan), in *Ishihama sensei koki kinen Tōyōgaku ronsō* 石濱先生古稀記念東洋學論叢 (Oriental studies in honor of Juntaro Ishihama on the occasion of his seventieth birthday). Osaka, 1958.

Osborne, Milton E. *The French Presence in Cochinchina and Cambodia: Rule and Response (1859–1905)*. Ithaca, Cornell University Press, 1969.

Otake Fumio 小竹文夫. "Shindai ni okeru Chūgoku no gaikoku ryūgakusei" 清代に於ける中國の外國留學生 (Chinese who studied abroad during the Ch'ing dynasty), in Hayashi Tomoharu 林友春 comp., *Kinsei Chūgoku kyōikushi kenkyū* 近世中國教育史研究 (Studies in the educational history of modern China). Tokyo, 1958.

Palmer, Spencer J. *Korea and Christianity: The Problem of Identification with Tradition*. Seoul, 1967.

Pearl, Cyril. *Morrison of Peking*. Sydney, Angus and Robertson, 1967.

Pelcovits, Nathan A. *Old China Hands and the Foreign Office*. New York, Institute of Pacific Relations, 1948.

Porter, Jonathan. *Tseng Kuo-fan's Private Bureaucracy*. Berkeley, Center for Chinese Studies, University of California, 1972.

Price, Don. "The Chinese Intelligentsia's Image of Russia, 1896–1911." Ph.D. dissertation, Harvard University, 1967.

Pulleyblank, E. G. "Chinese Historical Criticism: Liu Chih-chi and Ssu-ma

Kuang," in W. G. Beasley and E. G. Pulleyblank, *Historians of China and Japan.*

Rankin, Mary Backus. "The Revolutionary Movement in Chekiang: A Study in the Tenacity of Tradition," in Mary C. Wright, *China in Revolution: The First Phase, 1900–1913.*

Records of the General Conference of the Protestant Missionaries of China Held at Shanghai, May 7–20, 1890. Shanghai, 1890.

Report of the Directors to the Sixtieth General Meeting of the Missionary Society, Usually Called the London Missionary Society, on Thursday, May 11th, 1854, The. London, 1854.

Report of the Directors to the Sixty-First General Meeting of the Missionary Society, Usually Called the London Missionary Society, on Thursday, May 10th, 1855, The. London, 1855.

Reynolds, Robert L. *Europe Emerges: Transition Toward an Industrial World-Wide Society, 600–1750.* Madison, University of Wisconsin Press, 1961.

Ride, Lindsay. "Biographical Note," in James Legge, *The Chinese Classics*, vol. 1.

Sanetō Keishū 實藤惠秀. "Ō Tō no raiyū to Nihon bunjin" 王韜の來遊と日本文人 (Wang T'ao's visit to Japan and Japanese men of letters), in his *Kindai Nisshi bunka ron* 近代日支文化論 (On modern Sino-Japanese culture). Tokyo, 1941.

Schiffrin, Harold Z. *Sun Yat-sen and the Origins of the Chinese Revolution.* Berkeley, University of California Press, 1968.

Schwartz, Benjamin. *In Search of Wealth and Power: Yen Fu and the West.* Cambridge, Mass., Harvard University Press, 1964.

Shang Yen-liu 商衍鎏. *T'ai-p'ing t'ien-kuo k'o-chü k'ao-shih chi-lüeh* 太平天國科舉考試紀略 (A brief account of the Taiping examination system). Shanghai, 1962.

Shen-pao 申報. 40 vols. Taipei, 1965.

Shin, Linda P. "China in Transition: The Role of Wu T'ing-fang (1842–1922)." Ph. D. dissertation, University of California (Los Angeles), 1970.

Shinjō Shinzō 新城新藏. *Tung-yang t'ien-wen-hsüeh shih yen-chiu* 東洋天文學史研究 (Studies in the history of Chinese astronomy), tr. Shen Chün 沈璿. Shanghai, 1933.

Shively, Donald H. "Nishimura Shigeki: A Confucian View of Modernization," in Marius B. Jansen, ed., *Changing Japanese Attitudes Toward Modernization.* Princeton, Princeton University Press, 1965.

Smith, Thomas C. *Political Change and Industrial Development in Japan: Government Enterprise, 1868–1880.* Stanford, Stanford University Press, 1955.

So Kwan-wai and Eugene P. Boardman (with the assistance of Ch'iu P'ing). "Hung Jen-kan, Taiping Prime Minister, 1859–1864," *Harvard Journal of Asiatic Studies* 20.1–2: 262–294 (June 1957).

Sombart, Werner. *The Quintessence of Capitalism*, tr. M. Epstein. New York, E. P. Dutton and Company, 1915.

Sone Toshitora 曾根俊虎. *Fa-Yüeh chiao-ping chi* 法越交兵紀 (A record of the French-Annamese conflict). Taipei, 1971.

Spector, Stanley. *Li Hung-chang and the Huai Army: A Study in Nineteenth-Century*

Chinese Regionalism. Seattle, University of Washington Press, 1964.

Stone, Lawrence. "Prosopography," *Daedalus: Journal of the American Academy of Arts and Sciences,* Winter 1971: 46–79.

Ta-Ch'ing Mu-tsung-i (T'ung-chih) huang-ti shih-lu 大清穆宗毅(同治)皇帝實錄 (The veritable records of the Ch'ing: T'ung-chih reign). 10 vols. Taipei, 1964.

T'ai-p'ing t'ien-kuo 太平天國 (The Taiping kingdom), comp. Hsiang Ta 向達 et al. 8 vols. Shanghai, 1957.

T'ai-p'ing t'ien-kuo wen-shu 太平天國文書 (Taiping documents). Peiping, 1933.

T'an Cheng-pi 譚正璧, comp. *Chung-kuo wen-hsüeh-chia ta tz'u-tien* 中國文學家大辭典 (A dictionary of Chinese men of letters). Shanghai, 1934.

T'ang Chih-chün 湯志鈞. *Wu-hsü pien-fa shih lun-ts'ung* 戊戌變法史論叢 (A collection of essays on the history of the reform movement of 1898). Wuhan, 1957.

Teng Ssu-yü. *Historiography of the Taiping Rebellion.* Cambridge, Mass., East Asian Research Center, Harvard University, 1962.

—————— and John K. Fairbank. *China's Response to the West: A Documentary Survey, 1839–1923.* Cambridge, Mass., Harvard University Press, 1954.

Teng Y. C. "The Failure of Hung Jen-kan's Foreign Policy," *Journal of Asian Studies* 28: 125–138 (November 1968).

Thompson, R. Wardlaw. *Griffith John: The Story of Fifty Years in China.* New York, A. C. Armstrong and Son, 1906.

Tseng Hsü-pai 曾虛白, comp. *Chung-kuo hsin-wen shih* 中國新聞史 (A history of Chinese journalism). 2 vols. Taipei, 1966.

Wakeman, Frederic, Jr. "The Opening of China," in Joseph R. Levenson, ed., *Modern China: An Interpretive Anthology.* New York, The Macmillan Company, 1971.

—————— "High Ch'ing: 1683–1839," in James B. Crowley, *Modern East Asia: Essays in Interpretation.*

Walker, Richard L. *The Multi-State System of Ancient China.* Hamden, Conn., The Shoe String Press, 1953.

Wan-kuo kung-pao 萬國公報 (The globe magazine; Review of the times). Shanghai, 1875–1883, 1889–1907.

Wang Chih-ch'un 王之春. *Ko-kuo t'ung-shang shih-mo chi* 各國通商始末記 (A complete account of trade with foreign countries). 20 chüan. 1895.

Wang Gungwu. "Early Ming Relations with Southeast Asia: A Background Essay," in John K. Fairbank, ed., *The Chinese World Order: Traditional China's Foreign Relations.* Cambridge, Mass., Harvard University Press, 1968.

Wang P'ing 王萍. *Hsi-fang li-suan-hsüeh chih shu-ju* 西方曆算學之輸入 (The introduction of Western astronomical and mathematical sciences into China). Taipei, 1966.

Wang Shu-huai 王樹槐. *Wai-jen yü wu-hsü pien-fa* 外人與戊戌變法 (Foreigners and the 1898 reform movement). Taipei, 1965.

Wang T'ao 王韜. "T'iao-hua-lu jih-chih" 苕花廬日志 (A daily record from the Tecoma flower cottage), June 11–22, 1849 (unpublished).

—————— "Ming-hsiang-liao jih-chi" 茗薌寮日記 (Diary from a tea-scented hut), July 17–October 12, 1852 (unpublished).

———— "Ying-juan tsa-chi" 瀛壖雜記 (Sundry notes from Shanghai), October 13, 1852–April 17, 1853 (unpublished).

———— "Hu-ch'eng wen-chien lu" 滬城聞見錄 (A record of experiences in Shanghai), July–September 1853 (unpublished).

———— "Ying-juan jih-chih" 瀛壖日志 (A daily record from Shanghai), April 18, 1853–January 29, 1854 (unpublished).

———— "Heng-hua-kuan jih-chi" 蘅花館日記 (Diary from the Asarum flower studio), September 22, 1854–May 4, 1855 (unpublished).

———— *P'u-Fa chan-chi* 普法戰紀 (Account of the Franco-Prussian war). 14 chüan. Hong Kong, 1873.

———— *Ying-juan tsa-chih* 瀛壖雜志 (Sundry notes on Shanghai). 6 chüan. 1875.

———— ed. *Yen-shih ts'ung-ch'ao* 豓史叢鈔 (A collection of writings about amorous women). 8 ts'e. 1878.

———— *Tun-k'u lan-yen* 遯窟讕言 (Fanciful stories from my hideaway). 12 chüan. 1880.

———— *T'ao-yüan ch'ih-tu* 弢園尺牘 (The letters of Wang T'ao). 12 chüan. 1880.

———— *Heng-hua-kuan shih-lu* 蘅華館詩錄 (The poems of Wang T'ao). 5 chüan. Tokyo, 1881.

———— *Huo-ch'i lüeh-shuo* 火器略說 (Introductory treatise on firearms). 1 ts'e. Hong Kong, 1881.

———— *T'ao-yüan wen-lu wai-pien* 弢園文錄外編 (Additional essays of Wang T'ao). 10 chüan. Hong Kong, 1883. 2 additional chüan (chüan 11–12) subsequently published (n.d.).

———— *P'u-Fa chan-chi* 普法戰紀 (Account of the Franco-Prussian war). 20 chüan. 1886.

———— *Sung-yin man-lu* 淞隱漫錄 (Random jottings of a Woosung recluse). 12 chüan. Shanghai, 1887.

———— *T'ao-yüan ch'ih-tu hsü-ch'ao* 弢園尺牘續鈔 (Additional letters of Wang T'ao). 6 chüan. Shanghai, 1889.

———— *T'ao-yüan chu-shu tsung-mu* 弢園著述總目 (A catalogue of Wang T'ao's writings). Shanghai, 1889.

———— comp. *Hsi-hsüeh chi-ts'un liu-chung* 西學輯存六種 (Six treatises on Western learning). 2 ts'e. Shanghai, 1889–1890.

———— *Hsi-hsüeh t'u-shuo* 西學圖說 (An illustrated exposition of Western learning), in Wang T'ao, *Hsi-hsüeh chi-ts'un liu-chung*, ts'e 1.

———— *Hsi-hsüeh yüan-shih k'ao* 西學源始考 (An inquiry into the beginnings of Western learning), in Wang T'ao, *Hsi-hsüeh chi-ts'un liu-chung*, ts'e 2.

———— *Fa-kuo chih-lüeh* 法國志略 (General history of France). 24 chüan. 1890.

———— "Ko-lun-pu ch'uan-tsan" 哥倫布傳贊 (In praise of Columbus), *Wan-kuo kung-pao*, no. 42: 11–12b (July 1892).

———— "Chiu-shih ch'u-i" 救時芻議 (My proposals for saving the times), 1st part, *Wan-kuo kung-pao*, no. 43: 12–13b (August 1892); 2nd part, *Wan-kuo kung-pao*, no. 44: 14–16 (September 1892).

———— "Lun i hsing chih-tsao i kuang mao-i" 論宜興製造以廣貿易 (On the need to promote manufacture in order to expand trade), *Wan-kuo kung-pao*, no. 45: 2b–4 (October 1892).

———— "Lun i te-jen i li-ts'ai" 論宜得人以理財 (On the need to obtain men of ability to deal with economic matters), *Wan-kuo kung-pao*, no. 46: 7b–9 (November 1892).

———— "Lun Ch'uan-tung she-li yang-wu hsüeh-shu" 論川東設立洋務學塾 (The establishment of a foreign affairs school in Chungking), *Wan-kuo kung-pao*, no. 47: 9b–11b (December 1892).

———— "Lun i she shang-chü i wang shang-wu" 論宜設商局以旺商務 (On the need to establish a bureau of trade for the promotion of commerce), *Wan-kuo kung-pao*, no. 49: 6–7b (February 1893).

———— "Yüeh Te-kuo Shih-hao ch'uan-ch'ang chang-ch'eng shu-hou" 閱德國 什好船廠章程書後 (A colophon written after perusing the regulations of Germany's Shih-hao shipyard), *Wan-kuo kung-pao*, no 51: 3–4b (April 1893).

———— "Lun hsün-yüeh p'ao-t'ai" 論巡閱砲臺 (On the inspection tour of gun emplacements), *Wan-kuo kung-pao*, no. 56: 10b–11b (September 1893).

———— "Lun Chung-kuo mei-t'ieh chih fu Mei-kuo chin-yin chih fu" 論中國煤鐵 之富美國金銀之富 (On China's abundance of coal and iron and America's abundance of gold and silver), *Wan-kuo kung-pao*, no. 57: 8–9 (October 1893).

———— "Lun ch'u-shih hsü ch'iu chen-ts'ai" 論出使須求眞才 (On the need to seek out true talent in the diplomatic field), *Wan-kuo kung-pao*, no. 58: 5b–6b (November 1893).

———— "Lun so t'an yang-wu chung nan tso-yen ch'i-hsing" 論所談洋務終難坐 言起行 (On the difficulty of getting the actions of those who discuss foreign affairs to accord with their words), *Wan-kuo kung-pao*, no. 59: 4b–5b (December 1893).

———— *Sung-pin so-hua* 淞濱瑣話 (Tales of trivia from the banks of the Woosung). 12 chüan. Shanghai, 1893.

———— *P'u-Fa chan-chi* 普法戰紀 (Account of the Franco-Prussian war). 20 chüan. 1895.

———— ed. *Tzu-ch'iang-chai pao-fu hsing-kuo lun ch'u-pien* 自強齋保富興國論初編 (Essays from the Self-Strengthening Studio on the safeguarding of China's wealth and the revival of the nation: First collection). 6 chüan. Shanghai, 1897.

———— *Sung-pin so-hua* 淞濱瑣話 (Tales of trivia from the banks of the Woosung). Shanghai, 1934.

———— *T'ao-yüan pi-chi* 弢園筆記 (The notebooks of Wang T'ao). Shanghai, 1934.

———— *Weng-yu yü-t'an* 甕牖餘談 (Gossip from a poor man's window), in *Ch'ing-tai pi-chi ts'ung-k'an* 清代筆記叢刊 (Collection of Ch'ing dynasty notebooks), ts'e 119–120. Shanghai, 1936.

———— *Ch'un-ch'iu li-hsüeh san-chung* 春秋歷學三種 (Three works on the chronology of the Spring and Autumn period). Peking, 1959.

———— *Man-yu sui-lu* 漫遊隨錄 (The record of my wanderings), in *Hsiao-fang-hu-chai yü-ti ts'ung-ch'ao* 小方壺齋輿地叢鈔 (Collection of geographical works from the Hsiao-fang-hu studio), comp. Wang Hsi-ch'i 王錫祺, vol. 62. Taipei, 1962.

———— *Fu-sang yu-chi* 扶桑遊記 (A record of travels in Japan), in *Hsiao-fang-hu-chai yü-ti ts'ung-ch'ao*, vol. 52.

———— "Ch'ü hsüeh-hsiao chi-pi i hsing jen-ts'ai lun" 去學校積弊以興人材論

(The elimination of bad practices in the schools as a means of fostering men of ability), in *Huang-ch'ao ching-shih-wen san-pien* 皇朝經世文三編 (Third collection of Ch'ing essays on statecraft), comp. Ch'en Chung-i 陳忠倚, vol. 2. Taipei, 1965.

——— "Li-chüan pi lun" 釐捐弊論 (On the evils of the likin tax), in *Huang-ch'ao ching-shih-wen san-pien*, vol. 1.

——— comp. "Chou-i chi-shih" 周易集釋 (Collected commentaries on the *I-ching*). 1 ts'e. Manuscript in New York Public Library. N.d.

——— comp. "Li-chi chi-shih" 禮記集釋 (Collected commentaries on the *Li-chi*). Manuscript in New York Public Library. N.d.

——— comp. "Mao-shih chi-shih" 毛詩集釋 (Collected commentaries on the Mao version of the *Shih-ching*). 30 chüan. Manuscript in New York Public Library. N.d.

Wang Wei-ch'eng 王維誠. "Wang T'ao ti ssu-hsiang" 王韜的思想 (Wang T'ao's thought), in *Chung-kuo chin-tai ssu-hsiang shih lun-wen chi.*

Wang, Y. C. *Chinese Intellectuals and the West, 1872–1949*. Chapel Hill, University of North Carolina Press, 1966.

Wang Yung-k'ang 王永康. "Cheng Kuan-ying ch'i jen chi ch'i ssu-hsiang" 鄭觀應其人及其思想 (Cheng Kuan-ying: The man and his thought), *Shih-hsüeh yüeh-k'an* 史學月刊 (Historical studies monthly), no. 1: 34–40 (January 1958).

Ward, Robert E. "Epilogue," in Robert E. Ward, ed., *Political Development in Modern Japan*. Princeton, Princeton University Press, 1968.

Watanabe Tetsuhiro 渡邊哲弘. "Ka Kei Ko Reien no shinseiron" 何啟胡禮垣の新政論 (The administrative reform proposals of Ho Kai and Hu Li-yüan), *Ritsumeikan bungaku* 立命館文學 (The monthly journal of cultural sciences), no. 11: 939–955 (November 1961).

Watson, Burton. *Ssu-ma Ch'ien: Grand Historian of China*. New York, Columbia University Press, 1958.

Weiner, Myron. "Introduction," in Myron Weiner, *Modernization: The Dynamics of Growth*.

Wen-hsien ts'ung-pien 文獻叢編 (Collected documents from the Historical Records Office). 46 ts'e. Peiping, 1930–1943.

Wong, K. Chimin and Lien-teh Wu. *History of Chinese Medicine*. 2nd ed. Shanghai, 1936.

Worthy, Edmund H., Jr. "Yung Wing in America," *Pacific Historical Review* 34: 265–287 (August 1965).

Wright, Arnold, ed. *Twentieth-Century Impressions of Hong Kong, Shanghai, and Other Treaty Ports of China: Their History, People, Commerce, Industries and Resources*. London, Lloyds Greater Britain Publishing Company, 1908.

Wright, Arthur F. "The Study of Chinese Civilization," *Journal of the History of Ideas* 21: 233–255 (1960).

Wright, Mary C. *The Last Stand of Chinese Conservatism: The T'ung-chih Restoration, 1862–1874*. Stanford, Stanford University Press, 1957.

——— "Introduction: The Rising Tide of Change," in Mary C. Wright, *China in Revolution: The First Phase, 1900–1913*.

Wu Ching-shan 吳靜山. "Wang T'ao shih-chi k'ao-lüeh" 王韜事蹟考略 (A

brief inquiry into the life of Wang T'ao), in *Shang-hai yen-chiu tzu-liao* 上海研究資料 (Materials for the study of Shanghai). Shanghai, 1936.

Wu Hsing-lien 吳醒濂. *Hsiang-kang Hua-jen ming-jen shih-lüeh* 香港華人名人史略 (Sketches of prominent Chinese of Hong Kong). Hong Kong, 1937.

Wu Yen-nan 吳雁南. "Shih lun Wang T'ao ti kai-liang-chu-i ssu-hsiang" 試論王韜的改良主義思想 (A tentative discussion of Wang T'ao's reformist thought), *Shih-hsüeh yüeh-k'an*, no. 4: 17–21 (April 1958).

Wylie, Alexander (Wei-lieh-ya-li 偉烈亞力) and Wang T'ao 王韜. *Hsi-kuo t'ien-hsüeh yüan-liu* 西國天學源流 (The genesis and growth of Western astronomy), in Wang T'ao, *Hsi-hsüeh chi-ts'un liu-chung*, ts'e 1.

—— *Hua-Ying t'ung-shang shih-lüeh* 華英通商事略 (A general account of Sino-British trade), in Wang T'ao, *Hsi-hsüeh chi-ts'un liu-chung*, ts'e 2.

—— *Chinese Researches*. Shanghai, 1897.

—— *Notes on Chinese Literature*. 2nd ed. New York, Paragon Reprint Corporation, 1964.

—— *Memorials of Protestant Missionaries to the Chinese*. Taipei, 1967.

Yang Lien-sheng 楊聯陞. "Ch'ao-tai chien ti pi-sai" 朝代間的比賽 (Dynastic comparison and dynastic competition), in *Ch'ing-chu Li Chi hsien-sheng ch'i-shih-sui lun-wen chi* 慶祝李濟先生七十歲論文集 (Symposium in honor of Dr. Li Chi on his seventieth birthday), vol. 1. Taipei, 1965.

—— "Toward a Study of Dynastic Configurations in Chinese History," in his *Studies in Chinese Institutional History*. Cambridge, Mass., Harvard University Press, 1963.

Yung Wing. *My Life in China and America*. New York, Henry Holt and Company, 1909.

Yüan Ch'ang-ch'ao 袁昶超. *Chung-kuo pao-yeh hsiao-shih* 中國報業小史 (A short history of Chinese journalism). Hong Kong, 1957.

GLOSSARY

Chang Chih-tung 張之洞
Chang Fei 張芾
Chang Ssu-kuei 張斯桂
Chang Tsung-liang 張宗良
Chang Yüeh 張曜
Ch'ang-mao chuang-yüan 長毛狀元
Ch'ang-shan 常山
Chao Lieh-wen 趙烈文
Chao-wen hsin-pao 昭文新報
Chen-shu 枕書
Ch'en Ai-t'ing 陳藹廷
Ch'en Chih 陳熾
Ch'en Ch'iu 陳虬
Ch'en Kuei-shih 陳桂士
Ch'en Lan-pin 陳蘭彬
Ch'en Shao-pai 陳少白
Ch'en Yen 陳言
Cheng-chai 正齋
cheng-chiao i-t'i 政教一體
Cheng Hsüan 鄭玄
Cheng Kuan-ying 鄭觀應
cheng-shih 正史
Cheng Shih-liang 鄭士良
Cheng Tsao-ju 鄭藻如
"Chi Ying-kuo cheng-chih 紀英國政治
ch'i (vital force) 氣
ch'i (technology, physical realm) 器
Ch'i-Feng 岐豐
Ch'i-pao 七寶
Chia I 賈誼

chia-tsu chu-i 家族主義
Chiang Chien-jen 蔣劍人
Chiang I-li 蔣益澧
Chiang Kai-shek (Chiang Chieh-shih) 蔣介石
Chiang Tun-fu 蔣敦復
ch'iang 強
Chiao-hui hsin-pao 教會新報
chien-chü 薦舉
Ch'ien Cheng 錢徵
Ch'ien-Han-shu 前漢書
chih 志
Chih-fang wai-chi 職方外紀
chih-min 治民
chih-ping 治兵
ch'ih pu jo Hsi-kuo 恥不若西國
chin-shih 進士
Chin-shih pien-lu 近事編錄
Ching-hua yüan 鏡花緣
ching-shih 經世
ch'ing-i 清議
Chou T'eng-hu 周騰虎
Ch'ou-jen chuan 疇人傳
Ch'ou-yang ch'u-i 籌洋芻議
Chu-chai 諸翟
Chu Hsi 朱熹
Chu-t'ieh-an tu-shu ying-shih sui-pi 鑄鐵庵讀書應事隨筆
ch'uan-t'ung 傳統
Ch'uang-shih chi 創世記

chun chu t'ien-tao 準諸天道
Ch'un-ch'iu 春秋
"Ch'un-ch'iu Tso-shih-chuan chi-shih"
　春秋左氏傳集釋
Chung-fa 中法
Chung-hsüeh 中學
Chung-hsüeh ch'ien-shuo 重學淺說
Chung-hua yin-wu tsung-chü 中華印務總
　局
Chung-kuo 中國
"Chung-min" 重民
Chung-wai hsin-pao 中外新報
Chung-yung 中庸
chü-jen 舉人
Ch'ü Yüan 屈原
ch'üan chu jen-shih 權諸人事
ch'üan-li 權利
Ch'üan-shu 權書
chün 君
chün-ch'en kung-chih 君臣共治
chün-chu 君主
chün chu yü shang erh min chu yü hsia
　君主於上而民主於下
chün-min chih hsin 君民之心
chün-min kung-chih 君民共治
chün-min kung-chu 君民共主
chün-min t'ung-chih 君民同治
chün-tzu pu ch'i 君子不器
ch'ün-ts'e ch'ün-li 群策群力

Dai Nihon shi 大日本史

Fa-chih 法志
Fa-kuo t'u-shuo 法國圖說
Fa-lan-hsi chih 法蘭西志
Fang Ming-shan 方銘山
Fang Yao 方耀
Feng Chün-kuang 馮焌光
Feng Kuei-fen 馮桂芬
feng-shui 風水
feng-su jen-hsin 風俗人心
fu-ch'iang 富強
Fujita Mokichi 藤田茂吉
fu-kuo ch'iang-ping 富國強兵
fu-kuo erh tsu-min 富國而足民
Fukuzawa Yukichi 福澤諭吉
Fu-li 甫里
Fu Sheng 伏生
fu-shou i t'ing-ming 俯首以聽命
Fu-yün 福雲

Hai-hsiu-ta 海修遠

Hai-kuo t'u-chih 海國圖志
Hai-t'ien san-yu 海天三友
Han-chien 漢奸
Han Kao-tsu 漢高祖
Hōchi shimbun 報知新聞
Ho Ching 何璟
Ho Fu-t'ang 何福堂
Ho Ju-chang 何如璋
Ho Kai (Ho Ch'i) 何啟
Ho-ma 和馬
Hoshino Tsune 星野恒
Hou Liao-chai chih-i 後聊齋志異
Hsi-fa 西法
Hsi-hsüeh 西學
"Hsi ku-shih" 西古史
"Hsi-shih fan" 西事凡
Hsien-t'an hsiao-hsia lu 閒談消夏錄
Hsin wu-tai shih 新五代史
Hsing-Chung hui 興中會
hsing-li 性理
hsiu-ts'ai 秀才
Hsiung Chao-chou 熊兆周
Hsiung-nu 匈奴
Hsü Chi-yü 徐繼畬
Hsü Yu-jen 徐有壬
Hsüeh Fu-ch'eng 薛福成
Hsüeh Huan 薛煥
Hu Li-yüan 胡禮垣
"Hua-hsü shih-lu" 華胥實錄
Hua-pao 畫報
Hua-tzu jih-pao 華字日報
Huang Hsieh-hsüan 黃協塤
Huang Hsing 黃興
Huang Tsun-hsien 黃遵憲
Huang Tsung-hsi 黃宗羲
Huang Wan 黃畹
Hui-pao 匯報
Hung-ch'iao 虹橋
Hung Hsiu-ch'üan 洪秀全
Hung Jen-kan 洪仁玕
Hung Kan-fu 洪幹甫
Hung Shih-wei 洪士偉
huo-luan 霍亂

I-ching 易經
i-hsüeh (public school) 義學
i-hsüeh (technical studies) 藝學
i-pien 一變
i-shih shih Wang T'ao 逸史氏王韜
"I-t'an" 臆譚
Itō Hirobumi 伊藤博文
Iwaya Ichiroku 岩谷一六

I-yen 易言

i-yüan 議院

jen 人
jen-shih 人事
Jen-shu 壬叔
jen-tao 人道
jen-ts'ai 人材
Jih-pen kuo-chih 日本國志
Jih-pen tsa-shih shih 日本雜事詩
jōi 攘夷
ju 儒
Juan Yüan 阮元

Kan-wang 干王
K'ang Yu-wei 康有爲
Kao Yao 皋陶
k'ao-cheng (kōsho) 考證
Kihara Genrei 木原元禮
Kōa kai 興亞會
"Ko-chih hsin-hsüeh t'i-kang" 格致新學
  提綱
Ko-chih shu-yüan 格致書院
Komaki Masanari 小牧昌業
ko-ming 革命
Ku Yen-wu 顧炎武
Kuan Chung 管仲
kuan-tu shang-pan 官督商辦
Kuang-hsü 光緒
"Kuang-hsüeh t'u-shuo" 光學圖說
Kung Ch'eng 龔橙
kung-chü 公舉
kung-ho 共和
kung-ho chih cheng 共和之政
Kung Tzu-chen 龔自珍
Kung-yang 公羊
K'ung An-kuo 孔安國
K'ung chih tao jen tao yeh 孔之道人道也
kuo-chia chih ch'üan 國家之權
kuo-chia chu-i 國家主義
kuo-hui 國會
Kuo Sung-tao 郭嵩燾
kuo-yün 國運
Kurimoto Joun 栗本鋤雲

Lan-chin 懶今
Lan-ch'ing 蘭卿
Lao-min 老民
li (profit, material gain) 利
li (physical power) 力
li (officials) 吏
Li Chao-t'ang 黎兆棠

Li-chi 禮記
li-chin 釐金
li-ch'üan 利權
Li Hsiao-ch'ih 李小池
Li Hsiu-ch'eng 李秀成
Li Hung-chang 李鴻章
Li-pin 利賓
Li-sao 離騷
Li Shan-lan 李善蘭
Li Ssu 李斯
li-ts'ai 理財
Liang Ch'i-ch'ao 梁啟超
Lin Tse-hsü 林則徐
Liu Chao-chün 劉肇均
Liu Chih-chi 劉知幾
Liu Hsi-hung 劉錫鴻
Liu K'un-i 劉坤一
Liu Ming-ch'uan 劉銘傳
Lu Hao-tung 陸皓東
Lu Hsün 魯迅
luan 亂

Ma Chien-chung 馬建忠
Ma Hsiang-po 馬相伯
Ma Liang 馬良
Ma-shih wen-t'ung 馬氏文通
Ma Tuan-lin 馬端臨
mai-wen 賣文
Mao Tse-tung 毛澤東
Masanao 正直
Massatsu Hakase 抹殺博士
Meiji shibun 明治詩文
Mei-po 某伯
Meirokusha 明六社
Meiroku zasshi 明六雜誌
min-ch'i 民氣
min-chien 民間
min-chih 民治
min-ch'ing 民情
min-chu 民主
min-ch'üan (minken) 民權
min-ping 民兵
min-sheng 民生
min wei pang pen pen ku pang ning
  民惟邦本本固邦寧
ming-chiao 名教
Ming-i tai-fang lu 明夷待訪錄
Ming-shih 明史
Mishima Chūshū 三島中州
mo 末
Mo-hai shu-kuan 墨海書館
Mo-tzu 墨子

mu-fu 幕府
mu-shih 牧師

Nagaoka Moriyoshi 長岡護美
Nai-tuan 奈端
Nakamura Keiu 中村敬宇
nei 內
neng tzu wei chih 能自為之

Oka juku 岡塾
Oka Senjin 岡千仞
Ou-chi-li-te 歐几利德
Ou Feng-ch'ih 區鳳墀
Ou-yang Hsiu 歐陽修

pa-tao 覇道
P'an Ying 潘瑩
Pao Shih-ch'en 包世臣
pen 本
pien-fa 變法
ping-li 兵力
ping-min pu-fen 兵民不分
Po I 伯夷
Pu-shih-ko-la 布士哥拉
P'u 普
P'u Sung-ling 蒲松齡

Sada Hakubō 佐田白茅
San i-min 三異民
"Sao-Ch'in" 掃秦
Seng-ko-lin-ch'in 僧格林沁
"Shang-chan" 商戰
"Shang-chien" 尚簡
shang-chü 商局
shang-li 商力
Shang-ti 上帝
Shang Yang 商鞅
Shao Yu-lien 邵友濂
Shen Kung 申公
Shen Pao-chen 沈葆楨
sheng chi erh shuai 盛極而衰
Sheng Hsüan-huai 盛宣懷
Shigeno Yasutsugu 重野安繹
shih ch'i so ch'ang 師其所長
Shih Chien-ju 史堅如
Shih-ching 詩經
shih-jen 士人
Shih Ta-k'ai 石達開
Shih-wu pao 時務報
Shikamon (Rokumon) 鹿門
Shu-ching 書經
shu kuo-wei 樹國威

shu-yüan 書院
shui-shih yüan 水師院
Shun 舜
Shuo-wen 說文
Sone Toshitora 曾根俊虎
Ssu-ma Ch'ien 司馬遷
"Ssu-ming pu-ch'eng" 四溟補乘
Ssu-shu 四書
Su Hsün 蘇洵
Sun Ch'i-chü 孫啟榘
Sun Yat-sen (Sun I-hsien) 孫逸仙

ta 達
Ta-ching 大境
ta-i 大義
ta-t'ung 大同
Ta Ying-kuo chih 大英國志
T'a-li-ssu 他里斯
t'ai-p'ing 太平
T'ai-p'ing t'ien-kuo 太平天國
T'ai-tsu 太祖
T'ang T'ing-shu 唐廷樞
tao 道
tao pi ta-t'ung 道必大同
T'ao-yüan shu-chü 弢園書局
te 德
te-jen 得人
ti-k'ang-li 抵抗力
t'i 體
t'i-yung 體用
t'ien 天
t'ien-ch'uan 天船
t'ien-hsia 天下
t'ien-hsin 天心
t'ien-tao 天道
t'ien-tao hsün-huan 天道循環
T'ien-wang 天王
Ting Jih-ch'ang 丁日昌
Tong King-sing (T'ang Ching-hsing)
    唐景星
Toyotomi Hideyoshi 豐臣秀吉
tsai-hsiang 宰相
Ts'ai Erh-k'ang 蔡爾康
tsao-wu-che 造物者
Tse Tsan-tai (Hsieh Tsuan-t'ai) 謝纘泰
Tseng Kuo-fan 曾國藩
Tso-chuan 左傳
Tso Tou-shan 左斗山
Tso Tsung-t'ang 左宗棠
Tsou-Lu 鄒魯
Tsui-yen 罪言
Tu Mu 杜牧

Tung-lai fa 東來法
Tung-lin 東林
T'ung-chih 同治
T'ung-meng hui 同盟會
T'ung-wen kuan 同文館
Tzu-cheng hsin-p'ien 資政新篇
tzu-ch'iang 自強
tzu-yu ch'üan-li (jiyū kenri) 自由權利

wai 外
wai-ch'iang chung-kao 外強中槁
wai-kuo 外國
wai-kuo chuan 外國傳
Wang An-shih 王安石
Wang Ch'ang-kuei 王昌桂
Wang-chia-ssu 王家寺
Wang Chih-fu 王質甫
Wang Fu-chih 王夫之
Wang Han 王瀚
Wang K'ang-nien 汪康年
Wang Mang 王莽
wang-tao 王道
Wang T'ao 王韜
Wang Tzu-ch'üan 王紫詮
Washizu Kidō 鷲津毅堂
Watanabe Kōki 渡邊洪基
Wei Yüan 魏源
wen 文
wen-hsüeh 文學
Wo-jen 倭仁
wo li-ch'üan 握利權
Wong Foon (Huang K'uan) 黃寬
Wong Shing (Huang Sheng) 黃勝

Wong Wing-sheung (Huang Yung-shang) 黃詠商
wu 武
wu ch'ang-ch'iang chih kuo 無常強之國
Wu Hsü 吳煦
wu-pei yüan 武備院
wu-tao chih hu-lang Ch'in 無道之虎狼秦
Wu T'ing-fang 伍廷芳
wu-ts'ai 務財

yang-wu 洋務
Yang Yin-ch'uan 楊引傳
Yao 堯
Yao Hsieh 姚燮
Yeh Ming-ch'en 葉名琛
Yen Fu 嚴復
yen-lu 言路
Yen-shou hsin-fa 延壽新法
"Ying-hai pi-chi" 瀛海筆記
Ying Lung-t'ien 應龍田
Ying Yü-keng 應雨畊
Yoshida Shōin 吉田松蔭
yung 用
Yung Wing (Jung Hung) 容閎
Yü Ch'ien-chih 余謙之
yü-lun chih mei-o shih-fei 輿論之美惡是非
yü min kung ch'i li 與民共其利
yü-p'ing 輿評
Yü Sung-nien 郁松年
Yü Yün-mei 余雲眉
"Yüan-hsüeh" 原學
"Yüan-jen" 原人

INDEX

Harvard East Asian Monographs

STUDIES IN THE MODERNIZATION OF THE REPUBLIC OF KOREA: 1945–1975

90. Noel F. McGinn, Donald R. Snodgrass, Yung Bong Kim, Shin-Bok Kim, and Quee-Young Kim, *Education and Development in Korea*

91. Leroy P. Jones and Il SaKong, *Government, Business and Entrepreneurship in Economic Development: The Korean Case*

92. Edward S. Mason, Dwight H. Perkins, Kwang Suk Kim, David C. Cole, Mahn Je Kim, et al., *The Economic and Social Modernization of the Republic of Korea*

93. Robert Repetto, Tai Hwan Kwon, Son-Ung Kim, Dae Young Kim, John E. Sloboda, and Peter J. Donaldson, *Economic Development, Population Policy, and Demographic Transition in the Republic of Korea*

106. David C. Cole and Yung Chul Park, *Financial Development in Korea, 1945-1978*

107. Roy Bahl, Chuk Kyo Kim, and Chong Kee Park, *Public Finances during the Korean Modernization Process*

94. Parks M. Coble, *The Shanghai Capitalists and the Nationalist Government, 1927-1937*

95. Noriko Kamachi, *Reform in China: Huang Tsun-hsien and the Japanese Model*

96. Richard Wich, *Sino-Soviet Crisis Politics: A Study of Political Change and Communication*

97. Lillian M. Li, *China's Silk Trade: Traditional Industry in the Modern World, 1842-1937*

98. R. David Arkush, *Fei Xiaotong and Sociology in Revolutionary China*

99. Kenneth Alan Grossberg, *Japan's Renaissance: The Politics of the Muromachi Bakufu*

100. James Reeve Pusey, *China and Charles Darwin*

101. Hoyt Cleveland Tillman, *Utilitarian Confucianism: Ch'en Liang's Challenge to Chu Hsi*

102. Thomas A. Stanley, *Ōsugi Sakae, Anarchist in Taishō Japan: The Creativity of the Ego*

103. Jonathan K. Ocko, *Bureaucratic Reform in Provincial China: Ting Jih-ch'ang in Restoration Kiangsu, 1867-1870*

104. James Reed, *The Missionary Mind and American East Asia Policy, 1911-1915*

105. Neil L. Waters, *Japan's Local Pragmatists: The Transition from Bakumatsu to Meiji in the Kawasaki Region*

108. William D. Wray, *Mitsubishi and the N.Y.K., 1870-1914: Business Strategy in the Japanese Shipping Industry*

109. Ralph William Huenemann, *The Dragon and the Iron Horse: The Economics of Railroads in China, 1876-1937*

110. Benjamin A. Elman, *From Philosophy to Philology: Intellectual and Social Aspects of Change in Late Imperial China*

111. Jane Kate Leonard, *Wei Yuan and China's Rediscovery of the Maritime World*

112. Luke S. K. Kwong, *A Mosaic of the Hundred Days: Personalities, Politics, and Ideas of 1898*

113. John E. Wills, Jr., *Embassies and Illusions: Dutch and Portuguese Envoys to K'ang-hsi, 1666-1687*

114. Joshua A. Fogel, *Politics and Sinology: The Case of Naitō Konan (1866-1934)*

115. Jeffrey C. Kinkley, ed., *After Mao: Chinese Literature and Society, 1978-1981*

116. C. Andrew Gerstle, *Circles of Fantasy: Convention in the Plays of Chikamatsu*

117. Andrew Gordon, *The Evolution of Labor Relations in Japan: Heavy Industry, 1853-1955*

118. Daniel K. Gardner, *Chu Hsi and the* Ta Hsueh: *Neo-Confucian Reflection on the Confucian Canon*

119. Christine Guth Kanda, *Shinzō: Hachiman Imagery and its Development*

120. Robert Borgen, *Sugawara no Michizane and the Early Heian Court*

121. Chang-tai Hung, *Going to the People: Chinese Intellectuals and Folk Literature, 1918-1937*

122. Michael A. Cusumano, *The Japanese Automobile Industry: Technology and Management at Nissan and Toyota*

124. Steven D. Carter, *The Road to Komatsubara: A Classical Reading of the Renga Hyakuin*

125. Katherine F. Bruner, John K. Fairbank, and Richard T. Smith, *Entering China's Service: Robert Hart's Journals, 1854-1863*

126. Bob Tadashi Wakabayashi, *Anti-Foreignism and Western Learning in Early Modern Japan: The* New Theses *of 1825*

127. Atsuko Hirai, *Individualism and Socialism: The Life and Thought of Kawai Eijirō (1891-1944)*

128. Ellen Widmer, *The Margins of Utopia:* Shui-hu hou-chuan *and the Literature of Ming Loyalism*

129. R. Kent Guy, *The Emperor's Four Treasuries: Scholars and the State in the Late Ch'ien-lung Era*

130. Peter C. Perdue, *Exhausting the Earth: State and Peasant in Hunan, 1500-1850*